CHOCOLATE

HarperCollins*Publishers*

CHOCOLATE

FROM SIMPLE COOKIES TO EXTRAVAGANT SHOWSTOPPERS

NICK MALGIERI

PHOTOGRAPHS BY TOM ECKERLE

HarperCollins books may be purchased for educational, business, or sales
promotional use. For information please write: Special Markets Department,
HarperCollins Publishers, Inc., 10 East 53rd Street, New York, NY 10022.
FIRST EDITION

Designed by Joel Avirom and Jason Snyder
Design Assistant: Meghan Day Healey

Illustrations by Laura Hartman Maestro

Food styling by Bianca Borges Henry, Tom Cutler,
Michelle Tampakis, and Andrea Tutunjian
Props by Ceci Gallini

Library of Congress Cataloging-in-Publication Data

Malgieri, Nick.
    Chocolate : from simple cookies to extravagant showstoppers / Nick Malgieri.
        p.   cm.
    Includes bibliographical references and index.
    ISBN 0-06-018711-5
        1. Cookery (Chocolate) 2. Chocolate. I. Title.
TX767.C5M35   1998
641.6'374—dc21   97-53168

98 99 00 01 02 ❖/RRD 10 9 8 7 6 5 4 3 2 1

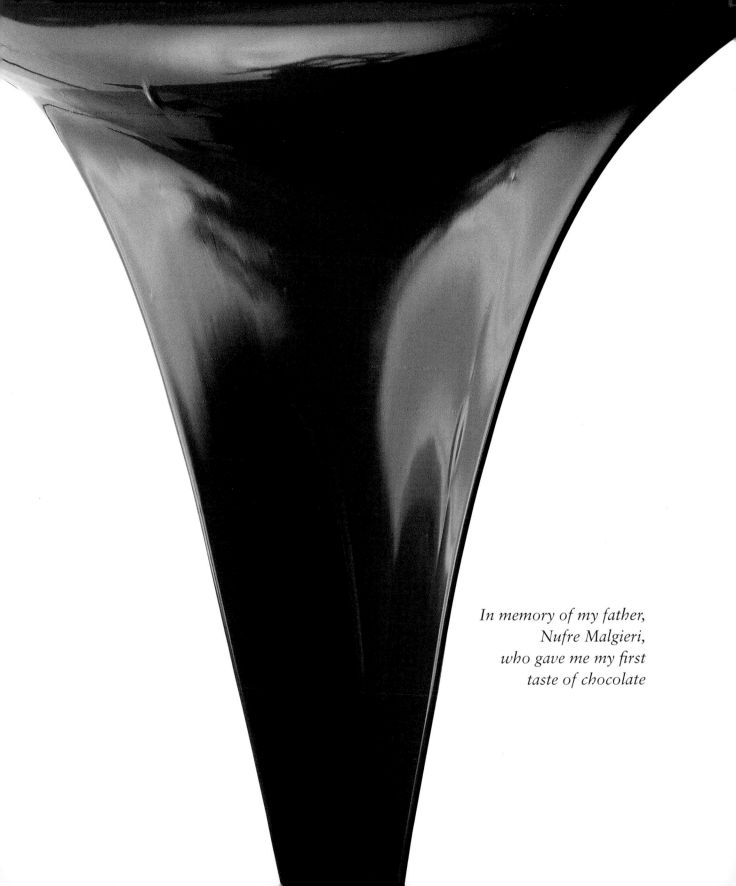

In memory of my father,
Nufre Malgieri,
who gave me my first
taste of chocolate

CONTENTS

ACKNOWLEDGMENTS

Many thanks are due to the following people, without whom this book would not exist: Susan Friedland, my editor; Phyllis Wender, my agent; Nancy Nicholas, who edited the manuscript; everyone at HarperCollins who worked on the book, especially, Sharon Bowers and Ellen Morrissey, Susan's assistants, Estelle Laurence, copy editor, and Chris Tanigawa, production editor; Joel Avirom, for the striking design; Tom Eckerle, whose beautiful photographs enliven the text; Ceci Gallini, brilliant prop stylist; Denise Figlar of Calvin Klein Home and Lisa Schorr of Simon Pearce for kindly lending props; Bianca Borges Henry, Tom Cutler, Richard Simpson, Michelle Tampakis, and Andrea Tutunjian, for preparing food for photography and developing and testing recipes; all my friends at Peter Kump's, especially Christine Mangone and Gerri Weiner who helped with ordering food for photography; all the students who helped in preparing food for photography; all my friends and colleagues who contributed recipes, including Ellen Baumwoll, Fran Bigelow, Marilynn Brass, Sheila Brass, Miriam Brickman, Anna Teresa Callen, Sandra Church, Amanda Cushman, Liza Davies, Kyra Effren, Peter Fresulone, Elaine Gonzalez, Dorie Greenspan, Michael Grossman, Anne-Marie Hadda, Ceri Hadda, Maida Heatter, Pierre Hermé, Stephen Hoffman, Paul Kinberg, Sandy Leonard, Karen Ludwig, Copeland Marks, Michael McLaughlin, Jennifer Migliorelli, Marie Ostrowski, Scott Peacock, David Perkins, Dorothy May Perkins, Sheri Portwood, Julie Rocco, Vicki Russell, Stephan Schiesser, Betty Shaw, Marie Simmons, Allen Smith, Jacques Torres, Hans Tschirren, Andrea Tutunjian, and Carole Walter; my friends at Switzerland Tourism, Erika Lieben and Evelyne Mock; Pat and Ed Opler of World's Finest Chocolate for putting me in touch with Mark Guiltinan, magical provider of cocoa pods, and Arthur Boehm for accompanying me on the cocoa pod chase; David Perkins and Larry Ritner for providing and delivering Mexican chocolate and artifacts; Bernard Duclos of Chocolaterie Valrhona for generous provisions of chocolate for testing and photography; Andrea Tutunjian especially for her hard work on the early stages of the manuscript and Jennifer Harvey Williams for her tireless work on the last stages of the manuscript; and a big hug to my friend Dorie Greenspan who listened, suggested, and was always there. Thanks, Dorie.

INTRODUCTION

Though my father, Nufre Malgieri, was not particularly fond of sweets, he did like chocolate. The selection of chocolate candy available in our 1950s inner-city neighborhood was nothing compared to what is available nowadays; nevertheless, there still were many to choose among besides the ubiquitous Hershey bars, both plain and with almonds. My father once brought me a surprise when I was about five or six years old. He unwrapped a small, thin candy bar about four inches square and said, "Guess what this is." I looked—it was an off-white color and was marked in squares like a chocolate bar. I sniffed—it had a scent of orange. I tasted—it was like sweet chocolate perfumed with a delicate orange flavor. The bar was a then common Dutch brand of orange-flavored white chocolate (yes, I know white chocolate isn't really chocolate). I was delighted.

Thus my obsession with chocolate began.

Another of my early chocolate memories is of going with my grandfather to his club on a Saturday afternoon. The bartender kept chocolate bars in the refrigerator behind the bar and I always got a cold, firm milk chocolate bar to break apart square by square and eat while my grandfather greeted his friends.

And every Easter was a time when my cousins and I received enormous baskets of chocolates and other confections from parents, grandparents, godparents, aunts, and uncles. Every basket had as its centerpiece a large milk chocolate bunny or egg, richly decorated with dark chocolate and piped flowers made of hard sugar icing, probably royal icing. There were also little eggs, hollow or filled with chocolate or sometimes nut pastes or gianduja, and of course the inevitable jelly beans and marshmallow chicks.

I think the first chocolate dessert I remember enjoying was my grandmother's pizza di crema, a kind of pie with a sweet crust filled with chocolate pastry cream scented with vanilla and cinnamon and studded with candied citron. It was a typical Easter dessert (a wonder we could eat dessert after all the chocolate in the Easter baskets) and was always part of the selection of sweet and savory ricotta and cream pies that my maternal grandmother, Clotilda Lo Conte, made for the holiday.

My grandmother made lots of delicate cakes and pastries, and although I never learned a recipe from her, watching her and observing the pleasure that her baking brought everyone inspired a love of baking in me.

I started experimenting on my own in my late teens. One of the first things I tried was a fancy chocolate dessert involving ladyfingers and a rich chocolate filling. I found the recipe in a not very precisely translated cookbook by a French countess. The imposing-sounding recipe called for soaking the ladyfingers in ½ cup of kirsch diluted with an equal amount of water, and then adding another half cup of kirsch to the chocolate filling.

Unfortunately the resulting strong, alcoholic flavor made the dessert inedible. Undaunted, I tried the recipe again (this time with about a tenth of the kirsch) and began my lifelong passion for collecting recipes for chocolate desserts and confections.

My quest for additions to my collection has taken me from southern France to British Columbia—it's never too long a trip if there is chocolate at the end of it.

Before I knew it I had finished college—still experimenting with cooking and baking at every chance—and decided to attend culinary school instead of graduate school.

My first great chocolate mentor was my teacher Albert Kumin. In his classes at the Culinary Institute of America, Albert created beautiful, decorative, and edible confections with chocolate and sugar. Before, I had only seen art like his made in porcelain.

His ability with chocolate was and is unsurpassed. It was he who convinced me that I should go to Switzerland for an apprencticeship after graduation. In the early 1970s there was no better place for a chocolate lover. I was fascinated with the beautiful chocolate cakes and the precisely uniform and perfect pralinés—the Swiss name for dipped chocolate candies, like the ones on pages 338 to 346—in the windows of elegant and expensive pastry shops in Zurich, where I worked, and in the other cities and towns I visited. The air in Switzerland seemed chocolate-scented and in some places it actually was, as I discovered when I first visited Kilchberg on Lake Zurich, the site of the Lindt chocolate factory. My recipe collection increased as I traded school recipes with fellow apprentices and assistant pastry chefs and made weekly rounds of the city's pastry shops. I sketched and made notes on the contents of window displays and occasionally scraped a few extra francs together from my meager pay to buy a few chocolate truffles or some intricately decorated little pastries.

Visits in Switzerland and France to stores that sold professional equipment started my collection of chocolate molds, cutters, dipping forks, and thermometers. Fortunately, nowadays all these pieces of equipment are easily available from importers in the United States (see Sources, page 442).

After working in Switzerland, Monaco, and France for about five years, I returned to New York to work with Albert Kumin at Windows on the World when it opened in 1976. We made one chocolate extravaganza after another. Another of my great chocolate inspirations has been Robert Linxe, of La Maison du Chocolat in Paris and New York. The first time Monsieur Linxe came to Peter Kump's Cooking School in New York, I assisted him in preparing for his class—a great experience. His knowledge of chocolate is unsurpassed. He is equally at home preparing sumptuous chocolate desserts or beautiful confections. He is, in fact, the only person I have ever known who can judge the temper of chocolate by just looking at it: one stir and he knows if the chocolate is at the right degree of viscosity and temperature.

His skill fanned the flames of my passion for chocolate and I decided to return to France to learn more. Thanks to the kind efforts of my friend Rachel Akselrod I spent a whirlwind week working in the Valrhona factory, at Tain-l'Hermitage, near Valence in France. Under the able tutelage of Valrhona's head of research and development, Paul Bernard-Bret, I spent that week molding, dipping, and preparing confections of every type imaginable. It was like a short stay at a chocolate Harvard!

Since then I have taught innumerable classes in making chocolates and chocolate desserts, and although my previous books have all had a goodly amount of chocolate desserts in them, this is my first all-chocolate book. I hope you enjoy using it as much as I have enjoyed writing it.

CHOCOLATE

CHOCOLATE BASICS

A SHORT HISTORY OF CHOCOLATE

• • •

Throughout most of its three-thousand-year history, chocolate has been exclusively used as a beverage. After its introduction to Europe in the sixteenth and seventeenth centuries, various other uses were found, bringing chocolate into use as an ingredient in desserts and cakes, up to the point in the nineteenth century when eating chocolate of the type we know today came into common use.

For a fascinating read, look at Sophie D. Coe and Michael D. Coe's *The True History of Chocolate* (Thames and Hudson, 1996). The Coes have traced the history of chocolate from its beginnings in the lowlands of Mexico to its present-day use as one of the most popular food products in the world. Because they are scholars in the true sense of the word (Mrs. Coe is deceased, and her husband is a professor at Yale University) they have no axes to grind and, aside from a few swipes at food writers, have traced the origin and development of chocolate throughout its history with great objectivity and impartiality.

The main milestones in the history of chocolate are:

Cocoa beans were discovered, processed, and first made into a beverage by the Olmec, an ancient Mexican civilization that flourished during the last millennium B.C.E.

Use of chocolate as a beverage passed from the Olmec to the Maya, the Toltec, and finally the Aztecs. The Aztecs incorporated chocolate beverages of different types even into their religious rites and began to use cocoa beans as currency. They used a *metate*, the grinding stone pictured at right to crush the roasted cocoa beans into a paste.

When the first Spanish Conquistadores came to Mexico early in the sixteenth century, they tasted chocolate beverages and began to adapt them to their own use, finally exporting cocoa beans to Spain toward the end of the sixteenth century.

During the seventeenth century, use of chocolate as a beverage spread to both Italy and France, mainly by religious who had been to Mexico and returned to their convents and monasteries in those countries. By the middle of the sixteenth century chocolate was also introduced into Britain, perhaps by pirates who had preyed on ships headed for Spain. The chocolate used at this time would resemble a coarse version of present-day

unsweetened chocolate, though it was sometimes sold in a sweetened form, resembling the disks of chocolate available from Mexican chocolate companies to this day, used for making hot chocolate.

During the eighteenth century, the use of chocolate as a beverage became more widespread throughout Europe and the first efforts at using chocolate as an ingredient in dessert recipes began. It has a prominent entry in Diderot's *Encyclopedia,* where the roasting and grinding processes are well illustrated.

The nineteenth century saw the development of the types of chocolates that we know today. Treating cocoa powder with alkali occurred in Holland when Conrad van Houten invented the process in 1828. This gave the cocoa a darker color and a somewhat milder flavor and the use of this type of cocoa powder persists to this day.

Candy bars first appeared in England in the middle of the nineteenth century, though it wasn't until the last quarter of the century that the Swiss chocolatier Rudolphe Lindt invented the process of conching (see page 8), making the resulting chocolate smoother and creamier.

Jean Tobler, another Swiss chocolate technician, is said to have discovered the need for and the process of tempering at the very end of the nineteenth century, when he realized that the addition of extra cocoa butter to the mixture for eating chocolate made it more palatable. Milk chocolate had been invented by another Swiss, Daniel Peter, when he used some of Henri Nestlé's dry milk in a formula for chocolate years before.

American chocolate pioneers include James Baker, who opened a chocolate factory in Massachusetts in 1765 to manufacture chocolate for beverages. His grandson, Walter Baker, took over the business, which still exists, supplying baking chocolate to this day. Milton Hershey discovered a process of using actual milk, rather than milk powder, in the manufacture of milk chocolate and that process is still used to this day to manufacture the many tons of Hershey's chocolate produced.

Today's fancy chocolate cakes and candies are a far cry from the Aztec beverage that the Conquistadores discovered a little more than 450 years ago. We are fortunate to live in a world where the use of chocolate has become so developed and refined so that there are chocolates and chocolate recipes available for almost every mood. The history of chocolate will continue to unfold for many centuries to come.

WHERE CHOCOLATE COMES FROM

. . .

THE CHOCOLATE TREE

All chocolate comes from the tree that is botanically identified as *Theobroma cacao*—one of about 20 species of the genus *Theobroma*, from the Greek meaning "food of the gods." Only one other species is edible—*Theobroma bicolor*—and it is used to make a beverage in Mexico and part of Latin America.

The tree, which originated in the lowlands of southern Mexico, grows in a belt around the world delineated by 20 degrees north and south of the equator in Africa, the Caribbean, Hawaii, South America, and the South Seas.

There are three varieties of *Theobroma cacao*: Criollo (creole), a frail plant which produces very high-quality chocolate; Forastero (foreigner), a more robust plant which makes a less delicate chocolate; and Trinitario (trinitarian), a natural cross between the two other varieties, which occurred in Trinidad.

High temperatures, high humidity, and an abundance of the little insects known as midges, which pollinate the flowers as they bloom, are necessary to the growth of the Theobroma tree. It produces flowers constantly in tufts of bark all over its trunk and branches. Though only a small percentage of flowers actually produce fruit, they bloom throughout the year, without a particular flowering season, unlike fruit trees that grow in temperate climates. If the flowers do produce fruit, the result is large pods that may range from bright orange to brown in color, surrounding a white, acidic flesh and a center of about 20 to 40 almond-shaped beans. The beans are the part that becomes chocolate. Both the tree and its fruit are referred to as *cacao*, although the chocolate-producing beans are referred to as cocoa beans.

After the pods are harvested, they are broken open—usually with a machete—and the beans are removed. Though I have heard that a beverage similar to lemonade is made from the flesh, I know of no commercial use for it.

The beans, which are covered with a white skin, are first piled on the ground, covered, and allowed to ferment. During fermentation, when the beans germinate—at a temperature of about 120 degrees—the first sign of chocolate flavor develops.

After the beans have fermented, they are uncovered and exposed to the sun to dry and arrest the fermentation.

The next step is to roast them. Though beans are often roasted where they are grown, it is just as common for fermented and dried beans to be roasted far from the growing site in the factory where the beans will be made into chocolate.

After roasting, the husks, which have become dry and papery, are removed. This is usually done by crushing the beans slightly until they break into smaller pieces known as nibs. Then the skin is easy to remove. Often a chocolate factory will purchase fully processed nibs to use for making chocolate.

HOW CHOCOLATE IS MANUFACTURED

· · ·

At the chocolate factory, the process of making chocolate may begin with either nibs or beans. Chocolates made from a blend of different beans usually start with dried, unroasted beans, whereas chocolates made from one type of bean usually start with nibs that were roasted and skinned where they were grown. Of course there are exceptions to both cases.

The first step is to crush the skinned nibs into chocolate liquor—a misleading term because it is only liquid when it is heated and it contains no alcohol. Chocolate liquor, also confusingly known as cocoa solid or solids, is the pure essence of the roasted and skinned cocoa bean, and is commonly available as unsweetened chocolate.

Chocolate liquor may also be pressed to extract its natural fat, cocoa butter, which is used in both the confectionery and cosmetic industries. What remains of chocolate liquor after most (about 85 percent) of the cocoa butter has been pressed out is called a "cake." Cakes are sometimes further defatted and ground to become cocoa powder. Cocoa treated with an alkali during processing is referred to as alkalized or Dutch process cocoa.

For the manufacture of other types of chocolate, finely pulverized sugar and flavoring (usually artificial vanilla) are added to the paste of crushed nibs. Lecithin, an emulsifying agent derived from soybeans, is also added to keep the chocolate mixture from separating during manufacture or when the chocolate is melted. Often extra cocoa butter is added at this point, especially if the end product is to be high-quality chocolate.

After all the ingredients are mixed together they are conched. Conching refers to the process of beating the chocolate mixture constantly for a period of sometimes several days. This decreases bitterness and diminishes the particle size, giving the chocolate a smoother "mouth feel."

After conching, the chocolate is tempered (for a full explanation of tempering, see pages 20–23) and molded into large or small bars, depending on its destination. After this, all that remains is the wrapping and shipping.

If the chocolate is to be made into candies, after tempering it usually goes by pipeline directly to be mixed with other ingredients or molded into candies.

CHOCOLATE TYPES

• • •

The many different brands and flavors of chocolate may be easily grouped into several types.

Cocoa Powder: Available as both nonalkalized and alkalized (Dutch process) cocoa. Cocoa is used in baking and in making candies as well as in beverages. When used as an ingredient in recipes in this book, alkalized or nonalkalized cocoa is always specified. If you have no alkalized cocoa powder and must substitute nonalkalized cocoa, add a pinch of baking soda to the cocoa.

Powdered Chocolate or Ground Chocolate: More available in Europe than North America, ground chocolate is a sweet powder made from semisweet chocolate that does not have a very high cocoa butter content. It is best used as a flavoring for whipped cream or as a beverage mix. I don't usually use it for baking.

Baking Chocolate: These are the 1-ounce squares of chocolate commonly available in the supermarket. They usually come in semisweet and unsweetened varieties, and are best used in recipes in which chocolate is one of many ingredients. With the possible exception

WHAT'S THE BEST CHOCOLATE?

Chocolate must adhere to strict laws governing its content, as you can easily see from the FDA's chart of obligatory percentages of ingredients opposite. Even so, wide differences exist in the flavor and performance of chocolate. How can you tell which is the best?

First of all, use chocolate for the purpose for which it was intended. Don't try to make a truffle center with baking chocolate or to coat a mold with chocolate that isn't fluid enough. Once you know the right type of chocolate for your recipe, the best chocolate is the one that tastes best to you. Remember, texture and smoothness matter a lot with chocolate, especially when the chocolate is used with few or no other ingredients. Chocolate should be smooth, not grainy on the tongue and palate, and should melt easily. So taste a few different brands before you invest in a lot of any one particular chocolate.

of high-quality unsweetened chocolate used in some confections, this type of chocolate is almost always used only in baking.

Couverture Chocolate: The name means "covering" and it derives from the fact that this type of chocolate may be tempered and used for molding and dipping. But confusingly there are also many eating or "candy bar" type chocolates that qualify as couverture. Basically, the chocolate has to have enough added cocoa butter to make it fluid when it melts because otherwise it would be impossible to pour into molds or use for dipping. Couverture may also be used for almost any other purpose—its high cocoa butter content does not make it unsuitable for use in candies or in baking, although the most costly couvertures would be wasted if combined with other ingredients and baked.

Eating Chocolate: Though many chocolates sold for eating are enhanced with additives that contribute flavor or texture, plain bars—especially the 3- or 4-ounce bars of imported eating chocolate—are ideal for tempering. To test this, melt an ounce or two of chocolate in a heatproof bowl placed in another bowl of hot tap water. If the melted chocolate flows freely when you lift some of it with a spoon it will be good for tempering.

Compound Coating: Though this is not really chocolate, the best coatings are chocolate products, which contain some pure chocolate. Compounds are chocolate-flavored products in which the cocoa butter is enhanced or replaced by hard vegetable fat, a practice that occurs in the preparation of some confections and the manufacture of "candy melts" or other types of nonchocolate coatings. Compounds are used because they require no tempering, though the best compounds are merely an inferior substitute for chocolate. Some of these are manufactured to be used for glazing cakes and pastries, as the French name *pâte à glacer* (icing or glazing paste) would suggest. The best compounds taste good—though never as good as pure chocolate. Beware of little disks called candy melts, sold in candy-molding hobby stores: Taste one and you'll know why. Compound coatings come in many different colors (in fact, they used to be referred to as summer coatings, because they are harder and therefore less likely to melt in hot weather) and are sometimes used in the preparations of certain chocolate decorations.

CHOCOLATE FLAVORS

. . .

Although describing chocolate flavors really has to do with semantics and percentages of cocoa solid, here are the norms used for defining the different types of chocolate according to the minimum percentages of chocolate liquor, sugar, and other ingredients used by the FDA:

	CHOCOLATE LIQUOR	SUGAR	EMULSIFIER	FLAVOR ADDITIVES
UNSWEETENED	100%	—	1%	Variable
BITTERSWEET	35%	Variable	1%	Variable
SEMISWEET	35%	Variable	1%	Variable
SWEET	15%	Variable	1%	Variable
MILK	10%	Variable	1%	12% whole milk

Note: White confectionery bars, not to say white "chocolate," contain no chocolate liquor; therefore, they may not strictly be called chocolate.

NONCHOCOLATE INGREDIENTS

...

To prepare the recipes in this book you will need ingredients other than chocolate. What follows are descriptions and specifications for the nonchocolate ingredients used in the recipes.

Flour: Both all-purpose flour and cake flour are called for. Although you may not substitute one for the other (all-purpose flour contains a higher percentage of gluten-forming proteins and is better used for pastry doughs), I don't think it matters if you use bleached or unbleached all-purpose flour. All cake flour is bleached. In the cake chapter, some recipes use all-purpose flour for cakes. I use self-rising cake flour for angel food cake, but not for any other recipe. And remember: Always measure flour or any other dry ingredient by gently spooning it into a dry measuring cup, then leveling the cup with the back of a knife or with a spatula.

Other starches used in the recipes that follow are cornstarch and bread crumbs. If you purchase dry bread crumbs instead of preparing your own by pulverizing stale bread in the food processor, make sure you buy the unflavored kind. Occasionally a recipe may call specifically for fresh bread crumbs. To make them, reduce fresh white bread, crust removed, to fine, moist crumbs in the food processor. A variation on a recipe to make a Passover cake may suggest substituting potato starch, matzoh meal, or a combination.

Sugars: I always use plain granulated, not superfine, sugar. When a recipe calls for dark or light brown sugar, use that exact type for best results. The only difference between them is the strength of the molasses flavor, which is more pronounced in dark brown sugar. Don't hesitate to substitute granulated light brown sugar for the moist type. For accurate measuring always remember to pack and press moist brown sugar into a dry-measure cup. Confectioners' sugar is called for in some recipes, often for dusting a finished cake or pastry—do not use it as a substitute for granulated sugar.

Liquid Sugars: Light and dark corn syrup, honey, molasses, and maple syrup are called for in some recipes. Corn syrup contributes smoothness to preparations from candy centers to ices. Honey, molasses, and maple syrup are only used when their flavor is desired.

Dairy Products: When milk is specified in recipes it refers to whole milk. Cream is always heavy whipping cream, though I like to use half and half for crème anglaise and some ice cream mixtures, but in those cases I specify it in the recipe. Butter is always unsalted and eggs are always graded large.

Other dairy products found in the recipes include cream cheese and sour cream. Be careful not to purchase the "light" or fat-free versions, which will not perform the same way as the full-fat version. Mascarpone, the Italian cream cheese, is called for in a recipe or two as is crème fraîche, the slightly fermented French cream.

Leaveners: Double-acting baking powder, baking soda, active dry yeast, and compressed yeast are called for in recipes. Do not substitute instant or rapid-rise yeast for dry yeast. If you buy dry yeast in bulk, use 2½ teaspoons of dry yeast for one envelope.

Nuts: Many nut products are used in the preparation of chocolate candies and desserts. Always be sure nuts are fresh. If possible, taste them where you buy them—if nuts have become rancid, they taste bitter. Rancid nuts will render any recipe inedible. Store all nuts in heavy-duty plastic bags in the freezer. If you will be keeping them only a short time before using them, store dry and airtight at a cool room temperature.

Almond Products: Whole almonds are available as natural almonds, with the skins on, or blanched, with the skins removed. To blanch almonds, place them in a saucepan and cover with water. Bring to a boil over medium heat and drain in a strainer or colander. Place the hot, wet almonds on a clean kitchen towel, then fold the towel over them and rub—most of the almonds will separate from the skins and the ones that have not will pop out easily if you squeeze them.

Sliced almonds are flat slices of whole almonds, either blanched or natural. Slivered almonds are cut into matchstick shapes and granulated almonds are slivered almonds that have been cut across into little cubes. If you can't find granulated almonds, hand-chopped slivered almonds are a good substitute. Almond flour is the commercial form of ground almonds—great if you can find it because it's finer than you can grind it your-self. To make your own, pulse room-temperature almonds repeatedly in the food processor, stopping occasionally to scrape down the inside bottom of the bowl with a metal spatula. Stop pulsing the machine before the almonds become sticky. If you want to grind almonds that have been stored in the freezer, let them come to room temperature first or the condensation will make them pasty—or warm them slightly on a jelly-roll pan in a 350-degree oven, then cool them to room temperature before grinding. Always buy almond paste that comes in a can. The type that comes in a cellophane-wrapped cylinder has little almond flavor and is usually dried out.

Hazelnut Products: Hazelnuts or filberts come in all the above forms except slivered and granulated. Sliced hazelnuts are rare, though they exist. To blanch hazelnuts, toast them at 350 degrees on a jelly-roll pan for 10 or 15 minutes, or until the skins crack and shatter off easily. Then rub the nuts in a towel—damp terry cloth works best—and separate the nuts from the skins.

Praline paste, a rich mixture of hazelnuts and sugar the consistency of peanut butter, is called for in some recipes. It is also made from almonds or a combination of almonds and hazelnuts. See Sources, page 442, for purchasing.

Pecans: Pecans are sold shelled as halves or pieces or a combination—the latter is an economical choice for pies, tarts, and candies.

Walnuts: Walnuts are available like pecans; neither needs to be blanched. They may both be ground in the food processor, but be careful, they turn to paste easily. I find that hand-chopping pecans and walnuts works better.

Pistachios: The best come from Sicily and are all but unavailable outside Europe. Always buy pistachios in a Middle Eastern grocery store and try to get Turkish or other imported varieties, which are greener and more flavorful than the California ones. Blanch pistachios—an essential step when cooking with them—like almonds.

Macadamias: These expensive nuts usually come salted. Most of the time, all traces of salt can be removed by bringing the nuts to a boil in fresh water and rinsing in running cold water after draining. Place on a jelly-roll pan and dry out at 300 degrees in the oven for 5 minutes. Cool before using.

Pine Nuts: Buy these in bulk at an import store—the tiny jars in the supermarket are ridiculously high in price. Always taste pine nuts before using. They are highly subject to turning rancid.

Peanuts: I like to use the honey-roasted type for the occasional cookie or candy. For peanut butter, grind warm, skinned, toasted peanuts in a food processor. They will turn into a slightly chunky butter much better than the salt- and oil-laden supermarket varieties.

Oils: I always use a mild oil, such as canola or corn.

Herbs and Spices: Keep these tightly covered in a cool, dark place—I don't even keep mine in the kitchen anymore. Don't buy large quantities—it is much better to buy herbs and spices often than to use inferior-tasting ones. See Sources, page 442, for mail-order suppliers.

Liquors and Liqueurs: Don't skimp here. The best available are often the most expensive, but by using the best, you will avoid adding an off flavor to your dessert or candy. Fine liquors and liqueurs (sweetened liquors) should enhance the flavor of chocolate and good desserts—they should never dominate the flavor or taste bitter.

Instant Espresso: This comes in a 1-ounce jar; if you can't find instant espresso, use 1½ times the quantity in regular instant coffee.

SPECIAL EQUIPMENT FOR WORKING WITH CHOCOLATE
· · ·

Though you need a minimum of special equipment to prepare the recipes in this book, if you wish to acquire specialized equipment you may wish to know about the possibilities.

Thermometers: I prefer a mercury-gauge chocolate thermometer (see Sources, page 442). Though digital thermometers are tempting, only the most expensive ones are accurate. A small instant-read thermometer works well for testing doneness on a loaf of bread or a roast, but it is not accurate enough for tempering chocolate.

Chocolate Molds: Old-fashioned chocolate molds were made of heavy base metal that was silver-plated on the inside. Though you may encounter these occasionally in flea markets or antique stores, they are not very practical, and are mainly collectibles nowadays. If you have an old mold and you absolutely have your heart set on using it, have the inside resilvered (check Yellow Pages for this) and it will work well for molding. Most contemporary chocolate molds are made of polycarbonate or other plastic. I prefer clear to opaque molds because it is easy to see if the chocolate has set and shrunk from the mold. Remember: Any shiny-surfaced metal, glass, or plastic vessel may be used as a chocolate mold—even an inflated balloon.

Dipping Forks: Best to use the professional type available in kitchenware stores (opposite) or see Sources for mail order. To approximate one, bend the middle two tines back on a cheap, lightweight stainless-steel table fork—or use a long, thin, two- or three-tined fork, or a fondue fork.

Offset Spatula: This type of metal spatula works like a trowel—the blade is set about an inch lower than the handle and makes spreading batters and frostings easier.

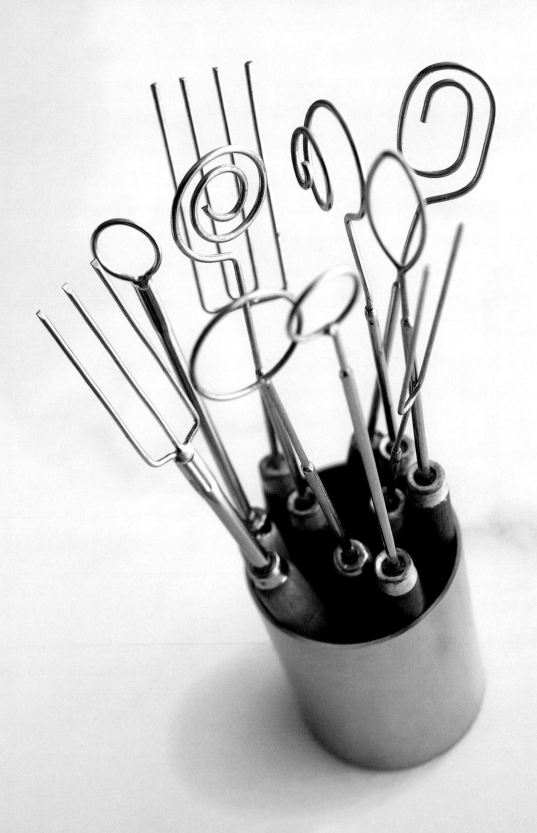

Tempering Machines: One of these is useful if you are doing a lot of tempering, although even the cheaper ones are quite an investment. There are three basic ones available. A Hilliard will hold 5 pounds of chocolate and is the one for large-quantity work. It costs about $1,200. An A.C.M.C. tempering machine will hold almost as much, but costs about $700. A Sinsation chocolate maker, meant for small-quantity home use, holds about a pound, but only costs about $325—probably the best investment if you are not going into large-scale production. See Sources, page 442, for ordering information.

GENERAL BAKING EQUIPMENT

• • •

Electric Mixer: Although you may use a hand mixer for most of the recipes here, I use a Kitchen-Aid 5-quart mixer for all general mixing and whipping.

Food Processor: This is no longer an optional piece of equipment. I use a seven-cup food processor for many purposes such as grinding nuts and mixing pastry doughs.

Pans and Molds: Buy the best, heavy-duty aluminum baking pans you can afford. Though they may be easy to find in kitchenware stores, be sure to check local restaurant supply stores for the best quality at more reasonable prices. For catalog sales, see Sources, page 442. Recipes in this book will call for 8-, 9-, or 10-inch-diameter pans that are 2 inches deep.

Pie Pans: I always use a plain 9-inch Pyrex pie pan. This is *not* the one with a fluted edge and two handles, which is deeper and holds almost twice as much as the plain one.

Tart Pans: I use the fluted-sided, removable-bottom type, which are usually available in tinned metal. I prefer these to the black steel ones, which are prone to rust and sometimes make baked goods turn out too dark.

Aluminum Foil Baking Pans: If you are going to try a recipe and don't have a particular size pan, it can be practical to pick up a foil pan in the supermarket. One caveat: Be sure to place the aluminum foil pan on a cookie sheet or jelly-roll pan before filling it. This will prevent it from buckling when full of batter and insulate it a little better during baking. I especially like the 4-ounce pleated foil cups for individual cakes, such as the Warm Chocolate-Chili Cakes on page 124.

Cake Circles or Cardboards: These come in a variety of sizes from a cake-decorating or specialty store. See Sources at the end of the book.

PRIMARY LESSONS IN WORKING WITH CHOCOLATE
▪ ▪ ▪

STORAGE

The best chocolate in the world can't survive improper storage and handling. Though a little bloom (cocoa butter or sugar rising to the surface of chocolate blocks that have warmed up and cooled down again) won't necessarily hurt what you are preparing, it's better to keep your chocolate at a uniform 65 degrees with about 50 percent humidity to avoid having this happen.

If you live in a warm climate, store in an air-conditioned room; failing that, refrigerate or freeze, but if you do, be on the lookout for condensation. This can be a problem, especially on chocolate that is to be melted—then the little beads of moisture can cause the chocolate to become grainy while it is melting.

If chocolate becomes dry and grainy and hardens (the process is called seizing) while it is melting, add a teaspoon of vegetable oil and stir until the chocolate is smooth again. Adding the oil will not affect your recipe if you are going to bake the resulting dough or batter. Chocolate that has seized cannot be tempered (see pages 20–23). Adding oil to smooth out seized chocolate makes it no longer pure chocolate and only pure chocolate can be tempered.

To chop small pieces of chocolate such as 1-ounce squares, a sharp chef's knife or even a serrated knife (makes the job easy but is bad for the blade) works well. If you want chocolate very finely chopped, cut it into ¼-inch pieces by hand, then pulse pieces in the food processor with metal blade until finely chopped.

A four-tined ice pick makes quick work of chopping large blocks of chocolate—you will likely find one at the hardware store.

For all the recipes in this book, chocolate should be cut into ¼-inch pieces.

MELTING

To melt large quantities of chocolate, put it in a roasting pan and place in an oven with a pilot light—in several hours the chocolate will melt slowly and perfectly.

In a microwave oven, place the chocolate in a microwave-safe bowl and set oven at half power. Microwave for 30 seconds at a time, stirring chocolate between zaps.

On the stove, bring a saucepan half filled with water to a boil; turn off heat. Put chocolate in a heatproof bowl and place the bowl over the hot water. Stir occasionally as chocolate melts.

When melting chocolate with hot ingredients, add cut-up chocolate to hot ingredients in the bowl or pan, then wait a minute or two so that the heat of the cream, melted butter, or sugar syrup can penetrate the chocolate. Then, after you are sure the chocolate has melted, whisk the mixture smooth.

TEMPERING

Though there are entire books written about tempering, what follows is a fast, simple description of how to accomplish this process with a minimum of laboratory talk and incomprehensible statistics.

Why temper? When you raise the temperature of chocolate above 91.5 degrees and melt it, the crystals of cocoa butter (all hard saturated fats form crystals) melt and lose their shape. When the chocolate cools back to about 80 degrees it will harden again, but the crystals, having been rendered unstable by the rise in temperature during melting, will not automatically resume their previous shape. The resulting chocolate will look dull and streaky rather than shiny and its texture will be grainy rather than smooth. Tempering is a process of manipulating the temperature of melted chocolate to make the cocoa butter crystals resume their previous shape so that the chocolate returns to the stable condition it was in before you melted it.

Tempering is necessary if the chocolate is to be used for molding, dipping, or coating. It is not necessary if the melted chocolate is to be used in a baked item or in a candy center that contains other ingredients. Tempering is only for when the chocolate is unadulterated. The exception to this rule is when preparing simple candies such as clusters or bark, where nuts and/or broken candy are added to the chocolate. If the chocolate is not tempered, the clusters will not have the right consistency or appearance. To temper accurately you *must* have a chocolate thermometer (see Sources, page 442).

How to temper: Melt, cool, reheat—three simple steps, but you need to monitor the temperature of the chocolate exactly.

1. *Melt the chocolate.* You may use any method you choose, but make sure the temperature of the chocolate rises to between 115 and 120 degrees. If the chocolate melts but doesn't get hot enough, the crystals of cocoa butter will not melt completely and it will be impossible to temper the chocolate—even if you accomplish the other two steps perfectly. This is the single greatest cause of failure in tempering chocolate. Warm, untempered, melted chocolate is referred to as virgin chocolate.

2. *Cool the chocolate.* My favorite way is to do nothing—leave the chocolate at a cool room temperature, stirring it occasionally, until the temperature drops into the low eighties. You can tell this is happening when the chocolate starts to set around the top edge in the bowl.

Other ways of cooling the chocolate are tabling and seeding.

TABLING: Pour about half the melted chocolate out onto a smooth non-porous surface, such as a marble slab. Spread the chocolate back and forth with a metal spatula until it starts to cool and to thicken slightly. Keeping it moving constantly, scrape it back into the bowl of virgin chocolate. *Pitfall to avoid*: Leaving the chocolate on the marble too long and having it solidify. This is to be avoided, but if it happens, just scrape the hardened chocolate into a clean, dry bowl and remelt it by whatever method you used.

SEEDING: Add some large chunks of unmelted chocolate to the virgin chocolate to bring down the temperature—this is the same principle as using ice cubes in a drink. The unmelted chocolate not only cools, it also seeds the virgin chocolate with stable crystals, encouraging the chocolate to be in good temper. *Pitfalls to avoid*: Adding too much seed and having the chocolate solidify in the bowl. The right amount to add is about 20 percent of the weight of the virgin chocolate.

3. *Reheat the chocolate:* After you have cooled the chocolate into the low eighties, the last step is to raise the temperature of the chocolate into the tempered range. This is 88 to 91 for dark chocolate and 86 to 88 for milk chocolate and white chocolate. The best way to do this is to lower the bowl with the chocolate over a pan of hot, not simmering, water for a few seconds at a time. Use your thermometer to gauge the temperature of the chocolate accurately. *Pitfall to avoid*: If you heat the chocolate above the high end of the tempered range, you must start all over again, and remelt the chocolate to between 115 and 120 degrees, or the chocolate will not be in good temper.

When you really need to temper: For anything molded or coated or dipped, the chocolate must be in good temper. For truffles, I do a quick temper when I am going to roll the truffles in cocoa, confectioners' sugar, grated chocolate, or ground nuts—in this case I just melt the chocolate and cool it to about 90 degrees, and it works well all the time.

Keeping chocolate in temper: There are many ways to keep chocolate in temper once you have gotten it to the correct temperature. One way is to add small amounts of virgin chocolate to the tempered chocolate as the tempered chocolate cools. But, if you add too much and the temperature goes above the tempered range, you must start all over again. Other ways to keep chocolate in good temper: place the bowl of chocolate on a heating pad wrapped in a thick towel and safely placed inside a plastic bag, with the heating pad set at low. I have done this successfully on many occasions. Still another way is to keep the bowl of tempered chocolate half in the aura of a 250-watt heat lamp set about a foot from the top of the bowl. This method has to be monitored—the chocolate may overheat.

BASIC CAKE LAYERS FOR CHOCOLATE CAKES

• • •

Chocolate Genoise

Plain Genoise

Genoise Sheet

Chocolate Sponge Cake

Plain Sponge Cake

Sponge Cake Sheet

PLAIN CAKES

• • •

Easy Fudgy Loaf Cake

Torta Caprese
(*Neapolitan Chocolate Walnut Cake*)

Cocoa Angel Food Cake
with Raspberry Compote

Chocolate Sour Cream Cake

Cocoa Banana Coffee Cake

Chocolate Honey Cake

Grand-maman's Chocolate Cake

Chocolate Rum Raisin Loaf Cake

Chocolate Chip Pound Cake

Chocolate Walnut Pound Cake
with Shiny Chocolate Glaze

German Chocolate Marble Cake

Milk Chocolate Gugelhupf

Chocolate Mayonnaise Cake

Chocolate Chunk Pecan Crunch Cake

Chocolate Pecan Bourbon Cake

ONE-LAYER CAKES

• • •

Vermont Farmhouse Devil's Food Cake

Easy Flourless Chocolate Cake

Coffee-Flavored Flourless Chocolate Cake

Torta Divina
(*Chocolate Mousse Cake with Liqueur*)

Rich Cocoa Mousse Cake

Fudge Cake

Slivered Almond Fudge Cake

Slivered Almond Fudge Passover Cake

Texas Sheet Cake

Yogurt Poppy Seed Cake
with White Chocolate Frosting

Total Heaven Chocolate Almond Cake

Chocolate Pudding Cake

Triple Chocolate Cheesecake

ROLLED CAKES

• • •

Swiss Roll

Traditional Bûche de Noël

Chocolate Soufflé Roll
with Striped Chocolate Filling

LAYER CAKES

• • •

Old-fashioned Chocolate Layer Cake

Chocolate Orange Cake

Chocolate Chestnut Cake

Traditional Black Forest Cake

Raspberry Devil's Food Cake

Lemon-Scented White Cake
with Milk Chocolate Frosting

The Horseradish Grill's
Chocolate Chocolate Cake

Texas Chocolate Prune Cake

Chocolate Velvet Cake
Chocolate Velvet Coffee Cake

Blanc et Noir
(*Black and White Cake*)

Chocolate Walnut Nougatine Cake

Chocolate Walnut Crown

Chocolate Mocha Heart

Chocolate Hazelnut Pavé

Swiss Chocolate Hazelnut Cake

Chocolate Banana Layer Cake

CHOCOLATE
MERINGUE CAKES
...

Chocolate Meringue Cake

Quadruple Chocolate Cake

Chocolate Meringue Heart

Chocolate Pavlova
Chocolate Meringue Shell

MOLDED CAKES
...

Dark and White Chocolate Mousse Cake

Venetian Chocolate Cake

Chocolate Raspberry Bavarian Cake

Chocolate Hazelnut Mousse Cake

Chocolate Raspberry Cream Cake

Golden Chocolate Charlotte

Rigotorte

CAKES IN BOWLS
...

Chocolate and Vanilla Trifle

Chocolate Orange Trifle

INDIVIDUAL CAKES
...

Pierre Hermé's Warm
Chocolate-Chili Cakes
with Caramelized Bananas

Petits Fondants au Chocolat
(*Little Chocolate Mousse Cakes*)

Chocolate Orange Slices

Chocolate Buttermilk Cupcakes
with Boiled Icing

If cakes mean celebrations, chocolate cakes mean extra special ones. The recipes in this chapter are varied. Some of the cakes are simple ones—what I call "mix-bake-eat." Others are more elaborate—they consist of several component parts, such as a moistening syrup, a filling, a frosting, and decorations to create the finished cake.

Remember, it is not necessary to prepare every one of these component parts on the same day you intend to serve the cake. Elaborate desserts are best made in stages over a period of several days. Cake layers may always be frozen in advance and syrups can wait in a covered container in the refrigerator. Some fillings, such as ganache, must be made in advance, so that they have time to cool and achieve spreading consistency before use. And decorations such as toasted nuts or chocolate shavings keep almost indefinitely. Let your experiences with preparing cakes for friends and family be relaxed and pleasant rather than harried and rushed. Remember, baking elaborate desserts, as some of these are, should be an enjoyable pastime, not a rigorous obligation.

These are the types of cakes you will encounter in this chapter:

Cake Layers: Basic cakes—such as genoise, the French sponge cake—not used on their own, but always in conjunction with frostings and fillings and finishes to make more elaborate desserts. Sponge cakes such as these are used when there is a stronger emphasis on frostings than on the cake itself, and are really a delicate and simple vehicle for these more elaborate finishes.

Plain Cakes: Some loaf, pound, and other rich cakes that are left unfinished except for a sprinkling of confectioners' sugar or perhaps a drizzle of glaze. These keep well frozen and are great to have on hand in the freezer. Also, these are among the best cakes for "bringing." They transport easily in any weather and won't get ruined if they have to survive a few bumps in the trunk of the car.

Layer Cakes: For these, you either prepare a single cake and divide it into separate layers with a knife, or bake a series of individual layers to be assembled with a filling later on. In general, if the layer is a sponge cake, it is usually baked as a large layer and then cut. Butter cakes—recipes that start out with butter beaten with sugar, with eggs and other ingredients added afterward—are usually baked as separate layers.

Rolled Cakes: These are prepared as rectangular sheets, spread with filling and rolled up. The simplest ones are just sprinkled with confectioners' sugar on the outside, though more elaborate ones are spread with glaze or frosting.

Molded Cakes: Cakes that are assembled with fillings inside a pan or mold. Frequently the filling is a mousse or other soft filling that must be refrigerated to set before the cake can be unmolded and finished.

BASIC CAKE LAYERS FOR CHOCOLATE CAKES

. . .

The following recipes are for cake layers used later in this chapter. Though each recipe makes a cake that stands alone, each is really best suited to being finished in one way or another.

CHOCOLATE GENOISE

. . .

Makes I round layer, 9 or 10 inches
in diameter by 2 inches deep

⅓ cup cake flour

⅓ cup cornstarch

¼ cup alkalized (Dutch process) cocoa powder

3 large eggs plus 3 large egg yolks

¾ cup sugar

Pinch salt

One 9 or 10 × 2-inch round layer pan, or a 9-inch springform pan, buttered and the bottom lined with a disk of parchment or wax paper

This versatile French sponge cake may be used in any number of ways—usually it is filled and frosted or rolled.

I. Set a rack at the middle level of the oven and preheat to 350 degrees.

2. Sift together the cake flour, cornstarch, and cocoa through a fine-meshed strainer over a piece of wax paper to break up any small lumps in the cocoa. Set sifted ingredients aside with the strainer.

3. Whisk together the eggs, yolks, sugar, and salt in the bowl of an electric mixer. Place the bowl over a pan of simmering water and continue whisking gently until the mixture is lukewarm, about 100 degrees. This should take only a minute or two.

4. Whip with the electric mixer on high speed until the mixture is cooled and increased in volume, about 3 to 4 minutes.

5. Remove bowl from mixer and sift in dry ingredients, in three additions, gently folding each third in with a rubber spatula. Pour the batter into the prepared pan and spread the top even with a spatula.

6. Bake the layer about 30 minutes, until it is well risen and the center is firm to the touch.

7. If necessary, loosen the layer from the side of the pan with a small knife or spatula and invert the cake onto a rack. Place another rack on the cake and invert again. Remove the top rack, so that the layer cools right side up, still on the paper.

STORAGE: Double-wrap the layer in plastic wrap and refrigerate for several days or freeze for several months.

HINTS FOR SUCCESS: Keep the egg and sugar mixture just warm. If the temperature gets higher, the mixture will not whip up well, and the cake layer will not rise as much while baking.

VARIATIONS

PLAIN GENOISE Omit the cocoa powder and use ½ cup cake flour and ¼ cup cornstarch.

GENOISE SHEET Bake batter at 400 degrees in a 10 × 15 × 1-inch or 11 × 17-inch jelly-roll pan, buttered and lined with parchment or wax paper. The cake will take about 15 minutes to bake, until it is well risen and the center is firm to the touch. Be careful not to overbake, especially if the layer is to be rolled. Loosen the cake from the sides of the pan and slide it, still stuck to the paper, onto a work surface to cool—this helps keep the finished cake moist.

CHOCOLATE SPONGE CAKE

. . .

Makes I round layer, 9 or 10 inches
in diameter by 2 inches deep

⅓ cup all-purpose flour

⅓ cup cornstarch

⅓ cup alkalized (Dutch process)
cocoa powder

4 large eggs, separated

¾ cup sugar, divided

1 teaspoon vanilla extract

Pinch salt

One 9 or 10 × 2-inch round layer
pan, or a 9-inch springform pan,
buttered and the bottom lined
with a disk of parchment or wax
paper

This version of a sponge cake uses separated eggs to assemble the batter and yields a particularly tender and chocolaty result.

1. Set a rack at the middle level of the oven and preheat to 350 degrees.

2. Sift the flour, cornstarch, and cocoa together through a fine-meshed strainer onto a piece of wax paper to break up any small lumps in the cocoa. Set sifted ingredients aside with the strainer.

3. Whisk the yolks with half the sugar and the vanilla in the bowl of an electric mixer. Whip with the electric mixer on medium speed for about 4 minutes, until the mixture is pale, fluffy, and lemon-colored. Set aside.

4. In a clean, dry mixer bowl, combine the egg whites and salt. Whip on medium speed until white and opaque and beginning to hold a very soft peak. Increase speed and whip in remaining sugar gradually, until the whites hold a firm peak.

5. Fold the yolk mixture into the whipped whites, using a rubber spatula. In three additions, sift in dry ingredients, gently folding each third in with the spatula. Pour the batter into the prepared pan and spread the top even with the spatula.

6. Bake the layer about 30 minutes, until well risen and firm to the touch in the center.

7. If necessary, loosen the layer from the side of the pan with a small knife or spatula and invert the cake onto a rack. Place another rack on the cake and invert again, removing the top rack, so that the layer cools right side up, still on the paper.

STORAGE: Double-wrap the layer in plastic wrap and refrigerate for several days or freeze for several months.

PLAIN SPONGE CAKE Omit the cocoa powder and use ½ cup all-purpose flour and ½ cup cornstarch.

SPONGE CAKE SHEET Bake batter at 400 degrees in a 10½ × 15½ × 1-inch jelly-roll pan, buttered and lined with parchment or buttered wax paper. The cake will take 10 to 15 minutes to bake, until it is well risen and the center is firm to the touch. Be careful not to overbake, especially if the layer is to be rolled. Loosen the cake from the sides of the pan and slide it, still stuck to the paper, out onto the work surface to cool—this helps keep the finished cake moist.

. . .

Although these cakes are anything but plain in flavor and texture, they are so called because they are served unadorned by filling or frosting. These are all great cakes to take on picnics or pack in lunches. Serve them for tea or for those odd hours of the day when you "just want something."

EASY FUDGY LOAF CAKE

. . .

Makes one 8½ × 4½ × 2¾-inch loaf cake

2 cups cake flour

2 teaspoons baking powder

¼ teaspoon salt

8 tablespoons (1 stick) unsalted butter, softened

½ cup granulated sugar

½ cup light brown sugar

2 ounces unsweetened chocolate, melted and cooled

1 large egg

¾ cup milk

1 teaspoon vanilla extract

One 8½ × 4½ × 2¾-inch loaf pan, buttered and the bottom lined with parchment or wax paper

This easy cake may be served as it is or adorned with some whipped cream.

1. Set a rack at the middle of the oven and preheat to 325 degrees.

2. In a small bowl, stir together the flour, baking powder, and salt.

3. Use an electric mixer set at medium speed to beat the butter and sugars together until light, about 5 minutes. Beat in the chocolate and continue beating until smooth. Scrape bowl and beater(s) and beat in the egg. Continue beating until creamy and smooth, another minute or two.

4. By hand, using a rubber spatula, stir in half the flour mixture, making sure to scrape the sides of the bowl well. Stir in the milk and vanilla, then the remaining flour mixture.

5. Scrape the batter into the prepared pan and smooth the top. Bake for about an hour, or until well risen and a toothpick inserted into the middle comes out clean. Cool in the pan for 5 minutes, then unmold, remove paper, and finish cooling on a rack.

SERVING: You may serve it with tea or coffee or as a snack.

STORAGE: Keep the cake wrapped in plastic at room temperature for several days. For longer storage, wrap and freeze.

TORTA CAPRESE

Neapolitan Chocolate Walnut Cake

■ ■ ■

Makes one 10-inch round cake,
about 10 servings

10 tablespoons (1¼ sticks) unsalted
butter, softened

¾ cup sugar, divided

8 ounces semisweet chocolate,
melted and cooled

7 large eggs, separated

1½ cups walnut pieces, about 6
ounces

⅓ cup all-purpose flour

Confectioners' sugar for finishing

One 10-inch round cake pan, 2
inches deep, buttered and the
bottom lined with parchment or
wax paper

This rich cake, which contains very little flour,
derives its intense flavor from walnuts and
chocolate. It is not difficult to prepare and also
keeps well.

1. Set a rack at the middle level of the oven and
preheat to 350 degrees.

2. In a large mixer bowl, beat the butter with half
the sugar until soft and light. Beat in the melted
chocolate, then the yolks, one at a time, scraping
bowl and beater(s) often. Continue beating until the
mixture is smooth and light.

3. Place the walnuts in the bowl of a food processor
and grind them finely, pulsing the machine on and off
at 1-second intervals. Be careful that the walnuts do
not become gummy. Stir the walnuts into the batter,
then the flour.

4. In a clean, dry bowl, beat the egg whites until
they hold a very soft peak, then beat in the remaining
sugar in a slow stream. Continue to beat until the whites hold a soft, glossy
peak. Stir ¼ of the whites into the batter, then with a rubber spatula fold in the
rest so that no streaks remain.

5. Pour the batter into the prepared pan and smooth the top. Bake about 40
minutes, until the center is firm when pressed with a fingertip.

6. Cool the cake in the pan for 10 minutes. The cake may sink slightly, though
this does not affect its texture. Trim off any loose crust and invert the cake on
a rack, remove the pan and paper, and allow to cool completely.

SERVING: Dust the cake with confectioners' sugar and slide onto a platter.

STORAGE: Keep cake under a cake dome at room temperature.

COCOA ANGEL FOOD CAKE WITH RASPBERRY COMPOTE

. . .

Makes one 10-inch cake, 10 to 12 servings

CAKE BATTER

1 cup self-rising cake flour

⅓ cup alkalized (Dutch process) cocoa powder, sifted before measuring

1¼ cups sugar, divided

1½ cups egg whites (about 12 or 13 from large eggs)

¼ teaspoon salt

2 teaspoons vanilla extract

RASPBERRY COMPOTE

Two ½-pint baskets fresh raspberries

¼ cup sugar

1 tablespoon raspberry liqueur

1 teaspoon lemon juice

1 ungreased 10-inch tube pan with removable bottom, *not nonstick*

Serving an angel cake with a compote always dresses it up.

1. Set a rack at the middle level of the oven and preheat to 325 degrees.

2. Combine the self-rising cake flour, cocoa, and ½ cup of the sugar in a small mixing bowl and stir well with a small whisk to combine. Set aside.

3. In a clean, dry bowl, use an electric mixer on medium speed to whip the egg whites with the salt until they are frothy. Continue beating the egg whites until they are white and opaque, and are beginning to hold their shape when the beaters are lifted. Increase the speed to high and gradually whip in the remaining ¾ cup sugar, continuing to whip the egg whites until they hold a soft, glossy peak. Beat in the vanilla extract.

4. Remove bowl from mixer and sift a third of the cocoa mixture over the whites. Use a rubber spatula to fold gently. Repeat with another third of the cocoa mixture, then fold in the remaining cocoa mixture. Fold slowly and deliberately, scraping across the bottom of the bowl with the spatula often. This will prevent the cocoa mixture from accumulating there and forming lumps. Scrape the batter into the pan, then cut into the batter with a series of side-by-side vertical chops, to break up any large air bubbles in the batter. Smooth the top.

5. Bake the cake for about 40 to 45 minutes, until it is well risen and firm when pressed with a fingertip.

6. Immediately after removing the cake from the oven, invert the pan and hang it with the center tube over the neck of a bottle (don't worry, the cake won't fall out). Cool the cake completely.

7. After it is cool, take the pan off the bottle. Insert a thin knife between cake and pan and scrape against the pan, all the way around to loosen the cake. To remove the cake from the pan lift the central tube, then slide knife all around between pan bottom and cake, then around central tube. Invert the cake to a platter or cake stand.

8. For the compote, crush one quarter of the berries and combine with the sugar, liqueur, and lemon juice. Gently fold in the remaining raspberries.

SERVING: To cut an angel food cake, use a sharp serrated knife and cut back and forth with a sawing motion, rather than cutting straight down, which would only compress the cake. Serve each slice with some of the compote on the side.

STORAGE: Keep under a cake dome at room temperature or wrap well and freeze. Defrost and bring to room temperature before serving. Store the compote tightly covered and in the refrigerator.

CHOCOLATE SOUR CREAM CAKE

▪ ▪ ▪

Makes one 10 × 5-inch loaf cake,
about 12 servings

1½ cups all-purpose flour

½ cup alkalized (Dutch process) cocoa powder

1 teaspoon baking powder

¼ teaspoon baking soda

16 tablespoons (2 sticks) unsalted butter, softened

1⅓ cups sugar

2 large eggs, at room temperature

One 8-ounce container sour cream

One 10 × 5-inch loaf pan, buttered and the bottom lined with parchment or buttered wax paper, cut to fit

This elegant loaf cake is adapted from a recipe by my friend Dorie Greenspan, baker and prize-winning author of *Baking with Julia* (Morrow, 1996). The recipe appeared in Dorie's first book, *Sweet Times* (Morrow, 1991).

1. Set a rack at the middle level of the oven and preheat to 350 degrees.

2. Combine the flour, cocoa, baking powder, and baking soda in a mixing bowl and stir well to mix. Sift the dry ingredients onto a piece of parchment or wax paper and set aside.

3. Beat the butter and sugar together in an electric mixer set at medium speed. Beat in the eggs, one at a time, beating smooth after each addition.

4. Lower mixer speed to low and beat in half the dry ingredients. Scrape bowl and beater(s) well. Add the sour cream and scrape again, then beat in the remainder of the dry ingredients.

5. Scrape batter into prepared pan and bake cake 55 to 65 minutes, or until well risen and a toothpick or knife inserted into the center of the cake emerges clean.

6. Cool in pan on a rack for 5 minutes, then turn out of pan. Turn cake over again so it stands right side up to finish cooling.

SERVING: Cut thin slices of cake and serve with whipped cream or even chocolate sauce.

STORAGE: Wrap cake in plastic and keep at room temperature or freeze. If frozen, bring to room temperature before serving.

COCOA BANANA
COFFEE CAKE
• • •

Makes 1 Bundt cake, about 12 large servings

1½ cups mashed *very* ripe bananas (about 4)

One 8-ounce container sour cream

1¼ cups all-purpose flour

¾ cup alkalized (Dutch process) cocoa powder

1½ teaspoons baking soda

¾ teaspoon salt

12 tablespoons (1½ sticks) unsalted butter, softened

1½ cups sugar

3 large eggs

One 10-cup Bundt pan, buttered and floured, tapped to remove excess flour

The recipe for this excellent and easy cake comes from my friend Jennifer Migliorelli.

1. Set a rack at the middle level of the oven and preheat to 350 degrees.

2. In a mixing bowl, mix together the bananas and sour cream; set aside.

3. Sift together the flour, cocoa, baking soda, and salt onto a piece of wax paper and set aside.

4. Use an electric mixer set at medium speed to beat the butter and sugar until well combined, then beat in the eggs, one at a time, beating until smooth after each addition.

5. Beat in half the flour mixture. Scrape bowl and beater(s) well. Beat in the banana mixture, scrape bowl again, then beat in the remaining flour mixture and scrape well again.

6. Bake 55 to 65 minutes until well risen and a toothpick inserted halfway between the side of the pan and the tube emerges clean.

CAKES

SERVING: This is great with chocolate ice cream.

STORAGE: Keep cake under a cake dome at room temperature.

CHOCOLATE HONEY CAKE

• • •

Makes one 10-inch round Bundt cake

1¾ cups cake flour

¼ cup Dutch process (alkalized) cocoa powder

¼ teaspoon salt

1 teaspoon baking soda

½ teaspoon ground ginger

½ teaspoon ground cinnamon

8 tablespoons (1 stick) unsalted butter, softened

1 cup dark flavorful honey

1 egg

½ cup buttermilk

One 10-cup Bundt pan, buttered and dusted with fine dry bread crumbs

This unusual recipe comes from my friends Sheila and Marilynn Brass, who created it as a variation on a traditional Jewish honey cake.

1. Set a rack at the lower third of the oven and preheat to 350 degrees.

2. Sift together the flour, cocoa, salt, soda, ginger, and cinnamon once onto a piece of parchment or wax paper. Set aside.

3. Use an electric mixer set on medium speed to beat the butter with the honey until light, about 3 minutes. Beat in the egg and continue beating until smooth and light, another 2 minutes.

4. On low speed, beat in half the dry ingredients, then scrape down bowl and beater(s) with a rubber spatula. Beat in the buttermilk and scrape down again, then repeat with remaining dry ingredients.

5. Spoon the batter into the prepared pan and bake the cake for about 30 to 35 minutes, or until a toothpick inserted halfway between the side of the pan and the center tube emerges clean.

6. Cool the cake in the pan on a rack for 10 minutes, then invert onto a rack, remove pan, and finish cooling.

SERVING: Marilynn and Sheila suggest serving this with butter pecan ice cream. It's also great alone as a tea cake.

STORAGE: Keep the cake at room temperature under a cake dome or double-wrap in plastic and freeze.

GRAND-MAMAN'S CHOCOLATE CAKE

• • •

Makes one 8-inch round cake, about 8 servings

3 large eggs

¾ cup sugar

8 tablespoons (1 stick) unsalted butter, very soft

4½ ounces bittersweet chocolate, melted and cooled

¾ cup all-purpose flour

Confectioners' sugar for finishing

One 8-inch round cake pan, 2 inches deep, buttered and lined with parchment or wax paper

In France, this popular chocolate cake is one of the simple desserts almost everyone prepares at home. This version is adapted from *Le Patissier Chocolatier* by Daniel Giraud (Edition S.E.G.G., 1986), who has a beautiful pastry shop in Valence, not far from Lyons in France.

1. Set a rack at the middle level of the oven and preheat to 350 degrees.

2. In an electric mixer fitted with the whisk attachment, whip eggs and sugar on medium speed for 4 to 5 minutes, until very light and increased in volume. Whip in the butter, then the chocolate, beating until smooth after each addition.

3. Remove the bowl from the mixer and use a rubber spatula to fold in the flour by hand. Scrape the batter into the prepared pan and smooth the top.

4. Bake the cake about 30 minutes, until well risen and still moist in the very center.

5. Cool in the pan for 5 minutes, then invert onto a rack to cool. When cool, peel off the paper and slide onto a platter. Dust with confectioners' sugar just before serving.

SERVING: This plain cake is great with any kind of ice cream accompaniment.

STORAGE: Keep the cake at room temperature under a cake dome or wrap and freeze for longer storage.

CHOCOLATE RUM RAISIN
LOAF CAKE
. . .

Makes one 9 × 5 × 3-inch loaf cake

1 cup dark raisins

½ cup candied orange peel, cut into
 ¼-inch dice

¼ cup dark rum

1 cup all-purpose flour

3 tablespoons alkalized (Dutch
 process) cocoa powder

1 teaspoon baking powder

¼ teaspoon salt

8 tablespoons (1 stick) unsalted
 butter, softened

⅔ cup sugar

2 ounces bittersweet chocolate,
 melted and cooled

4 large eggs

One 9 × 5 × 3-inch loaf pan,
 buttered and the bottom lined
 with parchment or wax paper,
 cut to fit

This cake was the result of my experiments in trying to develop a chocolate fruitcake. It's much lighter and more appealing than a standard fruit-cake would be and will be gobbled up rather than put away and remailed every Christmas to another unsuspecting relative.

1. A few hours, or the day, before preparing the cake, place the raisins in a saucepan and cover them with water. Bring to a simmer over low heat. Drain the raisins and place in a bowl. Add the orange peel and rum and stir together. Cover with plastic wrap and allow to macerate a few hours or overnight.

2. When ready to prepare the cake, set a rack at the middle level of the oven and preheat to 350 degrees.

3. Sift together the flour, cocoa, baking powder, and salt to break any lumps in the cocoa. Set aside until needed.

4. Use an electric mixer to beat the butter and sugar until soft and light. Beat in the chocolate, then one of the eggs, then a second. Beat in half the flour mixture, then the other two eggs, one at a time. Beat well and scrape down bowl and beater(s) after each addition. Beat in the remaining flour mixture. Stir in the raisins, peel, and rum mixture. Pour batter into prepared pan.

5. Bake the cake about an hour, or until a toothpick or thin knife inserted in the center emerges clean.

6. Cool the cake in the pan for about 5 minutes, then unmold to a rack to cool. Peel off paper.

SERVING: Serve as a tea cake or with whipped cream or ice cream for dessert.

STORAGE: The cake keeps well wrapped in plastic at room temperature. Freeze for longer storage.

CHOCOLATE CHIP POUND CAKE
. . .
Makes one 10-inch cake

3 cups all-purpose flour

2 teaspoons baking powder

½ teaspoon salt, plus a pinch for the egg whites

One 12-ounce bag semisweet chocolate chips

1 cup coarsely chopped walnuts or pecans, about 4 ounces

16 tablespoons (2 sticks) unsalted butter, softened

2 cups sugar

4 large eggs, separated

1 teaspoon vanilla extract

1 cup whole milk

Confectioners' sugar for finishing

One 10-cup (10-inch) Bundt or tube pan, buttered and floured

Don't neglect to try this one—it's easy and delicious and one of those cakes to make when you just want to have something terrific in the house, although it's also perfect for special occasions.

The recipe comes from my cousin, Karen Ludwig. It originally came from Karen's stepmother, Julie Rocco.

1. Set a rack at the middle level of the oven and preheat to 350 degrees.

2. Stir the flour, baking powder, and salt together in a bowl. Combine the chocolate chips and chopped nuts in another bowl and toss them with a tablespoon of the flour mixture.

3. In a large mixer bowl beat the butter and sugar at medium speed until the mixture is light in color and fluffy, about 5 minutes. Add the egg yolks, one at a time, beating smooth between each addition. Beat in the vanilla.

4. On lowest speed, beat in a third of the flour mixture, scrape bowl and beater(s), then beat in half the milk, scrape bowl and beaters again and do so after each addition. Continue to alternate adding another third of the flour, the remaining milk, and the remaining flour, scraping well after each addition.

5. In a clean, dry mixer bowl, beat the egg whites with a pinch of salt. Continue beating until the egg whites hold a soft peak. Stir about a third of the egg whites into the batter to lighten it, then fold in the remaining egg whites with a rubber spatula. Stir in the chocolate chips and nuts. Pour the batter into the prepared pan and smooth the top with the spatula.

6. Bake the cake for 65 to 75 minutes, or until it is well risen and a thin knife inserted midway between the side of the pan and the central tube emerges clean.

7. Cool the cake in the pan for about 5 minutes, then invert over a rack and remove the pan. Cool completely.

8. Dust the cake lightly with confectioners' sugar before serving.

SERVING: Great by itself, this is also a good cake to serve with ice cream or some crushed, sweetened berries.

STORAGE: Keeps well at room temperature under a cake dome or securely wrapped in plastic wrap for several days. Or wrap and freeze for up to several months.

CHOCOLATE WALNUT POUND CAKE WITH SHINY CHOCOLATE GLAZE

• • •

Makes one Bundt cake,
10 to 12 servings

CAKE BATTER

2 cups walnut pieces, about 7 to 8 ounces

8 ounces semisweet chocolate, cut into ¼-inch pieces

16 tablespoons (2 sticks) unsalted butter, softened

1 cup sugar, divided

8 eggs, separated

1 cup all-purpose flour

¼ teaspoon salt

CHOCOLATE GLAZE

¼ cup water

¼ cup light corn syrup

⅔ cup sugar

6 ounces semisweet chocolate

One 10-cup Bundt or other tube pan, buttered

Almonds or hazelnuts make a good substitute for the walnuts in this recipe.

1. Set a rack at the middle level of the oven and preheat to 350 degrees.

2. Place walnuts in the bowl of a food processor fitted with the steel blade and pulse until finely ground.

3. Bring a small pan of water to a boil and remove from heat. Place chocolate in a heatproof bowl and set over the pan of water, stirring occasionally, until chocolate melts. Remove bowl from pan and set aside to cool slightly.

4. In a large mixer bowl beat the butter and ½ cup of the sugar until soft and light. Beat in the chocolate and scrape bowl and beater(s). Beat in the egg yolks, one at a time. Scrape bowl and beater(s). Stir in the ground walnuts and the flour by hand.

5. In a clean, dry mixer bowl, on medium speed, whip the egg whites and the salt until they are frothy. Continue whipping the egg whites until they are white and opaque, and beginning to hold their shape when the beaters are lifted. Increase the speed and gradually beat in the remaining ½ cup of sugar. Continue to whip the egg whites until they hold a soft, glossy peak.

6. Stir a quarter of the egg whites into the batter to lighten it, then fold in the remaining egg whites with a rubber spatula, until no streaks of egg white remain. Scrape the batter into the prepared pan.

7. Bake the cake about 45 to 55 minutes, until it is well risen and a toothpick or skewer inserted midway between the edge of the pan and the central tube emerges fairly clean. Do not bake the cake until it is dry. Place a rack on the pan and invert cake and pan onto rack. Remove pan after 5 minutes and allow cake to cool.

8. For glaze, combine water, corn syrup, and sugar in a saucepan and stir well to mix. Place over low heat and bring to a boil, stirring occasionally to dissolve sugar. Remove from heat and add chocolate. Swirl pan so that chocolate is submerged in hot syrup, then allow to stand 2 minutes. Whisk glaze smooth. Pour glaze from pan onto the highest point of the cake. Pour all around circle of cake, allowing glaze to drip down outside and center of cake. Transfer cake to a platter while glaze is still wet to avoid having it crack.

SERVING: Serve in slices with ice cream, if you wish.

STORAGE: Keep cake under a cake dome at room temperature.

GERMAN CHOCOLATE
MARBLE CAKE
▪ ▪ ▪

Makes one 10-inch tube cake or two loaves

9 ounces bittersweet chocolate, cut
  into ¼-inch pieces

2½ cups all-purpose flour

2 teaspoons baking powder

Pinch salt

24 tablespoons (3 sticks) unsalted
  butter, softened

1¾ cups sugar

7 large eggs, at room temperature

Grated zest and strained juice of 1
  large lemon (about 1 tablespoon
  zest and 4 tablespoons juice)

5 tablespoons dark rum, divided

3 tablespoons milk

½ teaspoon baking soda

One 10-inch tube or Bundt pan, or
  two 9 × 5 × 3-inch loaf pans,
  buttered and then dusted with
  flour or dry bread crumbs

I've been listening to my friend Ceri Hadda go on about this cake for the past fifteen years. It's a specialty of her mother, Anne-Marie Hadda, who brought the recipe with her from Germany. This version is adapted from Ceri's book, *Coffeecakes* (Simon & Schuster, 1992).

1. Set a rack at the middle level of the oven and preheat to 350 degrees.

2. Put the chocolate in a heatproof bowl and place the bowl over a pan of hot, not simmering, water to melt. Remove the bowl from the pan when the chocolate has melted, stir, then allow the chocolate to cool while preparing the rest of the ingredients.

3. Combine the flour, baking powder, and salt in a bowl and stir well to mix. Set aside.

4. Use an electric mixer set at medium speed to beat the butter and sugar until light, about 3 minutes. Beat in the eggs, one or two at a time, beating well between each addition. (After all the eggs are added, the mixture may seem separated—this does not matter.)

5. Beat in the lemon zest, juice, and 2 tablespoons of the rum.

6. Gradually beat the flour mixture into the butter mixture.

7. Remove 3 cups of the batter to a bowl. Stir the remaining 3 tablespoons rum, the milk, and the baking soda into the melted chocolate and immediately beat the chocolate mixture into the 3 cups batter.

8. Spread the chocolate or white batter evenly in the prepared pan(s), then top with the other batter. Plunge a knife or spatula into the cake batter and cut up and down through the batter. Repeat every inch around the cake to marbleize the two batters. Or place alternating spoonfuls of the two batters into the pan(s), then gently stir through once.

9. Bake the tube cake about 1 hour, or until a knife inserted halfway between the edge of the pan and the tube emerges clean. Bake the loaves about 45 minutes, testing them the same way.

10. Cool the cake(s) in the pan(s) on a rack for 15 minutes, then invert to a rack to cool completely.

SERVING: Cut thick slices. This cake needs no accompaniment.

STORAGE: Store under a cake dome or wrap well and freeze.

MILK CHOCOLATE GUGELHUPF

. . .

10 to 12 servings

BATTER

1 cup cake flour

⅔ cup cornstarch

2 teaspoons baking powder

1 cup sugar

14 tablespoons (1¾ sticks) unsalted
   butter, softened

Grated zest of 1 orange

5 large eggs

¼ cup milk

One 12-ounce package milk
   chocolate chips, coarsely
   chopped in the food processor

GLAZE

¼ cup water

¼ cup light corn syrup

¾ cup sugar

6 ounces milk chocolate, cut into
   ¼-inch pieces

One 2-quart or larger Gugelhupf
   mold or Bundt pan, buttered and
   dusted with flour

This classic Viennese coffee cake is leavened with baking powder. For a slightly different taste, use semisweet, white, and milk chocolate chips.

1. Set a rack at the middle level of the oven and preheat to 350 degrees.

2. To mix the batter, sift the cake flour, cornstarch, and baking powder into an electric mixer bowl. Add sugar and mix on low speed. Add butter and orange zest and mix until smooth, 3 minutes.

3. Combine eggs and milk and add half to batter. Mix 5 minutes. Scrape bowl and beater and add half the remaining liquid and continue mixing 2 more minutes. Scrape again, add remaining liquid and mix 2 more minutes.

4. Fold chips into batter by hand. Pour batter into prepared pan and smooth top. Bake for about 50 minutes, until well risen and deep golden brown and a thin knife inserted in the thickest part of the cake emerges clean. Cool the cake in the pan for 5 minutes, then invert onto a rack, remove mold, and cool completely.

5. To make the glaze, combine water, corn syrup, and sugar in a saucepan. Place over low heat and bring to a boil, stirring occasionally. Off heat, add chocolate and let stand 3 to 4 minutes. Whisk smooth and place in a plastic bag or a wax paper or parchment cone. Snip off corner of bag or end of cone and drizzle glaze over cake. Leave cake on rack until glaze is set, then transfer to a platter.

SERVING: Serve in wedges for dessert or tea.

STORAGE: Keep under a cake dome or well wrapped at room temperature.

CHOCOLATE MAYONNAISE CAKE
• • •

Makes one 9-inch round or square cake

2 cups all-purpose flour

1 cup sugar

½ cup alkalized (Dutch process) cocoa powder, sifted after measuring

1½ teaspoons baking soda

1 cup buttermilk (or whole milk plus 1 tablespoon distilled white vinegar or lemon juice)

1 cup bottled mayonnaise (I always use Hellman's)

1 teaspoon vanilla extract

Confectioners' sugar for finishing

One 9-inch round cake pan, 2 inches deep, or a 9 × 9 × 2-inch square pan, buttered and the bottom lined with parchment or wax paper

Chocolate mayonnaise cake was invented in the thirties by the wife of a grocery salesman, to boost his mayonnaise sales. The mayonnaise adds a richness and moistness to the cake. This recipe was shared by biochemist Liza Davies, a friend and colleague from the King's Supermarket cooking schools in New Jersey.

Chocolate mayonnaise cake will always have a special place in my heart. On September 30, 1987 (also my fortieth birthday), I prepared the presentation cake (shaped like a 5-foot-tall jar of mayonnaise, complete with gold-leaf label) for Hellman's mayonnaise's seventy-fifth anniversary celebration.

1. Set a rack at the middle level of the oven and preheat to 350 degrees.

2. In a large mixing bowl, combine the flour, sugar, cocoa, and baking soda and stir well to mix.

3. In another bowl, whisk together the buttermilk, mayonnaise, and vanilla; stir into the dry ingredients to form a smooth batter.

4. Pour the batter into the prepared pan and bake for 45 to 50 minutes, or until risen and a small knife or toothpick inserted in the center of the cake emerges clean.

5. Cool the cake in the pan for 5 minutes, then invert onto a rack and peel off the paper. Cool completely.

6. To serve, dust lightly with confectioners' sugar.

SERVING: Serve unadorned, accompanied by fruit, or cover the cake with Old-Fashioned Boiled Frosting, page 52.

STORAGE: Keep the cake at room temperature under a cake dome, or double-wrap in plastic and freeze. Defrost and bring to room temperature before serving.

CHOCOLATE CHUNK PECAN CRUNCH CAKE

• • •

Makes one 10-inch Bundt cake,
about 16 servings

PECAN CRUNCH

2 tablespoons (¼ stick) unsalted butter, softened

½ cup light brown sugar, firmly packed

2 tablespoons all-purpose flour

1 teaspoon ground cinnamon

¾ cup coarsely chopped pecan pieces, about 3 ounces

CAKE BATTER

3 cups all-purpose flour

2 teaspoons baking powder

½ teaspoon baking soda

¼ teaspoon salt

16 tablespoons (2 sticks) unsalted butter, softened

1½ cups granulated sugar

3 large eggs, at room temperature

2 teaspoons vanilla extract

Grated zest of 1 large orange

1½ cups sour cream

4 ounces bittersweet chocolate, cut into ¼-inch chunks

One 10-inch Bundt pan, buttered and floured, excess flour tapped out

This fun cake is the creation of my friend, Dallas caterer Sheri Portwood. The bottom of the pan is lined with a pecan crunch mixture, so that the crunch is on top when the cake is unmolded.

1. Set a rack at the middle level of the oven and preheat to 350 degrees.

2. To make the crunch, beat butter in a mixing bowl with a rubber spatula until smooth. Beat in the sugar, then beat in the remaining crunch ingredients until the mixture is a crumble. Use a spoon to scatter the crumble evenly on the bottom of the prepared pan.

3. To make the batter, in a mixing bowl combine the flour, baking powder, baking soda, and salt and mix well. Sift onto a sheet of parchment or wax paper.

4. Use an electric mixer on medium speed to beat butter and sugar until mixed, about a minute. Beat in the eggs, one at a time, beating smooth after each addition. Beat in the vanilla and the orange zest.

5. Beat in a third of the dry ingredients. Scrape bowl and beater(s) well. Beat in half the sour cream, then another third of the dry ingredients, scraping well. Beat in the remaining sour cream, then the remaining dry ingredients. Scrape well one more time.

6. Fold the chocolate chunks into the batter by hand and pour it into the pecan-crunch-lined pan.

7. Bake the cake for 65 to 75 minutes, until a toothpick inserted halfway between the side of the pan and the tube emerges clean.

8. Cool in pan on a rack for 5 minutes, then turn cake over onto a rack, remove pan, and cool completely.

SERVING: This cake cries out for ice cream to accompany it, although it is also wonderful plain with tea or coffee.

STORAGE: Keep at room temperature under a cake dome or well wrapped in plastic. Or double-wrap in plastic and freeze.

CHOCOLATE PECAN
BOURBON CAKE
• • •

Makes one 9-inch cake, about 10 servings

2 ounces semisweet chocolate, cut
   into ¼-inch pieces

2 ounces unsweetened chocolate,
   cut into ¼-inch pieces

8 tablespoons (1 stick) unsalted
   butter

2 tablespoons Bourbon

1½ cups pecan pieces, about 6
   ounces

1½ cups sugar, divided

¾ cup all-purpose flour

1 cup egg whites (from about 7 or 8
   large eggs)

¼ teaspoon salt

One 9-inch cake pan, 2 inches deep,
   or a 9-inch springform pan,
   buttered and the bottom lined
   with parchment or wax paper

This rich, elegant Southern cake needs nothing more than a dusting of confectioners' sugar to finish it off.

1. Set a rack at the middle level of the oven and preheat to 350 degrees.

2. Bring a small pan of water to a boil and remove from heat. Combine the chocolates and the butter in a heatproof bowl and set over the pan of water, stirring occasionally, until melted. Remove bowl from pan, stir in Bourbon, and set aside.

3. Combine the pecans and ¾ cup of the sugar in the bowl of a food processor fitted with the steel blade and pulse continually until nuts are finely ground. Pour into a bowl and stir in the flour.

4. In a clean, dry mixer bowl, whip the egg whites with the salt on medium speed, until they are frothy. Continue whipping the egg whites until they are white and opaque, and are beginning to hold their shape when the beaters are lifted. Increase the speed to high and gradually beat in the remaining ¾ cup sugar. Continue to whip the egg whites until they hold a soft, glossy peak.

5. Remove bowl from mixer and use a rubber spatula to stir in the pecan mixture. Don't worry about overmixing—the batter deflates when the butter and chocolate mixture is added. After the dry ingredients are incorporated, fold in the chocolate and butter mixture, continuing to fold until no streaks remain.

6. Scrape the batter into the prepared pan and smooth the top. Bake the cake about 50 minutes, until well risen and a toothpick or skewer inserted in the center emerges clean. Loosen with a knife around the side, then invert the cake onto a rack to cool. When cool peel off the paper.

SERVING: Dust cake lightly with confectioners' sugar before serving.

STORAGE: Keep cake under a cake dome at room temperature.

These single-layer cakes with frosting are a little more elaborate than plain cakes. Although still quick and easy to put together for a birthday or special occasion, the addition of frosting or whipped cream dresses them up.

VERMONT FARMHOUSE DEVIL'S FOOD CAKE

. . .

Makes one 10-inch cake, about 12 servings

CAKE BATTER

2½ cups cake flour

1 teaspoon baking soda

½ teaspoon salt

8 tablespoons (1 stick) unsalted
    butter, softened

2½ cups dark brown sugar

3½ ounces unsweetened chocolate,
    melted and cooled

3 large eggs

½ cup sour cream

2 teaspoons vanilla extract

1 cup boiling water

OLD-FASHIONED BOILED FROSTING

3 egg whites, about 6 tablespoons

1 cup granulated sugar

⅓ cup light corn syrup

Pinch salt

One 10-inch springform pan,
    buttered and the bottom lined
    with parchment or wax paper

This recipe was given to me by Copeland Marks, the famous teacher of Asian and Latin American cooking.

1. Set a rack at the middle level of the oven and preheat to 350 degrees.

2. Sift flour, baking soda, and salt once, then set aside. With an electric mixer set at medium speed, beat butter until soft and light. Add sugar and continue beating until very light, about 5 minutes. Beat in chocolate, then eggs, one at a time. Continue beating until light and smooth.

3. Beat in half the sour cream, then half the flour mixture, scraping bowl and beater(s). Repeat with remaining sour cream and flour mixture, scraping again. Combine vanilla and boiling water and gently beat into batter. Pour batter into prepared pan and bake for about 45 minutes, until firm and well risen. Cool in pan on rack for 5 minutes, then unmold and cool on a rack.

4. For the frosting, combine all ingredients in bowl of mixer. Whisk to combine, then place over a pan of simmering water, gently whisking until mixture is hot and sugar is dissolved. Use electric mixer on medium speed to beat until cooled, but not dry.

5. To finish, cover top and sides of cake with frosting, swirling it from the center outward.

SERVING: Cut the cake with a moist knife, wiping the blade with a wet cloth between each cut.

STORAGE: Keep cake under a cake dome at room temperature.

EASY FLOURLESS CHOCOLATE CAKE

• • •

Makes one 9-inch cake, about 10 servings

CAKE

8 tablespoons (1 stick) unsalted butter, softened to room temperature

¾ cup sugar

7 large eggs, separated

8 ounces semisweet chocolate, melted and cooled

Pinch salt

FINISHING

¼ cup seedless raspberry preserves

1 cup heavy whipping cream

3 tablespoons sugar

One 9-inch springform pan, buttered and the bottom lined with a disk of parchment or wax paper

CHOCOLATE

This has to be one of the fastest and easiest recipes ever and just the thing for last-minute entertaining. You can have it in and out of the oven in an hour. Thanks to New York chef and teacher Amanda Cushman for sharing the recipe.

1. Set a rack at the middle level of the oven and preheat to 350 degrees.

2. Beat butter and sugar until light: by hand, with a hand mixer set at medium speed, or in a heavy-duty mixer fitted with the paddle attachment, about 3 to 5 minutes.

3. Add the yolks, one at a time, beating until smooth after each addition. Beat in the chocolate.

4. In a clean, dry bowl, beat the egg whites with the salt until soft peaks form. Stir about a third of the egg whites into the batter, then, using a rubber spatula, gently fold in the remaining egg whites.

5. Pour the batter into the prepared pan and smooth to make the top even. Bake the cake for about 40 minutes, until well risen and the center is firm and elastic to a fingertip.

6. Cool the cake in the pan for 5 minutes, then invert onto a rack to cool completely. Slide the cake from the rack onto a platter.

7. To finish, place the preserves in a small pan and stir over low heat to melt. Pour preserves into center of cake and allow to cool to room temperature.

8. Whip the cream with the sugar until soft peaks form. Spread the cream over the top of the cake, covering the preserves, shortly before serving.

SERVING: Cut this rich cake into 10 or 12 wedges. Serve with some fresh fruit or berries on the side, if you wish, though it really needs no embellishment.

STORAGE: To make the cake ahead, cool and double-wrap in plastic wrap. Store in the refrigerator several days or in the freezer several months. Bring the cake to room temperature before finishing it. This can be done a short time before serving. Pour the preserves over it and leave at room temperature. Whip the cream and refrigerate it. Spread the cream on the cake shortly before serving.

COFFEE-FLAVORED FLOURLESS CHOCOLATE CAKE For a coffee flavor, add 2 tablespoons instant espresso coffee dissolved in 1 tablespoon water or rum to the batter after the egg yolks. Omit the raspberry preserves and garnish the whipped cream with some chocolate shavings.

TORTA DIVINA

Chocolate Mousse Cake with Liqueur

▪ ▪ ▪

Makes one very rich 8-inch cake, about 8 to 10 servings

BATTER

½ cup granulated sugar

½ cup water

8 tablespoons (1 stick) unsalted butter, softened

12 ounces semisweet or bittersweet chocolate, cut into ¼-inch pieces

⅓ cup sweet liqueur, such as Cointreau or Chambord

6 eggs

FINISHING

1 cup heavy whipping cream

2 tablespoons sugar

One ½-pint basket fresh raspberries, optional

One 8-inch round pan, buttered and the bottom lined with buttered parchment or buttered wax paper, cut to fit

This unusual cake may be made in advance. Just make sure to bring it to room temperature before serving.

1. Set a rack at the middle level of the oven and preheat to 325 degrees.

2. Combine the sugar and water in a saucepan and bring to a boil over low heat, stirring occasionally to make sure all the sugar crystals dissolve.

3. Remove the syrup from the heat and stir in the butter and chocolate; allow to stand 5 minutes. Whisk smooth.

4. Whisk liqueur, then the eggs, one at a time, into the chocolate mixture. Be careful not to overmix.

5. Pour the batter into the pan and place in a small roasting pan. Pour 1 inch of warm water into the roasting pan. Bake about 45 minutes, until dessert is set and slightly dry on the surface. Remove cake pan from roasting pan. Cool to room temperature, then cover with plastic wrap. Refrigerate dessert in pan several hours or until chilled. To unmold, run a knife between the dessert and the pan and pass the bottom of the pan over heat for no more than 10 seconds. Invert onto a platter.

6. To finish, whip the cream with the sugar until it holds a soft peak. Spread the whipped cream over the top of the dessert. If you wish, decorate the top with the raspberries.

STORAGE: Cover and refrigerate leftovers; bring to room temperature before serving.

RICH COCOA MOUSSE CAKE

■ ■ ■

Makes I very rich 8-inch cake,
about 8 to 10 servings

½ cup water

⅔ cup sugar

¼ teaspoon salt

16 tablespoons (2 sticks)
unsalted butter

6 ounces semisweet chocolate

⅔ cup alkalized (Dutch process)
cocoa powder

4 large eggs

¼ cup orange liqueur or other
sweet liqueur

WHIPPED CREAM

1 cup heavy whipping cream

2 tablespoons sugar

One 8-inch round cake pan,
2 inches deep, buttered and the
bottom lined with a disk of
parchment or wax paper and
set in a small roasting pan

This dessert gets its strong chocolate flavor from cocoa as well as chocolate. Though it may be prepared several days in advance and stored in the refrigerator, it is so easy to make that such advance preparation hardly seems necessary. For delightful excess, garnish the dessert with whipped cream.

1. Set a rack at the middle level of the oven and preheat to 325 degrees.

2. Combine the water, sugar, and salt in a saucepan and bring to a boil over medium heat, stirring occasionally. Combine the butter and chocolate in a heatproof bowl and place over a pan of hot, but not simmering water to melt. Stir occasionally. Sift the cocoa into a mixing bowl. Slowly whisk the boiling liquid into the cocoa, keeping the mixture smooth and free of lumps. Whisk in the melted chocolate and butter, then whisk in the eggs, one at a time, then the liqueur.

3. Pour the batter into the prepared pan and pour warm tap water into the roasting pan to a depth of 1 inch. Bake the dessert 45 minutes, until it is slightly puffed and firm when gently pressed with a fingertip.

4. Remove from the pan of hot water and cool on a rack at room temperature. Refrigerate the dessert for several hours until it is firm.

5. To unmold, taking no more than 10 seconds, place the pan on a burner set at low heat and rotate it so that the heat reaches the entire bottom of the pan. Run a small, sharp knife between the dessert and the pan, then invert a platter over the pan. Invert and remove the pan. Peel off the paper and cover loosely with plastic wrap. Refrigerate until serving time.

6. Whip the cream with the sugar until it holds a soft peak. To serve, cut the dessert into wedges and serve some of the whipped cream on the side.

STORAGE: Cover and refrigerate leftovers; bring to room temperature before serving.

FUDGE CAKE

• • •

Makes one 10-inch cake, about 12 servings

FUDGE CAKE BATTER

  1 cup sugar

  1 cup flour

  16 tablespoons (2 sticks) unsalted
    butter, softened

  ¼ cup strong coffee

  6 eggs

  12 ounces bittersweet chocolate,
    melted and cooled

WHIPPED CREAM

  1 cup heavy whipping cream

  2 tablespoons sugar

  1 teaspoon vanilla extract

  One 10-inch round cake pan,
    buttered and the bottom lined
    with parchment or wax paper

This rich and satisfying cake needs only a bit of whipped cream to finish it.

1. Set a rack at the middle level of the oven and preheat to 325 degrees.

2. Put sugar, flour, and butter in the bowl of an electric mixer. Beat on lowest speed 3 minutes.

3. Add coffee and 3 of the eggs to the chocolate; whisk to combine. Add to bowl and mix on slow speed 1 minute. Stop, scrape bowl and beater(s), and beat on medium speed 3 minutes. Scrape again.

4. Add remaining eggs and beat 1 minute on second speed. Stop, scrape, and beat for 1 more minute.

5. Pour into prepared pan and bake about 45 to 55 minutes, or until the cake forms a peak in the center, or until a thin knife or a toothpick inserted in the center of the cake emerges with only a little batter clinging to it—do not bake the cake until it is dry. Cool in pan on a rack, then turn out and refrigerate covered with plastic wrap.

6. To finish, whip the cream with the sugar and vanilla until it holds a soft peak. Spread the whipped cream over the top of the cake.

SERVING: Serve in wedges with some berries or alone.

STORAGE: Refrigerate cake until time to serve and bring to room temperature before serving.

SLIVERED ALMOND
FUDGE CAKE
• • •

Makes one very rich 9-inch cake,
about 12 servings

FUDGE CAKE BATTER

16 tablespoons (2 sticks) unsalted
butter, softened

½ cup granulated sugar

½ cup dark brown sugar, firmly
packed

1 tablespoon instant espresso coffee
powder

½ teaspoon almond extract

4 ounces unsweetened chocolate,
melted

4 large eggs, at room temperature

1 cup all-purpose flour

1 cup slivered almonds, toasted

FINISHING

1 cup heavy whipping cream

2 tablespoons sugar

1 teaspoon vanilla extract

¼ cup slivered almonds, toasted

One 9-inch springform pan,
buttered

The crisp matchsticks of toasted almond give
this rich cake a bit of crunch.

1. Set a rack at the middle level of the oven and
preheat to 350 degrees.

2. Use an electric mixer on medium speed to beat
together the butter and sugars until light, about 2
minutes. Beat in the instant coffee, almond extract,
and chocolate, then the eggs, one at a time, beating
well after each addition. Beat in flour, then almonds.

3. Scrape the batter into the prepared pan and
smooth the top. Bake the cake 30 to 40 minutes, until
it is fairly firm in the center, but still somewhat soft in
general. Do not overbake or cake will be very dry.
Cool the cake on a rack.

4. To finish the cake, run the blade of a small knife
between the side of the pan and the cake all around
to loosen it. Unbuckle the springform side and
remove it, but leave the cake on the base.

5. To make the whipped cream, combine the cream,
sugar, and vanilla in the bowl of an electric mixer and
whip until the cream holds soft peaks. Spread the
cream over the top of the cake and sprinkle with the
slivered almonds. If you are preparing the cake early
in the day, leave it covered at room temperature and
whip the cream and refrigerate it. Rewhip the cream
if it has separated, spread it on the cake, and sprinkle
with the almonds right before serving.

SERVING: Cut the cake into wedges. It needs no accompaniment.

STORAGE: For advance preparation, bake the cake, cool, wrap, and refrigerate
or freeze it. Bring cake to room temperature and finish as above.

VARIATION

SLIVERED ALMOND FUDGE PASSOVER CAKE Substitute ¾ cup matzoh
cake meal for the flour.

TEXAS SHEET CAKE

• • •

Makes one 13 × 9 × 2-inch cake,
about twenty-four 2-inch squares

CAKE LAYER

  2 cups all-purpose flour

  2 cups sugar

  1 teaspoon ground cinnamon

  1 teaspoon baking soda

  16 tablespoons (2 sticks) unsalted
    butter

  ¼ cup alkalized (Dutch process)
    cocoa powder

  1 cup water

  ½ cup buttermilk or milk

  2 large eggs

  1 teaspoon vanilla extract

FROSTING

  8 tablespoons (1 stick) unsalted
    butter

  ⅓ cup heavy whipping cream

  ¼ cup alkalized (Dutch process)
    cocoa powder

  1 teaspoon vanilla extract

  4 cups (one 1-pound box)
    confectioners' sugar

  1 cup chopped pecans

  1⅓ cups sweetened shredded
    coconut

One 13 × 9 × 2-inch pan, buttered
  and floured

There are many versions of this popular cake. This one comes from a combination of recipes from two friends from Texas, Allen Smith and Dorothy Perkins, mother of my friend David Perkins.

1. Set a rack at the middle level of the oven and preheat to 350 degrees.

2. In a large mixing bowl combine the flour, sugar, cinnamon, and baking soda. Stir well to mix.

3. Combine the butter, cocoa, water, and buttermilk in a saucepan and place over low heat. Stir occasionally until the mixture comes to a simmer and the butter is completely melted.

4. Add the contents of the saucepan to the dry ingredients and quickly stir them together. Stir in the eggs and vanilla extract, but stop mixing when the batter is smooth.

5. Scrape the batter into the prepared pan and smooth the top. Bake for about 30 minutes, or until cake is well risen and springs back slightly in the center when touched with a fingertip. Place the pan on a rack to cool for about 15 minutes before spreading on the frosting, which should be applied to the warm cake.

6. To make the frosting, combine the butter, cream, and cocoa in a saucepan and bring to a boil over low heat, stirring occasionally. Remove from heat and add remaining frosting ingredients. Mix well and spread over the top of the still-warm cake. Allow the cake to cool, then cover with plastic wrap.

SERVING: This cake is usually served alone, on the day after it is made. Cut into squares right in the pan and use a wide spatula to lift the squares of cake onto plates. Great with ice cream.

STORAGE: Cover the pan with plastic wrap to keep the cake fresh and moist.

YOGURT POPPY SEED CAKE WITH WHITE CHOCOLATE FROSTING

· · ·

Makes one 13 × 9 × 2-inch cake,
about twenty-four 2-inch squares

CAKE BATTER

3 large eggs

1½ cups sugar

½ cup vegetable oil

1 cup poppy seeds

1⅓ cups sweetened shredded
coconut

1 cup all-purpose flour

1 teaspoon baking powder

½ teaspoon salt

One 8-ounce container plain low-
fat (not fat-free) yogurt

WHITE CHOCOLATE GANACHE

½ cup heavy whipping cream

4 tablespoons (½ stick) unsalted
butter

6 ounces white chocolate, cut into
¼-inch pieces

FINISHING

White chocolate shavings, page 392

One 13 × 9 × 2-inch pan, buttered
and the bottom lined with
parchment or wax paper

This recipe comes from South Africa, where my friend Kyra Effren found it while visiting her family there several years ago.

1. Set a rack at the middle level of the oven and preheat to 350 degrees.

2. In a large mixing bowl, whisk the eggs until liquid, then whisk in the sugar. Continue whisking for a minute or two until the mixture lightens slightly.

3. Whisk in the oil until it is combined.

4. In another bowl mix the poppy seeds, coconut, flour, baking powder, and salt and stir half into the egg mixture. Stir in the yogurt, then stir in the remaining poppy seed mixture.

5. Spread the batter in the prepared pan and smooth the top. Bake the cake for about 30 minutes, until it is well risen, deep golden, and a knife or toothpick inserted in the center emerges clean.

6. Cool the cake on a rack for 5 minutes, then unmold it onto a rack to cool. Peel off the paper and invert the cake on another rack so it cools right side up.

7. To make the frosting, bring the cream and the butter to a boil in a saucepan. Remove from heat and add the white chocolate. Let stand 3 minutes, then whisk smooth. Pour the ganache into a bowl and refrigerate until it thickens to spreading consistency.

8. When the ganache is ready, place the cake on a cardboard or platter and spread the ganache evenly over the top of the cake, swirling it into points and peaks. Sprinkle the chocolate shavings over the ganache.

SERVING: Cut the cake into squares for serving.

STORAGE: Keep the cake loosely covered with plastic wrap at a cool room temperature.

TOTAL HEAVEN CHOCOLATE ALMOND CAKE
. . .

Makes one 10-inch cake, about 12 servings

CAKE BATTER

1 cup whole almonds, about 4 ounces

1½ cups fresh white bread or cake crumbs, see Note

1 teaspoon ground cinnamon

12 tablespoons (1½ sticks) unsalted butter, softened

¾ cup sugar, divided

4 ounces bittersweet chocolate, melted and cooled

8 large eggs, separated

½ teaspoon almond extract

Pinch salt

1 batch Ganache Glaze, page 76

¼ cup toasted sliced almonds for finishing

One 10-inch round cake pan, buttered and the bottom lined with parchment or buttered wax paper, cut to fit

Although this dessert tastes heavenly, that isn't the whole reason for its name. It was one of our best-selling items at the Total Heaven Baking Company when I owned it with Peter Fresulone and Bill Liederman in the early 1980s.

1. Set a rack at the middle level of the oven and preheat to 350 degrees.

2. Place the almonds in the bowl of a food processor and pulse until finely ground. Combine with the crumbs and cinnamon in a bowl and set aside.

3. Use an electric mixer on medium speed to beat the butter and half the sugar together for about 2 minutes. Then beat in chocolate.

4. Beat in the egg yolks, one a time, beating well after each addition, and scraping down the bowl and beater(s) occasionally with a rubber spatula. Beat in the almond extract.

5. Remove bowl from mixer and stir in almond and crumb mixture.

6. In a clean dry mixer bowl, whip egg whites and salt on medium speed until they are white and opaque and beginning to hold a very soft peak. Increase the speed to high and whip in the remaining sugar 1 tablespoon at a time. Continue to whip the egg whites until they hold a soft peak.

7. Stir a quarter of the whipped egg whites into the chocolate batter to lighten it, then fold in the remaining egg whites with a rubber spatula.

8. Scrape the batter into the prepared pan and smooth the top. Bake the cake for 45 minutes, or until it is well risen and a knife or toothpick inserted in the center emerges with only a small amount of batter clinging to it.

9. Cool the cake in the pan on a rack for 5 minutes, then unmold the cake onto the rack to cool. The center of the cake will sink slightly in as it cools. Turn the cooled cake over again so that what was the top while the cake was baking is on top. Use a sharp serrated knife to cut away any high edges and to trim the top of the cake even.

10. Before you glaze the cake, chill it for an hour. Prepare the glaze and let it cool. Invert the cake (so that what was the bottom is now uppermost) onto a piece of cardboard or a springform base and use a small metal offset icing spatula to spread some of the glaze over the entire outside of the cake to seal it. Use no more than a few tablespoons of the glaze. Refrigerate the cake 15 minutes to set the glaze.

11. Set the chilled and masked cake on a rack in a jelly-roll pan and pour the rest of the glaze over the cake as in the instructions on page 76. Scatter the almonds around the rim of the cake before the glaze sets.

SERVING: Serve wedges of the cake with whipped cream.

STORAGE: Keep the cake at a cool room temperature until time to serve it. Wrap and refrigerate leftovers but bring them to room temperature before serving.

NOTE: To make fresh, white bread crumbs, trim crusts from firm white or French bread and pulse the bread in the food processor to make fine crumbs. When we made this cake for the baking company, we saved all the scraps from trimming cakes and used those as the bread crumbs. If you want to do this, make your first cake with bread crumbs, then freeze the scraps you trim away until the next time you make it. Use the scraps plus enough bread to make up the quantity of crumbs needed.

CHOCOLATE PUDDING CAKE

. . .

Makes one thin 10-inch cake,
about 8 servings

CAKE BATTER

1 cup all-purpose flour

2 tablespoons alkalized (Dutch process) cocoa powder

1½ teaspoons baking powder

¼ teaspoon salt

2 tablespoons unsalted butter, softened

⅔ cup granulated sugar

½ cup milk

TOPPING

½ cup granulated sugar

½ cup granulated light brown sugar

½ cup alkalized (Dutch process) cocoa powder

½ cup chopped pecan pieces

1¼ cups boiling water

One 10-inch round layer pan, 2 inches deep, buttered and floured

This is a wonderful old-fashioned recipe. The cake elements in the batter separate during baking to form a chocolate cake and a fudgy chocolate sauce. This is an adaptation of a James Beard recipe that appears in his *American Cookery* (Little, Brown, 1972).

1. Set a rack at the middle level of the oven and preheat to 350 degrees.

2. To make the cake, combine the flour, cocoa, baking powder, and salt in a mixing bowl and stir well to mix. Sift the dry ingredients onto a piece of parchment or wax paper and set aside.

3. In a mixing bowl, beat together the butter and sugar until well mixed—you may use an electric hand mixer, but if the butter is soft, a rubber spatula works just as well.

4. Mix in half the dry ingredients, the milk, then the remaining dry ingredients.

5. Spread the batter in the prepared pan.

6. To make the topping, combine the sugars in a mixing bowl and sift the cocoa powder over the bowl. Mix well, then mix in the pecans. Scatter this mixture over the batter in the cake pan. Pour the boiling water over this topping, then place the cake in the oven.

7. Bake for about 30 minutes, or until the cake feels firm when pressed with a fingertip. Cool on a rack.

SERVING: Serve the cake right from the pan it baked in either warm or at room temperature with whipped cream.

STORAGE: This cake is really only good on the day it is baked. By all means, keep leftovers covered at room temperature, but the fresh, warm cake is best.

TRIPLE CHOCOLATE CHEESECAKE
• • •

Makes one 9-inch cheesecake,
about 12 servings

1 batch Dark Sweet Chocolate
Dough, page 267

CHEESECAKE BATTER

24 ounces softened cream cheese

¾ cup sugar

4 ounces unsweetened chocolate,
melted

4 ounces bittersweet chocolate,
melted

4 ounces milk chocolate, melted

2 teaspoons vanilla extract

4 large eggs

One 9-inch springform pan,
buttered, plus a small roasting pan

The combination of three chocolates gives it a chocolate flavor with a lot of depth.

1. Set a rack at the middle level of the oven and preheat to 350 degrees.

2. Divide the dough in half and wrap and freeze one piece for another cheesecake. Lightly flour the dough and roll it on a floured surface into a round a little less than 9 inches. Fold the dough in half and transfer it to the prepared pan. Unfold it and arrange it evenly in the bottom of the pan. Trim the sides of the dough so they don't come up the sides of the pan. Pierce the dough all over with a fork and bake it for about 15 to 20 minutes, until it is firm and dull, rather than shiny-looking. Cool on a rack.

3. To make the cheesecake batter, set an electric mixer at lowest speed. Beat the cream cheese until smooth, no more than 30 seconds. Stop mixer and scrape bowl and beater. Add the sugar in a stream, mixing for no more than 30 seconds. Stop and scrape. Add the melted chocolate and mix only until absorbed, no more than 30 seconds. Beat in the vanilla extract, then the eggs, one at a time, mixing only until each is absorbed. Stop and scrape after each addition.

4. Wrap aluminum foil around the bottom of the springform pan to at least 2 inches up the side. Pour the filling into the prepared pan over the crust. Place the pan in a small roasting pan with ½ inch of warm water in it.

5. Bake the cheesecake for 50 to 60 minutes, or until lightly colored and firm except for the very center. Remove from the pan of hot water.

6. Run the tip of a small knife between the cheesecake and the pan to about ¼-inch depth to loosen the top edge all around. Scrape the knife against the pan—this will help to prevent the cheesecake from cracking as it cools.

7. Remove the foil and cool the cheesecake completely in its pan on a rack. Wrap in plastic and chill overnight before unmolding.

SERVING: Serve in wedges; a few fresh raspberries make a good accompaniment.

STORAGE: Wrap in plastic and refrigerate for up to several days. Bring the cheesecake to room temperature for an hour before serving.

ROLLED CAKES

• • •

Neat and easy to serve, rolled cakes deserve to be more popular than they are. The few here are classics—you can serve them as a dessert for the most elegant occasion.

SWISS ROLL

• • •

Makes one 16-inch-long roll, about 12 generous servings

VANILLA SYRUP

¼ cup water

¼ cup sugar

2 teaspoons vanilla extract

WHIPPED CREAM

3 cups heavy whipping cream

⅓ cup sugar

2 teaspoons vanilla extract

1 batch Genoise Sheet, page 31, baked in an 11 × 17-inch jelly-roll pan

FINISHING

1 cup dark or milk chocolate shavings, page 392

This is the British name for a cocoa sponge sheet rolled around a whipped cream filling. This one dresses up the plain sponge roll with a little splash of vanilla syrup—more for moisture than flavor—and some chocolate shavings to finish the outside. This is an ideal recipe to prepare in advance—you can make the cake and syrup one day, then whip the cream and finish the cake early on the day you plan to serve it. Thanks to Paul Kinberg and Vicki Russell for sharing their recipes for Swiss rolls.

1. To make the syrup, combine the water and sugar in a small saucepan and bring to a boil over low heat. Cool and add the vanilla.

2. For the whipped cream, combine all ingredients in the bowl of an electric mixer and whip on medium speed until firm but not grainy.

3. To assemble the roll, turn the cooled genoise layer over onto a cookie sheet or cutting board and peel off the paper. Replace with a clean sheet of paper over the layer, then cover paper with another cookie sheet or board and turn the whole stack over again, so that the genoise is right side up on the clean paper. Remove both cookie sheets or boards and leave the genoise on the paper on your work surface.

4. Use a brush to paint the layer with the syrup. Apply it evenly over the whole surface of the layer and use it all.

5. Spread the layer with half of the whipped cream. Arrange the paper so that one of the long sides of the cake is parallel with the edge of the work surface nearest you. Fold ½ inch of that long side of the cake over onto the cream, then, holding the paper to help guide you, let the cake roll up on itself. To tighten the cake and make it a perfect cylinder, position it in the center of the paper and wrap one end of the paper around the cake the long way so that the edges of the paper meet. Hold the bottom paper and use a piece of stiff cardboard or a cookie sheet, held at a 45-degree angle to the cake, to tighten the top piece around the cake, as in the illustration.

6. Trim the ends of the roll on a diagonal and roll it off the paper onto a platter. Spread the outside of the cake with the remaining whipped cream and sprinkle the cream evenly with the chocolate shavings.

SERVING: Cut the cake into 1-inch-thick slices. A few raspberries or sliced sweetened strawberries would be a good accompaniment.

STORAGE: Loosely cover the roll with plastic wrap and refrigerate it until you plan to serve it. Cover and refrigerate leftovers.

TRADITIONAL BÛCHE DE NOËL

• • •

Makes one 14-inch-long rolled cake,
about 12 to 15 servings

MERINGUE MUSHROOMS

Whites of 3 large eggs

Pinch salt

¾ cup sugar, divided

Cocoa powder for finishing the
mushrooms

GANACHE FILLING AND FROSTING

2 cups heavy whipping cream

3 tablespoons unsalted butter

3 tablespoons light corn syrup

24 ounces bittersweet chocolate,
cut into ¼-inch pieces

MOISTENING SYRUP

¼ cup water

¼ cup sugar

¼ cup dark rum or kirsch

1 batch Plain Genoise, page 31,
baked in an 11 × 17-inch
jelly-roll pan

FINISHING

Confectioners' sugar

2 cookie sheets or jelly-roll pans
lined with parchment or foil for
the mushrooms

There are so many ways to prepare this typical French Christmas log cake that it's hard to distinguish what's really traditional. This one is made with a genoise, filled and frosted with a rich ganache, and decorated with meringue mushrooms. I like to use a plain, rather than a chocolate, genoise for the bûche so there is a better contrast between the color of the cake and that of the ganache. Because this cake is rich and yields a lot of portions, it is a perfect item for a holiday buffet on which you are serving several desserts.

1. To make the mushrooms, set racks in the upper and lower thirds of the oven and preheat to 250 degrees.

2. Use an electric mixer on medium speed to whip egg whites and salt until they are white and opaque and beginning to hold a soft peak. Increase speed to high and, 1 tablespoon at a time, whip in half the sugar. Continue to whip until the egg white and sugar mixture is very stiff, but not dry.

3. Remove bowl from mixer and add remaining sugar all at once. Gently fold it in with a rubber spatula.

4. Fill a pastry bag fitted with a ½-inch plain tube (Ateco #6 or #806) with half the meringue. Hold the bag straight up and down, perpendicular to the pan, and about an inch above it, and pipe out 1½- to 2-inch half-rounded drops—the mushroom caps—

about an inch apart. To avoid leaving a point on the mushroom caps, when you have piped one, release pressure and pull away sideways, rather than straight up. Fill the first pan with the mushroom caps.

5. To make the mushroom stems, refill the bag with the remaining meringue and hold it in the same position, but only about ½ inch away from the pan. Pipe ½-inch-wide stems about 1½ to 2 inches tall by pulling the bag up gently as the meringue touches the pan. When the meringue pedestal is the right height, release the pressure on the bag and pull straight up to leave a point. This will help attach the stems to the caps later on. Dust a little cocoa through a strainer on the mushroom stems and caps.

6. Bake the mushroom stems and caps for about 45 minutes, until the stems are dry and crisp and the caps are still moist in the center. They are easier to assemble that way. Cool the meringues on the pans.

7. To make the ganache, bring the cream, butter, and corn syrup to a simmer in a large saucepan over medium heat. Remove from heat and add chocolate. Gently shake the pan to make sure all the chocolate is covered by the hot liquid. Let stand 5 minutes, then whisk smooth. Allow the ganache to cool at room temperature to spreading consistency, several hours or overnight.

8. To make the syrup, bring the water and sugar to a boil in a small saucepan. Cool the syrup, then stir in the rum or kirsch.

9. First assemble the mushrooms. Remove ¼ cup of the ganache from the bowl to a separate smaller bowl. This is to avoid getting meringue crumbs in the filling and frosting ganache. Use a small metal icing spatula or a table knife to spread a dab of ganache on the flat side of each mushroom cap. Then push the pointed end of a stem into a cap. If the insides of the caps are dry, you may have to use the point of a knife or a vegetable peeler to make a small hole in the flat side of the caps. Don't put the ganache on the caps; dip the point of a stem into the ganache and press it into the opening in the cap. Set the assembled mushrooms on a paper-covered pan or on a platter until they are needed. Continue until all the mushrooms are ready.

10. To create the bûche, turn the cooled genoise layer over onto a cookie sheet or cutting board and peel off the paper. Replace with a clean sheet of paper and top the layer with another cookie sheet or board, then turn the whole stack over again so the genoise is right side up on the clean paper. Remove both cookie sheets or boards and leave the genoise on the paper on your work surface.

11. Use a brush to paint the layer with the syrup. Apply it evenly over the whole surface and use it all.

12. Spread the layer with half the remaining ganache. Arrange the paper so the long side of the cake is lined up with the edge of the work surface nearest you. Fold ½ inch of that long edge over onto the ganache, then, holding the paper to help guide you, let the cake roll up on itself. To tighten the cake and make it a perfect cylinder, position it in the center of the paper and wrap one long end up around the cake until the edges of the paper meet. Hold the bottom paper and use a piece of stiff cardboard, held at a 45-degree angle to the cake, to tighten the top piece of paper around the cake, as in the illustration on page 67.

13. Make a diagonal cut about 3 inches in from one of the ends of the roll to make a side branch, then trim the other end parallel, but as close to the end as possible. Use a dab of ganache to stick the side branch to the top of the cake a third of the way down the top and just in from the right end of the bûche.

14. Place the bûche on a platter or narrow rectangular cardboard and cover the outside of the bûche with the ganache, making sure to leave the ends and the top of the side branch uncovered to show the spiral pattern of the filling. A small metal icing spatula or table knife works best for this. After covering the outside of the bûche, scrape the ganache all over with a fork to make it look like bark. Arrange the mushrooms on the bûche and around the platter, then dust lightly with confectioners' sugar to simulate snow, if you wish.

SERVING: Cut the bûche into thin slices and serve a mushroom or two with each serving.

STORAGE: Keep loosely covered at a cool room temperature on the day it is made. Refrigerate leftovers and bring to room temperature before serving.

NOTE: If you want to prepare this in advance, roll and frost the log, but do not decorate with mushrooms. Leave them aside in a cool place loosely covered with plastic wrap. Place bûche in refrigerator or freezer until ganache is firm, then wrap and chill for several days or freeze for up to a week. Unwrap and decorate the bûche with mushrooms on the day you intend to serve.

CHOCOLATE SOUFFLÉ ROLL WITH STRIPED CHOCOLATE FILLING

• • •

Makes one 15-inch roll, about 12 servings

BATTER

6 ounces bittersweet or semisweet chocolate, cut into ¼-inch pieces

4 tablespoons liqueur or water

2 tablespoons unsalted butter

6 large eggs, separated

Pinch salt

¼ cup sugar

WHITE CHOCOLATE FILLING

6 ounces white chocolate, cut into ¼-inch pieces

3 tablespoons unsalted butter

⅔ cup heavy whipping cream

MILK CHOCOLATE FILLING

6 ounces milk chocolate, cut into ¼-inch pieces

3 tablespoons unsalted butter

⅔ cup heavy whipping cream

FINISHING

Confectioners' sugar

One 10 × 15-inch jelly-roll pan, buttered and lined with parchment or wax paper

This presentation with striped filling looks particularly attractive when the roll is cut—there will be alternating squares of light and dark fillings in rows throughout the spiraled slice of cake.

1. Set a rack at the middle level of the oven and preheat to 350 degrees.

2. For the cake layer, combine the chocolate with the liqueur or water and the butter in a heatproof bowl. Place the bowl over a pan of hot, but not simmering, water and stir occasionally until the chocolate is melted and the mixture is smooth. Whisk in the yolks, one at a time.

3. Whip the egg whites with the salt until they just begin to hold a very soft peak; then, beating faster, whip in the sugar in a slow stream until the whites hold a soft peak. Stir a quarter of the egg whites into the chocolate batter, then fold in the remaining egg whites.

4. Pour the batter into the prepared pan and smooth the top. Bake for about 15 minutes, until firm to the touch.

5. Remove the pan from the oven and loosen the cake with a small, sharp knife. Use the paper to pull up the layer and slide it onto a work surface to cool, about 20 minutes.

6. To make the fillings, follow the same directions with the different chocolates. Place chocolate and butter in a small heatproof bowl over a pan of hot, not simmering, water. Stir to melt. Remove bowl from pan and gradually whisk in cream, until mixture is smooth. Cover and chill until cooled and thickened.

7. To finish the roll, slide a pan or cookie sheet under the layer. Cover the layer with a clean piece of parchment or wax paper and another pan; invert the cake between the pans. Lift off the top pan and peel away the paper stuck to the layer. Replace with clean paper and replace the pan. Invert again and remove the top pan and paper.

8. Whip the white filling to lighten it and use it to fill a pastry bag fitted with a ½-inch plain tube. Pipe the white filling onto the layer in stripes parallel to the long edges of the cake. Skip a space as wide as the stripe is before piping the next one. Repeat with the milk chocolate filling and pipe it into the spaces left between the stripes of white filling. Gently roll the cake up by grasping the paper and rolling away from you. Chill to set fillings.

9. Arrange roll on platter, seam side down. Trim ends and dust with confectioners' sugar.

SERVING: Cut 1-inch slices of the roll and serve them cut side down on a plate, to show the alternating colors of the filling.

STORAGE: Keep the roll at a cool room temperature until serving time. Cover and refrigerate leftovers.

• • •

Perhaps the most popular of all cakes, layer cakes are the mainstay of the cake repertoire. Since they require the extra work of assembly after the layer or layers and filling are made, why not divide the work among several sessions, as professional bakers do? If you prepare the cake layers one day, wrap and chill them. Then prepare the frosting and finish the cake early in the day you plan to serve it. Unless the cake is finished with whipped cream—you'll need to refrigerate it—you may leave the cake in a cool place until you plan to serve.

OLD-FASHIONED CHOCOLATE LAYER CAKE

• • •

Makes one 8-inch 2-layer cake,
about 10 servings

CAKE BATTER

2 cups cake flour

2 teaspoons baking powder

¼ teaspoon salt

8 tablespoons (1 stick) unsalted butter, softened

1 cup sugar

6 large egg yolks

1 teaspoon vanilla extract

½ cup milk

CHOCOLATE CREAM FROSTING

1¼ cups heavy whipping cream

4 tablespoons (½ stick) unsalted butter

¼ cup light corn syrup

16 ounces semisweet chocolate, cut into ¼-inch pieces

It was typical in the past to use a white or yellow cake for the layers with a rich chocolate frosting instead of all-chocolate layers and frosting. This particular version uses tender yellow cake and a fudgy frosting.

1. Set a rack at the middle level of the oven and preheat to 350 degrees.

2. In a small bowl, stir together the flour, baking powder, and salt.

3. Use an electric mixer set at medium speed to beat the butter and sugar together. Continue beating until light, about 5 minutes. Beat in the egg yolks, two at a time, beating smooth between each addition. Beat in the vanilla.

4. By hand, using a rubber spatula, stir half the flour mixture into the batter, making sure to scrape the sides of the bowl well. Stir in the milk, then the remaining flour mixture. Scrape well after each addition.

Chocolate shavings, page 392, optional

Two 8-inch round cake pans, 2 inches deep, buttered and the bottoms lined with parchment or wax paper

5. Divide the batter between the prepared pans and smooth the top. Bake the layers for about 35 to 45 minutes, or until well risen and a toothpick or a thin knife inserted in the center emerges clean. Cool in the pans for 5 minutes, then unmold and finish cooling the layers on racks. Peel off papers.

6. To make the chocolate cream frosting, combine the cream, butter, and corn syrup in a saucepan. Place over medium heat and bring to a boil, stirring occasionally. Remove from heat, add chocolate, and shake pan gently so that all the chocolate is covered by the hot liquid. Let stand 5 minutes, then whisk smooth. Scrape the frosting into a bowl and let cool to spreading consistency, either in the refrigerator or at room temperature.

7. To assemble the cake, place one of the cooled layers on a cardboard or platter. Spread about half the frosting over the first layer. Top with the second cake layer, flat bottom side up, and spread the top and sides of the cake with the remaining frosting. If you wish, using a spatula, press some chocolate shavings into the frosting on the sides of the cake. (If you try to use your hands, the chocolate will melt from the heat of your hands).

SERVING: Serve the cake in wedges—it needs no accompaniment.

STORAGE: If the cake is made early on the day it is to be served, keep it under a cake dome at a cool room temperature. If you prepare the layers in advance, wrap and freeze them until you are ready to finish the cake. If you prepare the frosting in advance, wrap and refrigerate it, then bring it back to room temperature for several hours so that it turns to spreading consistency.

CHOCOLATE
ORANGE CAKE
▪ ▪ ▪

Makes one 9-inch three-layer cake,
about 12 servings

ORANGE SYRUP

¼ cup sugar

⅓ cup water

¼ cup orange liqueur

GANACHE FILLING

1¼ cups heavy whipping cream

16 ounces semisweet chocolate, cut
into ¼-inch pieces

2 tablespoons (¼ stick) unsalted
butter

2 tablespoons light corn syrup

ORANGE FILLING

⅓ cup orange marmalade

1 tablespoon orange liqueur

One 9-inch round Chocolate
Genoise, page 30, baked and
cooled

GANACHE GLAZE

1 cup heavy whipping cream

8 ounces semisweet chocolate, cut
into ¼-inch pieces

A jelly-roll pan and rack for glazing
the cake

This rich mixture of chocolate cake and two different kinds of ganache is a perfect party dessert. But
beware, it's very rich, so serve in small portions.

1. For the syrup, combine the sugar and water, bring
to a boil and cool. Stir in the liqueur.

2. To make the ganache filling, bring the cream to a
boil, then remove from heat. Add the chocolate,
allow to stand 2 minutes, whisk in the butter and
corn syrup until smooth. Cool until thickened.

3. To make the orange filling, stir the marmalade and
the liqueur together.

4. To assemble, slice cake into three horizontal
layers and place one on a cardboard or springform
base. Sprinkle layer with syrup and spread with half
the orange filling. Spread with a third of the ganache
filling. Repeat with remaining layers, syrup,
marmalade, and ganache filling. Spread the outside of
the cake with the remaining ganache but reserve
enough to pipe some rosettes on the outside of the
cake. Chill cake to set.

5. To make the glaze, bring the cream to a boil, then
remove from the heat. Add the chocolate, allow to
stand 2 minutes, then whisk until smooth. Strain into
a bowl and cool to room temperature.

6. Place the chilled cake on a rack over a roasting
pan and pour the glaze over it, starting in center of
cake and pouring outward in larger and larger circles
to the edge, ending at top edge. Let the glaze run
down and cover the sides of the cake. Allow to stand about 5 minutes to set
glaze. Use a pastry bag fitted with a small star tip to pipe rosettes around top
edge of cake. To keep the glaze shiny, avoid refrigerating the cake.

SERVING: Cut the cake into wedges with a sharp, thin knife wet with warm
water and wiped between each cut.

STORAGE: Loosely cover and refrigerate leftovers. Bring to room temperature
before serving.

CHOCOLATE CHESTNUT CAKE

• • •

Makes one 9-inch 3-layer cake,
about 12 servings

KIRSCH SYRUP

⅓ cup water

⅓ cup sugar

¼ cup kirsch

2 teaspoons vanilla extract

CHESTNUT BUTTER CREAM

24 tablespoons (3 sticks) unsalted
butter, softened

1½ cups sweetened chestnut spread,
see Note

2 tablespoons kirsch

GANACHE GLAZE

1 cup heavy whipping cream

8 ounces semisweet chocolate, cut
into ¼-inch pieces

One 9-inch round Chocolate
Genoise, page 30, baked and
cooled

FINISHING

Chocolate shavings, page 392
Crystallized violets

A jelly-roll pan and rack for glazing
the cake

This is a really great dessert for the holiday season. You can make this cake entirely the day before and chill it. Just bring it to room temperature before serving.

1. To make the syrup, combine water and sugar in a small saucepan and bring to a boil over low heat. Cool, then stir in the kirsch and vanilla.

2. To make the butter cream, use an electric mixer on medium speed to beat the butter until it is soft and light. Add the chestnut spread, scrape down bowl and beater(s), and continue beating until the butter cream is smooth and light, about 5 minutes. Beat in the kirsch a little at a time, so the butter cream doesn't separate.

3. To make the glaze, bring the cream to a simmer in a saucepan over low heat. Remove from heat and add chocolate all at once. Shake the pan to make sure all the chocolate is submerged in the hot liquid. Let stand 5 minutes, then whisk smooth. Strain into another pan and leave to cool while you assemble the cake.

4. Use a sharp serrated knife to cut the cake into three horizontal layers. Place the layer that was the top of the cake bottom up on a cardboard or springform base. Brush a third of the syrup onto the layer to moisten it. Use an offset icing spatula to spread the layer with a quarter of the butter cream. Cover with the middle layer and moisten it with another third of the syrup and spread it with another quarter of the butter cream. Place the last layer on the cake, so that what was the flat bottom of the cake is now the top surface. Moisten the layer with the remaining syrup.

5. Cover the top and sides of the cake with another quarter of the butter cream, thinly applied. Chill the cake for an hour. Leave the last quarter of the butter cream at room temperature.

6. Place the chilled cake on the rack in the jelly-roll pan and glaze the cake according to the instructions on page 76.

7. Let the cake stand on the rack for a few minutes until the glaze sets, then use a wide spatula to lift the cake from the rack. Use a spatula to press chocolate shavings into the frosting around the bottom edge of the cake.

8. Place the remaining butter cream in a pastry bag fitted with a small star tube and pipe 12 rosettes, equidistant from each other, around the rim of the cake. Top each rosette with a small piece of crystallized violet.

SERVING: Cut the cake into wedges with a knife warmed in hot water and wiped dry between each slice. This rich cake needs no accompaniment.

STORAGE: Keep the cake at a cool room temperature on the day it is made or refrigerate it until the next day. Bring the cake to room temperature before serving. Wrap and refrigerate leftovers.

NOTE: The correct chestnut product for this cake is sweetened chestnut cream, sometimes also called chestnut spread. If you only have unsweetened chestnut puree, use 1¼ cups chestnut puree beaten with ½ cup light corn syrup. See Sources, page 442, for mail-order purchasing.

VARIATION

Omit the chocolate glaze and cover the entire outside of the cake with chocolate shavings. To pipe the rosettes on the shavings, use the tip of a spoon to push the shavings away from the place where you wish to pipe a rosette and make sure the butter cream you are piping touches the butter cream on the cake.

TRADITIONAL BLACK FOREST CAKE

． ． ．

Makes one 9-inch 3-layer cake,
about 12 servings

KIRSCH SYRUP

⅓ cup water

⅓ cup sugar

⅓ cup kirsch

SOUR CHERRY FILLING

2 pounds sour cherries, canned or
frozen, drained

½ cup sugar

¼ teaspoon ground cinnamon

3 tablespoons kirsch

2 tablespoons cornstarch

CHOCOLATE FILLING

1 cup heavy whipping cream

8 ounces semisweet chocolate, cut
into ¼-inch pieces

WHIPPED CREAM

3 cups heavy whipping cream

⅓ cup sugar

2 teaspoons vanilla extract

One 9-inch round Chocolate
Genoise, page 30, baked and
cooled

FINISHING

Chocolate shavings, page 392
Confectioners' sugar

This dessert classic got its name because both the sour cherries and the kirsch are typical products of the Black Forest in southern Germany.

1. To make the syrup, bring water and sugar to a boil in a small pan. Cool and stir in the kirsch.

2. To make the sour cherry filling, combine cherries, sugar, and cinnamon in a saucepan. Bring to a boil and simmer about 5 minutes to concentrate juices; lower heat until barely simmering. Stir kirsch and cornstarch together, then stir in several spoonfuls of the hot liquid from the cherries. Stir the starch mixture into the simmering cherries and continue cooking, stirring often, until clear and thickened. Set aside 12 of the best cherries for decorating the cake. Pour the remaining filling into a bowl and refrigerate.

3. For the chocolate filling, bring cream to a boil, then remove from heat. Add chocolate and allow to stand 2 minutes. Whisk smooth and refrigerate until slightly thickened and cooled.

4. To make the whipped cream, whip all ingredients until soft peaks form.

5. To assemble, slice genoise into three layers and place one on cardboard. Moisten with a third of the syrup and spread with half the chocolate filling. Strew with half the cherries, then spread with some whipped cream. Repeat with second layer. Place the last layer on and moisten with remaining syrup. Spread outside of cake evenly with whipped cream and press chocolate shavings against sides. Save ½ cup whipped cream and some chocolate shavings for the top.

6. To decorate, pipe 12 rosettes of whipped cream around top border of cake. Place a reserved cherry on each rosette. Pile chocolate shavings in center of cake and dust them lightly with the confectioners' sugar.

SERVING: Serve this cake as a dessert for an important dinner.

STORAGE: Keep the cake in the refrigerator, or the whipped cream might melt.

RASPBERRY DEVIL'S FOOD CAKE

. . .

Makes one 10-inch 4-layer cake,
about 16 servings

CAKE BATTER

2¼ cups cake flour

¾ cup alkalized (Dutch process)
    cocoa powder

2¼ cups sugar

1 teaspoon salt

2½ teaspoons baking powder

1 teaspoon baking soda

12 tablespoons (1½ sticks) unsalted
    butter, very soft

1¾ cups buttermilk, divided

4 large eggs

FILLING

One 10-ounce package frozen
    raspberries, with their liquid

1½ cups heavy whipping cream

8 tablespoons (1 stick) unsalted
    butter

1¼ pounds semisweet chocolate,
    cut into ¼-inch pieces

½ cup raspberry preserves

FINISHING

Chocolate shavings, page 392

Two 10-inch round cake pans, 2
    inches deep, buttered and the
    bottoms lined with a circle of
    parchment or wax paper

This cake batter is mixed according to the high-ratio method in which the weight of the sugar equals or exceeds the weight of the flour. Using this method guarantees a batter that is not likely to separate during mixing, making for a smoother-textured baked cake.

1. Set a rack at the middle level of the oven and preheat to 375 degrees.

2. For the cake batter, sift dry ingredients into a mixer bowl and add butter. Mix 2 minutes on low speed. Add half the buttermilk and continue mixing 5 more minutes. Scrape bowl and beater(s). Mix remaining buttermilk with the eggs, and add a third at a time to the batter, stopping and scraping between each addition.

3. Divide batter between prepared pans and bake for 30 minutes, until layers are well risen and firm.

4. Unmold layers immediately and cool right side up on a rack.

5. For the filling, bring raspberries to a boil and reduce slightly. Use a food mill or a fine sieve to puree berries and strain away seeds. Cool the puree. Bring cream and butter to a boil, remove from heat, and add chocolate. Let stand 2 minutes, then whisk smooth. Whisk in raspberry puree and cool until thickened.

6. Slice each cooled layer in two horizontally. Place one layer on a piece of cardboard or a platter and spread thinly with preserves. Spread with filling. Repeat with remaining layers. Mask outside of cake with remaining filling, then press chocolate shavings onto all surfaces of cake.

SERVING: This makes a great dessert after a light meal.

STORAGE: Keep under a cake dome or well wrapped at room temperature.

LEMON-SCENTED WHITE CAKE WITH MILK CHOCOLATE FROSTING

• • •

Makes one 9-inch 2-layer cake,
about 12 servings

LEMONY WHITE CAKE

2¼ cups cake flour

3 teaspoons baking powder

½ teaspoon salt

8 tablespoons (1 stick) unsalted
butter, softened

1½ cups sugar

2 teaspoons finely grated lemon zest

½ teaspoon lemon extract

½ cup egg whites (from about 4
large eggs)

1¼ cups milk

MILK CHOCOLATE GANACHE

Zest of 2 lemons removed in long
strips with a vegetable peeler

2 cups heavy whipping cream

4 tablespoons (½ stick) unsalted
butter, softened

20 ounces milk chocolate, cut into
¼-inch pieces

4 ounces bittersweet chocolate, cut
into ¼-inch pieces

Two 9-inch round pans, 1½ to 2
inches deep, buttered and lined
with buttered parchment or wax
paper

The unusual flavoring for this cake is lemon zest. It is used in both the light, moist cake and the milk chocolate ganache and it delicately perfumes and complements both. It works because the lemon zest, which is rich in the essential oil of lemon, transmits a lemon perfume without any of the acidity of lemon juice, which would mar the chocolate flavor.

1. Set a rack at the middle level of the oven and preheat to 350 degrees.

2. Sift the cake flour, baking powder, and salt onto a piece of parchment or wax paper and set aside.

3. Use an electric mixer set at medium speed to beat the butter and sugar until light, about 3 minutes. Beat in the lemon zest and extract.

4. In a bowl, whisk together the egg whites and milk.

5. Add a third of the flour mixture to the butter and sugar mixture and beat until smooth. Scrape down bowl and beater(s). Beat in half the milk and egg white mixture until incorporated, then beat in another third of the flour mixture. Scrape bowl and beater(s). Beat in remaining liquid until absorbed, followed by remaining flour mixture. Scrape well after each addition.

6. Divide batter between prepared pans and smooth tops evenly. Bake for about 30 to 35 minutes, until well risen and a toothpick inserted in the center emerges clean. Cool layers in pans for 5 minutes, then invert to racks to cool. Peel off paper. If prepared in advance, double-wrap layers in plastic wrap and chill for up to several days or freeze.

7. To make the ganache, place the pieces of zest in a saucepan and add the cream. Place over low heat and bring to a simmer. Remove from heat and allow to steep about 5 minutes. Remove zests from cream with a slotted spoon and discard them. Add butter to the cream and bring to a boil over low heat. Remove from heat and add chocolates. Shake pan to submerge chocolate and allow to stand 5 minutes. Whisk smooth, then cool to room temperature. Ganache will thicken to spreading consistency.

8. To finish, put one layer right side up on a platter or cardboard. Place ganache in mixer bowl and beat until light, about 20 seconds. Using an offset spatula, spread the layer with a little more than a third of the ganache. Place the other cake layer upside down on the ganache, so that the smooth bottom of the cake layer is uppermost. Spread the top and sides of the cake evenly with most of the remaining ganache.

SERVING: This rich cake needs no accompaniment.

STORAGE: Keep the cake at a cool room temperature before serving. Keep leftovers under a cake dome at a cool room temperature or covered with plastic wrap in the refrigerator.

THE HORSERADISH GRILL'S CHOCOLATE CHOCOLATE CAKE
• • •

Makes one 9-inch 2-layer cake,
about 12 servings

CAKE BATTER

2 cups sugar

1½ cups flour

½ teaspoon salt

¾ teaspoon baking soda

4 ounces unsweetened chocolate,
cut into ¼-inch pieces

1 cup double-strength hot brewed
coffee

2 large eggs, at room temperature

½ cup vegetable oil

1½ teaspoons vanilla extract

½ cup sour cream

CHOCOLATE BUTTER FROSTING

1 cup heavy whipping cream

8 tablespoons (1 stick) unsalted
butter

⅓ cup sugar

¼ teaspoon salt

16 ounces semisweet chocolate, cut
into ¼-inch pieces

¼ cup double-strength brewed
coffee

1 teaspoon vanilla extract

Two 9-inch round pans, 2 inches
deep, buttered and the bottoms
lined with parchment or wax
paper

When I was on my book tour for *How to Bake*, I had a memorable lunch at the Horseradish Grill in Atlanta with Edna Lewis and Lenada Merrick. For dessert we had an excellent chocolate cake and I promised myself I'd get the recipe at once. Then-chef Scott Peacock sent it to me soon after and here it is.

1. Set a rack at the middle level of the oven and preheat to 325 degrees.

2. In a mixing bowl, stir together the sugar, flour, salt, and baking soda and set aside.

3. Place the cut-up chocolate in a bowl and pour the hot coffee over it. Let stand while the chocolate melts and you are preparing other ingredients.

4. In a large mixing bowl, whisk the eggs until liquid, then whisk in the oil, vanilla, and sour cream, one at a time.

5. Whisk the chocolate and coffee mixture smooth and scrape it into the egg mixture; whisk smooth.

6. Use a rubber spatula to fold a third of the flour mixture into the chocolate batter. Repeat until all dry ingredients are incorporated.

7. Divide the batter between the prepared pans and smooth the tops. Bake the cake about 30 minutes, or until well risen and a toothpick inserted in the center emerges clean. Cool cakes in pans on racks for 5 minutes, then invert each onto a rack, peel off paper, and invert again onto other racks to cool right side up.

8. To make the frosting, combine the cream, butter, sugar, and salt in a saucepan and bring to a simmer over low heat. Remove from heat and whisk once to make sure butter is melted, then add chocolate. Shake pan to make sure all the chocolate is covered, then allow to stand 5 minutes. Whisk frosting smooth and whisk in coffee and vanilla. Scrape the frosting into a bowl and chill it until it is of spreading consistency. (Be careful not to leave it in the refrigerator too long, or it will set very hard. If it does, divide the hardened filling into 8 or 10 pieces and stir in a bowl over warm water to spreading consistency.)

9. To finish, place one of the layers right side up on a cardboard or platter. Spread with a third of the frosting. Place the other layer on the frosting so that the smooth bottom of the layer is uppermost. Spread the remaining frosting over the top and sides of the cake.

SERVING: Serve alone or if you are really pulling out all the stops, with home-made vanilla ice cream.

STORAGE: Keep the cake under a cake dome at a cool room temperature.

TEXAS CHOCOLATE PRUNE CAKE

• • •

Makes one 10-inch 2-layer cake, about 16 servings

CAKE BATTER

12 ounces pitted prunes

Several cups weak brewed tea, optional

2 cups all-purpose flour

3 tablespoons alkalized (Dutch process) cocoa powder

4 teaspoons baking powder

½ teaspoon baking soda

12 tablespoons (1½ sticks) unsalted butter, softened

1½ cups sugar

3 large eggs

1 cup milk

1 batch Chocolate Butter Frosting, page 84

Two 10-inch round layer pans, 2 inches deep, buttered and the bottoms lined with parchment or buttered wax paper, cut to fit

This recipe comes from my friend David Perkins's mother, Dorothy May Perkins of Sherman, Texas. It is part of a legacy of family recipes that she inherited from her maternal grandmother, Hattie Hawkins May, born in 1864 and the daughter of a Confederate captain.

The prunes contribute a lot of flavor and moisture to this simple cake and I urge you to try it, even if you are not a prune lover. The cake is pure chocolate indulgence and not at all "pruney."

1. Place the prunes in a 2-quart saucepan and cover them with water or weak tea. Bring to a simmer and allow to cook until the prunes are very tender, about 30 minutes. Add more water if necessary to keep the prunes covered with liquid. Cool the prunes in the liquid, then drain it off and reserve it. Measure 2 cups stewed prunes and set them aside. Store any remaining prunes in the liquid for another use. Puree the 2 cups of prunes in the food processor and set aside.

2. Set a rack at the middle level of the oven and preheat to 350 degrees.

3. In a medium mixing bowl combine the flour, cocoa, baking powder, and baking soda and stir well to mix. Sift the dry ingredients onto a piece of parchment or wax paper.

4. Use an electric mixer on medium speed to beat the butter with the sugar until light, about 2 minutes. Beat in the eggs, one at a time, beating well after each addition. Beat in a third of the dry ingredients, then combine the prune puree with the milk and beat in half of that. Scrape the bowl and beater(s) well, then beat in another third of the dry ingredients, followed by the remaining liquid mixture. Scrape bowl and beater(s) well and beat in the remaining dry ingredients.

5. Divide the batter between the prepared pans and smooth tops. Bake the cakes for about 30 to 40 minutes, or until they are well risen and a toothpick or knife inserted in the center of one of the layers emerges clean. Cool layers in pans for 10 minutes and turn them over onto racks. Turn the layers back over so that they cool right side up.

6. When the layers are cool, peel off the papers and place one of the layers right side up on a plate or cardboard. Spread with a little more than a third of the frosting. Place the other layer on the frosting so that its smooth bottom is uppermost. Spread the remaining frosting over the top and sides of the cake.

SERVING: Serve alone or with homemade vanilla ice cream.

STORAGE: Keep the cake under a cake dome at a cool room temperature.

CAKES

CHOCOLATE VELVET CAKE

■ ■ ■

Makes one 10-inch 2-layer cake,
about 12 servings

1 tablespoon strained lemon juice

1 cup milk

2¼ cups cake flour

2½ teaspoons baking powder

1 teaspoon salt

8 tablespoons (1 stick) unsalted
butter, softened

1½ cups sugar

3 ounces unsweetened chocolate,
melted and cooled

2 large eggs

¼ teaspoon baking soda

2 tablespoons hot tap water

FINISHING

1 batch Chocolate Butter Frosting,
page 84

¾ cup toasted sliced almonds

One 10-inch springform pan,
buttered and the bottom lined
with parchment or wax paper

This rich and satisfying cake is from Sheila and Marilynn Brass, who got the recipe from their mother, Dorothy Brass, a passionate baker well known for her luscious cakes in their hometown of Winthrop, Massachusetts. The name of the cake refers to the delicate, smooth crumb of the baked cake.

1. Set a rack at the middle level of the oven and preheat to 350 degrees.

2. In a small bowl, stir the lemon juice into the milk and set aside while preparing the other ingredients.

3. Combine the cake flour with the baking powder and salt in a mixing bowl and stir well to mix. Set aside.

4. Use an electric mixer set at medium speed to beat the butter and sugar until light, about 3 minutes. Beat in the chocolate until combined, then the eggs, one at a time. Scrape bowl and beater(s) well after each addition.

5. Mix the baking soda into the hot water, then beat into batter. Beat in half the dry ingredients, scraping bowl and beater(s) well after they are absorbed. Beat in the milk and lemon juice mixture, scrape again. Beat in the remaining dry ingredients.

6. Put the batter into the prepared pan and bake for about 35 to 45 minutes, or until well risen and a knife or toothpick inserted in the center of the cake emerges clean. Cool the cake in the pan on a rack for 5 minutes, then invert on the rack, remove pan and paper, and cool completely.

7. To finish the cake, divide the cake into two horizontal layers using a sharp serrated knife. Place one layer on a platter or cardboard and spread a little less than half the frosting evenly on it. Place the other layer on the frosting and spread the remaining frosting evenly all over the top and sides of the cake. Press the almonds into the frosting around the sides of the cake.

SERVING: This is a great "anytime" cake—don't wait until dessert to serve it. It needs no accompaniment.

STORAGE: Keep the cake under a cake dome at a cool room temperature. For advance preparation, double-wrap and freeze the cake layer, then defrost it at room temperature before finishing.

VARIATION

CHOCOLATE VELVET COFFEE CAKE Bake the cake in a buttered Bundt pan that has been dusted with fine, dry bread crumbs. It should take about 35 minutes to bake: test by inserting a knife or toothpick halfway between the side of the pan and the central tube—it should emerge clean. Don't frost, but dust with confectioners' sugar before serving or drizzle with 1 batch Chocolate Glaze, page 44.

BLANC ET NOIR

Black and White Cake

. . .

Makes one 4¹/₂ × 12-inch 4-layer cake,
about 16 servings

CHOCOLATE LAYER CAKE

16 ounces bittersweet chocolate,
cut into ¼-inch pieces

10 large eggs, separated

1 cup sugar, divided

Pinch salt

16 tablespoons (2 sticks) unsalted
butter, softened

WHITE CHOCOLATE GANACHE FILLING

1 cup heavy whipping cream

12 ounces white chocolate, cut into
¼-inch pieces

CHOCOLATE GLAZE

1¼ cups heavy whipping cream

12 ounces bittersweet chocolate,
cut into ¼-inch pieces

FINISHING

1 ounce milk chocolate, cut into ¼-
inch pieces

1 ounce white chocolate, cut into
¼-inch pieces

One 12 × 18-inch or 11 × 17-inch
jelly-roll pan, buttered and lined
with buttered parchment paper
or foil

This delicious and easy cake, perfect for a special occasion, comes from Seattle chocolate maven Fran Bigelow, owner and operator of Fran's Chocolates Limited, a Seattle institution for the past fifteen years.

1. Set a rack at the middle level of the oven and preheat to 300 degrees.

2. For the cake layer, bring a pan of water to a boil and remove from heat. Put chocolate in a heatproof bowl and place over water. Stir occasionally to melt chocolate. When chocolate is melted, remove bowl from pan and allow to cool slightly.

3. Place yolks in bowl of electric mixer and whip until frothy, about 15 seconds. Gradually beat in half the sugar and continue to beat until the mixture is light and thick. Set aside.

4. Use an electric mixer, set on medium speed, and a clean, dry bowl with clean, dry beater(s) to whip the whites with the salt until they are opaque and beginning to hold their shape. Increase speed to high and gradually add remaining sugar. Continue to whip until the whites hold a firm peak.

5. Quickly beat the butter into the chocolate, then fold the chocolate mixture into the yolk mixture. Finally, use a rubber spatula to fold in the egg whites.

6. Spread the batter in the prepared pan and smooth the top with a metal spatula. Bake the cake layer for about 25 to 30 minutes, until it is well risen and firm to the touch. Cool the cake in the pan on a rack—it will shrink and fall slightly as it cools. If cake was prepared in advance, tightly wrap cake, pan and all, in plastic wrap and refrigerate several days or freeze for up to a month. Defrost cake at room temperature and continue with recipe.

7. To make the filling, bring the cream to a boil and remove from heat. Add white chocolate and allow to stand 2 minutes. Whisk smooth and cool to room temperature, several hours or overnight.

8. For glaze, bring cream to a boil and remove from heat. Add chocolate and allow to stand 2 minutes, whisk smooth and strain into a bowl. Cool to room temperature while assembling and chilling cake.

9. To assemble cake, cut a cardboard rectangle about 12 × 4½ inches. Cut the cake into four quarters, each 12 × 4½ inches. If you've used an 11 × 17-inch pan, make the cardboard 11 × 4 inches. Cut right through the paper under the cake. Lift one of the layers by the paper and invert it onto the cardboard. Peel off the paper. Use an electric mixer on medium speed to beat the white chocolate filling for about 10 seconds, then spread a third of the frosting over the layer. Top with another layer, peel off its paper, and repeat with another third of the filling. Repeat with another peeled cake layer and the remaining filling. Top with the last peeled layer, pressing it down and making the cake even. Smooth any of the filling that oozes out around the sides of the cake with a metal spatula. Chill the cake; in the meantime, cool the glaze to room temperature.

10. To finish the cake, place the milk chocolate and white chocolate for finishing in separate plastic bags. Immerse each bag about a third in a bowl of warm tap water, to melt the chocolate. Be sure the bags are tightly closed and no water can get in. Before beginning to glaze the cake, make sure the chocolates have melted completely, then remove the bags from the water and dry the outsides with paper towels. Set a pair of scissors and a toothpick by the two bags of chocolate.

11. Place the cake on a rack over a jelly-roll pan and pour the glaze over the cake, beginning at one of the short ends. Use a metal spatula to pick up the glaze that dripped into the pan and use it to patch up any bare spots.

12. Quickly snip the corner of the bag of white chocolate and pipe 4 lines of white chocolate along the length of the top of the cake; they should be equidistant from one another. Repeat with the milk chocolate, placing it between the white chocolate lines. Use the toothpick to pull across the lines of chocolate. Pull the first from the left, the second from the right and continue, at ½-inch intervals, down the length of the top of the cake. Place the cake on a platter to serve.

SERVING: Cut ¾-inch slices of cake with a sharp serrated knife rinsed in hot water and dried between each slice.

STORAGE: Cover the cake loosely with plastic wrap and refrigerate leftovers. If prepared in advance, keep the cake at a cool room temperature or refrigerate it. Remember to bring it to room temperature for an hour or so before serving.

NOTE: See page 390 for instructions on feathering the glazes.

CHOCOLATE WALNUT NOUGATINE CAKE

. . .

Makes one 10-inch 2-layer cake, about 12 servings

BATTER

6 ounces semisweet chocolate, cut into ¼-inch pieces

12 tablespoons (1½ sticks) unsalted butter, softened

⅔ cup sugar, divided

8 large eggs, separated

1⅓ cups ground walnuts

⅔ cup dry bread crumbs

WALNUT NOUGATINE

½ cup sugar

½ teaspoon lemon juice

1 cup toasted walnuts

CHOCOLATE BUTTER CREAM

2 egg whites (about ¼ cup)

⅓ cup sugar

12 tablespoons (1½ sticks) unsalted butter

3 tablespoons water

4 ounces bittersweet chocolate, cut into ¼-inch pieces

1 tablespoon dark rum

One 10-inch cake pan, buttered and the bottom lined with parchment or wax paper

One jelly-roll pan, oiled, for the nougatine

The crunch of the walnut nougatine tempers the richness of cake and filling and provides a good contrast in texture.

1. Set a rack at the middle level of the oven and preheat to 350 degrees.

2. For the batter, place the chocolate in a small bowl over hot water to melt. Stir occasionally. Beat the butter with half the sugar until soft and light. Beat in the chocolate, then the yolks, one at a time. Combine the walnuts and crumbs and stir in.

3. In a dry, clean bowl beat the egg whites until they hold a very soft peak, then beat in the remaining sugar in a slow stream. Beat the whites until they hold a firm peak. Stir a quarter of the whites into the batter, then fold in the rest with a rubber spatula. Pour the batter into the prepared pan and bake about 40 minutes. Unmold the cake onto a rack to cool.

4. To make the nougatine, combine the sugar and lemon juice in a small saucepan. Meanwhile, oil a jelly-roll pan and have it ready. Place the saucepan over medium heat and begin to melt the sugar. At the first sign of smoke, stir the caramel and continue stirring occasionally for about 3 to 5 minutes until the caramel is a golden amber—when the caramel becomes liquid and starts to color, watch it carefully or it may become too dark and be too bitter to use. Off the heat, stir in the walnuts and pour on the oiled jelly-roll pan to cool and harden. By hand, break the nougatine into 1-inch pieces. Grind the nougatine finely in the food processor.

5. For the butter cream, combine the egg whites and sugar in a heatproof bowl and whisk over simmering water. When the mixture becomes hot, use an electric mixer on medium speed to beat them cool. Beat in butter, continuing to beat until smooth. Bring the 3 tablespoons water to a boil in a small saucepan, then remove from heat and add chocolate. Allow to melt 3 minutes, then whisk smooth and cool. Beat chocolate and rum into butter cream.

6. Slice the cake into two layers and place one on a cardboard. Spread with half the butter cream. Place the other layer on the butter cream and press the layers together so they stick. Cover the outside of the cake with the remaining butter cream. Press the ground nougatine into the butter cream. Chill to set the butter cream.

SERVING: Cut the cake into wedges—it needs no accompaniment.

STORAGE: Keep the cake in a cool place until serving time. Wrap and refrigerate leftovers; bring to room temperature for 1 hour before serving again.

CHOCOLATE WALNUT CROWN

· · ·

Makes one 10-inch 4-layer cake, about 12 servings

CAKE BATTER

6 ounces semisweet chocolate, cut into ¼-inch pieces

12 tablespoons (1½ sticks) unsalted butter, softened

¾ cup sugar, divided

8 large eggs, separated

1 cup ground walnuts

1 cup dry bread crumbs

WALNUT NOUGATINE

1 cup sugar

½ teaspoon lemon juice

2 cups coarsely chopped toasted walnuts

CHOCOLATE BUTTER CREAM FILLING

8 ounces semisweet chocolate, melted

4 tablespoons dark rum

⅔ cup egg whites

1 cup sugar

24 tablespoons (3 sticks) unsalted butter, softened

FINISHING

Dark rum, optional

One 2-quart ring mold or 10-cup Bundt pan, buttered and floured

---

This elegant cake, loosely based on a German classic called a "Frankfurt Crown," is easy to prepare in advance.

1. Set a rack at the middle level of the oven and preheat to 350 degrees.

2. To make the batter, place the chocolate in a small heatproof bowl over hot but not simmering water to melt, stirring occasionally. Beat the butter with half the sugar until soft and light. Beat in the melted chocolate, then the yolks, one at a time. Combine the walnuts and crumbs and stir in.

3. In a dry, clean bowl beat the egg whites until they hold a very soft peak, then beat in the remaining sugar in a slow stream. Beat the whites until they hold a soft, glossy peak. Stir a quarter of the whites into the batter, then fold in the rest with a rubber spatula. Spread the cake batter in the prepared pan and bake for about 30 minutes, or until a knife or toothpick inserted between the side of the pan and the central tube emerges clean. Cool in the pan for 5 minutes, then turn the cake out onto a rack to cool completely.

4. To make walnut nougatine, butter a jelly-roll pan and set it aside. Combine sugar and lemon juice in a saucepan and stir well to mix. Place over low heat and stir occasionally, until sugar melts and caramelizes. Stir in walnuts and pour out onto a buttered pan. Cool, break it into 1-inch pieces, then grind it coarsely in a food processor.

5. For the filling, combine chocolate and rum, then let cool. Combine egg whites and sugar in mixer bowl and place over a pan of simmering water, whisking gently, until egg whites are hot and sugar is dissolved. Beat at medium speed until cooled. Beat in butter and continue beating until smooth. Beat cooled chocolate into butter cream.

6. To assemble cake, place baked cake on a cardboard or platter and slice into four layers. Sprinkle layers with rum while assembling, if desired. Reassemble cake with chocolate butter cream between layers, then spread outside with remaining butter cream. Press the nougatine against the sides to cover the surface of the frosting completely Chill briefly to set butter cream.

SERVING: Cut this rich cake into thin slices—it needs no accompaniment.

STORAGE: Keep covered at a cool room temperature.

CHOCOLATE MOCHA HEART
∎ ∎ ∎

Makes one 10-inch cake, about 12 servings

CHOCOLATE CAKE LAYER

9 tablespoons (1 stick plus 1 tablespoon) unsalted butter, softened

1 cup sugar, divided

5 ounces bittersweet or semisweet chocolate, melted and cooled

6 eggs, separated

1 cup cake flour

RUM SYRUP

⅓ cup sugar

½ cup water

¼ cup dark rum

COFFEE BUTTER CREAM

4 egg whites (½ cup)

⅔ cup sugar

24 tablespoons (3 sticks) unsalted butter, softened

3 tablespoons dark rum

3 tablespoons instant espresso coffee

FINISHING

2 ounces semisweet chocolate, melted

Chocolate shavings, page 392

One 10-inch cake pan, 2 inches deep, buttered and the bottom lined with parchment or wax paper

This versatile cake is cut into a heart shape after baking so there's no need for a special pan, or you can simply leave it as a round cake.

1. Set a rack at the middle level of the oven and preheat to 350 degrees.

2. For the batter, use the electric mixer to beat the butter until soft and light, then beat in half the sugar. Continue beating until very light. Beat in the melted chocolate, then the yolks, one at a time, scraping the bowl often. Continue beating until very light.

3. In a dry, clean bowl beat the egg whites until they hold a very soft peak, then raise mixer speed and beat in the rest of the sugar in a slow stream. Continue beating, until the egg whites hold a firm peak. Stir the flour into the chocolate batter. Stir a quarter of the egg whites into the batter, then fold in the rest. Pour the batter into the prepared pan. Bake the cake about 30 minutes. Unmold the cake and cool it, right side up, on a rack.

4. Draw a heart-shaped pattern, large enough to cover the entire cake layer. Use the pattern to cut out a piece of stiff cardboard to make a base for the cake. Place the pattern on the cake and cut around it. Reserve the trimmings. Then slice the heart-shaped cake layer horizontally to make two layers. Slice the trimmings in half as well, so that they are the same thickness as the layers.

5. To make the syrup, combine the sugar and water in a saucepan, bring to a boil, and cool. Add the rum.

6. To make the butter cream, combine the egg whites and sugar in the bowl of an electric mixer. Whisk over a pan of simmering water until egg whites are hot and sugar is dissolved. Use the electric mixer to beat on medium speed until cooled. Beat in butter and continue beating until butter cream is smooth. Combine rum and instant coffee, stir to dissolve, and beat into butter cream a little at a time.

7. Place the first heart-shaped layer on the cardboard heart and moisten with a third of the syrup. Spread with a thin layer of the butter cream. Cover the butter cream with the trimmings as evenly as possible, then moisten the trimmings. (The trimmings won't make a complete layer, but after the cake is completed, it won't be apparent.) Cover the trimmings with more butter cream, making an even surface. Cover with the last cake layer, and moisten it.

8. Frost the outside of the cake with half the remaining butter cream. Chill the cake to set the frosting. Cover with a second coat of the remaining butter cream, smoothing it well.

9. Place the melted chocolate in a squeeze bottle or the corner of a nonpleated plastic bag and use it to streak the top of the heart. Press the chocolate shavings into the frosting around the sides of the cake.

SERVING: To serve, cut the cake once from indentation to bottom point of heart, then cut each half into slices perpendicular to the first cut.

STORAGE: Keep the cake at a cool room temperature until time to serve it. Wrap and refrigerate leftovers. Bring to room temperature before serving.

NOTE: To leave this as a round cake, cut it into three horizontal layers.

CHOCOLATE HAZELNUT PAVÉ

■ ■ ■

Makes one 4 × 17-inch or 4 × 18-inch
3-layer cake, about 16 servings

CHOCOLATE HAZELNUT SPONGE

6 eggs

½ cup firmly packed light brown
sugar

⅓ cup alkalized (Dutch process)
cocoa powder

¼ cup all-purpose flour

2 cups ground hazelnuts, about
8 ounces

Pinch salt

½ cup granulated sugar

CHOCOLATE HAZELNUT FILLING

1½ cups heavy whipping cream

18 ounces bittersweet or semisweet
chocolate, cut into ¼-inch pieces

8 tablespoons (1 stick) unsalted
butter

½ cup praline paste, about 5
ounces, see Sources

RUM SYRUP

¼ cup sugar

½ cup water

¼ cup dark rum

2 teaspoons vanilla extract

FINISHING

Large chocolate shavings, page 392

Confectioners' sugar

One 12 × 18-inch or 11 × 17-inch
jelly-roll pan, buttered and lined
with parchment or wax paper

This rich combination of chocolate and hazelnuts qualifies as much as a confection as it does as a dessert.

1. Set a rack at the middle level of the oven and preheat to 350 degrees.

2. For chocolate hazelnut sponge, separate the eggs and whip the yolks by machine until liquid. Beat in the brown sugar a little at a time and continue beating on medium speed until very light.

3. Sift the cocoa and the flour several times and combine with the ground hazelnuts.

4. Beat the whites with the salt on medium speed. When they are white and opaque, increase the speed to maximum and beat in the granulated sugar in a stream. Beat until the whites hold a firm peak. Fold the yolks into the whites, then fold in the hazelnut mixture.

5. Spread the batter in the prepared pan and bake about 15 minutes. Immediately after removing the layer from the oven, loosen it and slide it off the pan to cool.

6. For chocolate hazelnut filling, bring cream to a boil and remove from heat. Add chocolate to cream and allow to stand several minutes. Stir the ganache smooth. Strain, then cool at room temperature or over cold water to speed cooling.

7. Use an electric mixer on medium speed to beat butter until softened. Beat in praline paste and beat smooth, scraping sides down several times. Beat in cooled ganache and continue beating to lighten.

8. For rum syrup, bring sugar and water to a boil. Remove from heat and cool. Stir in rum and vanilla.

9. To assemble, cut the hazelnut sponge into three strips, 4 × 18 inches. If you've used the smaller pan, cut into three equal strips. Place one strip on a platter or cardboard and moisten it with a third of the syrup. Spread with a quarter of the filling.

10. Top with the second layer and repeat. Place the third layer on and moisten with the remaining syrup. Spread the top and sides of the pavé with the remaining filling.

11. Decorate the top with large chocolate shavings and dust very lightly with confectioners' sugar.

SERVING: Cut thin slices of this rich cake.

STORAGE: Keep the cake at a cool room temperature until time to serve it. Wrap and refrigerate leftovers.

SWISS CHOCOLATE HAZELNUT CAKE

• • •

Makes one 5 × 10-inch 3-Layer cake,
about 12 servings

CHOCOLATE HAZELNUT CAKE

12 tablespoons (1½ sticks) unsalted
butter, softened

⅔ cup sugar, divided

7 ounces semisweet chocolate,
melted

8 large eggs, separated

1½ cups ground hazelnuts

⅓ cup all-purpose flour

½ teaspoon ground cinnamon

FILLING

1¼ cups heavy whipping cream

2 tablespoons (¼ stick) unsalted
butter

2 tablespoons light corn syrup

16 ounces semisweet chocolate, cut
into ¼-inch pieces

FINISHING

1 cup toasted and skinned
hazelnuts, chopped

1 batch Chocolate Sheet, page 391

Alkalized (Dutch process) cocoa
powder

One 10 × 15-inch jelly-roll pan
lined with parchment or buttered
wax paper

This is an adaptation of a cake I tasted at the beautiful Confiserie Schiesser in Basel. I spent a morning visiting the pastry shop, which has been run by the same family since 1870, now guided by Stephan Schiesser, great-grandson of the original owner. The recipe for Swiss Chocolate S's on page 164 is also a Schiesser specialty.

1. Set a rack at the middle level of the oven and preheat to 350 degrees.

2. Beat the butter with half the sugar until soft and light. Beat in the chocolate, then the yolks, one at a time. Combine the hazelnuts, flour, and cinnamon and stir in.

3. In a dry, clean bowl whip the egg whites until they hold a very soft peak and beat in the remaining sugar

in a slow stream. Continue whipping the whites until they hold a firm peak. Stir a quarter of the whites into the batter, then fold in the rest with a rubber spatula. Pour the batter into the prepared pan and bake about 25 minutes, until well risen and firm in the center. Turn the cake over onto a rack and allow to stand a few minutes, then lift off the pan and paper and cool completely.

4. To make the filling, bring cream to a boil with butter and corn syrup. Off heat, add chocolate and shake pan to make sure all chocolate is submerged. Whisk smooth, pour into a bowl and cool to room temperature.

5. Divide cake into thirds, each 10 × 5 inches. Place one layer on a cardboard or platter and spread with a third of the filling. Place another layer on top and spread with another third of the filling. Top with the last layer and mask the top and sides of the cake with the remaining ganache. Press the chopped hazelnuts into the frosting on the sides of the cake.

6. To decorate the top, break the chocolate sheet into irregular pieces about 2 to 3 inches across. Cover the entire top of the cake with the chocolate pieces, placing the straight edges of the chocolate sheet at the edges of the top of the cake. Dust very lightly with cocoa powder to make the chocolate shapes stand out.

SERVING: Use a sharp knife that has been warmed in hot water and wiped to cut through the chocolate sheet.

STORAGE: Keep the cake at a cool room temperature on the day you intend to serve it. Wrap and refrigerate leftovers and bring to room temperature before serving.

VARIATIONS

The cake may be made and finished with almonds, pecans, or walnuts replacing the hazelnuts.

CHOCOLATE BANANA LAYER CAKE

• • •

CHOCOLATE

Makes one 9-inch 4-layer cake,
about 12 servings

WHIPPED CREAM

3 cups heavy whipping cream

⅓ cup sugar

1 tablespoon vanilla extract

BANANAS

2 large very ripe bananas

Two 9-inch chocolate cake layers,
from the Horseradish Grill's
Chocolate Chocolate Cake,
page 84

FINISHING

¼ cup chocolate shavings, page 392

This cake is like the chocolate equivalent of a fruit shortcake and it never fails to elicit requests for seconds. For best results, make sure the bananas are really ripe—the skin should be evenly spotted with brown "sugar spots" when the bananas are ready.

I. Combine all ingredients for the whipped cream, and whip by machine on medium speed until the cream holds a firm peak.

2. Peel the bananas and slice into ¼-inch diagonal pieces, right before you assemble the cake.

3. To assemble the cake, slice each cake layer once horizontally, making four layers, and place one on a cardboard or platter. Spread the layer with a thin coat of whipped cream and top with a third of the banana slices. Spread another thin layer of cream over the banana slices and top with another cake layer. Repeat the cream-banana-cream layering and top with third layer. Repeat the cream-banana-cream layering again and top with the last layer. Spread the top of the cake with the remaining whipped cream and scatter the chocolate shavings over it.

SERVING: When you cut the cake, let each slice fall sideways onto a wide spatula—don't attempt to stand wedges of this cake up.

STORAGE: Refrigerate the cake after assembling it or the whipped cream will soften and run. Wrap and refrigerate leftovers.

CHOCOLATE MERINGUE CAKES

. . .

Crunchy and chewy, meringue is the ideal medium for luscious fillings such as ganache and chocolate whipped cream. Use the following few recipes that utilize chocolate meringue as starting points for your own creations.

CHOCOLATE MERINGUE CAKE

. . .

Makes one 9-inch cake, about 12 servings

CHOCOLATE MERINGUE

10 large egg whites (1¼ cups)

Pinch salt

1¼ cups granulated sugar

2 cups confectioners' sugar

⅓ cup alkalized (Dutch process) cocoa powder

CHOCOLATE FILLING

12 ounces semisweet or bittersweet chocolate

1 cup heavy whipping cream

8 tablespoons (1 stick) unsalted butter, softened

3 tablespoons orange liqueur

FINISHING

Confectioners' sugar

4 baking pans or cookie sheets lined with parchment paper and with a 9-inch circle traced on two of the pieces of paper, the papers then inverted

This is my personal version of a classic French cake called Concorde, originated in the early seventies by the famous French pastry chef Gaston Lenôtre.

1. If your oven has four racks, place them equidistantly. If not, set racks in the upper and lower thirds of the oven and preheat to 300 degrees.

2. Place the egg whites in the bowl of an electric mixer and add the salt. Beat on medium speed using the whip attachment until white and opaque, about 3 to 4 minutes. Increase the speed to maximum and add the granulated sugar in a stream. Continue beating until the egg whites hold a very stiff peak. Sift the confectioners' sugar and cocoa powder together several times and fold into the beaten egg whites with a rubber spatula.

3. Fit a pastry bag with a ½-inch plain tube (Ateco #6 or #806) and pipe the meringue in a concentric pattern to fill the two traced circles on the cookie sheets. Pipe small oval mounds of the remaining meringue onto the other two paper-covered pans.

4. Bake the meringues for about 45 minutes until firm on the outside and almost baked through. Cool the meringue layers and ovals on the pans.

5. Cut up the chocolate and set it aside. In a saucepan, bring the cream to a boil and then remove from the heat. Add the chocolate and shake the pan so

that the cream covers it completely. Allow to stand for 2 minutes, then beat smooth. Cool to room temperature.

6. On medium speed beat the butter with an electric mixer until soft and light. Add the chocolate mixture all at once and continue to beat until the filling is light. Beat in the liqueur a little at a time.

7. To assemble, trim the two meringues to even 9-inch disks. Place one on a platter or cardboard and spread it with half the chocolate filling. Top with the other disk and press the meringues together so they adhere. Cover the top and sides smoothly with the remaining filling. Stick the meringue ovals to the filling all over the top and sides of the cake.

8. Chill the cake for an hour to set the filling. Dust very lightly with confectioners' sugar before serving.

SERVING: If you intend to serve the cake on the day it is made, keep it at a cool room temperature after chilling briefly.

STORAGE: Keep leftovers covered with plastic at a cool room temperature.

QUADRUPLE
CHOCOLATE CAKE
• • •

Makes one 9-inch cake, about 12 servings

CHOCOLATE SUCCÈS

¾ cup whole hazelnuts

1 cup confectioners' sugar

¼ cup alkalized (Dutch process)
   cocoa powder

4 egg whites (½ cup)

½ cup granulated sugar

RUM SYRUP

⅓ cup sugar

¼ cup water

¼ cup dark rum

GANACHE

12 ounces semisweet chocolate

1 cup heavy whipping cream

One 9-inch round Chocolate
   Genoise, page 30, baked and
   cooled

Chocolate shavings, page 392,
   optional

FINISHING

Cocoa powder

Confectioners' sugar

2 cookie sheets or jelly-roll pans
   lined with parchment or wax
   paper, with a 9-inch circle traced
   on each, the paper then inverted

A rich combination of chocolate meringue, chocolate cake, and chocolate filling, this cake may be prepared several days in advance.

1. Set racks in upper and lower thirds of the oven and preheat to 325 degrees.

2. For the Chocolate Succès, combine the hazelnuts, confectioners' sugar, and cocoa in a food processor and grind until very fine. Beat the egg whites until they are white and opaque. Increase speed and beat in the granulated sugar in a stream. Continue beating until the whites are stiff. Fold in the cocoa mixture by hand. Fit a pastry bag with a ½-inch plain tube (Ateco #6 or #806) and use it to fill in the circles on the paper-lined pans. Bake for about 30 minutes.

3. To make the rum syrup, bring the sugar and water to a boil. Cool, then add the rum.

4. For the ganache, cut up the chocolate and set it aside. Bring the cream to a boil, then remove from heat. Add the chocolate and let stand several minutes. With a hand whip, beat the ganache smooth. Cool to room temperature or stir the ganache over a bowl of cold water to cool faster. Then use an electric mixer to beat the ganache until lightened.

5. Trim the meringue layers into even 9-inch disks. Place one layer on cardboard and spread with ganache. Place the genoise layer on the ganache and moisten with the syrup. Spread the ganache on the genoise layer and top with the other meringue layer. Spread the sides with remaining ganache and press crushed meringue scraps or chocolate shavings into it.

6. To decorate, dust top lightly with cocoa powder, then confectioners' sugar.

SERVING: Cut the cake into wedges with a sharp serrated knife wet in hot water and wiped clean before each cut.

STORAGE: Keep the cake at a cool room temperature on the day it is made. Wrap and refrigerate leftovers and bring to room temperature before serving.

CHOCOLATE MERINGUE HEART

■ ■ ■

Makes one 10-inch heart-shaped cake,
about 12 servings

CHOCOLATE MERINGUE

10 large egg whites (1¼ cups)

Pinch salt

1 cup granulated sugar

1½ cups confectioners' sugar

½ cup alkalized (Dutch process)
cocoa powder

WHITE CHOCOLATE FILLING

12 ounces white chocolate

6 tablespoons (¾ stick) unsalted
butter

⅔ cup heavy whipping cream

3 tablespoons orange or raspberry
liqueur

FINISHING

Cocoa powder

2 cookie sheets lined with
parchment paper and a 10-inch
heart or circle drawn on each,
the papers then inverted

Whether or not you prepare this delicate dessert in a heart shape, its taste and appearance are always spectacular.

1. Set racks at the lower and upper thirds of the oven and preheat to 300 degrees.

2. Place the egg whites in the bowl of an electric mixer and add the salt. Beat with the whip on medium speed until white and opaque, about 3 to 4 minutes. Increase the speed to maximum and add in the granulated sugar in a stream. Beat until the egg whites hold a very stiff peak. Sift the confectioners' sugar and cocoa powder together several times, then fold them, with a rubber spatula, into the beaten egg whites.

3. Fit a pastry bag with a ½-inch plain tube (Ateco #6 or #806), and use it to pipe the meringue in adjacent straight lines into the traced shapes on the parchment. Bake the meringue about 45 minutes, until firm on the outside and almost baked through. Cool the meringue layers on the pans.

4. For the filling, cut the chocolate into small pieces and combine it with the butter in a heatproof bowl. Place bowl over a pan of hot but not simmering water and stir to melt the chocolate. Remove bowl from water and stir in the cream in four additions. Stir in the liqueur. Cover the filling with plastic wrap and cool at room temperature.

5. Trim each of the meringues into an even shape. Place one on a platter or cardboard and spread it with the chocolate filling. Top with the other meringue and press to make the layers adhere. Chill to set. Dust lightly with the cocoa immediately before serving.

CHOCOLATE PAVLOVA

. . .

Makes one 10-inch-diameter Pavlova,
about 12 servings

MERINGUE SHELL

4 egg whites (½ cup)

Pinch salt

1 teaspoon distilled white vinegar

1 cup sugar

1 teaspoon cornstarch or
potato starch

FRUIT FILLING

4 cups cut-up peeled fruit (cut into
½-inch slices or dice); mixture
may include kiwis, strawberries,
raspberries, bananas, mangoes,
papayas, and pineapple

¼ cup sugar

CHOCOLATE WHIPPED CREAM FILLING

1½ cups heavy whipping cream

8 ounces semisweet chocolate,
melted

½ cup warm water

1 cookie sheet lined with
parchment or foil, onto which a
10-inch circle has been traced,
the paper then inverted

This famous Australian dessert usually isn't made with chocolate, but I think this light chocolate whipped cream makes a perfect filling for the light, chewy meringue shell. This recipe comes from my friend Kyra Effren in Dallas.

1. For the meringue shell, set a rack at the middle level of the oven and preheat to 350 degrees.

2. Whip egg whites and salt with an electric mixer on medium speed and continue until egg whites are white, opaque, and just beginning to hold their shape. Add vinegar, then increase speed to medium-high and add sugar, 1 tablespoon at a time, until all sugar is added and meringue is stiff. Whip in the cornstarch.

3. Use the back of a spoon to spread the meringue on the prepared pan within the traced circle. Make the meringue concave in the center by spreading from center out. Place the meringue in the oven and bake 5 minutes. Then lower heat to 250 degrees and continue baking for 1 hour, until the meringue is firm, crisp on the outside, and still slightly moist within. Cool on the pan on a rack. When completely cooled, slide a spatula or knife between meringue shell and paper to loosen it. If you prepared this in advance, wrap meringue with plastic and store at room temperature.

4. Combine sliced fruit in a mixing bowl and sprinkle with sugar. Toss gently, cover, and refrigerate no more than several hours or until needed. Drain fruit well before assembling dessert.

5. To make the chocolate whipped cream, whip the cream until it holds a soft peak, then set it aside. Quickly, mix the chocolate and the water together in a large bowl and allow to cool to room temperature. As soon as it does, fold in the whipped cream.

3. For the white chocolate mousse, cut the chocolate finely and place it in a heatproof bowl over a pan of hot water to melt. Stir the chocolate frequently and when it is melted, soften the butter and beat it in smoothly. Beat in the liqueur.

4. Combine the egg whites and sugar in the bowl of the mixer and heat them over simmering water until the whites are hot and the sugar has dissolved. Beat the meringue on medium speed until it holds a very soft peak.

5. Beat the cream by hand until it is firm. Fold the meringue and the cream into the chocolate mixture.

6. For the liqueur syrup, bring the sugar and water to a boil and cool. Stir in the liqueur.

7. To assemble, slice the chocolate genoise into three layers, only two of which will be used for the dessert. Save the third for another use. Place the first layer in the bottom of a 10-inch springform pan or dessert ring. Moisten the layer with half the syrup. Pour on the dark chocolate mousse and spread it even. Repeat with the second layer and remaining syrup. Pour on the white chocolate mousse and smooth the top. Refrigerate to set the dessert.

8. Wipe the outside of the ring or springform with a cloth dipped in hot water and wrung out. Run a knife around between the ring and the dessert, loosen the ring with a knife and lift it off carefully. Roll the chocolate plastic out thin, dusting it and the surface with confectioners' sugar. Cut a band and fit it around the outside of the dessert. Use more of the chocolate plastic to decorate the top of the dessert, formed into either a bow or more ribbons. See pages 385–87 for more information on working and decorating with chocolate. Dust very lightly with confectioners' sugar.

SERVING: Cut the cake with a thin, sharp knife wet with warm water and wiped between each slice.

STORAGE: Keep the cake in a cool place until serving time. Wrap and refrigerate leftovers; bring to room temperature for 1 hour before serving again.

VENETIAN CHOCOLATE CAKE

. . .

Makes one 9-inch cake, about 12 servings

ESPRESSO SYRUP

½ cup sugar

¼ cup water

½ cup very strong brewed espresso

¼ cup Italian brandy or cognac
(not grappa)

GANACHE

1¼ cups heavy whipping cream

1 pound semisweet chocolate, cut
into ¼-inch pieces

ZABAGLIONE FILLING

3 egg yolks

⅓ cup sugar

⅓ cup sweet Marsala

½ pound Mascarpone, at room
temperature

1 cup heavy whipping cream

One 9-inch Chocolate Sponge
Cake, page 32, baked and cooled

FINISHING

Chocolate ribbons, page 385

Confectioners' sugar

One 9-inch springform pan

You may recognize this cake as a dressed-up chocolate version of *tiramisù*.

1. To make the syrup, combine the sugar and water in a saucepan and bring to a boil. Cool and stir in the coffee and brandy.

2. To make the ganache, bring cream to a boil and remove from heat. Add chocolate, allow to stand for 5 minutes, then whisk smooth. Cool to room temperature.

3. For the filling, make zabaglione by whisking the yolks in the bowl of an electric mixer, then beating in the sugar and the Marsala. Whisk over a pan of simmering water until thickened. Remove and use the machine to beat until cold. Smash the Mascarpone in a bowl with a rubber spatula until smooth. Fold in the zabaglione. Whip the cream and fold it in.

4. Cut the cake layer into thin, vertical slices. Use a third to make a layer to line the bottom of the springform pan and brush on one third of the syrup, until the slices are soaked. Spread with one third of the cooled ganache and half the filling. Repeat with the cake, more syrup, more ganache, and the rest of the filling. Place a last layer of genoise on the top and soak with the remaining syrup. (Reserve remaining ganache for finishing outside.) Chill overnight, until set.

5. To finish, run a knife around the side of the dessert and remove springform side. Spread top and sides with remaining ganache. Pound ribbon mixture with a rolling pin to soften, then pass through pasta machine on progressively thinner settings, ending with the next-to-last setting, to form a wide, thin ribbon. Wrap entire dessert with ribbon and sprinkle with confectioners' sugar.

SERVING: Cut into thin wedges with a thin sharp knife that has been dipped in warm water and wiped between each cut.

STORAGE: Keep the cake in the refrigerator until time to serve it. Wrap and refrigerate leftovers.

CHOCOLATE RASPBERRY BAVARIAN CAKE

. . .

Makes one 10-inch cake, about 12 servings

RASPBERRY SYRUP

¼ cup sugar

⅓ cup water

¼ cup raspberry liqueur

CHOCOLATE FILLING

½ cup heavy whipping cream

4 ounces semisweet chocolate, cut into ¼-inch pieces

2 tablespoons (¼ stick) unsalted butter

RASPBERRY BAVARIAN

Two 10-ounce packages frozen raspberries

¾ cup sugar

⅓ cup raspberry liqueur

1½ envelopes unflavored gelatin

2 cups heavy whipping cream

One 9-inch round Chocolate Genoise, page 30, baked and cooled

FINISHING

1 cup heavy whipping cream

Chocolate shavings, page 392

One ½-pint basket raspberries

Confectioners' sugar

One 10-inch springform pan

CHOCOLATE

The light raspberry Bavarian cream is a perfect foil to the moist genoise layers and thin layers of chocolate filling. Serve this for a very special occasion—especially since it can be made entirely in advance and just finished off on the day you'll serve it.

1. For the syrup, combine the sugar and water, bring to a boil and cool. Stir in the liqueur.

2. For the chocolate filling, bring the cream to a boil. Remove from heat, add the chocolate, and allow to stand 2 minutes. Whisk in the butter until smooth and cool.

3. To make the Bavarian, combine the raspberries and sugar in a saucepan. Bring to a boil and simmer 10 minutes. Use a food mill or a fine sieve to puree and strain away seeds. Cool. Combine the liqueur and gelatin in a small, heatproof bowl and soak 5 minutes. Place bowl over simmering water to make liquid again, then whisk into cooled puree. Whip cream and fold it in.

4. Slice genoise into two layers and place one in the bottom of a 10-inch springform pan. Moisten with half the syrup. Whip cooled chocolate filling to lighten and spread half of it over cake layer; pour on half the Bavarian. Repeat with remaining cake layer, syrup, chocolate filling, and Bavarian. Chill to set.

5. To unmold, run a small knife between dessert and mold and lift off side of pan. Whip the cream and spread over sides of dessert. Press some of the chocolate shavings into cream. Arrange raspberries on top in two concentric circles around the top rim, then sprinkle center with shavings and confectioners' sugar.

CHOCOLATE HAZELNUT MOUSSE CAKE

• • •

Makes one 10-inch cake, about 12 servings

CHOCOLATE HAZELNUT CAKE

4 eggs, separated

¾ cup sugar, divided

Pinch salt

1 cup ground unblanched hazelnuts

½ cup cake flour

3 tablespoons alkalized (Dutch process) cocoa powder

RUM SYRUP

⅓ cup sugar

⅓ cup water

⅓ cup dark rum

CHOCOLATE HAZELNUT MOUSSE

16 ounces bittersweet chocolate

1¼ cups heavy whipping cream

8 tablespoons (1 stick) unsalted butter, softened

3 tablespoons dark rum

4 egg whites (½ cup)

⅔ cup sugar

1 cup hazelnuts, toasted, skinned, and chopped

FINISHING

Dark chocolate ribbons, page 385 or chocolate shavings, page 392

Cocoa powder or confectioners' sugar

One 10-inch cake pan, buttered and the bottom lined with parchment or wax paper, plus a 10-inch springform pan

Another cake in which the richness of the filling is tempered by the crunch of the nuts—this time hazelnuts. The white chocolate ribbon dresses the cake up but it is not essential.

1. Set a rack at the middle level of the oven and preheat to 350 degrees.

2. For the cake layer, beat the yolks with half the sugar until light. In a dry, clean bowl beat the whites with the salt at medium speed until white and opaque. Increase speed and beat in remaining sugar in a stream. Fold yolks into whites, then add ground hazelnuts. Combine flour and cocoa, sift over the batter, and fold in. Pour batter into the prepared pan and bake about 30 minutes, until well risen and firm in the center. Unmold and cool on a rack.

3. For the syrup, bring sugar and water to a boil. Cool and add the rum.

4. For the mousse, cut up the chocolate and place in a heatproof bowl. Place over hot, but not simmering, water to melt. Bring cream to a boil and pour over chocolate; whisk until smooth and cool. Beat butter until soft and light, then beat in cooled chocolate mixture and rum. Heat egg whites and sugar, whisking constantly, until mixture is hot and sugar is dissolved, then use an electric mixer to whip until cooled. Fold into chocolate mixture. Fold in hazelnuts.

5. To assemble, slice cake into three horizontal layers and place one in the bottom of a 10-inch springform pan. Moisten with a third of the syrup and spread with a third of the mousse. Repeat with remaining layers, syrup, and mousse. Chill to set mousse.

6. To finish, unmold cake by loosening around the edges with a sharp knife and lifting off side of pan. Wrap a wide white chocolate ribbon around outside of cake, then cover center of cake with more ribbons. If you don't use ribbons, frost the sides with 1 cup whipped cream and finish with some white chocolate shavings. Dust lightly with cocoa powder or confectioners' sugar.

SERVING: Cut the cake with a thin, sharp knife wet with warm water and wiped between each slice.

STORAGE: Keep the cake in a cool place until serving time. Wrap and refrigerate leftovers; bring to room temperature for 1 hour before serving again.

CHOCOLATE RASPBERRY CREAM CAKE

. . .

Makes one 9-inch cake, about 12 servings

CHOCOLATE CAKE LAYER

3 ounces semisweet chocolate, cut into ¼-inch pieces

6 tablespoons (¾ stick) unsalted butter, softened

⅓ cup sugar

4 eggs

½ cup ground almonds

½ cup fresh bread crumbs, see Note, page 63

RASPBERRY BAVARIAN CREAM

Two 10-ounce packages frozen raspberries

¾ cup sugar

2 tablespoons raspberry liqueur

2 tablespoons water

1 envelope unflavored gelatin powder

1 cup heavy whipping cream

FINISHING

1 cup heavy whipping cream

2 tablespoons granulated sugar

One ½-pint basket fresh raspberries

Confectioners' sugar

One 10-inch springform pan, buttered and the bottom lined with parchment or wax paper, cut to fit

One 9-inch springform pan

Though this cake is made of a rich layer combined with a rich filling, the fruity result is surprisingly light as well as very satisfying.

1. Set a rack at the middle level of the oven and preheat to 350 degrees.

2. For the cake layer, in a heatproof bowl over a pan of hot, but not simmering, water melt the chocolate. Stir melted chocolate smooth and allow to cool.

3. Use electric mixer on medium speed to beat butter and sugar until soft and fluffy. Beat in chocolate and scrape bowl and beater(s). Beat in one of the eggs, then another, then beat in the ground almonds. Beat in remaining eggs one at a time, then bread crumbs. Scrape batter into the prepared 10-inch pan and smooth top. Bake for about 20 minutes, until well risen and firm. Cool cake in pan on a rack. Unmold cake, wrap in plastic, and chill until needed.

4. The day before you are going to serve, trim top of cake even. Then, using the *outside* of a 9-inch springform pan as a guide, cut cake to 9 inches in diameter. Put bottom into springform and force cake layer into pan. Chill cake in pan until ready to fill with mousse.

5. To make the mousse, combine raspberries and sugar in a nonreactive saucepan and bring to a boil over medium heat. Lower heat and simmer until slightly thickened. Puree in food processor, then strain away seeds. Chill puree.

6. To assemble mousse, pour liqueur and water into a heatproof bowl and sprinkle gelatin over surface. Allow to soak 5 minutes. Place bowl over gently simmering water until gelatin melts, then cool slightly. While gelatin is melting, whip cream until lightly firm, but not grainy. Whisk gelatin into puree, then fold puree into cream. Quickly pour mousse over chocolate layer in pan. Cover with plastic wrap and chill until set, 8 hours or overnight.

7. To finish dessert, whip cream with the granulated sugar and spread evenly over mousse. Chill to set cream, then run knife between cream and side of pan. Remove springform sides and place mousse, on pan bottom, on platter. Garnish top with raspberries and sprinkle berries with confectioners' sugar.

GOLDEN CHOCOLATE CHARLOTTE

• • •

SPONGE FINGERS

4 eggs, separated

½ cup sugar, divided

1 teaspoon vanilla extract

Pinch salt

1 cup cake flour

Confectioners' sugar

CHOCOLATE FILLING

1 pound semisweet chocolate

8 tablespoons (1 stick) unsalted butter

4 egg yolks

⅓ cup orange liqueur or other sweet liqueur

⅓ cup sugar

1 cup heavy whipping cream

FINISHING

½ cup light corn syrup

Gold leaf for decoration, see Note

2 cookie sheets or jelly-roll pans lined with parchment or wax paper, plus a 2½-quart charlotte mold or soufflé dish

With its classic charlotte shape, this dessert is as elegant in appearance as in flavor.

I. Set racks in the upper and lower thirds of the oven and preheat to 350 degrees.

2. Beat together the yolks and half the sugar and the vanilla until very light. Beat the whites with a pinch of salt and continue beating until they are white and opaque. Increase the speed and beat in the remaining sugar in a stream. Continue beating until whites hold a firm peak. Fold the yolks into the whites, then sift the cake flour over the eggs and fold it in. Fit a pastry bag with a ½-inch plain tube (Ateco #6 or #806) and use it to pipe the batter in 4-inch-long fingers on the paper-lined pans. Dust with confectioners' sugar and bake about 10 to 15 minutes, until just firm or beginning to turn gold.

3. Butter a 2½-quart charlotte mold and line with plastic wrap. Cut the ends of 6 or 8 of the sponge fingers into a point and fit the points together in the center, into the bottom of the mold. Line the inside of the mold with the remaining fingers, saving some to use to make a base after the mold is filled.

4. To make the mousse, cut up the chocolate and melt it over hot, but not simmering, water. Off heat, beat in butter. Beat together the yolks, liqueur, and sugar in a heatproof bowl. Place the bowl over a pan of simmering water and whisk until mixture thickens slightly. Use the electric mixer to beat until cool. Fold in chocolate-butter mixture. Whip cream, fold it in, and pour into lined mold. Cover with the reserved fingers and scraps. Chill the mousse about 8 hours or overnight to set.

5. Unmold the charlotte onto a platter. Bring the corn syrup to a simmer in a small saucepan over low heat. Brush the outside of the sponge fingers with corn syrup to moisten slightly. Press sheets of the gold leaf against the moistened fingers until they adhere.

SERVING: Cut the charlotte into wedges to serve.

STORAGE: Keep the charlotte loosely covered in the refrigerator. Bring it to room temperature 1 hour before serving. Wrap and refrigerate leftovers.

NOTE: Gold leaf is usually available in artists' supply stores, or see Sources, page 442. To be edible, it must be 23 karat or higher. Lower karat weight gold leaf contains too much copper to be edible.

RIGOTORTE

• • •

Makes one 8-inch cake, about 12 servings

CHOCOLATE PASTRY

1 cup all-purpose flour

¼ cup sugar

3 tablespoons alkalized (Dutch process) cocoa powder

½ teaspoon baking powder

4 tablespoons (½ stick) unsalted butter

1 egg

CHOCOLATE FILLING

16 ounces bittersweet or semisweet chocolate

1 cup heavy whipping cream

1 teaspoon vanilla extract

2 tablespoons dark rum

CHOCOLATE GLAZE

8 ounces bittersweet or semisweet chocolate

½ cup heavy whipping cream

One 8-inch springform pan, buttered

From the Viennese tradition, Rigotorte is one of the most elegant and satisfying chocolate desserts. A base of chocolate pastry is covered with a chocolate filling, then a chocolate glaze. Very simple and very rich.

1. Set a rack at the middle level of the oven and preheat to 350 degrees.

2. For the chocolate pastry, mix the dry ingredients together in a bowl. Rub in the butter by hand, beat the egg and stir it in with a fork. Press the dough into the bottom of the prepared springform pan and bake about 15 minutes. Cool the pastry in the pan at room temperature.

3. For the chocolate filling, cut chocolate finely and place in a mixing bowl. Bring the cream to a boil in a small saucepan. Pour cream over chocolate and allow to stand 3 minutes. Stir until smooth. Cover and chill until the cream is cool and just begins to set. Use an electric mixer to beat, on medium speed, until light. Beat in the vanilla and rum. Spread the filling in the pan over the chocolate pastry. Level the top. Chill while preparing the glaze.

4. For the chocolate glaze, cut chocolate finely and place in a mixing bowl. Bring the cream to a boil in a small saucepan. Pour cream over chocolate and allow to stand 3 minutes. Stir to smooth.

5. Pour the glaze over the filling and refrigerate the Rigotorte for about 2 hours, or until completely set.

6. To unmold the dessert, wipe the outside of the pan with a cloth dipped in hot water and wrung out. Use the point of a small knife to loosen first the very top of the dessert from the sides of the pan. Remove the sides of the pan and slide the Rigotorte onto a platter.

SERVING: Serve *small* wedges.

STORAGE: Bring the dessert to room temperature for about an hour before you serve it. Wrap and refrigerate leftovers.

CAKES IN BOWLS

• • •

These really aren't cakes at all, but cake layers used to construct trifles: layers of cake alternating with filling in glass bowls. Be sure to use a bowl in which the alternating layers and colors of cake and filling are easily visible—the attractive layers add so much to the enjoyment of a trifle.

CHOCOLATE
AND VANILLA TRIFLE

• • •

Makes one 3-quart trifle, about 16 servings

CUSTARD CREAMS

4 cups milk

1½ cups sugar, divided

12 large egg yolks

⅔ cup all-purpose flour

2 teaspoons vanilla extract

6 ounces semisweet chocolate

RUM SYRUP

¾ cup water

¾ cup sugar

½ cup dark rum

WHIPPED CREAM

2 cups heavy whipping cream

¼ cup sugar

2 teaspoons vanilla extract

1 batch Plain, page 33, or Chocolate Sponge Cake, page 32, baked and cooled

FINISHING

Chocolate shavings, page 392

Loosely based on the Italian sweet *Zuppa Inglese*, this trifle is easy to make in advance for holiday entertaining.

1. To make custard creams, bring milk to a boil with half the sugar in a heavy, nonreactive pan. Whisk yolks with remaining sugar. Sift flour over yolks, then whisk in. When milk boils, whisk a third into the yolk mixture. Return remaining milk to a boil and whisk yolk mixture into it. Lower heat and continue to whisk until mixture thickens and returns to a boil. Whisk constantly 30 seconds, then remove from heat and whisk in vanilla. Scrape half the cream into a bowl and cover with plastic wrap; refrigerate to cool. Whisk chocolate into remaining cream. Whisk until chocolate is melted then scrape into a bowl, cover, and cool.

2. To make syrup, bring water and sugar to a boil in a saucepan. Cool and stir in rum.

3. For whipped cream, combine all ingredients and whip to a soft peak.

4. To assemble, cut cake into thin, vertical slices. Place a layer of slices in the bottom of a 3-quart glass serving bowl and moisten with syrup. Spread with half the vanilla cream. Repeat layers of cake and syrup, but this

time spread the cake with chocolate custard; spread a layer of whipped cream directly on the chocolate custard. Repeat the layering process again from the beginning, so that the finished trifle is composed of cake, syrup, vanilla custard; cake, syrup, chocolate custard, whipped cream; cake, syrup, vanilla custard; cake, syrup, chocolate custard, whipped cream. Sprinkle lightly with chocolate shavings.

SERVING: Use a large spoon to serve the trifle in dessert bowls or on dessert plates.

STORAGE: Keep refrigerated until time to serve; wrap and refrigerate leftovers.

CHOCOLATE ORANGE TRIFLE

. . .

Makes one 3-quart trifle, about 16 servings

ORANGE SYRUP

¾ cup sugar

½ cup water

½ cup orange liqueur

FILLING

4 large oranges

⅔ cup toasted sliced almonds

CHOCOLATE CUSTARD

3 cups milk

¾ cup sugar

6 egg yolks

12 ounces bittersweet chocolate

WHIPPED CREAM

2 cups cream

⅓ cup sugar

2 teaspoons vanilla extract

2 tablespoons orange liqueur

One 9-inch round Chocolate Genoise, page 30, baked and cooled

FINISHING

Chocolate shavings, page 392

Confectioners' sugar

Try different combinations of fruit and flavoring in the trifle. A few raspberries or sliced strawberries will add a note of color and fragrance to it.

1. For the orange syrup, bring the sugar and water to a boil. Cool and add the liqueur.

2. For the filling, peel the oranges, so that all the pith is removed, halve, seed, and slice them. Reserve four slices for decorating the trifle.

3. For the chocolate custard, combine the milk and sugar and bring to a boil in a saucepan. Beat the yolks in a bowl and beat in a third of the boiling milk. Return the remaining milk to a boil and beat in the yolk mixture, continuing to beat until thickened, without returning to a boil. Remove from heat and beat in chocolate until melted and smooth. Refrigerate to cool.

4. For the whipped cream, combine the cream with sugar, vanilla, and liqueur and whip until it holds a soft peak. Reserve ½ cup whipped cream for finishing the trifle.

5. To assemble the trifle, slice the chocolate genoise in thin vertical slices. Place slices of the cake in a 2- to 2½-quart bowl and moisten with the syrup. Spread on a layer of the chocolate custard, some orange slices and almonds, then a layer of the whipped cream. Continue layering all the ingredients, ending with a layer of the cake slices and syrup. Spread the remaining whipped cream on the trifle and decorate with chocolate shavings and the reserved orange slices.

PETITS FONDANTS AU CHOCOLAT

Little Chocolate Mousse Cakes

∎ ∎ ∎

Makes about 12 to 15 little cakes,
depending on the molds used

BATTER

4 ounces bittersweet chocolate, cut
into ¼-inch pieces

¼ cup granulated sugar

¼ cup water

8 tablespoons (1 stick) unsalted
butter

1 tablespoon framboise (raspberry
eau de vie)

2 eggs

FINISHING

1 cup heavy whipping cream

2 tablespoons sugar

Milk chocolate shavings,
page 392

Confectioners' sugar

One ½-pint basket fresh
raspberries

RASPBERRY SAUCE

One 10-ounce package frozen
raspberries

⅓ cup sugar

1 tablespoon framboise

One 12-cavity miniature muffin pan
or other small molds, buttered
and the bottoms lined with
parchment or wax paper

These chocolate cakes should be tiny because
they are fairly rich. Large portions might be
overwhelming. The raspberry garnish dresses
them up beautifully.

1. Set racks at the lower and upper thirds of the oven
and preheat to 325 degrees.

2. Melt the chocolate over hot water, stirring occasionally, then set it aside to cool slightly.

3. Combine the sugar and water in a saucepan and
bring to a boil over low heat, stirring occasionally to
make sure all the sugar crystals dissolve.

4. Remove the syrup from the heat and stir in the
butter. When it has melted, stir in the framboise, then
the melted chocolate.

5. Beat the eggs until they become liquid, then whisk
them into the chocolate mixture in a stream. Be careful not to overmix.

6. Pour the batter into the molds and bake about 20
to 25 minutes. Cool briefly in the pans, then unmold
and peel off paper. Cool at room temperature.

7. Whip the cream with the sugar until it holds a soft
peak. Pipe a rosette of the whipped cream on each
tiny cake and top with a few chocolate shavings and
a light dusting of confectioners' sugar. Place 2 or 3
raspberries around the top of each.

8. For the raspberry sauce, bring the raspberries and
sugar to a boil and simmer 5 minutes. Puree in
blender, then strain away seeds. Cool and stir in framboise. Serve the fondants in a puddle of the sauce.

CHOCOLATE ORANGE SLICES

· · ·

Makes twelve 2½-inch-square
individual desserts

ORANGE ALMOND CAKE LAYER

1 cup blanched almonds

¾ cup cake flour

4 large eggs, separated

¾ cup sugar, divided

Grated zest of 1 orange

½ teaspoon orange extract

Pinch salt

CHOCOLATE ORANGE FILLING

1½ pounds semisweet chocolate

1½ cups heavy whipping cream

⅓ cup light corn syrup

3 tablespoons orange liqueur

ORANGE DECORATION

3 oranges

½ cup sugar

2 tablespoons water

ORANGE SYRUP

⅓ cup orange juice

¼ cup sugar

⅓ cup kirsch or orange liqueur

One 10 × 15-inch jelly-roll pan,
  buttered and the bottom lined
  with parchment or wax paper

These delicate individual pastries may also be made with raspberries or strawberries.

1. Set a rack at the middle level of the oven and preheat to 350 degrees.

2. To make the cake layer, grind almonds finely in a food processor and stir into sifted cake flour. Whip yolks with half the sugar, the grated orange zest, and the orange extract until light. Whip whites with salt, then whip in the rest of the sugar until whites hold a soft peak. Fold in yolks, then fold in almond and flour mixture. Spread in prepared pan and bake about 20 minutes. Turn out of pan onto a rack and cool.

3. For filling, cut chocolate finely and set aside. Bring cream and corn syrup to a boil; remove from heat and add chocolate. Allow to stand 5 minutes, then whisk in liqueur. Cool at room temperature or in the refrigerator until thickened and spreadable.

4. To make the decoration, use a sharp vegetable peeler to remove the zest from the oranges in large, wide strips. Cut zest into thin shreds, place in a small pan and cover with water. Bring to a boil, drain and rinse. Return zest to pan with sugar and the 2 table-spoons water and bring to a simmer. Cook briefly until zest candies. Remove zest from pan and lay on buttered paper to cool.

5. For the syrup, squeeze the zested orange and bring orange juice and sugar to a boil in a small saucepan. Cool and stir in liqueur.

6. To assemble, cut cake in half to make two 10 × 7½-inch layers. Place one layer on a cardboard and moisten with half the syrup. Spread with half the filling. Top with remaining layer, moisten and spread with remaining filling. Chill to set.

7. Cut cake into 2½-inch squares and decorate each with candied orange zest.

SERVING: Serve these delicate individual cakes for tea or dessert.

STORAGE: Chill until an hour before serving time, then bring to room temperature. Wrap and refrigerate leftovers.

CHOCOLATE BUTTERMILK CUPCAKES WITH BOILED ICING

■ ■ ■

Makes 12 standard-size cupcakes

1½ cups all-purpose flour

1½ teaspoons baking powder

¼ teaspoon salt

6 tablespoons (¾ stick) unsalted butter, softened

1 cup sugar

2 squares unsweetened chocolate, melted and cooled

2 large eggs

½ cup buttermilk or milk

1 teaspoon vanilla extract

1 batch Old-fashioned Boiled Frosting, page 52

One 12-cavity muffin pan lined with paper muffin cups

This is the classic combination: rich, fudgy little cakes topped with sweet, billowy frosting. Cupcakes are always great for kids, but I've never seen an adult refuse one either.

1. Set a rack at the middle level of the oven and preheat to 350 degrees.

2. In a small bowl, stir together the flour, baking powder, and salt.

3. Use an electric mixer set at medium speed to beat the butter and sugar together. Continue beating until light, about 5 minutes. Beat in the chocolate and continue beating until smooth. Scrape bowl and beater(s) and beat in the eggs. Continue beating until creamy and smooth, another minute or two.

4. With a rubber spatula stir in half the flour mixture, making sure to scrape the sides of the bowl well. Stir in the milk and vanilla, then the remaining flour mixture. Divide the batter evenly among the 12 lined cavities in the pan, filling each about three-quarters full.

5. Bake the cupcakes about 20 minutes, until well risen and firm to the touch, or until a toothpick or knife inserted in the center of one emerges clean.

6. Cool the cupcakes in the pan briefly, then lift them from the pan to a rack to cool completely.

7. To finish the cupcakes, spread a spoonful of the frosting on each, swirling it with a small spatula or the back of a soup spoon.

SERVING: Serve the cupcakes as they are—they need no accompaniment. Consider serving them as part of a dessert buffet for a large party—they are easy and convenient both to serve and to eat.

STORAGE: If you wish to prepare the cupcakes in advance, replace them, unfrosted, in the pans after they have cooled and then wrap the pans in plastic and freeze. Defrost the cupcakes at room temperature before frosting them. After the cupcakes are finished, keep them under a cake dome or loosely covered with plastic wrap until time to serve.

COOKIES

BROWNIES AND BAR COOKIES
. . .

Blondie Squares

Supernatural Brownies

Cakey Brownies

Cocoa Brownies

Caramel Pecan Brownies

Hardly-Any-Fat Fudge Brownies

Coconut Chocolate Chip Bars

Chocolate Spice Bars

DROP COOKIES
. . .

Spicy Chocolate Chunk
Pecan Meringues

Chocolate Fudge Cookies

Chocolate Hazelnut Crinkles

Peanut Butter and Cocoa Cookies

Iced Chocolate Pecan Drops

Chocolate Almond Tuiles
Chocolate-Covered Tuiles

Florentines

Old-fashioned Chocolate Chip Cookies

White Chunk Fudge Cookies

Hazelnut Rum Chocolate Chip Cookies

Orange Chocolate Chip Cookies

Chewy Oatmeal Chip Cookies

Peanut Butter Chip Cookies

Chewy Brownie Chip Cookies

REFRIGERATOR COOKIES
. . .

Chocolate Pecan Dollars

Peppery Chocolate Sablés
Chocolate Sablés
Triple Chocolate Sablés

Chocolate and Vanilla Pinwheels

PIPED COOKIES
. . .

Swiss Chocolate S's

French Chocolate Macaroons

Chocolate Walnut Macaroons

Chocolate Orange Macaroons

Sarah Bernhardts

Chocolate Almond Fingers
Chocolate Almond Fingers
with Chocolate Filling

ROLLED COOKIES
. . .

Chocolate Thumbprints

Chocolate Cinnamon Disks

Crisp Chocolate Wafers

Chocolate-Dipped Stars

Sicilian Easter Hearts

Chocolate Walnut Rugelach

Chicklet's Chocolate
Chocolate Chip Sand Tarts

Truffle Cookies

What could be better than a rich, chocolaty brownie or a couple of chocolate chip cookies? Cookies are among the most popular of all sweets not only because of their intrinsic goodness but also because, for the most part, they are fast and easy to prepare—they fall into the category of instant gratification sweets.

The recipes in this chapter follow the classic cookie categories of bar, drop, refrigerator, piped, rolled, and sandwich cookies. There are also biscotti and molded cookies. Each section in the chapter begins with a short explanation of the cookie type and hints for preparation.

BROWNIES AND BAR COOKIES

• • •

I'm a brownie fanatic and love all sorts of brownies. I even once ran home and baked a brownie recipe that was written on an index card I found on the sidewalk a few blocks from my apartment in New York! Brownies are great because they're practical, like all bar cookies. With just a little effort you can easily make enough for a crowd. I always bake the Supernatural Brownies in this section for Christmas—the holiday wouldn't be the same anymore without them.

Brownie Hints

- Don't overmix—this produces a cakey, dry brownie.

- Watch baking time carefully. Test brownies with a fingertip—they should be soft, but not liquid. An overbaked brownie is dry and uninteresting.

- Let brownies cool completely before attempting to cut. In fact, a few minutes in the refrigerator or freezer makes cutting the brownies much easier. For very moist, fudgy brownies, rinse knife in hot water and wipe between each cut.

- If you are going to store brownies for any length of time, wrap them individually in cellophane or plastic wrap.

BLONDIE SQUARES

• • •

Makes about thirty-six 2-inch squares

2½ cups all-purpose flour

½ teaspoon salt

1 teaspoon baking soda

16 tablespoons (2 sticks) unsalted butter, softened

1¼ cups granulated sugar

¾ cup firmly packed dark brown sugar

2 large eggs

1 teaspoon vanilla extract

½ cup coarsely chopped walnuts or pecans

2 cups (12 ounces) semisweet chocolate chips

One 10 × 15 × 1-inch jelly-roll pan, buttered and lined with buttered parchment or foil

This is a great variation on a classic chocolate chip cookie. The batter is not dropped and baked as separate cookies, but is spread in a pan and baked, then cut into chewy, luscious squares, like blond brownies.

1. Set a rack at the middle level of the oven and preheat to 350 degrees.

2. In a mixing bowl stir together the flour, salt, and baking soda to mix.

3. Beat the butter with the sugars until combined. Beat in the eggs, one at a time, and finally the vanilla extract.

4. Stir the flour mixture into the butter mixture, then the nuts and chips.

5. Spread the batter in the prepared pan and bake for about 30 minutes, until well risen and firm to the touch. Cool in the pan on a rack.

6. After cake is cool, invert onto a cutting board and peel away the paper. Cut into 2-inch squares.

STORAGE: Keep the blondies in a tin or plastic container with a tight-fitting lid. Or wrap individually and freeze in a tightly closed plastic container.

SUPERNATURAL BROWNIES

. . .

Makes, about twenty-four
2-inch-square brownies

16 tablespoons (2 sticks) unsalted
butter

8 ounces bittersweet or semisweet
chocolate, cut into ¼-inch pieces

4 large eggs

½ teaspoon salt

1 cup granulated sugar

1 cup firmly packed dark brown
sugar

2 teaspoons vanilla extract

1 cup all-purpose flour

One 13 × 9 × 2-inch pan, buttered
and lined with buttered
parchment or foil

Though the name sounds an exaggeration, you'll agree that these brownies are absolutely out of this world.

1. Set a rack at the middle level of the oven and preheat to 350 degrees.

2. Bring a saucepan of water to a boil and turn off heat. Combine butter and chocolate in a heatproof bowl and set over pan of water. Stir occasionally until melted.

3. Whisk eggs together in a large bowl, then whisk in salt, sugars, and vanilla. Stir in chocolate and butter mixture, then fold in flour.

4. Pour batter into prepared pan and spread evenly. Bake for about 45 minutes, until top has formed a shiny crust and batter is moderately firm. Cool in pan on a rack. Wrap pan in plastic wrap and keep at room temperature or refrigerated until next day.

5. To cut brownies, unmold onto a cutting board, remove paper, and replace with another cutting board. Turn cake right side up and trim away edges. Cut brownies into 2-inch squares.

SERVING: Serve the brownies on their own or with ice cream and Hot Fudge Sauce, page 369.

STORAGE: The best way to store brownies is to wrap them individually and keep them at room temperature in a tin or plastic container with a tight-fitting cover. Or freeze them.

NOTE: If you have a 12 × 18-inch commercial half-sheet pan, you may double this recipe easily.

VARIATION

Add 2 cups (½ pound) walnut or pecan pieces to the batter.

CAKEY BROWNIES

. . .

Makes sixteen 2-inch-square brownies

6 tablespoons (¾ stick) unsalted butter

2 ounces unsweetened chocolate, cut into ¼-inch pieces

⅓ cup granulated sugar

⅔ cup firmly packed dark brown sugar

2 large eggs

1 teaspoon vanilla extract

½ cup all-purpose flour

¼ teaspoon salt

1 cup chopped walnuts or pecans, about 4 ounces

One 8 × 8 × 2-inch pan, buttered and the bottom lined with a square of parchment or foil

This is a quick-to-prepare recipe that's easy to do at the last minute.

1. Set a rack at the middle level of the oven and preheat to 375 degrees.

2. In a 2-quart saucepan over low heat, melt the butter. When the butter is hot, add the chocolate and stir. If the chocolate does not melt completely, return the pan briefly to the heat and stir until it does. Remove from heat.

3. Stir the sugars into the pan of chocolate and butter, then stir in the eggs, one at a time, and the vanilla.

4. Fold in the flour and salt, then the nuts. Scrape the batter into the prepared pan and smooth the top.

5. Bake the brownies for about 20 to 25 minutes, or until they are firm but still somewhat soft in the center. Cool in the pan on a rack. When cooled, unmold the brownies onto a cutting board, peel away the paper, and use a sharp knife to cut them into 2-inch squares.

SERVING: Brownies are great at any time!

STORAGE: The best way to store brownies is to wrap them individually and keep them at room temperature in a tin or plastic container with tight-fitting cover. Or freeze them.

COCOA BROWNIES

. . .

Makes about twenty-four 2-inch-square
brownies

1⅓ cups all-purpose flour

⅔ cup alkalized (Dutch process)
    cocoa powder

½ teaspoon baking soda

3 large eggs

½ teaspoon salt

1 cup granulated sugar

1 cup firmly packed dark brown
    sugar

1½ teaspoons vanilla extract

16 tablespoons (2 sticks) unsalted
    butter, melted and cooled

2 cups (12 ounces) semisweet
    chocolate chips

One 10 × 15 × 1-inch jelly-roll pan,
    buttered and lined with buttered
    parchment or foil

These are different from traditional brownies in that they are made from a combination of cocoa and chocolate chips instead of chocolate. This makes them have a light background with the added richness of the chips. Be careful not to overbake these brownies or they will be very dry.

1. Set a rack in the middle level of the oven and preheat to 375 degrees.

2. In a mixing bowl, combine the flour, cocoa, and baking soda and stir well to mix. Sift the mixture onto a piece of parchment or wax paper and set aside.

3. In a large mixing bowl, whisk together the eggs and salt, then whisk in both sugars. Whisk in the vanilla, then the butter. Whisk just until combined. With a rubber spatula, fold in the flour and cocoa mixture, then fold in the chocolate chips. Spread the batter evenly in the prepared pan and smooth the top. Bake for about 35 to 40 minutes, until firm but not dry.

4. Cool on a rack, then invert onto a cutting board, peel off the paper, and cut into 2-inch squares.

STORAGE: Keep the brownies in a tin or plastic container with a tight-fitting lid. Or wrap individually and freeze in a tightly closed plastic container.

CARAMEL PECAN BROWNIES

• • •

**Makes about twenty-four
2-inch-square brownies**

BROWNIE LAYER

3 ounces semisweet chocolate, cut
into ¼-inch pieces

3 ounces unsweetened chocolate,
cut into ¼-inch pieces

16 tablespoons (2 sticks) unsalted
butter, cut into 16 pieces

4 large eggs

¼ teaspoon salt

¾ cup light brown sugar, firmly
packed

¾ cup granulated sugar

1 teaspoon vanilla extract

¾ cup all-purpose flour

CARAMEL LAYER

8 tablespoons (1 stick) unsalted
butter

1½ cups light brown sugar, firmly
packed

½ cup light corn syrup

1 cup heavy whipping cream

1 teaspoon vanilla extract

1½ cups pecan pieces, coarsely
chopped, about 6 ounces

One 13 × 9 × 2-inch pan, buttered
and lined with buttered
parchment or foil

These are the best version of this popular brownie variation I have ever tasted. The recipe is one from my friend, cookbook author Marie Simmons.

1. Set a rack at the middle level of the oven and preheat to 350 degrees.

2. To make the brownie layer, bring a pan of water to a boil and remove from heat. Combine the chocolates and butter in a heatproof bowl and place on the pan of water to melt, stirring occasionally. When melted, remove bowl from pan of water.

3. In a large mixing bowl, whisk the eggs and salt until liquid. Whisk in the two sugars, then the vanilla. Whisk for a minute, to aerate slightly, then whisk in the chocolate and butter mixture. Fold in the flour with a rubber spatula.

4. Scrape the batter into the prepared pan and smooth the top. Bake for about 25 to 30 minutes, or until firm, but not dry. Place on a rack to cool.

5. To make the caramel layer, place the butter in a heavy saucepan and over low heat to melt. Stir in the brown sugar and corn syrup and bring to a boil. Insert a candy thermometer and cook to the soft ball stage, 240 degrees. (If you don't have a thermometer, test caramel in a glass of ice water—a spoonful dropped into the glass should form a soft, pliable ball you can hold between thumb and forefinger.) Off heat, add the cream slowly and carefully. Stop if the mixture splatters a lot or starts to boil over. Insert the thermometer again and cook to the firm ball stage, 248 degrees. (Ice water test the same as before, but ball should be firmer and hold its shape better.) Remove from heat and stir in vanilla pecans. Allow to cool for about 30 minutes.

6. Pour the caramel layer over the brownies and spread even with a metal spatula. Place the pan in the freezer for an hour to firm the caramel layer.

7. Run the pan over a burner set on low heat to melt the butter between the pan and the paper lining. Loosen the baked cake all around the inside of the pan with a small, sharp knife. Turn the cake out onto a cutting board. Trim edges and cut into 2-inch squares. Turn over so that caramel layer is on top.

STORAGE: Keep the bars between sheets of wax paper in a tin or other container with a tight-fitting cover.

HARDLY-ANY-FAT FUDGE BROWNIES
▪ ▪ ▪

Makes sixteen 2-inch-square brownies

½ cup alkalized (Dutch process) cocoa powder

1 cup all-purpose flour

1 teaspoon baking powder

½ teaspoon salt

2 tablespoons (¼ stick) unsalted butter, softened

1½ cups sugar

2 large egg whites (¼ cup)

½ cup unsweetened applesauce

1 teaspoon vanilla extract

One 8 × 8 × 2-inch pan, buttered and the bottom lined with a square of parchment or wax paper

This is a great recipe if you want to make a dessert for someone on a severely fat-restricted diet. Though these brownies don't have the same richness that full-fat ones do, they have a great taste and texture of their own.

1. Set a rack at the middle level of the oven and preheat to 350 degrees.

2. In a medium bowl, sift together cocoa, flour, baking powder, and salt.

3. In a separate bowl, beat together butter and sugar. Whisk in egg whites, applesauce, and vanilla.

4. Stir flour mixture into applesauce mixture until combined.

5. Pour batter into prepared pan and bake for 35 to 40 minutes or until firm. Cool in pan before cutting into squares.

SERVING: To dress these up, serve with a raspberry or other fat-free berry sherbet.

STORAGE: Keep covered at room temperature, or wrap and freeze.

COCONUT CHOCOLATE
CHIP BARS

■ ■ ■

Makes thirty-five 2-inch squares

CRUST

16 tablespoons (2 sticks) unsalted
    butter, softened

½ cup granulated sugar

2 cups all-purpose flour

TOPPING

4 eggs

1 cup granulated sugar

1 cup light brown sugar, firmly
    packed

1 teaspoon baking powder

One 7-ounce bag (2⅔ cups)
    shredded sweetened coconut

2 cups (about 8 ounces) pecan
    pieces, coarsely chopped

2 cups (12 ounces) semisweet
    chocolate chips

One 10 × 15 × 1-inch pan, buttered

CHOCOLATE

These are old-fashioned, chewy bar cookies that combine coconut, pecans, and chocolate with a rich and satisfying result.

1. Set a rack at the lower third of the oven and preheat to 350 degrees.

2. To make the crust, use a rubber spatula to beat the butter in a mixing bowl. Beat in the sugar. Fold in the flour to form a crumbly dough.

3. Turn the dough out into the prepared pan and, using the floured palm of your hand, pat and press the dough out into an even layer over the bottom of the pan. Bake for 15 minutes, until crust begins to color. Remove to a rack and prepare the topping.

4. To make the topping, whisk the eggs together, then whisk in the granulated sugar. Whisk in the brown sugar, then the baking powder. Add the coconut, pecans, and chocolate chips and fold them in with a rubber spatula.

5. Distribute the topping all over the dough and spread it even with a small metal offset icing spatula or the back of a spoon. Bake the bars for 25 to 30 minutes, or until the topping is firm and golden. Cool on a rack.

6. Trim away ⅛ inch of the edges of the bars and cut into 2-inch squares. Lift them from the pan with a spatula.

SERVING: These are a good afternoon or tea cookie.

STORAGE: Keep the bars between sheets of wax paper in a tin or other container with a tight-fitting cover.

CHOCOLATE SPICE BARS

. . .

Makes about thirty-five 2-inch squares

¾ cup all-purpose flour

1 teaspoon ground cinnamon

½ teaspoon ground cloves

½ teaspoon ground allspice

¼ teaspoon salt

12 tablespoons (1½ sticks) unsalted butter, softened

1½ cups light brown sugar, firmly packed

3 ounces unsweetened chocolate, melted

3 large eggs

1 cup walnut pieces, about 4 ounces, coarsely chopped

One 10 × 15 × 1-inch pan, buttered and lined with parchment or foil

These are a spicy variation of a brownie that can be varied by changing the nuts or the spices.

1. Set a rack in the middle level of the oven and preheat to 375 degrees.

2. In a mixing bowl, combine the flour, spices, and salt. Stir well to mix and sift the dry ingredients onto a piece of parchment or wax paper.

3. In the bowl of an electric mixer, beat the butter with the sugar on low speed until just mixed. Beat in the chocolate, then the eggs, one at a time, beating smooth between each addition. Beat in the dry ingredients, scraping bowl and beater(s) several times. Off the mixer, fold in the chopped nuts.

4. Scrape the batter onto the prepared pan and smooth the top with an offset metal icing spatula or a rubber spatula.

5. Bake the bars for about 20 to 25 minutes, until firm, but not dry. Cool in the pan on a rack.

6. Trim ⅛ inch from the edges and cut the cooled sheet into 2-inch squares, using a sharp, thin-bladed knife.

STORAGE: Keep the bars between sheets of wax paper in a tin or other container with a tight-fitting cover.

DROP COOKIES

■ ■ ■

Quick to mix and easy to shape, the dough for most drop cookies may be scooped up with a spoon and, as the name indicates, plopped onto the pan.

Look for recipes for many chocolate chip cookie variations at the end of this section.

For Best Drop Cookies

■ Don't overmix the batter—it makes the cookies fill up with air, then puff and flatten out while they are baking.

■ Try to make cookies uniform so that they will be similar sizes—they will bake more evenly.

■ Remember to alternate racks in the oven during baking—reverse the cookies back to front after 8 or 10 minutes and place cookies from upper rack on the lower one and vice versa. Consider doubling the pan—baking on two pans stacked together—or using an insulated cookie sheet for the lower third of the oven, where there is strong bottom heat that can burn delicate cookies.

SPICY CHOCOLATE CHUNK PECAN MERINGUES

∎ ∎ ∎

Makes about 25 to 35 cookies,
depending on size

4 large egg whites

Pinch salt

½ cup granulated sugar

1 cup confectioners' sugar

1 teaspoon ground ginger

¼ teaspoon freshly ground white
  pepper

1 cup pecan pieces, lightly toasted
  and chopped into ¼-inch pieces,
  about 4 ounces

6 ounces semisweet or bittersweet
  chocolate, cut into ¼-inch pieces

2 cookie sheets or jelly-roll pans
  lined with parchment or foil

These delicious cookies were partly inspired by Maida Heatter's Hot and Sweet Meringues flavored with crystallized ginger and macadamia nuts. My recipe gets its bite from ground ginger and white pepper.

1. Set racks in the upper and lower thirds of the oven and preheat to 300 degrees.

2. In the bowl of an electric mixer, combine the egg whites and salt. Whip on medium speed until the egg whites are white and foamy and beginning to hold their shape. Increase speed to high and beat in granulated sugar, 1 tablespoon at a time, until egg whites are stiff, but not dry.

3. Remove bowl from mixer and sift confectioners' sugar over it. Fold in. Before the sugar is completely absorbed, sprinkle on the ginger, pepper, nuts, and chocolate and continue folding until the ingredients are all incorporated.

4. Use a tablespoon to drop meringue onto the prepared pans. Keep the cookies about 1½ inches from one another and from the sides of the pan.

5. Place the pans in the oven and immediately lower the temperature to 275 degrees. Bake about 30 to 35 minutes, until cookies are golden and firm, but not dry all the way through. Cool the meringues on the pans on racks.

STORAGE: Keep the meringues between sheets of wax paper in a tin or plastic container with a tight-fitting cover.

VARIATIONS

Use walnuts or toasted and skinned hazelnuts in place of the pecans. Or use milk chocolate or a combination of dark and milk chocolate for the dark chocolate.

CHOCOLATE FUDGE COOKIES

■ ■ ■

Makes about 60 cookies

2 cups all-purpose flour

2 teaspoons baking powder

5 ounces unsweetened chocolate

8 tablespoons (1 stick) unsalted butter

4 large eggs

Pinch salt

1 cup firmly packed dark brown sugar

1 cup granulated sugar

1 tablespoon dark rum

Confectioners' sugar

Several cookie sheets or jelly-roll pans lined with parchment or foil

These rich cookies are as easy to prepare as they are to consume!

I. Mix together flour and baking powder and set aside.

2. Bring a pan of water to a boil and remove from heat. Combine chocolate and butter in a heatproof bowl and set over pan of water, stirring occasionally until melted.

3. In a large bowl, whisk eggs with salt, then whisk in both sugars. Whisk in chocolate mixture, then rum.

4. Stir in flour to form a soft dough. Scrape dough onto a piece of plastic wrap and wrap tightly. Chill 2 hours.

5. Set racks in upper and lower thirds of the oven and preheat to 350 degrees. Flour your hands and roll the chilled dough into 2-teaspoon balls. They don't have to be too neat. Roll each ball in confectioners' sugar. Arrange well apart on prepared pans and bake about 12 minutes. Cool pans on a rack before removing cookies from pan.

STORAGE: Keep the cookies between sheets of wax paper in a tin or other container with a tight-fitting cover.

CHOCOLATE HAZELNUT
CRINKLES

. . .

Makes about 30 cookies

2 cups whole unblanched hazelnuts

3 ounces unsweetened chocolate,
cut into ¼-inch pieces

½ cup dry bread crumbs

2 tablespoons all-purpose flour

1 teaspoon ground cinnamon

½ teaspoon ground cloves

2 large eggs

1 cup sugar

FINISHING

Sugar

2 cookie sheets or jelly-roll pans
lined with parchment or foil

These cookies get their name from their attractively crinkled surface. The recipe is loosely based on one in *Just Desserts* (Obelensky, 1957) by Helen McCully and Eleanor Noderer.

1. Set racks in the upper and lower thirds of the oven and preheat to 325 degrees.

2. Place the hazelnuts in the bowl of a food processor fitted with the metal blade. Pulse repeatedly until coarsely ground. Add chocolate and continue pulsing until both are finely ground. Pour hazelnuts and chocolate into a bowl and add bread crumbs, flour, and spices.

3. In another mixing bowl, whisk the eggs with the sugar until light. Add the dry ingredients and use a rubber spatula to stir to a firm dough.

4. To shape the cookies, make the dough into 1-inch spheres and roll each in granulated sugar before placing about 3 inches apart on prepared pans.

5. Bake the cookies for about 15 minutes, or until they have spread and become crinkled on the surface. Slide parchment or foil from the pans to racks to cool.

STORAGE: Keep the cookies between sheets of wax paper in a tin or other container with a tight-fitting cover.

PEANUT BUTTER AND COCOA COOKIES

∎ ∎ ∎

Makes 40 cookies

1¼ cups all-purpose flour

½ cup alkalized (Dutch process) cocoa powder

½ teaspoon baking soda

12 tablespoons (1½ sticks) unsalted butter, softened

1 cup chunky peanut butter

½ cup granulated sugar

½ cup firmly packed dark brown sugar

1 large egg

1 teaspoon vanilla extract

2 cookie sheets or jelly-roll pans lined with parchment or foil

This is an easy variation on an old-fashioned peanut butter cookie. It uses some cocoa to give them a chocolate flavor.

1. Set racks in the upper and lower thirds of the oven and preheat to 350 degrees.

2. In a mixing bowl, combine the flour, cocoa, and baking soda and stir well to mix. Sift onto a sheet of parchment or wax paper.

3. Use an electric mixer on low speed to combine the butter and peanut butter. Raise speed to medium, beat in sugars, then continue to beat for about a minute, until light. Beat in the egg and vanilla and continue beating until smooth.

4. By hand, stir in the dry ingredients.

5. Divide the dough into four pieces and divide each into ten pieces.

6. Roll each piece of dough into a ball and place it about 2 inches from any other on the prepared pans. Press the back of a fork down on each cookie once, then press each again across the first marking.

7. Bake the cookies for about 15 minutes, until they are slightly puffed and no longer wet in appearance.

8. Slide the parchment or foil from the pans to racks to cool the cookies.

STORAGE: Keep the cookies between sheets of wax paper in a tin or other container with a tight-fitting cover.

ICED CHOCOLATE PECAN DROPS

• • •

Makes about 40 cookies, depending on
how large they are spooned out

COOKIE BATTER

1¾ cups all-purpose flour

½ teaspoon baking soda

½ teaspoon salt

8 tablespoons (1 stick) unsalted
butter, softened

½ cup granulated sugar

½ cup firmly packed dark brown
sugar

2 ounces unsweetened chocolate,
melted

1 large egg

1 teaspoon vanilla extract

¾ cup buttermilk or milk

1 cup pecan pieces, about 4 ounces,
coarsely chopped

CHOCOLATE ICING

2 tablespoons unsalted butter,
softened

4 tablespoons water

2 ounces unsweetened chocolate,
melted

1½ cups confectioners' sugar, sifted
after measuring

2 cookie sheets or jelly-roll pans
lined with parchment or foil

These easy cookies are dressed up with a small smear of chocolate icing.

1. Set racks in the upper and lower thirds of the oven and preheat to 350 degrees.

2. For the cookie batter, combine the flour, baking soda, and salt in a mixing bowl and stir well to mix. Sift the dry ingredients onto a piece of parchment or wax paper.

3. In the bowl of an electric mixer, combine the butter with the sugars. Beat on low speed until combined. Beat in the chocolate and continue beating just until mixed. Beat in the egg and vanilla, continuing to beat until the mixture is smooth.

4. Scrape bowl and beater(s) and beat in half the dry ingredients, then the buttermilk, then the other half of the dry ingredients, beating smooth between each addition. Beat in the chopped pecans.

5. Drop heaping teaspoons of the batter about 3 inches apart on the prepared pans. Bake the cookies for about 15 minutes, or until they have spread and puffed.

6. Slide the parchment or foil from the pans to racks to cool.

7. After the cookies have cooled, make the icing. Whisk the butter and water into the chocolate, then stir in the confectioners' sugar with a rubber spatula. With a small metal icing spatula or a table knife, spread about a teaspoon of the icing on each cookie. Let the icing set before packing away the cookies.

STORAGE: Keep the cookies between sheets of wax paper in a tin or other container that has a tight-fitting cover.

CHOCOLATE ALMOND TUILES

• • •

Makes about twenty-four 3-inch cookies

2 large eggs

½ cup sugar

1 teaspoon vanilla extract

3 cups sliced almonds, about 10 ounces

2 tablespoons all-purpose flour

2 tablespoons alkalized (Dutch process) cocoa powder

3 cookie sheets or jelly-roll pans, brushed with melted butter

Tuile means "tile" and the shape is similar to that of a curved overlapping clay roofing tile. These are easy to make, and if you don't want to curve all—or any—of the cookies, they taste exactly the same when they're flat. The variation following the recipes is for nonchocolate tuiles covered with tempered chocolate.

1. Set racks in the upper and lower thirds of the oven and preheat to 350 degrees.

2. Whisk the eggs in a bowl just to break them up. Whisk in the sugar in a stream, but do not whip to aerate. Stir in the vanilla. Mix the almonds and flour together and sift the cocoa powder over them. Stir into the egg mixture.

3. Drop small spoonfuls of the batter onto prepared pans, 3 inches from one another and from edges of pan. Flatten with the back of a fork. Bake for about 10 to 15 minutes, or until well spread out and firm.

4. Remove the hot tuiles from the pan with a spatula and curve them around a rolling pin or other cylindrical form. As they cool, they will quickly harden into the curved shape.

5. Repeat with the remaining batter.

SERVING: Tuiles are a wonderful accompaniment to any creamy or fruit dessert.

STORAGE: Keep them in a tin or plastic container with a tight-fitting cover, but they are so fragile that it doesn't make sense to prepare them for storage—they have the best flavor and texture when freshly made.

VARIATION

CHOCOLATE-COVERED TUILES Omit the cocoa from the batter (it isn't necessary to increase the flour to make up for it). Curve the tuiles or not, as you wish. After they are cool, use a small, dry brush to paint a thin layer of tempered chocolate (see pages 20–23) onto the flat side (the side that was against the pan) of each tuile.

FLORENTINES

. . .

Makes about 30 large cookies

½ cup heavy whipping cream

⅓ cup dark flavorful honey

1⅓ cups sugar

1½ cups candied orange peel, finely
   chopped

3 cups blanched sliced almonds,
   about 10 ounces

16 ounces bittersweet or semisweet
   chocolate, tempered, pages 20–23

3 cookie sheets or jelly-roll pans
   lined with parchment or
   buttered foil

These are really a combination cookie/candy. The sugary almond batter is baked, then one side is covered with tempered chocolate. Florentines are also good without the chocolate, but it's the tempered chocolate finish that lifts them from the ordinary to the sublime.

1. Set racks in the upper and lower thirds of the oven and preheat to 350 degrees.

2. Combine the cream, honey, and sugar in a medium saucepan over low heat and stir with a metal spoon to dissolve the sugar. When the mixture comes to a boil, stop stirring and insert a candy thermometer. Boil the mixture to 240 degrees, or until it forms a soft ball.

3. Remove the thermometer and quickly stir in the orange peel and the almonds.

4. Drop scant tablespoons of the mixture on the pans. Keep them about 4 inches apart, all around.

5. Bake the Florentines for 10 minutes, or until they start to bubble on the pan. Remove a pan from the oven and let the Florentines cool for a minute, then use the back of the tines of a fork to ease them back into a circular shape. Repeat with remaining cookies. Cool for another minute, then return the cookies to the oven to finish baking and become evenly golden.

6. Cool the cookies on the pans on racks.

7. After the cookies have cooled, peel them from the paper and arrange them on a clean, paper-covered pan.

8. Spread a thin layer of the tempered chocolate on the flat underside of each Florentine. Make decorative swirls in the chocolate with a decorating comb, the side of a serrated knife, or the edge of a spatula. Replace the Florentine on the pan chocolate side up. Repeat with remaining cookies.

SERVING: Serve these after a very special dinner or with an assortment of cookies and confections.

STORAGE: Keep the cookies between sheets of wax paper in a tin or other container with a tight-fitting cover.

VARIATION

Instead of coating the whole underside of each cookie with tempered chocolate, try streaking them instead. Line all the cookies up on pans, flat side up, and streak them with tempered chocolate from a paper cone, nonpleated plastic bag, or squeeze bottle. Let the chocolate set.

OLD-FASHIONED CHOCOLATE CHIP COOKIES
• • •

Makes about 30 cookies

1 cup all-purpose flour

½ teaspoon salt

½ teaspoon baking soda

8 tablespoons (1 stick) unsalted butter, softened

½ cup granulated sugar

¼ cup firmly packed dark brown sugar

1 large egg

1 teaspoon vanilla extract

½ cup walnut or pecan pieces, coarsely chopped

One 6-ounce bag semisweet chocolate chips

2 cookie sheets or jelly-roll pans lined with parchment or foil

No book of chocolate desserts would be complete without a recipe for this best and most beloved of all cookies.

1. Set racks in the upper and lower thirds of the oven and preheat to 375 degrees.

2. In a mixing bowl, stir together the flour, salt, and baking soda. Sift the dry ingredients onto a piece of parchment or wax paper.

3. By hand or with an electric mixer, beat together the butter and sugars. Beat in the egg and the vanilla extract until smooth. Stir in the dry ingredients, then the nuts and chocolate chips.

4. Drop the batter by heaping teaspoons onto the prepared pans, keeping the cookies about 3 inches apart on all sides.

5. Bake the cookies for about 12 to 15 minutes, until deep golden and firm. Slide parchment or foil from pans to racks to cool.

STORAGE: Keep the cookies between sheets of wax paper in a tin or other container with a tight-fitting cover.

WHITE CHUNK FUDGE COOKIES

∎ ∎ ∎

Makes about thirty-six 3-inch cookies

12 ounces bittersweet chocolate, cut into ¼-inch pieces

8 tablespoons (1 stick) unsalted butter, cut into 8 pieces

3 large eggs

1 cup sugar

½ teaspoon salt

½ teaspoon baking powder

1 cup all-purpose flour

12 ounces white chocolate, cut into ¼-inch pieces, or one 12-ounce bag white chocolate chips

2 or 3 cookie sheets or jelly-roll pans lined with parchment or foil

The contrasts in flavor and color in these are great—the bittersweet flavor of the dark chocolate tastes even better in contrast to the melting sweetness of the white chunks.

1. Set racks in the upper and lower thirds of the oven and preheat to 350 degrees.

2. Bring a saucepan of water to a boil and remove from heat. Combine the bittersweet chocolate with the butter in a heatproof bowl and place over the pan of water; stir occasionally until chocolate and butter are melted.

3. In a mixing bowl, whisk the eggs until liquid, then whisk in the sugar, salt, and baking powder. Stir in the chocolate and butter mixture, then fold in the flour and, lastly, the white chunks or chips.

4. Spoon 2-tablespoon-size mounds of the batter onto prepared pans, keeping the cookies about 3 inches from each other and the edges of the pan. If your oven ordinarily burns the bottoms of items on the lower shelves, place the cookies on two pans stacked together or use a special insulated pan.

5. Bake the cookies for about 15 minutes, until well puffed and slightly firm, but still soft in the center. Slide the parchment or foil off the pans to racks to cool.

STORAGE: Keep the cookies between layers of wax paper in a tin or plastic container with a tight-fitting cover.

HAZELNUT RUM CHOCOLATE CHIP COOKIES

■ ■ ■

Makes about 50 cookies

12 tablespoons (1½ sticks) unsalted butter, softened

1 cup light brown sugar

1 tablespoon dark rum

1 egg

1 egg yolk

1⅔ cups all-purpose flour

1 teaspoon baking soda

½ teaspoon salt

1 cup hazelnuts, toasted, skinned, and coarsely chopped

2 cups (12 ounces) semisweet chocolate chips

3 cookie sheets or jelly-roll pans lined with parchment paper

These are "adult chocolate chip cookies," although people of all ages love them.

1. Set racks at the upper and lower thirds of the oven and preheat to 375 degrees.

2. Beat butter with brown sugar until fluffy, then beat in rum, egg, and yolk.

3. Combine flour with baking soda and salt and stir into butter mixture. Stir in hazelnuts and chocolate chips.

4. Drop batter from teaspoon onto prepared pans.

5. Bake about 12 to 15 minutes, until risen and set. Cool on pans.

STORAGE: Keep the cookies between sheets of wax paper in a tin or other container with a tight-fitting cover.

ORANGE CHOCOLATE CHIP COOKIES

. . .

Makes about 40 cookies

2 cups all-purpose flour

2 teaspoons baking powder

½ teaspoon ground cinnamon

12 tablespoons (1½ sticks) unsalted butter, softened

1 cup sugar

Finely grated zest of 2 medium oranges

2 large eggs

One 12-ounce bag milk chocolate chips

2 cookie sheets or jelly-roll pans lined with parchment or foil

This is another great example of the happy combination between chocolate and orange flavors. These orange-scented cookies are studded with milk chocolate chips for a delicate variation on classic chocolate chip cookies.

1. Set racks in the upper and lower thirds of the oven and preheat to 350 degrees.

2. For the cookie batter, combine the flour, baking powder, and cinnamon in a mixing bowl and stir well to mix. Sift the dry ingredients onto a piece of parchment or wax paper.

3. In the bowl of an electric mixer, combine the butter with the sugar. Beat on low speed until combined. Beat in the orange zest, then the eggs, continuing to beat until the mixture is smooth.

4. Scrape bowl and beater(s) and beat in the dry ingredients. Beat in the chips.

5. Drop heaping teaspoons of the batter about 3 inches apart on the prepared pans. Bake the cookies for about 15 minutes, or until they have spread, puffed, and are a deep golden color.

6. Slide the parchment or foil from the pans to racks to cool.

STORAGE: Keep the cookies between sheets of wax paper in a tin or other container that has a tight-fitting cover.

CHEWY OATMEAL CHIP COOKIES

■ ■ ■

Makes about 45 cookies

8 tablespoons (1 stick) unsalted
   butter, softened

¾ cup light brown sugar

1 egg

1 teaspoon vanilla extract

¾ cup all-purpose flour

½ teaspoon baking soda

½ teaspoon ground cinnamon

¼ teaspoon salt

1½ cups rolled oats (regular
   oatmeal)

1 cup chocolate chips, 6 ounces

1 cup dark raisins, optional

2 cookie sheets or jelly-roll pans
   lined with parchment paper

These are addictive right out of the oven. If you manage to keep any, store them airtight to retain moisture.

1. Set racks at the upper and lower thirds of the oven and preheat to 350 degrees.

2. Beat butter and sugar until mixed, then beat in egg and vanilla. Continue to beat until smooth. Stir in flour, baking soda, cinnamon, and salt.

3. Stir in oatmeal, chips, and optional raisins. Drop by tablespoons onto paper-lined cookie sheets. Use the back of a fork to flatten the cookies slightly. Bake about 10 minutes, until golden and still moist. Cool on pans.

STORAGE: Keep the cookies between sheets of wax paper in a tin or other container with a tight-fitting cover.

PEANUT BUTTER CHIP COOKIES

∎ ∎ ∎

Makes about forty-eight 3-inch cookies

8 tablespoons (1 stick) unsalted butter, softened

1½ cups firmly packed dark brown sugar

½ cup granulated sugar

½ teaspoon salt

⅔ cup smooth peanut butter

2 large eggs

1½ teaspoons vanilla extract

2½ cups flour

2 teaspoons baking soda

2 cups semisweet chocolate chips, 12 ounces

2 cups chopped honey-roasted peanuts, about ½ pound

2 or 3 cookie sheets or jelly-roll pans lined with parchment or foil

These are my favorite variation on classic chocolate chip cookies. They have a real peanut crunch. My friend Jennifer Migliorelli developed this recipe when she was working as a chef in an American restaurant in Hong Kong.

1. Set racks in the upper and lower thirds of the oven and preheat to 350 degrees.

2. In an electric mixer, beat the butter, sugars, salt, and peanut butter just until smooth. Beat in the eggs, one at a time. Beat only until smooth after each addition. Beat in the vanilla.

3. Separately, in a small bowl, mix the flour with the baking soda, then beat into the peanut butter mixture, scraping the bowl and beater(s). Stir in the chocolate chips and peanuts.

4. Scoop or spoon 2-tablespoon-size mounds of the batter onto the prepared pans, leaving about 2 inches between cookies and from the edges of the pan. (If the batter is crumbly, roll the portions of dough into a rough sphere between the palms of your hands.) Flatten the cookies with the bottom of a glass. Bake about 12 to 15 minutes, until the cookies are well risen and golden.

5. Slide the parchment or foil from the pans to racks to cool.

STORAGE: Keep the cookies between layers of wax paper in a tin or plastic container with a tight-fitting cover.

CHEWY BROWNIE CHIP COOKIES

. . .

Makes about 30 cookies

¾ cup all-purpose flour

¼ cup alkalized (Dutch process) cocoa powder

½ teaspoon baking soda

Pinch salt

6 tablespoons (¾ stick) unsalted butter

6 ounces semisweet or bittersweet chocolate, cut into ¼-inch pieces

2 large eggs

1 cup sugar

2 teaspoons vanilla extract

1 cup semisweet chocolate chips, 6 ounces

2 cookie sheets or jelly-roll pans lined with parchment or foil

These rich cookies are like "drop" brownies. Be careful not to overbake them or they will be dry rather than moist and chewy.

1. Set racks in the upper and lower thirds of the oven and preheat to 350 degrees.

2. Mix together flour, cocoa, baking soda, and salt in a bowl and sift onto a piece of parchment or wax paper. Set aside.

3. Bring a pan of water to a boil and remove from heat. Put butter and the 6 ounces of semisweet or bittersweet chocolate in a heatproof bowl and place over the hot water, stirring occasionally until melted. Remove from heat and allow to cool slightly.

4. Use an electric mixer to whisk the eggs until liquid. Then whisk in the sugar and vanilla.

5. With a rubber spatula, fold in the melted chocolate and butter, then fold in the dry ingredients. Finally, fold in the chocolate chips.

6. Use a tablespoon measuring spoon to shape the cookies. Mound them about 1½ inches apart on the prepared pans.

7. Bake the cookies about 15 minutes, until well puffed but still very moist. Slide the parchment or foil off the pans to racks to cool.

STORAGE: Keep the cookies in a tin or plastic container with a tight-fitting lid. Or wrap individually and freeze in a tightly closed plastic container.

REFRIGERATOR COOKIES

. . .

When I was a child, these were still called "icebox cookies." I guess in the early fifties there were still a few old-fashioned iceboxes persisting where people didn't have electric refrigerators. In any case, these are practical cookies to prepare. The ancestors of industrially made "slice and bake" cookies, these may be made up and shaped days in advance and then cut and baked when it's convenient—or when you just want some freshly baked cookies.

To shape refrigerator cookies, flour the work surface and gently roll the dough into a cylinder. Divide it into the amount of separate pieces the recipe states, then place each on a piece of parchment or wax paper. Roll the cookie dough to the length stated in the recipe, then wrap the paper around it, making a tight cylinder. Chill the logs of dough until ready to slice and bake the cookies.

Give the paper-wrapped logs a second wrapping in plastic if you intend to freeze them—just remember to defrost the cookies in the refrigerator for half a day before trying to slice and bake them.

A hint about slicing the cookies: After you unwrap the log of chilled dough, place it on a cutting board and cut it with a sharp knife. Roll the log of dough a few degrees around every time you slice through it to avoid crushing the log by cutting repeatedly with the log in the same position.

CHOCOLATE PECAN DOLLARS

• • •

Makes about 70 cookies, depending on how thin you slice them

12 tablespoons (1½ sticks) unsalted butter, softened

1 cup light brown sugar

2 ounces unsweetened chocolate, melted and cooled

1 large egg

2 cups all-purpose flour

1 teaspoon baking powder

½ teaspoon ground cinnamon

¼ teaspoon salt

⅔ cup chopped pecans, about 2½ ounces

2 or 3 cookie sheets or jelly-roll pans lined with parchment or foil

These easy refrigerator cookies are great to have on hand. Chill or freeze the dough, then just slice some off and bake when you want cookies.

1. Use an electric mixer to beat the butter and sugar until light, about 2 minutes. Beat in the chocolate, then the egg, and continue beating until smooth, about a minute longer.

2. In a mixing bowl, combine the flour, baking powder, cinnamon, and salt and stir well to mix. Beat the dry ingredients into the butter and chocolate mixture. Scrape down bowl and beater(s) and beat in the pecans.

3. Transfer the dough to a lightly floured work surface, flour your hands, and form the dough into a cylinder. Cut cylinder in half and roll and pull each piece into a cylinder about 8 to 9 inches long. Roll a piece of parchment or wax paper around each piece of dough and tighten the paper around it by pressing in with the side of a cookie sheet or piece of cardboard as in the illustration for tightening the rolled cake, page 67. Chill the dough until firm. Or, at this stage it can be frozen, double-wrapped in plastic, and kept for up to several weeks.

4. When you are ready to bake the cookies, set racks in the upper and lower thirds of the oven and preheat the oven to 375 degrees. Remove one cylinder of dough from the refrigerator and unwrap it. Place it on a cutting board and use a sharp, serrated knife to slice it every ¼ inch. Arrange the slices about 2 inches apart on the prepared pans. If your oven tends to burn the bottoms of items baked on the lower shelves, place the cookies on two pans stacked together or use a special insulated pan.

5. Bake the cookies about 10 minutes, until puffed and beginning to become firm. Continue slicing and baking cookies, or freeze remaining dough to use on another occasion.

SERVING: These make a great accompaniment to ice cream or a simple dessert.

STORAGE: Keep the cookies between sheets of parchment or wax paper in a tin or plastic container that has a tight-fitting cover.

PEPPERY CHOCOLATE SABLÉS

• • •

Makes about 60 cookies

10 tablespoons (1¼ sticks) unsalted
   butter, softened

¾ cup sugar

1 teaspoon ground cinnamon

¼ teaspoon cayenne pepper

¼ teaspoon freshly ground black
   pepper

1 egg

1 large egg white

2 cups all-purpose flour

½ cup alkalized (Dutch process)
   cocoa powder

½ teaspoon baking soda

2 cookie sheets or jelly-roll pans
   lined with parchment or foil

These are based on a delicious cookie made by my friend and former student Stephen Hoffman.

1. Use an electric mixer to beat butter with sugar, cinnamon, and peppers until very light, about 5 minutes on medium speed.

2. Beat in egg, then egg white. Continue beating until smooth.

3. Sift flour, cocoa, and baking soda over batter, then stir in.

4. Divide dough in half, place each half on a sheet of parchment paper, and shape each into an 8-inch-long cylinder. Wrap parchment around dough and chill until firm.

5. Set racks in the upper and lower thirds of the oven and preheat to 325 degrees.

6. Slice dough every ¼ inch and arrange cookies on prepared pans. Bake 15 to 20 minutes. Cool on pans on a rack.

SERVING: These are great on their own or with a creamy dessert.

STORAGE: Keep the cookies between sheets of parchment or wax paper in a tin or plastic container that has a tight-fitting cover.

VARIATIONS

CHOCOLATE SABLÉS Omit the cinnamon, cayenne, and black pepper for a plain, but delicious, chocolate cookie.

TRIPLE CHOCOLATE SABLÉS Add ⅓ cup each dark, milk, and white chocolate chips to the batter for Chocolate Sablés. Not easy to slice after chilling, but a great chocolaty cookie.

CHOCOLATE AND VANILLA PINWHEELS

. . .

Makes about 35 cookies, depending how
thin you slice them

8 tablespoons (1 stick) unsalted
   butter, softened

½ cup sugar

1 large egg

1½ cups all-purpose flour

½ teaspoon baking powder

Pinch salt

1 tablespoon milk

1½ ounces unsweetened chocolate,
   melted and cooled

2 cookie sheets or jelly-roll pans
   lined with parchment or foil

These fun cookies are made by adding chocolate to half the dough and layering the two doughs together for a two-tone effect. Bake these carefully. If they get too dark during baking the pattern is obscured.

1. Use an electric mixer to beat butter and sugar until well mixed, about 30 seconds. Beat in the egg, and continue beating until smooth.

2. Mix together the flour, baking powder, and salt and beat into the butter mixture, making sure to scrape the sides of the bowl clean.

3. Remove a little more than half the dough from the bowl and thoroughly fold the milk and chocolate into the remaining dough with a rubber spatula.

4. On a floured piece of foil or wax paper pat each dough half into an 8-inch square. If the dough is extremely soft and sticky, slide the parchment onto a cookie sheet and chill briefly.

5. Use a pastry brush to paint the square of chocolate dough with water. Top it with the square of plain dough. Starting anywhere, roll up the two doughs like a jelly roll, keeping the roll straight and even. Roll dough onto a piece of plastic wrap and wrap and chill until firm. (You may leave the dough chilled for several days or even freeze it at this point. If the dough is frozen, defrost in the refrigerator before proceeding with the recipe.)

6. When you are ready to bake the cookies, set racks in the upper and lower thirds of the oven and preheat to 350 degrees. Slice the roll about every ¼ inch and arrange cookies on the prepared pans about 2 inches from one another and the edges of the pan. Bake for about 10 minutes, until cookies are firm and very lightly colored. Cool on the pans on racks.

STORAGE: Keep the cookies between sheets of wax paper in a tin or plastic container with a tight-fitting cover.

PIPED COOKIES

● ● ●

These are really drop cookies that we use a pastry bag and tube to shape. For this reason, they are some of the most tailored-looking cookies. Piping makes them have a uniform size and appearance that dropping the dough or batter from a spoon would never achieve.

For success in preparing piped cookies, always use the size tube specified in the recipe, unless you are very experienced at piping.

Remember, most piped cookies puff or spread, so leave at least the size of one of the piped cookies as a space before piping the next one.

Pipe cookies onto parchment or foil—though I prefer parchment.

SWISS CHOCOLATE S'S

● ● ●

Makes about thirty-six 2-inch S's

3 large egg whites

14 tablespoons sugar (measure 1 cup sugar, then remove 2 level tablespoons)

3 ounces unsweetened chocolate, melted and cooled

2 cookie sheets or jelly-roll pans lined with parchment

A Swiss classic, these chocolate meringue S's are fairly easy to prepare. The method in this recipe is simplified—usually the egg whites are whipped and a hot sugar syrup is poured over them, a process I find unnecessarily complicated. The easier technique of heating the egg whites and sugar provides similar—and excellent—results. My thanks to Stephan Schiesser of the Confiserie Schiesser in Basel for this recipe.

1. Set racks in the lower and upper thirds of the oven and preheat to 300 degrees.

2. Bring a pan of water to a boil and lower heat to a simmer. Combine egg whites and sugar in bowl of electric mixer and whip to combine. Place over pan of simmering water and use a wire whisk to stir gently and steadily, until egg white is hot and sugar is dissolved, about 4 or 5 minutes.

3. Place meringue in mixer and whip at medium speed until risen in volume and substantially cooled, but not dry.

4. Pour chocolate over meringue and fold it in with a rubber spatula.

5. Transfer the meringue to a pastry bag fitted with a ½-inch star tube (Ateco #4) and pipe S shapes, about 1½ inches apart, on the prepared pans. Bake the S's about 10 to 12 minutes, until crisp on the outside but still somewhat soft within.

SERVING: These are great as dessert with a simple ice cream or all alone.

STORAGE: Keep between sheets of wax paper in a tin or plastic container with a tight-fitting cover. They keep well, but are really best on the day they are made.

FRENCH CHOCOLATE MACAROONS

· · ·

Makes about 50 sandwiched macaroons

MACAROON MIXTURE

1¼ cups (about 5 ounces) whole, blanched almonds

2⅓ cups confectioners' sugar, divided

½ cup alkalized (Dutch process) cocoa powder, sifted after measuring

½ cup egg whites (about 4 large egg whites)

CHOCOLATE FILLING

½ cup heavy whipping cream

1 tablespoon unsalted butter

5 ounces semisweet chocolate, melted

1 tablespoon framboise (raspberry eau de vie) or raspberry-flavored vodka

2 heavy-duty cookie sheets or jelly-roll pans covered with parchment

This recipe for exquisitely smooth-textured French macaroons comes from Jacques Torres, the talented pastry chef of New York's famous Le Cirque 2000.

1. Set racks in the upper and lower thirds of the oven and preheat to 300 degrees.

2. Combine the almonds, 2 cups of the confectioners' sugar, and the cocoa in the bowl of a food processor. Pulse repeatedly, scraping down the inside bottom of the bowl occasionally with a metal spatula, until the mixture is very finely ground, about 5 minutes.

3. Use an electric mixer on medium speed to begin whipping the egg whites until they are foamy. Continue whipping until the egg whites hold a very soft peak. Increase the speed to high and add the remaining ⅓ cup confectioners' sugar, about 1 tablespoon at a time. Continue to whip the egg whites until they are stiff, but not dry.

4. With a rubber spatula fold the cocoa and almond mixture into the whipped egg whites. The mixture will become quite liquid.

5. Use a pastry bag fitted with a ½-inch plain tube (Ateco #6 or #806) to pipe the macaroon paste onto the prepared pans. Holding the bag straight up and down, perpendicular to and about an inch above the pan, pipe out ¾-inch macaroons an inch apart.

6. Bake them for 10 to 12 minutes, or until they have risen and the edges are crackled. Cool the macaroons on the pans on a rack.

7. To make the filling, bring the cream and butter to a simmer, then remove from heat. Let cool 5 minutes, then whisk into the chocolate. Whisk in the framboise. Let cool an hour or so, or until slightly thickened.

8. To fill the macaroons, detach them from the baking paper and turn half of them over so the flat bottom side is upward. Spread or pipe a dab of the filling onto each upside-down macaroon and top it with another macaroon, so the flat sides are together.

SERVING: These are best within 24 hours of preparing them.

STORAGE: Keep the filled macaroons in a cool place, not the refrigerator, loosely covered until you intend to serve them. You may freeze unfilled macaroons in a tin or plastic container with a tight-fitting lid, in layers between parchment or wax paper. If you freeze the macaroons, make the filling and fill them after you remove them from the freezer.

CHOCOLATE WALNUT MACAROONS

• • •

Makes about 48 macaroons

4 ounces canned almond paste

¾ cup walnut pieces, finely ground in the food processor, plus 2 cups (about 8 ounces) walnut halves

¾ cup sugar

¼ cup egg whites (from about 2 large eggs), plus 1 egg white, slightly beaten with a fork, for attaching the walnut halves

1 ounce bittersweet or semisweet chocolate, grated or finely ground in the food processor, optional

8 ounces tempered chocolate for finishing, pages 20–23, optional

2 cookie sheets or jelly-roll pans lined with parchment or foil

These unusual macaroons are a welcome change from the typical all-almond type.

1. Set racks in the upper and lower thirds of the oven and preheat to 375 degrees.

2. Cut the almond paste into ½-inch cubes and place in bowl of electric mixer. Add ground walnuts and half the sugar and mix on low speed until the almond paste is broken down into tiny crumbs—about 2 minutes. Beat in remaining sugar, then add the ¼ cup egg whites, about a tablespoon at a time, until the paste is smooth and evenly moistened. Do not over-beat. Beat in the grated or finely ground chocolate.

3. Remove the macaroon paste from the mixer and spoon a third of it into a pastry bag fitted with a ½-inch plain tube (Ateco #6 or #806). Hold the bag straight up and down, perpendicular to the prepared pan and about ½ inch above it. Squeeze out a macaroon about ¾ inch in diameter. When the macaroon is the right size, stop squeezing and pull away sideways to avoid leaving a point.

4. Dip the bottom of a walnut half in the remaining egg white and place it on a macaroon, gently pressing so it sticks. Repeat with remaining macaroons.

5. Bake the macaroons for about 20 minutes, until well puffed and crackled on the surface. Cool the macaroons in the pans on racks.

6. If the cooled macaroons do not come off the paper easily, turn paper over and moisten back of paper with hot water. Turn paper over again, so that macaroons are on top, and leave 5 minutes. Macaroons should release easily.

7. If you wish, dip the bottom half of each macaroon into tempered chocolate: Hold the macaroon by the walnut and submerge it halfway in the chocolate. Scrape the bottom clean against the side of the chocolate bowl and place chocolate side down on a paper-lined pan to set.

SERVING: These are great after dessert with coffee and liqueurs.

STORAGE: Keep the cookies between sheets of wax paper in a tin or other container with a tight-fitting cover.

CHOCOLATE ORANGE MACAROONS

. . .

Makes 60 cookies

8 ounces canned almond paste

¾ cup sugar

¼ cup alkalized (Dutch process) cocoa powder

1 teaspoon orange extract

Grated zest of 1 orange

3 egg whites

1 cookie sheet or jelly-roll pan lined with parchment

The best macaroons are made with canned almond paste—accept no substitute.

1. Set a rack at the middle level of the oven and preheat to 375 degrees.

2. With an electric mixer, mix almond paste, sugar, and cocoa on low speed. When crumbly, add extract, zest, and 1 egg white; mix until smooth. Add remaining egg whites and continue mixing until the macaroon paste is extremely smooth.

3. Use a ½-inch plain tube (Ateco #6 or #806) to pipe the macaroons on a paper-lined pan. Hold the bag perpendicular to the pan and about ½ inch above it and squeeze out a macaroon about ¾ inch in diameter. Stop squeezing and pull away sideways to avoid leaving a point. Wet a non-terry-cloth towel with warm water. Fold it into a narrow rectangle. Holding one end of the towel in each hand so that the towel hangs fairly loosely, let the towel touch the surface of the macaroons repeatedly to smooth them out.

4. Bake for about 10 to 12 minutes, or until the macaroons are well puffed and slightly firm—do not let them dry out.

STORAGE: Keep the cookies between sheets of wax paper in a tin or other container with a tight-fitting cover.

SARAH BERNHARDTS

• • •

Makes about 50 cookies

GANACHE

¾ cup heavy whipping cream

1½ tablespoons unsalted butter

1½ tablespoons light corn syrup

10 ounces bittersweet chocolate, melted

1 batch Chocolate Orange Macaroons, page 169

FINISHING

16 ounces tempered chocolate for dipping, pages 20–23

Silver dragees or pieces of crystallized violet

2 cookie sheets or jelly-roll pans lined with parchment or foil

Whenever I hear the name of this famous actress of the past I think of my mother's nickname for a bad-tempered neighbor child who was given to almost constant hysterics: Sarah Heartburn. My mother notwithstanding, these cookies are classics of the French and Swiss repertoires—a macaroon topped with a cone of ganache, then a silver dragee or shred of crystallized violet.

1. To make the ganache, combine the cream, butter, and corn syrup in a saucepan over low heat. Bring to a simmer and remove from heat. Cool 5 minutes. Whisk the cream mixture all at once into the chocolate. Place bowl of ganache in refrigerator to cool for about an hour, stirring occasionally, until the ganache has thickened.

2. Arrange the macaroons, rounded sides up, on one of the prepared pans. When the ganache is cool, beat it by machine to lighten, about 30 seconds on medium speed. Do not overbeat or the ganache will become dry and grainy.

3. Spoon the ganache into a pastry bag fitted with a ½-inch plain tube (Ateco #6 or #806) and pipe a cone of ganache onto the top of each macaroon. To achieve this, hold the bag perpendicular, straight up and down over the macaroon and about ½ inch above it. Squeeze the top of the bag so that the emerging ganache covers the macaroon entirely, then gradually pull away, still squeezing, but less firmly, for another second. When the ganache on the macaroon is about 1 inch tall, release pressure and pull the bag away, leaving a point. After you have used all the ganache to cover the macaroons with cones, chill them to set the ganache.

4. To dip the macaroons, remove the ganache-covered macaroons from the refrigerator and bring them to room temperature for a few minutes. Dip each macaroon into the tempered chocolate, holding the macaroon base and dipping the cones. Stand the dipped cookies on the other prepared pan and place a silver dragee on top of each as soon as you place it on the pan. Repeat with remaining cookies.

SERVING: Make these for a very special occasion—they are a delicate and elegant dessert or teatime treat.

STORAGE: These are best on the day they are made or soon afterward, though they will keep for several days in a cool, dry place. Just cover them loosely with plastic wrap.

CHOCOLATE ALMOND FINGERS

■ ■ ■

Makes about 40 cookies (20 if sandwiched)

8 tablespoons (1 stick) unsalted
   butter, softened

½ cup sugar

2 egg whites

½ cup all-purpose flour

2 tablespoons alkalized (Dutch
   Process) cocoa powder

1 cup ground almonds, about
   3½ ounces

2 cookie sheets or jelly-roll pans
   lined with parchment or foil

These crisp, rich cookies are just as good plain as sandwiched with the white chocolate filling in the variation that follows the recipe.

1. Set racks in the upper and lower thirds of the oven and preheat to 350 degrees.

2. Use an electric mixer to beat the butter on medium speed until light. Beat in the sugar in a stream and continue to beat until the mixture whitens.

3. Add the egg whites, one at a time, and continue beating until very creamy. Sift the flour and cocoa powder together several times, stir in the ground almonds, and stir into the batter.

4. Scrape the batter into a pastry bag fitted with a ½-inch plain tube (Ateco #6). Pipe dough out in fingers about 2 inches long by positioning the bag at a 45-degree angle to the pan and letting the bottom of the tube touch the paper. Squeeze and pull the tube about 2 inches toward you, then release pressure and pull the tube away and up to avoid leaving a tail on the cookie. Pipe the cookies about 2 inches apart.

5. Bake for about 10 to 12 minutes, or until cookies have spread and become matte-looking. Pull the parchment or foil off the pans onto racks to cool the cookies.

SERVING: These make a great accompaniment for any creamy dessert.

STORAGE: Keep in a tin or plastic container with a tight-fitting lid.

VARIATION

CHOCOLATE ALMOND FINGERS WITH CHOCOLATE FILLING Stir together ½ cup cold heavy whipping cream and ½ pound dark chocolate, melted and cooled. It should thicken immediately to spreading consistency. Spread or pipe the filling on the flat sides of half the cookies. Top with other cookies, flat sides against the filling.

TOP: *Chocolate Almond Fingers*
BOTTOM: *Chocolate Thumbprints (page 175)*

ROLLED COOKIES

. . .

Thin and delicate, rolled cookies can be as easy or as difficult to prepare as you choose to make them. Follow these simple steps for a pleasurable experience.

When instructed to chill dough before rolling it, press the dough out into a rectangle about ¼-inch thick on plastic wrap. Cover with more plastic wrap and chill until firm—the thin dough will chill quickly.

When you roll the chilled dough, divide it into several small pieces. Don't roll the whole batch at once or the dough will soften before you finish rolling it out and the process will become a nightmare. If you roll small pieces at a time, they will stay firm and easy to manage.

Save the scraps of dough, gently press them together, and chill again before rolling, for the most tender cookies.

Roll cookie dough between ⅛ and ¼ inch thick for best results, unless otherwise specified. Cookies that are too thin may burn easily while baking.

CHOCOLATE THUMBPRINTS

· · ·

Makes about 36 cookies

COOKIE DOUGH

8 tablespoons (1 stick) unsalted butter, softened

½ cup firmly packed light brown sugar

½ teaspoon salt

1 teaspoon vanilla extract

2 tablespoons milk

1½ cups all-purpose flour

FILLING

1 tablespoon butter, softened

2 tablespoons light corn syrup

1 tablespoon water

1 teaspoon vanilla extract

4 ounces semisweet chocolate, melted

2 cookie sheets or jelly-roll pans lined with parchment or foil

This is a great old-fashioned cookie usually filled with jelly or jam. These are filled with a chocolaty syrup that sets firm in the cookies.

1. Set racks in the upper and lower thirds of the oven and preheat to 325 degrees.

2. For the cookie dough, place butter in a mixing bowl and beat in sugar by hand with a rubber spatula. Beat in the salt, vanilla, and milk. Finally, fold in the flour to make a soft dough.

3. Divide the dough into three parts, then divide each part into twelve pieces. Roll each piece into a sphere and place on prepared pans about 2 inches apart.

4. Using the index finger of one hand, press a deep fingerprint into each cookie.

5. Bake the cookies for about 15 minutes, or until they are golden. Cool on pans on racks.

6. After the cookies have cooled, make the filling. In a small bowl, beat the butter, corn syrup, water, and vanilla. Stir in the chocolate. Using a small spoon, fill the indentation in each cooled cookie with the chocolate mixture. Leave the cookies on the pans until the chocolate filling has set.

STORAGE: Keep the cookies between sheets of wax paper in a tin or other container with a tight-fitting cover.

CHOCOLATE CINNAMON DISKS

• • •

Makes about 30 cookies, depending on size

1⅓ cups all-purpose flour

¼ cup alkalized (Dutch process) cocoa powder

2 teaspoons ground cinnamon

¼ teaspoon salt

8 tablespoons (1 stick) unsalted butter, softened

½ cup sugar

1 large egg

1 cup toasted and skinned hazelnuts, ground in the food processor

8 ounces tempered chocolate for finishing, optional

2 cookie sheets or jelly-roll pans lined with parchment or foil

This popular Swiss cookie is adapted from *Swiss Confectionery*, a publication of the Richemont Pastry School in Lucerne.

1. To make the dough, combine flour, cocoa, cinnamon, and salt in a mixing bowl and stir well to mix. Sift onto a sheet of parchment or wax paper.

2. Use an electric mixer on medium speed to beat the butter and sugar until mixed, about a minute. Beat in the egg and continue beating until smooth and light, about 2 minutes. Beat in the ground hazelnuts, then the dry ingredients.

3. Scrape the dough out of the bowl onto a piece of plastic wrap and press down so the dough is about ¼-inch thick. Bring the plastic wrap up around the dough to cover it and chill for about 20 minutes, or until firm. (You may leave the dough in the refrigerator for a day or two at this point.)

4. When you are ready to bake the cookies, set racks in the upper and lower thirds of the oven and preheat to 350 degrees.

5. Remove dough from the refrigerator and divide into thirds. Place one piece of dough on a floured surface and lightly flour dough. Press and pound dough with rolling pin to soften it. Roll dough about ⅛ inch thick and cut with a floured, fluted 2½-inch-diameter round cutter. Place cookies on prepared pans about an inch apart. Repeat with remaining pieces of dough. Mass together the scraps from all three rollings and roll them out once more. Discard scraps remaining after second rolling. They would make tough cookies.

6. Bake the cookies for 12 to 15 minutes, or until they are slightly puffed and dull in appearance. Cool the cookies on the pans on a rack.

7. If you wish to dip the cookies in chocolate, dip them halfway into a bowl of tempered chocolate (see pages 20–23). Scrape the dipped edge of the cookie against the side of the chocolate bowl on the way out and place dipped cookies on paper-lined pans to set.

STORAGE: Keep the cookies between sheets of wax paper in a tin or other container with a tight-fitting cover in a cool place.

CRISP CHOCOLATE WAFERS

■ ■ ■

Makes about 40 cookies

4 tablespoons (½ stick) unsalted
  butter, softened

½ cup light brown sugar

½ cup granulated sugar, plus more
  for finishing the cookies

1 teaspoon vanilla extract

2 large egg whites

¾ cup Dutch process (alkalized)
  cocoa powder

¾ cup all-purpose flour

¼ teaspoon salt

2 cookie sheets or jelly-roll pans
  lined with parchment or foil

This great recipe comes from my friend Marie Ostrowski, one of the backstage chefs at the Television Food Network.

1. Combine butter, sugars, and vanilla in the bowl of an electric mixer and beat on medium speed until light, about 5 minutes, scraping bowl and beater(s) occasionally. Beat in the egg whites, one at a time, beating smooth after each addition.

2. While the mixture is beating, sift the cocoa with the flour and salt. Stop mixer, scrape down bowl and beater(s) and add dry ingredients. Mix on low speed until incorporated.

3. Scrape the dough out onto a piece of plastic wrap. Cover with another piece of wrap and press the dough into a rough disk. Refrigerate the dough until it is firm—several hours or overnight.

4. About 20 minutes before you intend to bake the cookies, set a rack at the middle level of the oven and preheat to 350 degrees.

5. Divide the dough into three parts and roll one at a time on a lightly floured work surface into a 6-inch square. Cut the dough with a fluted or plain round cutter into nine 2-inch cookies and place them on the prepared pan. Continue with the remaining dough. After rolling all the dough, press the scraps back together and make about 12 to 14 more cookies. Pierce the cookies several times with a fork and sprinkle them lightly with granulated sugar.

6. Bake the cookies about 20 minutes, until slightly puffed and firm. Cool the cookies on the pan.

SERVING: Serve with any creamy or plain dessert, or ice cream. They're also great by themselves.

STORAGE: Keep the cookies between layers of wax paper in an airtight tin or plastic container.

CHOCOLATE-DIPPED STARS

* * *

Makes 50 cookies

COOKIE DOUGH

16 tablespoons (2 sticks)
   unsalted butter, softened

½ cup sugar

2 teaspoons vanilla

3 egg yolks

2½ cups cake flour

Egg wash: 1 egg beaten with
   a pinch of salt

DIPPING

About 1 pound of good-quality
   bittersweet or semisweet
   couverture chocolate, tempered,
   see pages 20–23

2 cookie sheets or jelly-roll pans
   lined with parchment, plus extra
   parchment for dipping

These are easy to make, with a base similar to shortbread. A quick dip in chocolate is the finishing touch for these simple, but exquisitely delicate cookies.

1. Use an electric mixer to beat the butter on medium speed until very soft. Beat in the sugar in a stream, then the vanilla, and continue beating until very light. Beat in the yolks, one at a time, beating until very smooth after each addition. After the yolks are beaten in, the mixture should look like butter cream.

2. Sift the cake flour and add it to the butter mixture. Pulse the mixer on and off on lowest speed only until the cake flour is absorbed. Mix no more than necessary to avoid toughening the dough.

3. Scrape the dough from the bowl onto a piece of plastic wrap. Wrap the dough tightly and refrigerate it until firm.

4. Set racks at the upper and lower thirds of the oven and preheat to 325 degrees.

5. Flour a work surface and the dough and roll it to slightly less than ¼-inch thickness. Paint the dough with the egg wash and score it with a fork, or roll over it with a grooved rolling pin or score the dough with a fork and paint it with the egg wash. Cut the dough with a star- or heart-shaped cutter and place the cookies on the prepared pans.

6. Bake for about 15 minutes, until lightly browned—they should still be quite pale. Cool on the pans.

7. Melt and temper the chocolate. Dip half of each cookie into the chocolate, so that the pattern on the surface still shows. Place the cookies on parchment paper to dry.

STORAGE: Store the cookies in a cool place in a tin or plastic container with a tight-fitting cover.

SICILIAN EASTER HEARTS

・ ・ ・

Makes about 15 large cookies

DOUGH

½ cup alkalized (Dutch process) cocoa powder, sifted after measuring

½ cup granulated sugar

⅔ to 1 cup all-purpose flour

1 cup whole almonds, finely ground in the food processor

½ teaspoon ground cinnamon

½ teaspoon ground cloves

1 teaspoon baking soda

⅓ cup honey

¼ cup water

ICING

2 cups confectioners' sugar

1 to 2 tablespoons water

Drop pink food coloring

ROYAL ICING

1 large egg white

1⅓ cups confectioners' sugar

Drop lemon juice

DECORATING

Chocolate chips

Silver dragees

Colored sugar

1 or 2 cookie sheets or jelly-roll pans lined with parchment or foil

These are traditionally made in Sicily for Easter. The dough typically used is dry and spiced and actually a little hard. This richer version is a lot better to eat.

1. Set a rack at the middle level of the oven and preheat to 325 degrees.

2. Combine dry ingredients in a mixing bowl. Make a well in the center of the dry ingredients and add the honey and water. Stir to form a smooth, sticky dough. Allow to stand a minute to absorb the liquid. If dough is too soft to handle, add another ⅓ cup flour.

3. Turn the dough out onto a generously floured surface. Flour dough and pat it into a rectangle, about ¼ inch thick. Use a 3- to 4-inch floured cutter to cut the dough into heart-shaped cookies, and as each is cut, place it on the cookie sheet. Bake for about 15 minutes or until they are puffed and slightly firm. Remove from pan to racks to cool.

4. To make the icing, combine the 2 cups confectioners' sugar, water, and coloring in a small saucepan and cook over low heat until creamy and thin. Brush the icing over the cookies.

5. While the icing is drying, make the royal icing. In a bowl mix egg white and the 1⅓ cups confectioners' sugar with an electric mixer on low speed until combined and smooth. Add lemon juice and continue beating until icing is fluffy and can hold its shape.

6. Use a pastry bag fitted with a small star tube (Ateco #2) to pipe the royal icing onto the cookies. Outline the edge with a series of rosettes or pipe a larger rosette in the center of the heart. Use the chocolate chips, dragees, and colored sugar to decorate the icing.

SERVING: These are perfect gift cookies—wrap them in clear plastic.

STORAGE: Once they are iced, they will keep almost indefinitely, especially if they are wrapped.

CHOCOLATE WALNUT RUGELACH

. . .

Makes about 36 small pastries

CREAM CHEESE DOUGH

8 tablespoons (1 stick) unsalted butter, softened

4 ounces cream cheese, softened

¼ teaspoon salt

1½ cups all-purpose flour

FILLING

¾ cup light brown sugar

1 teaspoon ground cinnamon

⅔ cup finely chopped walnut pieces, about 2½ ounces

1 cup semisweet chocolate chips, or 6 ounces semisweet chocolate cut into ¼-inch pieces

2 cookie sheets or jelly-roll pans lined with parchment or foil

This very typical Jewish pastry exists in many versions. A chocolate one like this is made in many bakeries.

1. To make the dough, beat the butter and cream cheese together until smooth and light by hand, with a hand mixer set at medium speed, or in a heavy-duty mixer fitted with the paddle attachment. Continue beating until the mixture is light and fluffy and looks like butter cream.

2. Beat in the salt. Sift the flour over the butter and cream cheese mixture, then fold it in using a rubber spatula.

3. To make this dough in a food processor, combine butter and cream cheese and pulse ten or twelve times to mix evenly, scraping down inside of work bowl several times with a metal spatula. Add salt and flour and pulse to form a soft dough (it will not form a ball).

4. Scrape the dough onto a floured work surface and divide it into three equal pieces. Form each third into a round about 5 inches in diameter. Wrap each in plastic wrap. Chill until firm, at least an hour.

5. When you are ready to bake the pastries, set racks in the upper and lower thirds of the oven and preheat to 350 degrees.

6. Mix the filling ingredients together in a small bowl.

7. Work with one piece of dough at a time. Remove it from the refrigerator, unwrap it, and place it on a lightly floured work surface. Flour the dough and roll it to a 10-inch circle. Cut the round into twelve equal wedges.

8. Use a pastry brush to paint the dough with water and scatter each piece evenly with the filling. Use about a third of the filling.

9. Starting from the edge opposite the point, roll up each wedge of dough. As each is rolled, place it on the prepared pans. Make sure to roll it tight enough that the filling doesn't fall out. Repeat with remaining dough and filling.

10. Bake the rugelach for about 30 minutes, until they are light golden and firm. Cool in the pans on racks.

SERVING: These are best when freshly baked.

STORAGE: Keep in a tin or plastic container with a tight-fitting lid.

VARIATION

To gild the lily, streak with Chocolate Glaze, page 44.

CHICKLET'S CHOCOLATE CHOCOLATE CHIP SAND TARTS

■ ■ ■

Makes about 48 cookies

16 tablespoons (2 sticks) unsalted butter, softened

½ teaspoon salt

½ cup confectioners' sugar, plus more for coating the cookies

¼ cup alkalized (Dutch process) cocoa powder

1½ cups all-purpose flour

½ cup mini chocolate chips

1 cup finely chopped pecan pieces, about 4 ounces

2 cookie sheets or jelly-roll pans lined with parchment or foil

The recipe for these intensely chocolaty cookies comes from my friend Allen Smith, chef, caterer, and cooking teacher.

1. Set racks in the lower and upper thirds of the oven and preheat to 350 degrees.

2. Use an electric mixer to beat butter with salt and ½ cup confectioners' sugar until light.

3. Sift together the cocoa and flour onto a piece of parchment or wax paper.

4. Add the cocoa and flour mixture to the butter and sugar, mixing only until just absorbed. Mix in the chips and pecans.

5. Roll about 1 tablespoon of dough into a little ball—or use a small ice cream or melon-ball scoop to shape it. Place balls on prepared pans about 2 inches from one another and from the edges of the pans.

6. Bake about 20 minutes, until cookies are slightly firm—do not overbake.

7. Cool the cookies in the pans on racks. Roll them in confectioners' sugar when they are still slightly warm.

STORAGE: Keep between sheets of wax paper in a tin or plastic container with a tight-fitting lid.

TRUFFLE COOKIES

Makes 40 cookies

∎ ∎ ∎

2 cups all-purpose flour

⅓ cup alkalized (Dutch process) cocoa powder

¼ teaspoon salt

1 teaspoon baking soda

8 tablespoons (1 stick) unsalted butter, softened

⅓ cup granulated sugar

⅓ cup dark corn syrup

Confectioners' sugar for finishing

2 cookie sheets or jelly-roll pans lined with parchment or foil

These look just like truffles, but one taste will reassure you they are cookies through and through.

1. Set racks in the upper and lower thirds of the oven and preheat to 350 degrees.

2. Combine flour, cocoa, salt, and baking soda in a mixing bowl and stir well to mix. Sift the dry ingredients onto a piece of parchment or wax paper.

3. Stir butter and sugar together with a rubber spatula. Stir in the corn syrup.

4. Add the dry ingredients and stir well to form a firm dough.

5. Divide the dough into four equal pieces, then divide each piece into ten pieces.

6. Roll each of the pieces of dough into a ball and place it an inch from any other on the prepared pans.

7. Bake the cookies for 10 to 12 minutes, until the surface crackles. Cool in the pans on racks.

8. After the cookies are cool, dust them lightly with confectioners' sugar.

STORAGE: Keep the cookies between sheets of wax paper in a tin or other container with a tight-fitting cover.

SANDWICH COOKIES

· · ·

These are all rolled or drop cookies with a filling—usually a bit of jam or ganache. Maybe it's because you get to eat two cookies at the same time, but sandwich cookies always seem more fun and festive to me.

For best results, don't overdo the filling or cookies will become uncontrollably messy. For most cookies between ¼ and ½ teaspoon of filling is enough.

CHOCOLATE BULL'S EYES

· · ·

Makes about 24 sandwich cookies

COOKIE DOUGH

16 tablespoons (2 sticks) unsalted butter, softened

1 cup unsifted confectioners' sugar

2 large egg yolks

2⅓ cups all-purpose flour

CHOCOLATE FILLING

6 ounces bittersweet chocolate

½ cup heavy whipping cream

1 tablespoon unsalted butter

1 tablespoon light corn syrup

FINISHING

2 tablespoons confectioners' sugar

2 cookie sheets or jelly-roll pans lined with parchment or foil

These are the chocolate-filled version of a cookie usually sandwiched with raspberry or apricot jam—either of these will also work well with the dough.

1. To make the dough, use an electric mixer set at medium speed to beat the butter until soft and light. Beat in sugar and continue beating until sugar is completely incorporated. Add yolks, one at a time, beating well and scraping bowl and beater(s) after each addition. Sift flour over butter and egg mixture and fold in with a rubber spatula, making sure flour is completely absorbed.

2. Stretch a piece of plastic wrap on a plate or cookie sheet and scrape dough onto wrap. Cover with another piece of plastic wrap and press dough into a 10-inch square, about ½ inch thick. Chill dough until firm, about 2 hours.

3. Set racks at the upper and lower thirds of the oven and preheat to 350 degrees.

4. Divide dough into quarters and roll one quarter at a time. Leave the rest of the dough in the refrigerator until ready to roll.

5. Place dough on a lightly floured work surface and lightly flour. Pound dough gently with rolling pin to soften it, then roll it out into an 8-inch square about 3/16 inch thick. Use a plain, round 1¾- to 2-inch cutter to cut dough. Arrange rounds on pans, about 1 inch apart, as they are cut. Repeat with remaining three pieces of dough. Refrigerate scraps after each rolling. When all four pieces of dough have been rolled and cut, press scraps together and reroll and cut them.

6. Count the bases and, using a pastry tube, cut a ½-inch hole in half of them. Place pans of cookies in oven and immediately lower temperature to 325 degrees.

7. Bake the cookies about 15 to 20 minutes, until they are pale golden and firm. Cool in pans on racks.

8. To make the filling, cut chocolate into fine pieces and set aside. Combine cream, butter, and corn syrup in a saucepan and bring to a boil over low heat. Remove from heat, add chocolate, and allow to stand several minutes. Whisk smooth, scrape into a bowl, and cool to room temperature. If cool filling has not thickened, chill for a few minutes until it is of spreading consistency.

9. To finish cookies, lightly dust the pierced cookie bases with confectioners' sugar. Arrange unpierced bases, upside down, on a clean pan. Spread unpierced bases with a dab of chocolate filling. Cover with pierced bases. Use a paper cone or a small spoon to place a drop of chocolate filling in the openings on tops of cookies.

SERVING: Serve these cookies on the day they are made.

STORAGE: Keep leftovers in a tin or tightly covered plastic container at a cool room temperature.

CHOCOLATE ORANGE HEARTS

. . .

Makes about 24 sandwich cookies

ORANGE COOKIE DOUGH

16 tablespoons (2 sticks)
  unsalted butter

½ cup sugar

1 teaspoon vanilla extract

1 teaspoon orange extract

1 teaspoon grated orange zest

2 egg yolks

2½ cups cake flour

ORANGE FILLING

⅔ cup orange marmalade

Zest and juice of 1 small orange

1 tablespoon orange liqueur

CHOCOLATE GLAZE

2 tablespoons water

2 tablespoons light corn syrup

⅓ cup sugar

3 ounces semisweet chocolate, cut
  into ¼-inch pieces

2 cookie sheets or jelly-roll pans
  lined with parchment or foil

These are great for Valentine's Day. Serve them at other times in other shapes.

1. To make the dough, with an electric mixer beat the butter and sugar on medium speed until very soft and light. Beat in the vanilla and orange extracts, the zest, and the yolks. Continue beating until smooth and shiny, about 3 more minutes. Stop the mixer, sift the cake flour, and add to the butter mixture. Pulse the mixer to incorporate the flour. Scrape the dough onto a piece of plastic, wrap, and chill it until firm.

2. Set a rack at the middle level of the oven and preheat to 325 degrees.

3. Divide the chilled dough into four or five pieces and place one on a lightly floured work surface. Return the remaining pieces of dough to the refrigerator. Flour the dough and pound it to soften and quickly roll the dough about 3/16 inch thick. Quickly cut the dough into heart shapes with a floured cutter. Transfer the hearts to the prepared pans. Repeat with the rest of the dough.

4. Bake the cookies about 15 to 20 minutes, or until they are a light golden brown. Cool in the pans.

5. To make the filling, combine all ingredients in a saucepan and bring to a boil over low heat, stirring occasionally. Allow to reduce slightly until thickened. Place about ½ to 1 teaspoon of the filling on half the cookies and top with the remaining cookies. Allow the filling to set.

6. To make the glaze, combine water, corn syrup, and sugar in a saucepan and bring to a boil over low heat, stirring occasionally. Remove from heat, add chocolate, and allow to stand 5 minutes to melt chocolate. Whisk smooth and allow to thicken before using. Use a paper cone or the end of a spoon to streak cookies with glaze. Or half-dip the cookies in hot glaze and allow them to drain on a rack over wax paper or a pan.

SERVING: Serve these cookies on the day they are made.

STORAGE: Keep leftovers between sheets of wax paper in a tin or plastic container with a tight-fitting lid.

SWISS CHOCOLATE SANDWICH COOKIES

• • •

Makes about 18 sandwich cookies

CHOCOLATE COOKIE DOUGH

12 tablespoons (1½ sticks) unsalted butter, softened

4 ounces semisweet chocolate, melted and cooled

1¾ cups all-purpose flour

GANACHE FILLING

⅓ cup heavy whipping cream

1 tablespoon unsalted butter

1 tablespoon light corn syrup

2 ounces bittersweet chocolate, cut into ¼-inch pieces

2 ounces milk chocolate, cut into ¼-inch pieces

FINISHING

Confectioners' sugar

2 cookie sheets or jelly-roll pans lined with parchment or foil

CHOCOLATE

This recipe is adapted from that great work *Swiss Baking and Confectionery* by Walter Bachmann, a Swiss pastry chef who lived in London after the Second World War.

1. To make the dough, beat the butter by hand in a medium bowl just until it is evenly softened. Quickly beat in the melted chocolate, then the flour. Continue to mix until dough is smooth.

2. Scrape the dough out onto a piece of plastic wrap and press it into a rectangle about ½ inch thick. Wrap and chill the dough until it is firm—about an hour.

3. While the dough is chilling, make the filling. Combine the cream, butter, and corn syrup in a saucepan and bring to a boil over low heat. Remove from heat and add both chocolates. Shake the pan gently to submerge chocolate in the hot liquid. Let stand 5 minutes, then whisk smooth and scrape filling into a bowl. Let stand at room temperature or in the refrigerator until of spreading consistency.

4. To bake the cookie bases, set racks in the upper and lower thirds of the oven and preheat to 350 degrees.

5. If the dough is very hard, pound it gently with the rolling pin to soften it so that it rolls out more easily. Divide dough in half and, on a floured surface, roll one half about ³⁄₁₆ inch thick. Use a fluted, round 2-inch cutter to cut the dough into cookies. Place them on prepared pans as they are cut, leaving about an inch between the cookies. Repeat with remaining dough. Save all the scraps. Reroll scraps and cut more cookies.

6. Bake the cookies 12 to 15 minutes, until they are firm and slightly colored. Cool the cookies in the pans on racks.

7. When cookies and filling have cooled, arrange half the cookies, flat side up. Place a dab of filling on them and cover with the remaining cookies, flat sides together. Dust cookies very lightly with confectioners' sugar before serving.

ROMANY CREAMS

• • •

Makes 30 sandwich cookies

COOKIE DOUGH

2 cups all-purpose flour

1 teaspoon baking powder

¼ teaspoon salt

⅓ cup alkalized (Dutch process)
  cocoa powder, sifted after
  measuring

¼ cup boiling water

16 tablespoons (2 sticks) unsalted
  butter, softened

1 cup sugar

1½ cups sweetened shredded
  coconut, finely ground in a food
  processor, about 4 ounces

FILLING

10 ounces milk chocolate, melted
  and cooled

2 cookie sheets or jelly-roll pans
  lined with parchment or foil

This delicious sandwich cookie comes a great friend and baker, Kyra Effren.

1. Set racks in the upper and lower thirds of the oven and preheat to 350 degrees.

2. In a mixing bowl, combine the flour, baking powder, and salt and stir well to mix. Sift the dry ingredients onto a sheet of parchment or wax paper.

3. Sift the cocoa into the same mixing bowl and stir in the boiling water. Set aside.

4. Use an electric mixer to beat the butter and sugar together until light, about 2 minutes. Beat in the coconut, then the dry ingredients, and finally the cocoa mixture to make a soft dough.

5. To shape the cookies, drop from a teaspoon onto the prepared pans. Keep the cookies about 2 inches apart. Before baking the cookies, slightly flatten each one with the floured palm of your hand.

6. Bake the cookies 10 to 12 minutes, until puffed and dry-looking. Slide the paper from the pans to racks to let the cookies cool.

7. Line up half the cookies, flat side up, on a work surface and spread each with some of the milk chocolate. Top with another cookie, flat sides together. Leave the cookies until the chocolate has set.

SERVING: These are a good dessert cookie with some ice cream or even just a cup of coffee.

STORAGE: Keep the cookies between sheets of wax paper in a tin or other container with a tight-fitting cover.

SWISS CHOCOLATE MERINGUE GLOBES
■ ■ ■

Makes about 30 sandwich cookies

CHOCOLATE ALMOND MERINGUE

8 large egg whites (1 cup)

Pinch salt

1¼ cups sugar

2 cups ground blanched almonds, about 8 ounces

3½ ounces unsweetened chocolate, melted and cooled

GANACHE FILLING

½ cup heavy whipping cream

2 tablespoons (¼ stick) unsalted butter

1 tablespoon light corn syrup

8 ounces bittersweet chocolate, cut into ¼-inch pieces

FINISHING

2 ounces dark or milk chocolate, melted and cooled

2 cookie sheets or jelly-roll pans covered with parchment or foil

Though these rich and satisfying cookies are a bit of a production to prepare, they are worth it.

1. Set racks in the upper and lower thirds of the oven and preheat to 300 degrees.

2. Use an electric mixer on medium speed to beat the egg whites and salt until whites are opaque and risen in volume. Increase speed to maximum and whip in sugar 1 tablespoon at a time. Continue whipping until egg whites are stiff, but not dry.

3. Remove meringue from mixer and fold in ground almonds, then chocolate.

4. Use a pastry bag fitted with a ½-inch plain tube (Ateco #6) to pipe the meringue. Position pastry bag perpendicular to prepared pan with tube about 1 inch above surface. Pipe a half-sphere of the meringue about 2 inches in diameter. Release pressure on tube before pulling it away sideways, to avoid leaving a point on the meringue. (If you do leave a point, use a fingertip to flatten it.) Pipe 30 meringue shells onto each pan.

5. Bake the meringues about 30 to 40 minutes, until crisp on the outside but still somewhat moist within. Slide the parchment or foil from the pans to racks to cool the meringues.

6. While the meringues are baking, make the filling. Combine the cream, butter, and corn syrup in a saucepan. Place over low heat and bring to a boil. Remove from heat and add chocolate. Shake pan to submerge chocolate and leave to melt for 5 minutes. Whisk smooth and scrape into a bowl. Allow ganache to cool at room temperature, or refrigerate briefly until it reaches spreading consistency.

7. When meringues and ganache are both cool, arrange half the meringues on a jelly-roll pan, flat side up. Whip the ganache briefly by machine until it lightens. Spread or pipe about 2 teaspoons of the ganache on each meringue and top with another meringue, flat sides together. When all the meringues have been joined, place the melted chocolate in a paper cone or in a nonpleated plastic bag. Snip end of paper cone or bag and streak tops of meringues with chocolate.

SERVING: These make a great dessert with a scoop of vanilla ice cream—the contrast of crisp and creamy is exquisite.

STORAGE: Keep the meringues at a cool room temperature—these are best on the day they are made. While they will keep for a few days, they just won't be as crisp and fresh-tasting.

BOURBON COOKIES

• • •

Makes 20 sandwich cookies

COOKIE DOUGH

1 cup all-purpose flour

3 tablespoons alkalized (Dutch process) cocoa powder

½ teaspoon baking powder

4 tablespoons (½ stick) unsalted butter, softened

¼ cup granulated sugar

1 large egg

FILLING

3 tablespoons strong brewed coffee or water

2 ounces semisweet chocolate, melted

¾ cup confectioners' sugar

2 cookie sheets or jelly-roll pans lined with parchment or foil

The name of these cookies is that of a popular industrially made cookie in South Africa, where my friend Kyra Effren got the recipe before she shared it with me.

1. Set racks in the upper and lower thirds of the oven and preheat to 325 degrees.

2. To make the dough, combine the flour, cocoa, and baking powder in a mixing bowl and stir well. Sift the dry ingredients onto a piece of parchment or wax paper.

3. In a medium mixing bowl, beat together the butter and sugar, then beat in the egg. Stir in the dry ingredients until the dough holds together.

4. Fold the dough over on itself several times, then place it on a floured surface. Flour the top of the dough and roll it out to form a 10-inch square. Cut the dough into 2½-inch strips, then cut each strip every inch, to make forty 1 × 2½-inch rectangles.

5. Arrange the cookies on the prepared pans and pierce each cookie about four times with a fork.

6. Bake the cookies for 20 minutes, or until they are dry and crisp. Cool in the pans on racks.

7. To make the filling, stir the coffee or water into the chocolate and stir in the confectioners' sugar. Turn half the cookies over so that they are bottom side up and spread with the filling. Top with the remaining cookies, flat sides together. Leave the cookies until the filling sets.

SERVINGS: Great with coffee or tea.

STORAGE: Keep the cookies between sheets of wax paper in a tin or other container with a tight-fitting cover.

BISCOTTI

. . .

Named for the Italian for "twice baked," these have recently become one of the most popular cookies in the United States. They all follow the same system: Divide the dough into several pieces and shape it into cylinders. Then place them on pans and bake until risen and firm. Cool and slice, rebaking the slices until crisp. Be careful about the following points in biscotti recipes:

- Make sure the first baking makes the logs of dough firm enough or they will have a heavy core after slicing and rebaking.

- Cool the baked logs completely or they may crumble when you try to slice them. Use a sharp knife and cut thin slices or the biscotti may be hard and not crisp.

- Store the biscotti airtight or they may soften. If they do, place them on a cookie sheet in one layer and bake again at 325 degrees for a few minutes to crisp them.

CRISP CHOCOLATE
BISCOTTI

• • •

Makes about 4 dozen biscotti

1¾ cups all-purpose flour

⅔ cup alkalized (Dutch process)
   cocoa powder

2 teaspoons baking powder

Pinch salt

1¼ cups sugar

1½ cups chopped skinned hazelnuts
   or walnuts

4 large eggs

1 teaspoon vanilla extract

2 cookie sheets or jelly-roll pans
   lined with parchment or foil

This is based on a recipe by Ellen Baumwoll, proprietor of Bijoux Doux in New York City.

1. Set a rack at the middle level of the oven and preheat to 325 degrees.

2. Mix together the flour, cocoa, baking powder, and salt and sift into a mixing bowl. Stir in the sugar and nuts.

3. Whisk the eggs and vanilla together and stir into the flour mixture to form a dough.

4. On a lightly floured surface, press dough together. Divide dough in half and roll each half into a log the length of the pan (14 to 18 inches). Place each log on a pan and flatten slightly. Bake for about 30 minutes, until well risen and firm. Cool the logs in the pans.

5. After the logs have cooled, lift them from the parchment and cut each into ½-inch-thick slices with a sharp serrated knife. Replace, cut side down, on paper-lined pans and bake again for about 20 minutes, until dry and crisp. Cool in pans.

SERVING: Serve the biscotti with coffee or ice cream.

STORAGE: Keep in a tin or plastic container with a tight-fitting lid.

VARIATION

CHOCOLATE ESPRESSO BISCOTTI Add 3 tablespoons instant espresso powder to the flour mixture.

DRIED CHERRY, CHOCOLATE CHIP, AND PISTACHIO BISCOTTI

• • •

Makes 60 to 70 biscotti

1¾ cups all-purpose flour

¾ cup sugar

1 teaspoon baking powder

¼ teaspoon salt

8 tablespoons (1 stick) unsalted butter

¾ cup dried cherries

1 cup semisweet chocolate chips, 6 ounces

1 cup unsalted pistachios, about 4 ounces

2 large eggs

2 teaspoons vanilla extract

1 cookie sheet or jelly-roll pan lined with parchment or foil

This great, easy recipe comes from Andrea Tutunjian, who teaches the career baking course at Peter Kump's New York Cooking School.

1. Set a rack at the middle level of the oven and preheat to 350 degrees.

2. In a mixing bowl, combine the flour, sugar, baking powder, and salt and stir well to mix.

3. Cut the butter into six or eight pieces and toss with the dry ingredients. Rub in the butter, as for a pastry dough. Squeeze the butter and dry ingredients with fingertips and rub the mixture between the palms of the hands. Keep bringing up the dry bits from the bottom of the bowl, and continue rubbing, until all the butter has been absorbed but the mixture remains cool and powdery. Stir in the cherries, chips, and pistachios.

4. Whisk the eggs and vanilla together and use a fork to stir them into the dry ingredients. Continue stirring until the dough masses together. Turn the dough out on a lightly floured surface and press it together. Flour your hands and form the dough into a 12-inch-long cylinder. Cut the cylinder in half, then roll and pull each half until it is 12 inches long. Place the two cylinders on the baking pan, spacing them so they are equidistant from the edges of the pan and each other.

5. Bake about 25 to 30 minutes, until the dough is well-colored and firm to the touch. Slide the parchment or foil off the pan onto a cutting board to cool the logs. For advance preparation wrap the logs in foil and use them within several days. Or, freeze the baked logs and use them within a month.

6. When the baked logs are cool, peel away the paper and place one log on the cutting board. Use a sharp, serrated knife to slice the log diagonally every ⅓ inch. As they are cut, line up the slices, cut side down, on a paper- or foil-lined cookie sheet (you may need a second pan). Bake the biscotti at 325 degrees about 15 to 20 minutes longer, until they are very light golden in color. Cool the biscotti on the pans on a rack.

SERVING: These are great as an accompaniment to ice cream or a fruit dessert.

STORAGE: Store in a tin or plastic container with a tight-fitting cover at room temperature.

VARIATIONS

Dried cranberries or raisins may be substituted for the dried cherries.

CHOCOLATE WALNUT BISCOTTI

• • •

Makes 60 biscotti or more, depending on how thin they are sliced

3 large eggs

Pinch salt

1 cup sugar

1 teaspoon vanilla extract

8 tablespoons (1 stick) butter, melted

1 cup coarsely chopped walnut pieces, about 4 ounces

2 cups semisweet chocolate chips, 12 ounces

2¼ cups unbleached all-purpose flour (spoon flour into cup and level off top to measure)

¼ cup alkalized (Dutch process) cocoa powder

1 tablespoon baking powder

1 teaspoon ground cinnamon

2 cookie sheets or jelly-roll pans lined with parchment or foil

These easy and delicious biscotti are based on a recipe for Mandelbrot from Carole Walter, author of *Great Pies and Tarts* (Potter, 1998).

1. Set a rack at the middle level of the oven and preheat to 350 degrees.

2. In a mixing bowl, whisk eggs and salt until liquid. Whisk in sugar and vanilla until smooth.

3. Whisk in melted butter, then stir in nuts and chips.

4. Combine flour with cocoa, baking powder, and cinnamon and sift over batter. Fold in until all the flour is absorbed. The dough will be very soft.

5. Spoon dough onto prepared pan to form two separate logs, each about 1 inch thick, 2½ inches wide, and about 15 inches long. Use a rubber or metal spatula to adjust the shape if necessary.

6. Bake the logs about 30 minutes, or until well risen and firm when pressed with a fingertip. Cool on pan to room temperature.

7. Use a sharp serrated knife to slice baked logs diagonally every ¼ to ½ inch. Return biscotti to pan, cut side down, and bake up to 20 minutes longer, or until biscotti are crisp and dry. Cool on pan.

STORAGE: Keep in a tin or plastic container with a tight-fitting lid.

The two molded cookies here use a shell-shaped mold and a pizzelle maker—a type of waffle iron for shaping. If you don't have the shell-shaped mold for the madeleines, a mini muffin pan will make a good substitute.

CHOCOLATE ORANGE MADELEINES

. . .

Makes 24 shell-shaped cookies

2 large eggs

Pinch salt

Finely grated zest of 1 large orange

½ teaspoon pure orange extract

½ cup sugar

8 tablespoons (1 stick) unsalted butter, melted

⅔ cup all-purpose flour

¼ cup alkalized (Dutch process) cocoa powder

Pinch baking soda

Two 12-cavity madeleine pans, buttered and floured, tapped to shake out the excess flour

To make these elegant cookies you'll need one or two plaques each with 12 of the 3-inch, classic madeleine shell-shaped cavities. (If you have only one pan you can reuse it for the second half of the batter.) See Sources, page 442, for easy places to find them. Though traditional madeleines aren't chocolate, I think the addition of cocoa makes these particularly good. Try streaking them with tempered chocolate, pages 20–23, or Chocolate Glaze, page 44.

1. Set a rack at the middle level of the oven and preheat to 375 degrees.

2. In a medium mixing bowl, whisk the eggs with the salt, orange zest, and orange extract. Whisk in the sugar, then continue whisking for about a minute, until the mixture lightens.

3. Add the butter and stir in with a rubber spatula.

4. Combine the flour, cocoa, and baking soda and sift into the egg mixture. Gently fold in with a rubber spatula.

5. Place about a tablespoon of the batter in each cavity. The molds should be about two-thirds full. If there is any batter left over, add an equal amount to each cavity.

6. Bake for about 15 minutes, until well risen and firm—do not overbake or the madeleines will be dry.

7. Cool in the pans on racks for 5 minutes, then turn out onto racks to finish cooling.

SERVING: Madeleines make a good accompaniment to a cup of tea—as we have read—or any creamy or ice cream dessert.

STORAGE: Keep the madeleines between sheets of wax paper in a tin or plastic container with a tight-fitting lid. Or, before finishing with chocolate or glaze, wrap individually and freeze in a tightly closed plastic container. Defrost before finishing with chocolate or glaze.

VARIATIONS

Madeleines are beautiful when dipped completely or partially in tempered chocolate.

LEMON MADELEINES WITH CHOCOLATE GLAZE Replace the orange zest and extract with lemon. Substitute 1 cup flour for the flour and cocoa. After the madeleines are baked and cooled, streak or dip them in Chocolate Glaze, page 44, or tempered chocolate, pages 20–23.

CHOCOLATE ALMOND PIZZELLE

• • •

Makes about eighteen 4-inch cookies

2 large eggs

½ cup sugar

¼ teaspoon salt

4 tablespoons (½ stick) unsalted butter, melted

1 cup all-purpose flour

3 tablespoons alkalized (Dutch process) cocoa powder

½ teaspoon ground cinnamon

1½ teaspoons baking powder

½ cup whole unblanched almonds, finely ground in the food processor

Oil for the iron

A pizzelle waffle iron

Although you need a special type of waffle iron to make these pizzelle (pronounced peet-sellay), it is easy to find and not very expensive. Divide the pizzelle into quarters with a sharp knife after they are baked, or mold them around a cone-shaped form to make delicious, easy ice cream cones like the ones on pages 250–51. Work quickly; the cookies become crisp as they cool.

1. Whisk the eggs with the sugar and salt until light. Stir in melted butter. Sift together the flour, cocoa, cinnamon, and baking powder and fold into batter. Stir in the almonds.

2. Oil the surface of the imprints and heat pizzelle iron. When hot, place 1 heaping teaspoon of batter on each imprint. Close iron and bake 30 seconds. Cool cookies on racks.

SERVING: These are great as an accompaniment to ice cream.

STORAGE: Keep in a tin or plastic container with a tight-fitting cover. If pizzelle lose their crispness, heat them in a 350-degree oven on a parchment or foil-covered cookie sheet for 5 minutes, then cool on racks.

Triple Chocolate Pudding

Old-fashioned Chocolate Pudding

Old-fashioned Chocolate Butterscotch Pudding

Mexican Chocolate Pudding

Bittersweet Chocolate Crème Brûlée

Individual Chocolate Crèmes Brûlées

Chocolate Brioche Pudding
with Raisins and Rum

Individual Chocolate Bread Puddings

Easy Brioche Loaf

Chocolate and Coffee Pots de Crème

Flan de Tres Leches y Chocolate
(**Mexican Chocolate Flan**)

Chocolate Caramel Custard

Caribbean Chocolate Custard

Chocolate Panna Cotta

Chocolate and Ricotta Custard

White Chocolate
and Coconut Baked Custard

Flourless Chocolate Soufflé

Chocolate Raspberry Soufflé

Chocolate Orange Soufflé

Milk Chocolate Soufflé

Chocolate Pecan Pudding
with Bourbon Sauce

Rich Chocolate Mousse

Swiss Chocolate Mousse

White Chocolate Mousse Layered
with Raspberry Compote

Blueberry Compote

Cranberry Compote

Layered Parfait of Orange
and Chocolate Mousses

*Layered Parfait of Mint
and Chocolate Mousses*

*Layered Parfait of Amaretto
and Chocolate Mousses*

Classic Chocolate Marquise
(**Marquise au Chocolat**)

Chocolate Orange Zabaglione

Chocolate Oeufs à la Neige

Chocolate Steamed Pudding

Semifreddo di Ricotta e Cioccolatto

"Instant" Chocolate Mousse

Instant Milk Chocolate Mousse

Instant White Chocolate Mousse

Striped Parfaits of Chocolate Mousse

Bittersweet Chocolate Terrine
with Raspberry Sauce

Chocolate Almond Terrine

Chocolate Pistachio Terrine

Chocolate Chestnut Terrine

Marbled Chocolate Terrine

T

hese are the desserts in which the meltingly sensuous texture of chocolate is as important as its flavor—and I think that is what defines the best in this type of dessert. That perfectly creamy, silky texture is all important. Nothing should interfere with it. Here are the categories these suavely smooth desserts fall into:

Puddings: Old-fashioned stirred puddings are really starch-thickened custard creams. The ones in this book, of course, are all flavored with chocolate. A steamed pudding batter is similar to a cake's, but usually includes bread crumbs instead of or in addition to flour. The batter is packed into a buttered, metal mold, covered with the mold's lid or a tight wrapping of foil, and steamed rather than baked (hence the name). Chocolate steamed puddings are among the best and most flavorful of all. Bread puddings are made by placing bread (or brioche) in a shallow or individual mold and pouring a custard mixture over the bread.

Custards: Sweet desserts based on eggs and milk or other liquids are called custards. The recipes that follow include chocolate versions of caramelized custards, both those baked in caramel-lined molds and those whose tops are caramelized after baking, the way crème brûlée is finished.

Soufflés: The word in French means "puffed up" and that is exactly what these mixtures are—baked batters lifted by whipped egg whites to twice their original size while baking. These must be served immediately after they are removed from the oven. Though the idea of a hot soufflé may be intimidating, really they are among the easiest of desserts to prepare.

Mousses: The name means "foam" in French. And a good mousse should have a light, foamy texture. Mousses here are both chocolate and nonchocolate so they can be combined and striped in a variety of ways.

Terrines: A borrowing from another kind of cooking. A terrine is a rectangular mold in which a pâté is baked. When that type of pâté is unmolded it too is known as a terrine. Because rich chocolate mixtures may be formed in the same types of molds, we now have chocolate terrines. For the recipes that follow a traditional terrine mold isn't necessary. These mixtures are molded in loaf pans and cut into slices for serving. They are convenient to serve and easy to prepare in advance.

TRIPLE CHOCOLATE PUDDING

. . .

Makes about 1½ pints pudding,
about 6 servings

2 cups whole milk, or use a combination of milk and heavy whipping cream, divided

⅓ cup sugar

2 ounces bittersweet chocolate, cut into ¼-inch pieces

2 ounces milk chocolate, cut into ¼-inch pieces

2 tablespoons cornstarch

2 tablespoons alkalized (Dutch process) cocoa powder

3 large eggs

2 teaspoons vanilla extract, rum, or a sweet liqueur

If your only experience with chocolate pudding is the packaged variety, you'll be surprised at how good—and easy—this homemade version is.

1. Combine 1½ cups milk with the sugar in a non-reactive saucepan. Whisk to mix. Place over medium heat and bring to a simmer. Remove from heat and add chocolates. Let stand 5 minutes, then whisk smooth.

2. Meanwhile, pour remaining ½ cup of milk in a mixing bowl; whisk in cornstarch, sift in cocoa, then whisk in eggs.

3. Return milk and chocolate mixture to a simmer over low heat, whisking often so it doesn't scorch. Whisk a third of the hot liquid into the egg mixture.

4. Return the remaining milk and chocolate mixture to a simmer and then slowly whisk in the egg mixture, whisking constantly until the mixture thickens and just comes to a boil.

5. Off heat, whisk in vanilla. Fill individual cups or glasses with the pudding and press a piece of plastic wrap against the surface of each, to prevent a skin from forming. Chill the puddings and serve cold, with a spoonful of whipped cream, if desired.

VARIATIONS

OLD-FASHIONED CHOCOLATE PUDDING This uses only semisweet chocolate and a sprinkling of walnuts for an old-fashioned flavor. Substitute 6 ounces
semisweet chocolate for the bittersweet and milk chocolates. Omit the cocoa
powder and increase the cornstarch to 3 tablespoons. Stir in ⅓ cup finely
chopped toasted walnuts or pecans after removing cooked pudding from heat.

OLD-FASHIONED CHOCOLATE BUTTERSCOTCH PUDDING Substitute
dark brown sugar for the white sugar. Whisk in 2 tablespoons butter after
removing cooked pudding from heat.

MEXICAN CHOCOLATE PUDDING

• • •

Makes about four ½-cup servings

2 cups milk, divided

3 tablespoons sugar

⅛ teaspoon salt

¼ cup cornstarch

2 tablespoons alkalized (Dutch process) cocoa powder

1 3-ounce tablet Mexican chocolate, cut into ¼-inch pieces

2 teaspoons vanilla extract

This sprightly variation on a classic chocolate pudding comes from my friend Sandy Leonard. To make it you will need some disks of Mexican chocolate used to make hot chocolate (see Sources, page 442).

1. In a heavy, nonreactive saucepan, bring 1½ cups milk, the sugar, and the salt to a boil over low heat.

2. Meanwhile, pour remaining ½ cup milk into a bowl and whisk in cornstarch and cocoa.

3. When the milk and sugar mixture comes to a boil, whisk about a third of it into the cornstarch mixture. Return the pan to the heat and bring the liquid to a simmer again and whisk in the cornstarch mixture. Whisk until the pudding thickens and returns to a boil. Cook, whisking constantly, about 30 seconds.

4. Off heat, whisk in the chocolate and the vanilla and keep whisking until chocolate has melted and pudding is smooth. Fill individual cups or glasses with the pudding and press a piece of plastic wrap against the surface of each to prevent a skin from forming on the surface. Chill the puddings and serve cold, with a spoonful of whipped cream, if desired.

VARIATIONS

Whisk any of the following into the Mexican Chocolate Pudding when removing from heat: 1 tablespoon instant coffee, 1 teaspoon ground cinnamon, 1 teaspoon grated orange zest.

BITTERSWEET CHOCOLATE CRÈME BRÛLÉE

■ ■ ■

Makes about 8 generous servings

CUSTARD CREAM

4 cups heavy whipping cream

½ cup sugar

12 ounces bittersweet chocolate

8 egg yolks

CARAMELIZING THE TOP

½ cup sugar

One 2-quart gratin or other flat baking dish set inside a roasting pan

This rich custard takes on a delicate complex flavor when chocolate is added.

1. Set a rack at the middle level of the oven and preheat to 300 degrees.

2. Bring cream and sugar to a boil in a nonreactive pan. Remove from heat, add chocolate, and allow to stand 3 minutes to melt. Whisk smooth.

3. Whisk yolks in a bowl, then whisk in chocolate mixture. Strain into gratin dish.

4. Place pans on oven rack. Add warm water to the bottom pan to about half the depth of the gratin dish. Bake about 1 hour, or until set. To test for doneness, insert a thin knife or toothpick in the center of the custard; it should emerge clean. Remove baking dish from roasting pan (leave the pan of water in the oven to cool) and chill custard.

5. To caramelize top, blot any moisture from top of chilled custard. Sprinkle evenly with sugar. Place under preheated broiler, or use blow torch or salamander to caramelize. Refrigerate until serving within several hours of caramelizing.

NOTE: If you use a blow torch for caramelizing the sugar, be careful. Strike a match first, then turn on the torch. Light the torch, then adjust the flame to medium. To caramelize the sugar, move the torch around in small circles, with the nozzle about an inch away from the top of the crème brûlée.

VARIATION

INDIVIDUAL CHOCOLATE CRÈMES BRÛLÉES Use shallow individual gratin dishes or even ramekins for individual versions of this dessert. Set individual molds in a shallow roasting pan and fill them. Carefully place the pan in the oven, then add hot water to the pan around them.

CHOCOLATE BRIOCHE PUDDING WITH RAISINS AND RUM

• • •

Makes about 12 generous servings

⅔ cup (6 ounces) golden or dark raisins

3 tablespoons dark rum

4 ounces (1 stick) unsalted butter

1 brioche loaf, page 209

1½ cups milk

1½ cups heavy whipping cream (or substitute 3 cups half and half for the milk and cream)

¾ cup sugar

1 vanilla bean, halved

16 ounces bittersweet chocolate

8 large eggs

One 2-quart baking dish, buttered

This luscious pudding combines a buttery brioche loaf with a creamy custard and just a touch of rum. If you don't have time to make the brioche loaf, substitute a bought loaf or a challah, which is probably easier to find than brioche.

1. The day before you want to serve this dessert, if possible, put raisins in a small saucepan, cover with water, and bring to a boil. Remove from heat and drain. Place plumped raisins in a plastic container with a tight-fitting cover and sprinkle with the rum. Cover and let macerate overnight.

2. Preheat the oven to 325 degrees. Melt the butter and cool it slightly.

3. Cut the brioche loaf in half, and cut one of the halves into thin slices. Cut remaining half brioche into ½-inch dice.

4. Put diced brioche in the bottom of the baking dish. Strew with the raisins and rum and half the butter. Dip one side of each slice of brioche into the butter and arrange, slightly overlapping and buttered side up, over the top of diced brioche and raisins.

5. Combine the milk, cream, sugar, and vanilla bean in a saucepan. Bring to a boil over medium heat. Remove from heat, add chocolate, and allow to stand 3 minutes; whisk smooth.

6. Whisk the eggs until liquid in a large mixing bowl, then strain the milk mixture into the eggs and beat them together. Do not overbeat or the custard will have a great deal of foam on the surface. Strain the custard back into the pan and use a large spoon to skim any foam from the surface. Pour the custard over the brioche in the dish, so that the bread is evenly soaked and rises to the surface.

7. Place the baking dish in another larger pan and pour warm water into it to come halfway up the side of the baking dish. Bake the bread pudding for about 45 minutes, until the custard is set and the brioche is an even color.

INDIVIDUAL CHOCOLATE
BREAD PUDDINGS
● ● ●

Makes 12 individual puddings

4 cups cut-up brioche, page 209, or leftover sponge cake (cut into ½-inch dice)

3 cups half and half, or 1½ cups milk and 1½ cups heavy whipping cream

¾ cup sugar

8 ounces bittersweet chocolate

4 whole eggs

8 egg yolks

2 tablespoons dark rum

Twelve 4- or 5-ounce ramekins or aluminum foil cups buttered and dusted with dry bread crumbs and arranged in a roasting pan

To make these you can use 4- or 5-ounce ramekins or 4-ounce pleated aluminum foil cups (see Sources, page 442)—either works very well.

1. Set a rack at the middle level of the oven and preheat to 325 degrees.

2. Distribute the diced brioche or cake evenly among the molds.

3. To make the custard mixture, combine the half and half and sugar and bring to a boil over medium heat. Off heat add chocolate. Don't stir.

4. Whisk eggs and yolks with rum. Whisk chocolate mixture smooth, then whisk into egg mixture. Strain through a fine wire-mesh sieve into a measuring jug or pitcher. Pour into the molds over the brioche. Wait until the brioche absorbs the chocolate custard, then add more of the custard mixture until the molds are full.

5. Place the roasting pan on the oven rack and pour an inch of warm tap water into it. Bake the puddings for about 45 minutes, until they are slightly puffed, firm to the touch, and the custard is no longer liquid. Remove pan from oven and use tongs or a spatula to remove molds to a rack to cool. Serve the puddings cooled to room temperature or chilled.

SERVING: Unmold each pudding onto a dessert plate. Serve Chocolate Sauce, page 370, or Crème Anglaise, page 372, with the pudding.

STORAGE: Keep the puddings at room temperature for no more than several hours before you serve them. If you must store longer, wrap individually in plastic wrap and refrigerate. Bring to room temperature again before serving.

EASY BRIOCHE LOAF

• • •

Makes one 9 × 5 × 3-inch loaf

½ cup milk

1 envelope (2 teaspoons) active
   dry yeast

2¼ cups unbleached all-purpose
   flour, divided

6 tablespoons (¾ stick)
   unsalted butter

3 tablespoons sugar

½ teaspoon salt

2 large eggs

One 9 × 5 × 3-inch loaf pan,
   buttered and the bottom lined
   with parchment or buttered wax
   paper

A relatively quick (about 20 minutes of preparation, plus about 90 minutes for rising and baking) brioche loaf can be made even more efficiently by preparing the dough in the evening, allowing the loaf to rise in the refrigerator overnight, and baking it the next morning.

1. In a small saucepan over low heat, warm the milk until it is just warm, about 110 degrees. Remove from heat and pour into a small bowl. Whisk in the yeast, then stir in 1 cup of the flour. Cover the bowl with plastic wrap and set aside at room temperature while preparing the other ingredients. It may begin to rise slightly before you add it to the other ingredients.

2. Cut the butter into six or eight pieces and combine with sugar and salt in the work bowl of a food processor fitted with the metal blade. Pulse at 1-second intervals until the butter is soft and smooth, scraping the inside of the bowl several times to ensure even mixing. Add the eggs, one at a time, and process until smooth. If the mixture appears curdled, continue to process for about 1 minute longer, until it looks smoother. (It may remain somewhat curdled in appearance, which is okay.) Add the remaining 1¼ cups flour, then the milk-yeast-flour mixture, scraping it from the bowl with a rubber spatula. Pulse at 1-second intervals until the ingredients form a soft, smooth dough. Then process continuously for 15 seconds.

3. Remove work bowl from base and remove blade. Turn dough out onto a generously floured work surface and fold it over on itself several times to make it more elastic. Press the dough into a rough rectangle, about 9 × 5 inches. Arrange it on the work surface with a short side facing you. Fold each side in about 1 inch toward the center and press firmly to seal. Then, starting at the short side at the top of the rectangle, fold the dough to the middle the way you would a business letter. Fold the bottom of the dough up past the seam and pinch to seal. Place the dough, seam side down, in the prepared pan. Press the top of the dough firmly with the palm of your hand to flatten it and make it fill the pan evenly. Cover with a piece of buttered plastic wrap or a towel and allow to rise to about 1 inch above the rim of the pan, about 1 hour.

4. About 40 to 45 minutes after you place the dough in the pan to rise, set a rack at the middle level of the oven and preheat to 350 degrees.

5. Use the corner of a razor blade or the tip of a sharp knife held at a 30-degree angle to the top of the loaf to cut a slash down the middle of the top beginning and ending about 1 inch from the ends of the loaf.

6. Bake for about 40 minutes, until it is well risen and a deep golden color. Place the pan on a rack to cool 5 minutes. Then invert the loaf onto the rack and turn it on its side to finish cooling.

STORAGE: Keep the loaf loosely covered at room temperature before you serve it. To use it for the bread pudding recipes, leave it until the next day and it will be easier to slice.

CHOCOLATE AND COFFEE POTS DE CRÈME

■ ■ ■

Makes about 8 servings

CUSTARD MIXTURE

2 cups heavy whipping cream

⅓ cup sugar

1 vanilla bean, split

6 egg yolks

12 ounces bittersweet chocolate, cut into ¼-inch pieces

½ cup very strong prepared espresso coffee

Eight 4- to 5-ounce pot de crème cups or ramekins

This rich and elegant dessert is perfect after a light dinner.

1. Bring the cream and sugar to a boil with the vanilla bean in a saucepan.

2. Whisk yolks in a bowl. Whisk about a third of the boiling cream into the yolks. Return remaining cream to a boil and whisk in yolk mixture. Continue to cook, whisking constantly, another 15 or 20 seconds, until slightly thickened.

3. Strain cream into a bowl and add chocolate. Whisk smooth, whisk in coffee, and pour into molds. Refrigerate until cooled.

SERVING: Serve the pots de crème alone, or with a crisp cookie, such as Chocolate Almond Fingers, page 172.

STORAGE: For advance preparation, cover the pots de crème with plastic wrap and refrigerate. Uncover and leave at room temperature for an hour before serving.

FLAN DE TRES LECHES Y CHOCOLATE

Mexican Chocolate Flan

• • •

Makes about 8 generous servings

FLAN MIXTURE

1 can evaporated milk, 12 ounces

1 can sweetened condensed milk, 14 ounces

1 cup fresh milk

1 cinnamon stick

4 strips lemon zest

8 ounces bittersweet chocolate, cut into ¼-inch pieces

8 eggs

1 tablespoon vanilla extract

CARAMEL

½ cup sugar

½ teaspoon plus 3 tablespoons water

One 6-cup ring mold, set inside a small roasting pan

The use of canned milk in different forms is common in recipes from the tropics, where there wasn't much refrigeration until recently. Although this version of baked custard uses fresh milk as one of the *leches*, that could be replaced by more evaporated milk, or even evaporated cream.

1. Set a rack at the middle level of the oven and preheat to 300 degrees.

2. To make the flan mixture, combine milks, cinnamon stick, and lemon zest in a saucepan. Bring the mixture to a boil, then turn off heat and allow to steep for 15 minutes. Add chocolate, and whisk until melted and smooth. In a large mixing bowl, whisk eggs with vanilla until liquid. Slowly whisk the milk into the eggs.

3. To make the caramel, combine sugar and ½ teaspoon water in a small saucepan. Stir well and place over low heat, stirring occasionally, until the mixture becomes amber in color. Add 3 tablespoons water, allow to return to a boil, then remove from heat.

4. Pour the caramel into the ring mold. Tilt to coat the inside completely, then invert the mold to drain off excess. Pour the flan mixture through a fine strainer into the mold in the roasting pan. Place on oven rack. Add warm water to the bottom pan to a depth of 1 inch. Bake for about 1 hour, or until the custard is set in the center and firm when gently pressed with a fingertip. Remove the ring mold from the roasting pan. (Leave the pan of water in the oven to cool.)

5. Cover the mold with plastic wrap and chill the custard. To unmold, run the point of a small paring knife around the custard to about ¼ inch down from the top of the mold to loosen. Invert a platter over the mold, then invert, hold platter and mold together, and shake several times to loosen custard from mold. Lift off mold and cover custard loosely with plastic wrap. Refrigerate until serving time.

SERVING: Serve thick slice of the custard. Accompany with a spoonful of whipped cream and/or a crisp cookie.

STORAGE: Cover leftovers with plastic wrap and refrigerate.

VARIATIONS

CHOCOLATE CARAMEL CUSTARD In the flan mixture, substitute 2 cups milk, 2 cups heavy whipping cream, and ⅓ cup sugar for the three milks; substitute 4 eggs and 4 egg yolks for the 8 eggs.

CARIBBEAN CHOCOLATE CUSTARD Add ¼ cup dark rum to either the basic recipe or its custard variation above.

CHOCOLATE PANNA COTTA

■ ■ ■

Makes 8 to 12 servings,
depending on the size of the molds used

1 cup milk

1 envelope unflavored gelatin

4 cups heavy whipping cream

⅓ cup sugar

½ vanilla bean, split

12 ounces bittersweet chocolate

Eight to twelve 4- to 6-ounce
    ramekins, set on a jelly-roll pan

The name of this classic Italian dessert literally means "cooked cream." This despite the fact that the cream is not cooked at all—just heated.

This chocolate version is definitely a departure from the original. Traditionally, the pudding is molded in a caramelized mold. I think a plain mold works better with chocolate, but if you wish to try a caramelized mold, follow the instructions given in the recipe for Mexican Chocolate Flan on page 212 for how to line a mold with caramel.

1. To prepare the cream, pour the milk into a bowl, then sprinkle the gelatin over the surface. Allow to stand and let the gelatin absorb the milk and soften. Bring the cream to a boil with the sugar and split vanilla bean; remove from heat; rinse, dry, and save the vanilla bean for another use. Whisk in chocolate until melted. Five minutes after, stir in the softened gelatin and return to a boil, stirring to dissolve the gelatin. Strain the mixture into a pitcher and fill the molds. Refrigerate until set, at least 6 hours—overnight is best.

2. To unmold, dip each mold briefly in hot water. Loosen the top of the dessert by running the point of a sharp paring knife around the mold about ¼ inch down between the cream and the mold. Place a plate over the mold and invert. Tap the bottom of the mold now on top and lift it off. Refrigerate the dessert until it is served.

SERVING: Serve with whipped cream, page 56, or Crème Anglaise, page 372.

STORAGE: Cover and refrigerate leftovers.

CHOCOLATE AND RICOTTA CUSTARD

• • •

Makes one 9-inch custard, about 10 servings

1½ pounds (3 cups) whole-milk
  ricotta

½ cup sugar

4 large eggs

1 teaspoon vanilla extract

1 teaspoon ground cinnamon,
  divided

6 ounces semisweet chocolate,
  cut into ¼-inch pieces

FINISHING

Confectioners' sugar

One 9-inch springform pan,
  buttered and dusted with fine,
  dry bread crumbs

The texture of this dessert after baking is some-what like that of a cheesecake. Baked in a springform pan, it unmolds easily and cuts into perfect wedges.

1. Set a rack at the middle level of the oven and preheat to 350 degrees.

2. In a mixing bowl, combine the ricotta and sugar and stir with a rubber spatula to mix. Mix in the eggs, one at a time.

3. Mix in the vanilla and half the cinnamon.

4. Place the chopped chocolate in a strainer and tap the strainer to sift away all the dusty particles that would cloud the color of the custard. Stir the remaining chunks of chocolate into the custard mixture.

5. Pour the mixture into the prepared pan and smooth the top. Sprinkle the remaining cinnamon on top of the custard.

6. Bake the custard for 45 minutes, until well risen and golden on top. Cool in the pan on a rack.

7. Chill the custard for several hours or overnight before serving.

8. To remove the springform pan, run a knife around the inside of the dessert, between it and the side of the pan. Unbuckle the ring and remove it. Use a long spatula to loosen the dessert from the springform base and to slide it to a platter. Dust lightly with confectioners' sugar before serving.

SERVING: A chocolate or raspberry sauce would be perfect with this.

STORAGE: Refrigerate leftovers covered with plastic wrap.

WHITE CHOCOLATE AND COCONUT BAKED CUSTARD

• • •

Makes one 1½-quart custard,
about 6 to 8 servings

3 cups milk

12 ounces white chocolate, cut into
¼-inch pieces

4 large eggs

4 large egg yolks

¼ cup white rum

1½ cups sweetened shredded
coconut

One 6-cup gratin dish or other
baking dish, buttered and set
inside another larger, shallow
pan, such as a small roasting pan

This rich combination of white chocolate, coconut, and rum makes as good a pie filling as it does a baked custard. See White Chocolate Coconut Cream Pie, page 276, for instructions.

1. Set a rack at the middle level of the oven and preheat to 325 degrees.

2. In a large saucepan, bring the milk to a simmer.

3. Remove the pan from the heat and whisk in the white chocolate until melted and smooth.

4. In a large mixing bowl, whisk together the eggs, yolks, and rum. Whisk in the milk mixture, then strain into another bowl. Stir in the coconut.

5. Pour the custard into the buttered pan and place on the oven rack. Add warm water to the bottom pan to about half the depth of the gratin dish.

6. Bake for about 45 minutes, or until the coconut on the surface is lightly colored and the custard is set and firm in the center when pressed with a fingertip. Remove the gratin dish from the pan. (Leave the pan of water in the oven to cool.) Cool the custard on a rack, then wrap it in plastic and chill it.

SERVING: Spoon the custard into bowls or plates and serve with some fresh fruit, such as the Orange Compote, page 232, or Crème Anglaise, page 372.

STORAGE: Cover and refrigerate leftovers.

FLOURLESS CHOCOLATE SOUFFLÉ

■ ■ ■

Makes 8 servings

7 ounces semisweet chocolate

¼ cup strong brewed coffee

4 tablespoons (½ stick) unsalted butter, softened

4 egg yolks

8 egg whites

Pinch salt

¼ cup sugar

Eight 4- to 5-ounce ramekins buttered and sugared, set on a jelly-roll pan

This a wonderful and easy way to make a chocolate soufflé. I always use 4- or 5-ounce individual ramekins. This is adapted from a recipe created by my late friend and associate Peter Kump, a real connoisseur of all things chocolate.

1. Set a rack at the lower third of the oven and preheat to 400 degrees.

2. Combine the chocolate with the coffee in a heatproof bowl. Place bowl over a pan of hot water and allow to melt, stirring occasionally. Stir smooth, remove from the heat, and stir in the butter. Cool to room temperature.

3. Stir in the yolks.

4. Use an electric mixer to whip egg whites with salt until they hold a very light peak. Add sugar gradually and continue to beat until whites form a soft peak.

5. Stir a quarter of the whites into the base. Using a rubber spatula, fold in the remaining whites.

6. Pour batter in buttered and sugared molds, filling molds to the top. Bake for approximately 12 to 15 minutes, or until the soufflés are well risen and baked through, except for the very center, which should remain soft and liquid. (Check one of the soufflés by taking the point of a spoon and using it to lift the top off on one side—it will fall right back into place.)

SERVING: Serve the soufflés immediately, on dessert plates. Pass Chocolate Sauce, page 371, and/or whipped cream, page 56, if you wish.

VARIATIONS

CHOCOLATE RASPBERRY SOUFFLÉ Substitute ¼ cup raspberry liqueur or 2 tablespoons raspberry eau de vie and 2 tablespoons water for the coffee. Serve the soufflé with Raspberry Sauce, page 126.

CHOCOLATE ORANGE SOUFFLÉ Substitute ¼ cup orange liqueur for the coffee.

MILK CHOCOLATE SOUFFLÉ Substitute 12 ounces milk chocolate for the semisweet chocolate. Reduce the sugar to 1 tablespoon.

CHOCOLATE PECAN PUDDING WITH BOURBON SAUCE

• • •

Makes about 6 generous servings

BATTER

4 ounces semisweet chocolate

3 tablespoons hot water

1½ cups pecan pieces (about 5 to 5½ ounces)

¼ cup dry bread crumbs

¼ teaspoon ground cinnamon

8 tablespoons (1 stick) unsalted butter, softened

⅓ cup sugar, divided

1 tablespoon bourbon

5 large eggs, separated

Pinch salt

BOURBON SAUCE

1 batch Vanilla Bean Crème Anglaise, page 373, plus 2 tablespoons bourbon

One 6-cup gratin dish or other baking dish, buttered, and a small roasting pan to hold the gratin dish

Two of my favorite flavor combinations are chocolate and pecans and bourbon and pecans. I merged the three several years ago in this pudding recipe that I devised for an article on comforting winter desserts for *Food & Wine* magazine. Don't worry too much about timing this—if it is done before you with to serve it, the pudding may sink slightly, but will be just as delicious.

1. Set rack at the middle level of the oven and preheat to 350 degrees.

2. Cut the chocolate into small pieces and place it in a small heatproof bowl. Add the water and place the bowl over a pan of hot, but not simmering water. Stir to melt the chocolate and combine it smoothly with the water. Use a whisk, if necessary, to mix smoothly. Remove the bowl from the heat and cool the chocolate to room temperature.

3. Place the pecan pieces in the bowl of a food processor and pulse, 2 seconds at a time, until the pecans are coarsely chopped. Remove ½ cup of the pecans and set aside. Continue to pulse until the remaining pecans are reduced to a fine powder. Be careful not to overprocess them and make them oily. Combine the ground pecans with the bread crumbs and cinnamon in a bowl, mix well, and set aside.

4. Use an electric mixer to beat the butter with half the sugar in a large bowl until soft. If you are using a hand mixer, set at medium speed. If you have a heavy-duty mixer on a stand, fit it with the paddle. Beat the cooled chocolate mixture into the batter, then the bourbon. Beat in the egg yolks, one at a time, and continue beating until the mixture is smooth. Stir in the pecan mixture.

5. Use a hand mixer with clean beaters, set at medium speed, or a heavy-duty mixer fitted with the whisk to whip the egg whites with the salt in a clean, dry bowl until they form a very soft peak. Beat in the remaining sugar in a very

slow stream, and continue whipping until the whites hold a soft peak. Stir a quarter of the beaten egg whites into the batter, then gently fold in the remaining egg whites.

6. Pour the batter into the baking dish and smooth the top. Scatter the reserved chopped pecans evenly over the surface. Place the baking dish in the larger, shallow pan and place on the oven rack. Add warm water to the bottom pan to halfway up the side of the baking dish. Bake the pudding about 30 to 40 minutes. The pudding will puff and feel slightly firm when pressed with the palm of the hand. Do not overbake the pudding or it will be lethally dry. Remove the dish from the pan. (Leave the pan of water in the oven to cool it.) Spoon the pudding onto warm dessert plates and serve 2 or 3 tablespoons of the Bourbon Sauce next to it.

SERVING: Serve the pudding right from the oven. Or allow it to cool, keep it loosely covered at room temperature, and serve it within a few hours.

VARIATIONS

Substitute walnuts or hazelnuts for the pecans. Serve with lightly sweetened whipped cream rather than the Bourbon Sauce.

CREAMS

RICH CHOCOLATE MOUSSE

.   .   .

Makes about 6 to 8 servings

12 ounces bittersweet or semisweet
   chocolate, cut into ¼-inch pieces

½ cup milk

2 cups heavy whipping cream

4 egg yolks

⅓ cup sugar

⅓ cup coffee, orange juice. or sweet
   liqueur (if using sweet liqueur,
   reduce sugar to 3 tablespoons)

Chocolate shavings, page 392,
   whipped cream, or both to
   garnish

The method used to cook the eggs in this recipe—making them into a sabayon—involves whisking the eggs with sugar and liquid over simmering water until they are hot and cooked. Cooking the eggs this way eliminates most of the danger of salmonella poisoning associated with mousses made from raw eggs.

Use this mousse to fill Free-Form Chocolate Tulip Cups, page 405, for a spectacular dessert.

1. Bring a saucepan of water to a boil and remove from heat. Put cut chocolate and milk in a heatproof bowl and place over the pan of hot water. Stir occasionally to melt chocolate evenly. Once chocolate has melted remove bowl from pan and whisk smooth.

2. While chocolate is melting, whip cream until it holds a soft peak. If it is warm in the room, cover and refrigerate the cream while preparing the sabayon.

3. Return the pan of water to a boil. In a heatproof bowl or the bowl of an electric mixer, whisk the yolks together by hand. Whisk in the sugar and the liquid flavoring. Replace the bowl over the pan of simmering water and beat constantly until the mixture thickens slightly. Remove from heat and use an electric mixer on medium speed to beat sabayon until cool and risen in volume. To finish, by hand whisk the bowl of hot sabayon over a bowl of cold water with a few ice cubes in it until cool and thickened. Do not let the sabayon become ice cold.

4. To assemble the mousse, whisk the chocolate mixture into the sabayon, and quickly fold in the whipped cream. Place mousse in a bowl or glasses and garnish with extra whipped cream, if desired, and chocolate shavings. Refrigerate until about an hour before serving.

SWISS CHOCOLATE MOUSSE

. . .

Makes about 1½ quarts mousse

2 cups heavy whipping cream

1 envelope unflavored gelatin

¼ cup cold water

1 cup egg whites (from about
 8 large eggs)

1 cup sugar

8 ounces bittersweet chocolate,
 melted and cooled

Chocolate shavings, page 392,
 for finishing

One 2-quart glass serving bowl

This extra-light, foamy mousse is perfect for a buffet when you are also serving other desserts—it adds just the right chocolate note without being overly rich. It is adapted from a recipe in *Swiss Confectionery*, a publication of the Richemont Pastry School in Lucerne. Because this mousse uses gelatin to help it to set, it is better to prepare it the day before you intend to serve it.

1. Whip the cream until it holds a soft peak and refrigerate while preparing other ingredients.

2. Sprinkle the gelatin over the water and allow to soften for 5 minutes.

3. Bring a saucepan of water to a boil, then lower to a simmer. Combine the egg whites and sugar in the bowl of an electric mixer and place over the simmering water. Whisk constantly by hand until egg whites are hot and the sugar is dissolved—about 3 minutes. Test a little between your thumb and forefinger—if the mixture is gritty, continue to heat until all the sugar is dissolved.

4. Whisk the softened gelatin into the hot egg whites, then use an electric mixer fitted with whisk attachment to beat whites until risen in volume, some-what cooled, and soft and creamy in appearance. Do not overbeat or the meringue will become dry or grainy.

5. Allow meringue to cool to room temperature, stirring occasionally if necessary. When it is cool whisk about a third of the meringue into the chocolate, then quickly fold the chocolate mixture back into the remaining meringue.

6. Quickly rewhip the cream if it has separated and fold it into the chocolate mixture. Pour the mousse into the waiting bowl, cover with plastic wrap, and refrigerate until set, several hours or overnight.

7. Before serving, decorate with the chocolate shavings.

WHITE CHOCOLATE MOUSSE LAYERED WITH RASPBERRY COMPOTE

• • •

Makes 6 generous servings

RASPBERRY COMPOTE

Two ½-pint baskets fresh raspberries, divided

¼ cup sugar

1 tablespoon raspberry liqueur or eau de vie

1 batch Instant White Chocolate Mousse, page 230

6 deep stemmed glasses, with a capacity of about 6 ounces each

This is a perfect dinner party dessert when you want to serve something rich, colorful, and satisfying.

1. To make the compote, reserve about 12 raspberries from one of the baskets to garnish the desserts, then combine the remainder of that basket with the sugar in a nonreactive saucepan. Reserve the other basket of berries for later. Bring to a simmer and cook until slightly thickened, about 3 minutes. Remove from heat, pour into a bowl, and cool. Fold in remaining berries and liqueur.

2. Prepare the mousse.

3. Place a tablespoon of the compote in the bottom of each glass, then half fill each glass with the mousse. Cover mousse with another tablespoon of the compote, then with half the remaining mousse. Repeat with remaining compote and remaining mousse.

4. Chill the mousse, loosely covered with plastic wrap.

SERVING: Remove plastic wrap and garnish with the reserved berries.

VARIATIONS

BLUEBERRY COMPOTE Substitute 2 cups blueberries, picked over, rinsed, and well drained, for the raspberries. Substitute white rum for the raspberry liqueur.

CRANBERRY COMPOTE Bring 2 cups cranberries and ½ cup sugar to a simmer in a nonreactive saucepan and cook down until slightly thickened, about 3 minutes. Cool and add 2 tablespoons orange liqueur. Do not garnish the dessert with any raw cranberries.

LAYERED PARFAIT OF ORANGE AND CHOCOLATE MOUSSES
. . .
Makes 6 servings

2 cups heavy whipping cream

1 envelope unflavored gelatin

¼ cup cold water

4 egg yolks

⅓ cup orange liqueur

¼ cup sugar

6 ounces bittersweet chocolate, melted and cooled

3 thin orange slices, quartered for decoration

6 deep stemmed glasses, about 6 or 7 ounces capacity each

This easy recipe may be adapted endlessly by changing the flavor of the liqueur. See photograph on pages 198–99.

1. Whip the cream until it holds a soft peak and set aside in the refrigerator.

2. Sprinkle the gelatin over the water in a heatproof bowl and set aside to soften.

3. Bring a saucepan of water to a boil, then lower to a simmer. Combine the yolks, liqueur, and sugar in the bowl of an electric mixer and whisk to mix. Place over simmering water and whisk constantly until mixture becomes foamy and slightly thickened, about 3 to 4 minutes. Remove the bowl from over the water and replace with bowl of gelatin. Leave gelatin over hot water until it is melted and clear.

4. Use an electric mixer fitted with whip to beat yolk mixture until cooled and increased in volume.

5. Whisk gelatin mixture into cooled yolk mixture, then divide mixture into two bowls. Quickly whisk the chocolate into one bowl.

6. Fold half the cream into the chocolate mixture, and the other half into the other bowl.

7. Spoon some of the chocolate mousse into each glass and top with a spoonful of the orange mousse. You will have more chocolate mousse than orange. Continue alternating the two mousses to form stripes up the glasses. Finish with either mousse.

8. Loosely cover glasses with plastic wrap and refrigerate to set mousse. Garnish each mousse with a slice or two of orange.

VARIATIONS

LAYERED PARFAIT OF MINT AND CHOCOLATE MOUSSES Substitute white crème de menthe for the orange liqueur. Garnish the parfaits with sprigs of mint.

LAYERED PARFAIT OF AMARETTO AND CHOCOLATE MOUSSES Substitute amaretto liqueur for the orange liqueur. Crumble a few amaretti cookies or any of the chocolate macaroons, pages 168–71, over the mousse before serving.

CLASSIC CHOCOLATE MARQUISE

Marquise au Chocolat

∎ ∎ ∎

Makes one 6-cup marquise,
about 10 servings

1 pound bittersweet or semisweet
chocolate, cut into ¼-inch pieces

8 tablespoons (1 stick) unsalted
butter, softened

1 cup heavy whipping cream

3 egg yolks

¼ cup sugar

⅓ cup coffee, orange juice, or sweet
liqueur (if you use sweet liqueur,
reduce sugar to 3 tablespoons)

One 6-cup Pyrex loaf pan, buttered
and lined with plastic wrap

This name has come to signify a rich chocolate loaf, somewhat like a terrine, served in slices with or without a sauce. This marquise is easy and particularly fragrant.

1. Bring a saucepan of water to a boil and remove from heat. Put cut chocolate in a heatproof bowl and place over the pan of hot water. Stir occasionally to melt chocolate evenly. Once chocolate has melted, remove bowl from pan and beat butter into chocolate.

2. While chocolate is melting, whip cream until it holds a soft peak. If the room is warm, cover and refrigerate the cream while preparing the remaining ingredients.

3. Return the pan of water to a boil, then lower heat so it simmers. In the bowl of an electric mixer, whisk the yolks together by hand. Whisk in the sugar and the liquid flavoring. Place the bowl over the pan of simmering water and whisk constantly until the mixture thickens slightly. Use an electric mixer on medium speed to heat the sabayon until cooled and risen in volume. To finish, by hand whisk the bowl of hot sabayon over a bowl of cold water—with a few ice cubes in it—until cooled and thickened. Do not let the sabayon become ice cold.

4. To finish the marquise, whisk the chocolate into the sabayon, then quickly fold in the whipped cream. Pour into mold and smooth top. Cover and refrigerate until set, at least overnight.

5. To unmold the marquise, wipe the outside of the loaf pan with a cloth dipped in hot water and wrung out. Cover the pan with a platter, invert and lift off the pan. Peel off the plastic wrap and smooth the outside of the marquise if necessary.

SERVING: Cut the marquise into ¾-inch slices with a sharp knife wet in warm water and wiped between each slice. Serve with chocolate shavings, page 392, whipped cream, page 56, Crème Anglaise, page 372, or some sliced and sweetened berries.

STORAGE: Refrigerate leftovers.

CHOCOLATE ORANGE ZABAGLIONE

. . .

Makes 4 generous servings

6 egg yolks

3 tablespoons sweet Marsala

¼ cup orange liqueur

¼ cup orange juice, strained

¼ cup sugar

4 ounces bittersweet chocolate, melted

Ground cinnamon or chocolate shavings, page 392, for finishing

4 deep stemmed or coupe glasses, about 5 ounces each

Zabaglione—or zabaione—is a classic Italian dessert made with egg yolks cooked and whisked until foamy with sugar and Marsala, the sweet Sicilian wine. This version with chocolate and orange liqueur was developed by my friend Peter Fresulone when he was pastry chef at Orso, a popular restaurant in Manhattan's theater district.

1. Half fill a saucepan with water and bring the water to a boil over medium heat. Reduce heat so water simmers.

2. In the bowl of an electric mixer, whisk together the yolks, then whisk in all the remaining ingredients, except the chocolate and the cinnamon for finishing. Place the bowl over the simmering water and whisk constantly until thickened and aerated, about 3 or 4 minutes.

3. Use an electric mixer fitted with the whisk and beat until cooled and further aerated, about 5 minutes.

4. Remove from mixer and whisk about a third of the zabaglione into the chocolate, then whisk that back into the remaining zabaglione.

5. Fill glasses. Decorate with a sprinkling of cinnamon or chocolate shavings.

SERVING: You can cover this dessert loosely with plastic wrap and chill briefly before serving, but it tastes better if it is consumed immediately after it is made.

CHOCOLATE OEUFS
À LA NEIGE
■ ■ ■

Makes about 6 servings

MERINGUE EGGS

½ cup egg whites (from about 4
large eggs)

⅔ cup sugar

POACHING LIQUID

1 cup milk

2 cups water

1 teaspoon vanilla extract

FINISHING

1 batch Chocolate Sauce, page 371,
or Chocolate Crème Anglaise,
page 373

Chocolate shavings, page 392

1 jelly-roll pan or cookie sheet

This dessert, the name of which means "snow eggs" in French, is often confused with Floating Island or *Île Flottante*, the large-size version, for which the meringue is baked in a mold and unmolded in one piece into a sea of crème anglaise. These delicate meringue eggs are poached in a combination of milk and water flavored with a little vanilla and then served with a rich chocolate sauce.

1. To make the meringue eggs, half fill a saucepan with water and bring it to a boil over medium heat. Lower heat so water simmers. Combine egg whites and sugar in the bowl of an electric mixer and place over the pan of simmering water, whisking constantly, until egg whites are hot and sugar is dissolved. Use an electric mixer fitted with the whisk to beat meringue until cooled and increased in volume. The meringue should remain smooth and creamy and not dry and grainy.

2. Prepare the poaching liquid. Combine the milk, water, and vanilla extract in a nonreactive preferably straight-sided shallow pan, such as a sauté pan. Place the pan on low heat and bring to a full boil. While the liquid is heating, line the jelly-roll pan or cookie sheet with paper toweling. This will be to drain the meringue eggs as they are poached.

3. To poach the meringue eggs, you will need two large tablespoons, a small bowl of water to help you form the eggs, and a slotted spoon to lift them out of the poaching liquid after they are cooked. Turn off heat under poaching liquid and skim the skin from surface with the slotted spoon. Dip one of the tablespoons in the bowl of water and scoop up a large spoonful of the meringue. Form it into a shape a little larger than an egg. Use the second spoon to ease it off the first one and into the hot liquid.

4. As quickly as possible form 5 more eggs and scrape them off the spoon and into the hot liquid. Quickly turn each over with the slotted spoon so that the bottom also cooks. Leave them about 10 seconds on the second side, then

remove from liquid with slotted spoon and poach 6 more eggs, forming and cooking them in the same way. If you make more than 12 eggs, skim and reheat the liquid before continuing.

5. Cover the tray of meringue eggs loosely with plastic wrap and refrigerate until time to serve.

6. To prepare a portion of the oeufs à la neige, place some of the sauce in the middle of a dessert plate or a dessert bowl and arrange two or three of the meringue eggs on it. Sprinkle with chocolate shavings. Repeat for each portion to be served. Alternately, place sauce in a glass bowl and float the eggs on the sauce and sprinkle them with the shavings. To serve, scoop up an egg or two and place on a plate, then surround with sauce.

MARBLED CHOCOLATE TERRINE
. . .
Makes about 8 servings

DARK CHOCOLATE MOUSSE

8 ounces semisweet chocolate

4 tablespoons (½ stick) unsalted butter

½ cup heavy whipping cream

1 tablespoon orange liqueur

WHITE CHOCOLATE MOUSSE

12 ounces white chocolate

6 tablespoons (¾ stick) unsalted butter

⅔ cup heavy whipping cream

1 tablespoon orange liqueur

MERINGUE FOR BOTH MOUSSES

3 large egg whites

⅓ cup sugar

ORANGE COMPOTE

4 large oranges

⅓ cup sugar

¼ cup water

3 tablespoons orange liqueur

One 6-cup Pyrex loaf pan, buttered and lined with plastic wrap

This striking presentation is the result of using two different chocolate mousses, one made with semisweet chocolate and the other with white chocolate. Be sure when you serve this dessert to use a very sharp, thin knife, rinsed in warm water and wiped so you make perfect slices. Try serving with some sugared berries and a bit of whipped cream flavored with the same liqueur you use in the terrine.

1. To make the dark chocolate mousse, cut the chocolate into small pieces and combine in a heat-proof bowl with the butter. Place bowl over a pan of hot but not simmering water and stir to melt the chocolate. Remove bowl from water and pour in liquid cream in four additions, stirring to incorporate after each. Stir in the liqueur. Cover the mousse with plastic wrap and cool at room temperature. Proceed the same way to make the white chocolate mousse.

2. To finish, place the dark mousse in the bowl of an electric mixer and beat at medium speed until light. If the mousse does not lighten considerably, it may be too warm. Stir over ice water for a minute or two and whip by machine again. Clean the bowl and beater(s) and repeat the process for the white chocolate mousse.

3. For the meringue, combine the egg whites and sugar in the bowl of an electric mixer. Place over simmering water and whisk gently until the egg whites are hot and the sugar is dissolved. Use an electric mixer on medium speed to whip until cool. Fold a third of the meringue into the dark mousse and two thirds into the white mousse.

4. To assemble the terrine, spoon the dark mousse out in five or six piles onto the white mousse. With a small rubber or metal spatula, cut through the two and swirl six or eight times. Do not overmix or there will not be distinct light and dark streaks. Pour the marbled mousse into the prepared pan and give the pan several raps on a towel-covered surface to settle the contents. Cover the

pan with plastic wrap and chill about 8 hours. The terrine may be prepared up to 3 days in advance at this point.

5. To unmold the terrine, wipe the outside of the loaf pan with a cloth dipped in hot water and wrung out. Cover the pan with a platter, invert, and lift off the pan. Peel off the plastic wrap and smooth the outside of the terrine if necessary.

6. For the compote, peel and section the oranges and place in a bowl. Bring sugar and water to a boil and pour over oranges. Cool, drain, and sprinkle with liqueur.

SERVING: Cut the terrine with a thin, sharp knife dipped in hot water and wiped between each slice. Serve some of the compote with each slice.

STORAGE: Cover and refrigerate the leftovers.

**Bittersweet Chocolate Sherbet
with Coconut Rum Sauce**

Chocolate Cognac Sherbet

Chocolate Granita

Pears with Chocolate Sherbet Hélène

Chocolate Orange Sherbet in Orange Shells

**Panera alla Gianduja
(*Italian Chocolate Hazelnut Gelato
with Cinnamon and Coffee*)**

Roman Chocolate Gelato

Rich Milk Chocolate Ice

Gelato Straciatella

Old-fashioned Chocolate Ice Cream

Philadelphia Vanilla Ice Cream

French Chocolate Ice Cream

French Vanilla Ice Cream

Chocolate Chip Ice Cream

Chocolate Rum Raisin Ice Cream

Black Forest Ice Cream

Mint Chip Ice Cream

Chocolate Walnut Crunch Ice Cream

Piquant Chocolate Ginger Ice Cream

Chocolate Fudge Swirl Ice Cream

Vanilla Fudge Ice Cream

Frozen Chocolate Mousse

Frozen Chocolate Charlotte

Frozen Devil's Food Cake

Frozen Chocolate Terrine

Frozen White Chocolate Terrine

Frozen Milk Chocolate Terrine

*Layered Milk Chocolate
and White Chocolate Terrine*

Frozen Cassata

Semifreddo alla Gianduja

Frozen Chocolate Bourbon Soufflé

Frozen Chocolate Chip Soufflé

Frozen Chocolate Rum Soufflé

White Chocolate and Lime Frozen Soufflé

Ice creams, sherbets, and gelati are certainly among the most popular desserts and snack foods. Their cool creaminess is always a welcome pleasure. These recipes require an ice cream maker to produce—though some of the sherbet mixtures may be frozen in a nonreactive pan in the freezer and stirred occasionally to produce a grainy-textured type of ice called a granita. Ice cream makers not only freeze, their churning process aerates the mixture, which contributes lightness to the dessert's final texture.

If you don't have an ice cream maker (see Ice Cream Freezers, page 239), see the recipes for various frozen soufflés, mousses, and parfaits in this chapter. These are ices in which different mixtures—usually whipped cream and whipped eggs or egg whites in some form—are combined and frozen in a mold. No special machinery is required. The lightness in these ices is produced by the air beaten into the egg mixtures and/or the whipped cream. So don't renounce ices just because you don't have an ice cream maker.

In general, sherbet refers to a water-based ice, though some recipes may have some milk or cream added. Sorbet is merely French for sherbet. Ice cream usually refers to a custard-based mixture containing eggs, though some old-fashioned American ice creams are made from sweetened cream mixtures without eggs. Gelato, Italian for ice (the word means frozen), usually refers to a milk-based ice mixture without eggs. In general gelati (the plural) are somewhat lighter than traditional French or American ice creams.

Frozen desserts fall into several categories. A frozen mousse may be frozen in a serving bowl and spooned out to serve, or in a springform or loaf pan and cut into wedges or slices for serving. A frozen soufflé is molded in a soufflé dish whose capacity has been extended with a paper collar, so that once the mixture is frozen and the collar removed, it extends above the rim of a dish in imitation of the way a hot soufflé rises above the dish in which it was baked. Semifreddo is a somewhat ambiguous Italian term that may refer to any of the frozen desserts mentioned in this paragraph, but may also be used to describe certain types of molded cakes with mousse and cream fillings.

BITTERSWEET CHOCOLATE SHERBET WITH COCONUT RUM SAUCE

• • •

Makes about 1½ pints sherbet, about 6 servings

SHERBET

½ cup sugar

2 cups water

½ cup light corn syrup

3 ounces unsweetened chocolate, cut into ¼-inch pieces

⅔ cup alkalized (Dutch process) cocoa powder

SAUCE

1 cup canned coconut cream, such as Coco Lopez

1 cup milk

4 egg yolks

1 teaspoon vanilla extract

2 tablespoons white rum

This smooth sherbet with a deep chocolate flavor is not excessively sweet. The coconut rum sauce adds just the right note of richness.

1. To make the sherbet, bring the sugar, water, and corn syrup to a boil. Off heat, add the finely cut chocolate, let stand 2 minutes, then whisk smooth.

2. Sift the cocoa powder through a very fine strainer into a small bowl. Whisk the syrup mixture into the cocoa a little at a time to prevent the cocoa from getting lumps. Strain the mixture.

3. Cool and freeze in an ice cream freezer. When it is frozen, place the sherbet in a covered plastic container and store in the freezer.

4. For the sauce, bring the coconut cream and the milk to a boil in a saucepan. Beat the yolks together in a bowl, then beat in a third of the boiling liquid. Return the remaining liquid to a boil and beat the yolk mixture into it. Continue beating over medium heat until the mixture thickens slightly. Do not allow to boil. Strain the sauce into a bowl and cool it. Stir in the vanilla and rum.

SERVING: Serve the sherbet in chilled glasses with a spoonful of the sauce on it.

STORAGE: To keep the sherbet after it has been frozen, press plastic wrap against the surface and store in the freezer.

VARIATIONS

CHOCOLATE COGNAC SHERBET Add 2 tablespoons cognac to the mixture. Increase the chocolate to 4 ounces (this will offset the softening effect of the alcohol). For other flavor variations, substitute any other strong, nonsweetened spirits such as bourbon, rum, brandy, or fruit eaux de vie for the cognac.

CHOCOLATE GRANITA Instead of freezing the mixture in an ice cream freezer, place in a stainless steel or other nonreactive pan in the freezer. When the mixture begins to freeze, remove it from the freezer and stir it up, scraping ice from the bottom and sides of the pan with a stainless steel spatula or pancake turner. Return to the freezer and stir and scrape it several more times during the next few hours until all the liquid has frozen to a slushy consistency. Scrape the granita into a chilled container and store it, covered, in the freezer. If the granita becomes hard, remove it from the freezer, roughly chop into 1- to 2-inch pieces and pulse, in a food processor, to restore the slushy consistency. Serve immediately after processing.

ICE CREAM FREEZERS

As a trip to any kitchenware store will show you, there are many fancy (and expensive) ice cream freezers available for home use. The top-of-the-line automatic models are electrically operated refrigerated machines that do all the work of making about a pint of ice cream at a time. The only inconvenience is emptying and refilling the churn when you want to make more than a small amount of ice cream.

There are a few models that have electrically driven mechanisms that you plug in, but place in the freezer to churn, though I don't have any experience using these.

And there are also small hand-operated freezers that have a container which you freeze, then place the ice cream mixture in, and churn by hand at room temperature to make the ice. These work fairly well, especially if you have the container very well frozen before you start.

Old-fashioned American ice cream freezers are worth looking into if you don't want to invest several hundred dollars. Though the oldest types were operated by a hand crank, the modern versions are electrically driven. These are not refrigerated and you must still surround the churn in which the ice cream will freeze with ice and salt. Department and cookware stores carry ice cream machines, especially in spring and summer.

PEARS WITH CHOCOLATE SHERBET HÉLÈNE

• • •

Makes 6 servings

1 batch Bittersweet Chocolate
   Sherbet, page 238, flavored with
   pear eau de vie

6 ripe fragrant medium Bartlett
   pears, about 1½ to 2 pounds

4 cups water

1 tray of ice cubes

2 tablespoons lemon juice

½ cup sugar

1 vanilla bean

Chocolate shavings, page 392,
   and/or chocolate cigarettes,
   page 385

This is a variation on the classic French dessert Poires Belle Hélène, or pears with vanilla ice cream and chocolate sauce. This version uses pears poached and chilled, then served with a pear eau de vie–flavored chocolate sherbet. If you like, serve with cold Chocolate Sauce, page 371.

1. The sherbet can be prepared up to several days in advance.

2. To poach the pears, place the 4 cups of water and the cubes from a tray of ice in a large saucepan. Add the lemon juice. Cut a piece of parchment or wax paper to fit the circumference of the saucepan. Cut a hole in the center. Peel the pears and cut them in half from the stem to the base; core the pears (a melon-ball scoop is perfect for coring) and immediately place each pear half in the acidulated ice water. When all the pears have been prepared, skim out any remaining ice and pour away excess water to leave the pears covered by about an inch of ice water. Add the sugar and vanilla bean.

3. Cover the top of the pan with the parchment or wax paper and press the paper down until it is below the surface of the liquid—this will help to keep the pears from bobbing up out of the liquid and becoming discolored. Bring to a boil over medium heat. Allow to boil for about a minute, then remove from heat. Let the pears cool in the liquid—they will be tender by the time they have cooled.

4. If you want to make this in advance, pack the pear halves in a plastic container and cover with syrup. Keep the rest of the syrup to cook another batch of pears—it will keep well in the freezer.

5. To assemble the dessert, arrange 2 pear halves, cut sides up, on a chilled plate or in a shallow stemmed glass. Place a small scoop of the chocolate sherbet on the wide end of each half. Sprinkle with chocolate shavings and serve immediately.

CHOCOLATE ORANGE SHERBET IN ORANGE SHELLS

• • •

Makes 6 generous servings

6 medium navel oranges

⅓ cup sugar

1 cup water

½ cup light corn syrup

3 ounces unsweetened chocolate, cut into ¼-inch pieces

⅔ cup alkalized (Dutch process) cocoa powder

2 tablespoons orange liqueur

1 small roasting pan lined with aluminum foil to hold the oranges in the freezer

CHOCOLATE

This is a bit of trouble, but well worth the effort for a special party. You can put the finished desserts in the freezer a day before your party, and remove them shortly before serving.

1. Cut a thin slice off the stem end of each orange so it sits levelly. Stand the oranges on the cut bases and cut off the top quarter of each. These will be the covers of the dessert. Scrape the orange flesh away from the top quarters and set it aside in a bowl. Reserve the orange tops.

2. Use a pointy spoon—or a grapefruit spoon if you have one—to hollow out the oranges. Put orange flesh with the other reserved flesh and place the empty orange skins and the tops on the prepared pan and freeze them. Place the orange flesh in a fine strainer over a bowl and press to extract juice. Reserve 1 cup of the orange juice. Discard the pulp.

3. To make the sherbet, bring the sugar, water, and corn syrup to a boil. Off heat, add the finely cut chocolate, let stand 2 minutes, then whisk smooth. Sift the cocoa powder through a very fine strainer into a small bowl. Whisk the syrup mixture into the cocoa a little at a time to prevent cocoa from forming lumps. Strain the syrup and whisk in the orange juice and orange liqueur. Cool the sherbet mixture and freeze in an ice cream freezer according to the manufacturer's directions.

4. When the sherbet is frozen, remove the orange shells one at a time from the freezer and fill each with sherbet, mounding it above the top of the shell. Perch a top on each filled orange, leaving the sherbet visible under it. Return the oranges to the freezer as they are filled.

5. After all the filled oranges have frozen solid, remove pan from freezer and wrap well in plastic wrap.

SERVING: Place the oranges in the refrigerator to soften slightly about an hour before you intend to serve them. Serve on a chilled plate.

STORAGE: Leftovers keep well individually wrapped in plastic and frozen.

COUPES

Coupes are the sundaes of elegant French, Italian, and Swiss pastry shops. In those countries, patrons commonly enjoy ice cream specialties in the tearoom/café part of a pastry shop even though there are elegant gelaterias in Italy and shops that prepare mostly ice cream in France and Switzerland. Until recently, industrially made ice cream, apart from prepared prefrozen cones, popsicles, and some dubiously fancy frozen desserts sold in grocery stores, was all but unknown in Europe and most ice cream was consumed outside the home.

Coupes are usually served in low, fairly shallow, stemmed silver dishes. A small glass dessert dish or even a martini glass will make a good coupe. Here are a few specialties that use some of the recipes in this and other chapters as components:

Coupe Jacques: Vanilla ice cream drizzled with Chocolate Sauce, page 371.

Chocolate Meringue Coupe: Chocolate or vanilla ice cream alternated with layers of crumbled Swiss Chocolate S's, page 164.

Coupe Belle Hélène: Chocolate or vanilla ice cream on half a poached pear, page 240, drizzled with Chocolate Sauce, page 371.

PANERA ALLA GIANDUJA

*Italian Chocolate Hazelnut Gelato
with Cinnamon and Coffee*

■ ■ ■

Makes about 2 quarts ice cream

1 quart plus ½ cup milk

3 tablespoons light corn syrup

1½ cups heavy whipping cream

1 cup sugar

1 teaspoon unflavored gelatin

½ cup nonfat dry milk

½ teaspoon ground cinnamon

10 ounces bittersweet chocolate, melted

½ cup strong prepared espresso coffee

½ cup praline paste, see Sources, page 442

This is my favorite ice cream, bar none. The combination of flavors blends to become a hauntingly delicious new taste, with none of the flavors predominating. This is loosely based on a recipe from *Il Gelato Artigianale Italiano* by G. Preti.

1. Combine the milk, corn syrup, and cream in a saucepan. Put the sugar, gelatin, and milk powder in a bowl and stir well to mix. Whisk the dry mixture into the milk mixture. Bring to a simmer over low heat, whisking occasionally.

2. Remove mixture from heat and whisk in remaining ingredients. Whisk smooth, then cool to room temperature, cover, and chill.

3. Freeze the mixture in an ice cream freezer according to the manufacturer's directions. Scoop the frozen gelato into a chilled container, press plastic wrap against the surface, and cover tightly. Freeze until ready to serve.

ROMAN CHOCOLATE GELATO

. . .

Makes about 2 quarts gelato

5 cups milk

3 tablespoons light corn syrup

1½ cups heavy whipping cream

1 cup sugar

1 teaspoon unflavored gelatin

½ cup nonfat dry milk

12 ounces bittersweet chocolate, melted

This is modeled after the light, slushy gelati found at such classic Roman establishments as Giolitti. The chocolate flavor is richer in this ice because the flavor of eggs doesn't interfere with it.

1. Put the milk, corn syrup, and cream in a saucepan. Combine the sugar, gelatin, and milk powder in a bowl and stir well to mix. Whisk the dry mixture into the milk mixture. Bring to a simmer over low heat, whisking occasionally.

2. Remove mixture from heat and whisk in melted chocolate. Cool to room temperature, cover, and chill.

3. Freeze in an ice cream freezer according to the manufacturer's directions. Place the frozen gelato in a chilled container, press plastic wrap against the surface, and cover tightly. Freeze until ready to serve.

RICH MILK CHOCOLATE ICE

. . .

Makes about 1 quart ice milk

3 cups whole milk, divided

1 pound best-quality milk chocolate, cut into ¼-inch pieces

This incredibly easy recipe comes my friend and mentor, Maida Heatter. Since it has only two ingredients, use the best chocolate you can find and afford.

1. Bring half the milk to a boil in a saucepan.

2. Remove from heat and add chocolate. Shake pan to make sure all the chocolate is covered, then let stand 5 minutes. Whisk smooth, then whisk in the remaining milk. Cool to room temperature.

3. Chill the mixture. If the chocolate rises to the top while the mixture is chilling, stir to reincorporate.

4. Freeze the mixture in an ice cream machine according to the manufacturer's directions. Place the frozen ice milk in a chilled container, press plastic wrap against the surface and cover tightly. Keep frozen until serving time.

STORAGE: Use the ice milk within a few days or it may become icy.

GELATO STRACIATELLA

▪ ▪ ▪

Makes about 2 quarts gelato

1 quart milk

3 tablespoons light corn syrup

1 pint heavy whipping cream

1 cup sugar

1 teaspoon unflavored gelatin

½ cup nonfat dry milk

1 teaspoon vanilla extract

4 ounces semisweet chocolate, melted

2 teaspoons mild vegetable oil, such as corn or canola

This is the Italian equivalent of chocolate chip ice cream. Melted chocolate is diluted with some oil to make it fluid and drizzled into the ice cream maker during the freezing process to make little flakes of chocolate throughout. One of my favorites.

I. Place the milk, corn syrup, and cream in a saucepan. Combine the sugar, gelatin, and milk powder in a bowl and stir well to mix. Whisk the dry mixture into the milk mixture. Bring to a simmer over low heat, whisking occasionally.

2. Remove mixture from heat and cool to room temperature, then whisk in the vanilla, cover, and chill.

3. Freeze the mixture in an ice cream freezer according to the manufacturer's directions. While the mixture is freezing, combine the melted chocolate with the oil. Drizzle the chocolate mixture into the ice mixture as it is turning in the machine. With some machines you may have to stop the rotation to remove the lid of the container. Leave it off until the chocolate is in, then replace it and continue. It's best if the ice cream is turning when the chocolate is poured in but it can't be if you have to stop the rotation to lift the lid. (Remember to use an amount of the chocolate mixture proportional to the quantity of ice cream. If your machine can only accommodate half the recipe, then only use half the chocolate at a time.) The chocolate will separate into little flakes throughout the ice cream.

4. Place the frozen gelato in a chilled container, press plastic wrap against the surface, and cover tightly. Freeze until ready to serve.

OLD-FASHIONED CHOCOLATE ICE CREAM

■ ■ ■

Makes about 1½ quarts ice cream

4 cups light cream, divided

⅓ cup sugar

12 ounces best-quality bittersweet chocolate, cut into ¼-inch pieces

2 teaspoons vanilla extract

My model for this recipe is old-fashioned Philadelphia ice cream, made with nothing but light cream, sugar, and flavoring. You'll find this creamy and chocolaty in the extreme, as well as quick and easy to prepare.

1. Bring half the cream and all the sugar to a simmer in a saucepan, stirring occasionally. Remove from heat and add chocolate, shaking pan to make sure all the chocolate is submerged. Let stand 5 minutes. Whisk the chocolate mixture smooth, then whisk in the vanilla and the remaining cream.

2. Chill, stirring occasionally.

3. Freeze in an ice cream machine according to the manufacturer's directions. Place the frozen ice cream in a chilled container, press plastic wrap against the surface, and cover tightly. Freeze until ready to serve.

VARIATION

PHILADELPHIA VANILLA ICE CREAM Omit chocolate; increase sugar to ½ cup. Heat half the cream with sugar to dissolve it, remove from heat and cool. Whisk in remaining cream and vanilla. Chill; freeze and store as above.

ICES

FRENCH CHOCOLATE
ICE CREAM
. . .

Makes about 2 quarts ice cream

4 cups milk

1 cup heavy whipping cream

1¼ cups sugar

10 egg yolks

1 cup alkalized (Dutch process)
cocoa powder

4 ounces best-quality bittersweet
chocolate

This is the ultimate rich ice cream made with a cooked custard base of milk, cream, sugar, and egg yolks—similar to the Crème Anglaise on page 372. This ice cream is creamier, richer, and better than anything you can buy. For best results, chill the ice cream mixture overnight before freezing it in an ice cream maker. This makes for a creamier texture in the finished ice cream. Use this as the master recipe for endless flavor variations.

1. Have ready a strainer set in a nonreactive pot or bowl. Set the pot or bowl in a larger bowl or pot half filled with a mixture of ice and water.

2. Combine the milk, cream, and sugar in a large saucepan and whisk once or twice to mix. Place over low heat and bring to a full boil.

3. Meantime, beat yolks together in a bowl until liquid, then whisk in a third of the boiling liquid. Return remaining liquid to a boil and whisk the yolk mixture into it, beating constantly until the custard thickens, about 20 seconds at the most. Be careful not to overcook the custard or it will scramble. Quickly whisk in the cocoa and chocolate.

4. Remove the pan from the heat, never ceasing to whisk, and pour it through the strainer into the pot or bowl set over the ice water. Whisk the strained custard for a few seconds to begin cooling it slightly, then let it cool, stirring occasionally, over the ice water. Cover and refrigerate the cooled custard overnight.

5. Freeze in an ice cream machine according to the manufacturer's directions. Place the frozen ice cream in a chilled container, press plastic wrap against the surface, and cover tightly. Freeze until ready to serve.

VARIATIONS

FRENCH VANILLA ICE CREAM Omit cocoa and chocolate. Add 2 vanilla beans, split lengthwise, to the milk and cream mixture. Cook as above—the vanilla beans will be removed when you strain the custard.

CHOCOLATE CHIP ICE CREAM Prepare a batch of chocolate or vanilla ice cream according to the above recipe. Melt 4 ounces chocolate with 2 teaspoons mild vegetable oil such as corn or canola. Drizzle the chocolate mixture into the ice cream as it is turning in the churn. Remember to divide the chocolate mixture proportionately if your machine won't hold all the ice cream at once.

CHOCOLATE RUM RAISIN ICE CREAM After preparing and chilling the ice cream mixture, place ⅔ cup dark raisins in a saucepan. Cover the raisins with water and bring to a boil. Drain the raisins and place them in a small bowl. Cool to room temperature, then stir in 3 tablespoons dark rum. Cover the raisins and place the bowl in the freezer. As soon as the chocolate ice cream is frozen, drain the raisins and stir them into the just-frozen ice cream. Cover and freeze immediately. Use vanilla ice cream as a base for plain rum raisin ice cream.

BLACK FOREST ICE CREAM Substitute dried cherries for the raisins, above. Substitute kirsch for the rum. Use chocolate ice cream.

MINT CHIP ICE CREAM Substitute 2 cups loosely packed fresh mint leaves, rinsed and dried, for the vanilla beans in the French Vanilla Ice Cream above. After you bring the milk, cream, sugar, and mint to a simmer, remove the pan from the heat and allow to stand 20 minutes. Return to a boil and continue with step 3 above, and cook the custard—the mint leaves will be removed when you strain the custard. (Add a tiny drop of green food coloring, if you wish.) Chill and freeze the ice cream. Melt 4 ounces chocolate with 2 teaspoons oil and finish as for Chocolate Chip Ice Cream, above.

CHOCOLATE WALNUT CRUNCH ICE CREAM Prepare a batch of Walnut Praline Topping (see recipe for Chocolate Walnut Crown, page 94). As soon as the ice cream is frozen, stir about half the praline in before you store it in the freezer. Save the rest of the praline to sprinkle over the ice cream when you serve it.

Substitute lightly toasted almonds, hazelnuts, macadamias, or pecans for the walnuts, if you wish.

PIQUANT CHOCOLATE GINGER ICE CREAM Add 1½ teaspoons ground ginger to the ice cream mixture along with the cocoa powder. When the ice cream is frozen, stir in ⅓ cup finely diced crystallized ginger. This contrast of hot and sweet is fun, but not for everybody.

FROM LEFT TO RIGHT:
Gelato Straciatella (page 246),
Chocolate Fudge Swirl Ice Cream
(page 252), Roman Chocolate
Gelato (page 245)

CHOCOLATE FUDGE SWIRL ICE CREAM

. . .

Makes about 1½ quarts ice cream

FUDGE MIXTURE

½ cup heavy whipping cream

½ cup light corn syrup

⅔ cup sugar

Pinch salt

2 ounces unsweetened chocolate, coarsely chopped

¼ cup alkalized (Dutch process) cocoa powder

1 teaspoon vanilla extract

1 batch French Chocolate Ice Cream, page 248

Use this as a master recipe to add a rich fudge swirl to any of the ice creams in this chapter.

1. Combine cream, corn syrup, and sugar in a non-reactive pan and bring to a boil, stirring often, until all the sugar crystals have melted.

2. Remove from heat and add the salt and the chocolate. Allow to stand 2 minutes, then whisk smooth.

3. Sift the cocoa into a mixing bowl and stir in enough of the chocolate syrup to make a paste. Stir the cocoa paste into the syrup mixture and keep stirring until smooth.

4. Whisk in the vanilla and cool to room temperature. Scrape the fudge mixture into a bowl and chill.

5. Spoon a thin layer of the ice cream into the bottom of the container, then drizzle in some of the fudge mixture. Continue alternating layers of the fudge mixture and the ice cream, ending with a layer of ice cream. Cover and store in the freezer.

VARIATION

VANILLA FUDGE ICE CREAM Substitute French Vanilla Ice Cream, page 248, for the chocolate ice cream above. The vanilla gelato mixture for straciatella without the added chocolate flakes, page 246, also makes a great base for Vanilla Fudge Ice Cream.

OLD-FASHIONED ICE CREAM SPECIALTIES

When I was in high school a typical after-school diversion was to congregate with friends from other schools at a local soda fountain called Gruning's. There were several branches in suburban Essex County, New Jersey, the main store being in South Orange Village. Gruning's was famous for its homemade ice cream as well as a line of hand-dipped chocolates—strictly American specialties such as fudge and buttercrunch.

Gruning's triumphs were its ice cream specialties. Throughout my high school years, until Gruning's and all its branches disappeared in the eighties, I was addicted to a sundae they made called a Dusty Road—vanilla ice cream drizzled with chocolate sauce and malted milk powder. If the fountain man was in a good mood, you could persuade him to use hot fudge sauce instead of plain chocolate syrup. This gave the sundae a whole new gooey dimension!

It can be fun to organize a casual ice cream sundae party. You'll need several flavors of ice cream, homemade or premium commercial, and some of the following fixings: whipped cream (page 56), hot fudge sauce (page 369), chocolate syrup (page 372), bananas, malt powder, nuts, and if you really want to be authentic, maraschino cherries.

The following are descriptions of some popular fountain combinations:

Hot Fudge Sundae: Pour a spoonful of hot fudge sauce into a deep, chilled stemmed glass. Alternate scoops of your favorite flavor ice cream with more sauce, ending with sauce. Top with whipped cream and a cherry.

Black and White Sundae: In a deep stemmed glass, alternate scoops of chocolate and vanilla ice cream with spoonfuls of chocolate syrup, ending with syrup. Top with whipped cream and a cherry.

Chocolate Banana Split: Peel and halve a banana lengthwise and place it in the bottom of an oval banana split dish. Drizzle with chocolate syrup and top with three scoops of ice cream, the same or different flavors. Drizzle with more chocolate syrup and top each scoop of ice cream with whipped cream and a cherry.

Dusty Road: In a deep stemmed glass, alternate scoops of chocolate or vanilla ice cream with spoonfuls of chocolate syrup or hot fudge sauce, sprinkling each layer with about a teaspoonful of malt powder. End with syrup or sauce and a generous tablespoon of the powder.

FROZEN CHOCOLATE MOUSSE

■ ■ ■

Makes about 1½ quarts mousse

2 cups heavy whipping cream

6 ounces bittersweet chocolate

6 ounces unsweetened chocolate

8 tablespoons (1 stick) unsalted butter

⅔ cup egg whites (from about 5 large eggs)

1½ cups sugar

Cocoa powder or chocolate shavings, page 392, for finishing

One 9-inch springform pan or other stainless steel mold

This is the richest and easiest to make of delicious frozen chocolate desserts. It rivals the best chocolate ice cream.

1. Place the 9-inch springform pan or other stainless steel mold in the freezer. Whip cream to a soft peak and refrigerate until needed.

2. Melt both chocolates over hot water, remove from heat and work in butter; set aside.

3. Combine egg whites and sugar in bowl of electric mixer, and place over pan of simmering water. Whisk gently until egg whites are hot and sugar is dissolved. Use an electric mixer with a whip to beat until cooled and increased in volume.

4. Quickly fold together chocolate mixture and meringue. Taste a spoonful to make sure the mixture is not any warmer than room temperature. If it is, let it cool for a few more minutes before folding in the whipped cream or the cream will melt and separate.

5. Scrape into frozen springform pan or mold and smooth the top with an offset metal spatula. Cover tightly with plastic wrap. Freeze overnight before serving.

6. To unmold, have a chilled platter ready. Dip a small, thin knife in hot water and run it around the inside of the pan to loosen dessert. Unbuckle side of springform and remove. Cover dessert with the chilled platter, invert, then lift off pan bottom. Dust very lightly with cocoa immediately before serving or stick chocolate shavings all over top and sides of mousse. Return to freezer until time to serve.

SERVING: This is great with a rich chocolate sauce or some crushed, sweetened berries.

VARIATION

FROZEN CHOCOLATE CHARLOTTE Line the sides and bottom of a springform pan with ladyfingers (see Golden Chocolate Charlotte, page 116, for the ladyfinger recipe). Pour in the chocolate mixture and freeze as above. To finish the charlotte, top with milk chocolate shavings, page 392, then remove the side of the springform and slide the dessert from the springform base to a platter, using a wide metal spatula. This can also be made in a classic charlotte shape, by using a charlotte mold instead of the springform pan and molding the charlotte according to the instructions on page 116.

FROZEN DEVIL'S FOOD CAKE Bake and cool a Vermont Farmhouse Devil's Food Cake, page 52. Slice the cake into three horizontal layers, each about ½ inch thick. Trim each to 9 inches using the *outside* of a 9-inch springform pan, so that the layer will fit tightly in the pan. Place a layer in the bottom of the 9-inch springform pan and cover with half the chocolate mixture. Cover with another layer and the remaining mousse. Top with the last layer. Wrap and freeze as above. Next day, or when you intend to serve the cake, unmold and mask the outside with sweetened whipped cream. Press milk or mixed milk and white chocolate shavings into the whipped cream. Return the cake to the freezer. About an hour before serving, place cake in refrigerator to soften slightly.

FROZEN CHOCOLATE TERRINE

■　■　■

About 1½ quarts mousse,
about 8 to 10 servings

9 ounces bittersweet chocolate, cut
　　into ¼-inch pieces

1½ cups heavy whipping cream

¾ cup milk

¾ cup sugar

5 large egg yolks

One 6-cup Pyrex loaf pan, buttered
　　and lined with plastic wrap

Make sure you use the best chocolate you can find—there is no flavor but chocolate in this easy but spectacular recipe.

1. Place the mold in the freezer before beginning to prepare the mousse.

2. Bring a pan of water to a boil and remove from heat. Place the chocolate in a heatproof bowl and place over the hot water. Stir occasionally until the chocolate has melted. Remove chocolate bowl from pan and cool slightly.

3. Use an electric mixer to whip the cream on medium speed until it forms soft peaks. Refrigerate.

4. Return the pan of water to a boil. Pour milk and sugar in bowl of electric mixer, then whisk in yolks. Place over simmering water and whisk constantly until thickened, about 3 or 4 minutes. Use electric mixer with whisk to beat until cooled to room temperature.

5. Remove cream from refrigerator and rewhip by hand if it has separated slightly. Quickly whisk the chocolate into the egg yolk and milk mixture and check that is no warmer than room temperature—if it is, let it cool for a few minutes before folding in the cream, or the cream will melt and separate on contact with the warm chocolate mixture. Quickly scrape the mousse into the prepared pan and smooth the top. Cover with plastic wrap pressed directly against the surface. Freeze the mousse for at least 8 hours or overnight.

6. To unmold the mousse, have a chilled platter ready. Dip the pan into a bowl of warm water and remove the plastic wrap covering the top. Cover the mold with the chilled platter, invert and lift off the mold—you may need to pull on the plastic wrap between the mousse and the mold to do this. The mold will come away as soon as the butter keeping the plastic wrap in place has softened or melted. If you are not going to serve the mousse right away, leave covered loosely with plastic wrap and return to the freezer.

SERVING: Serve the mousse in ¾-inch slices with a few berries or some Chocolate Sauce, page 371.

STORAGE: Wrap and freeze any leftover mousse. If you prepare the mousse in advance, double-wrap the mold in plastic wrap after the mousse has frozen—you may keep it in the freezer for up to a month before serving.

VARIATIONS

FROZEN WHITE CHOCOLATE TERRINE Reduce the sugar to ½ cup and use 10 ounces best-quality white chocolate, not chips.

FROZEN MILK CHOCOLATE TERRINE Follow instructions for Frozen White Chocolate Terrine above, but substitute milk chocolate.

LAYERED MILK CHOCOLATE AND WHITE CHOCOLATE TERRINE Prepare both mixtures and two 6-cup Pyrex molds. Pour a quarter of each mixture into each mold and freeze 15 minutes. Keep the rest of each mixture at a cool room temperature. Continue alternating the mousses in the molds, making four layers in each, and freezing each layer for 15 minutes. Unmold and serve as above.

FROZEN CASSATA

• • •

Makes about 1½ quarts frozen dessert

One 15-ounce container whole milk
　　ricotta

2 tablespoons white rum

1 cup heavy whipping cream

4 large egg whites (½ cup)

1 cup sugar

4 ounces semisweet eating or
　　couverture chocolate, cut into
　　¼-inch pieces, and little dusty
　　bits sifted away

½ cup finely diced candied orange
　　peel

½ cup blanched pistachios, see page
　　13, coarsely chopped and dusty
　　pieces sifted away

One 6-cup Pyrex loaf pan buttered
　　and lined with plastic wrap

A cassata is a classic Sicilian Easter dessert. This frozen version uses a ricotta mixture sweetened with a meringue and garnished with the classic chocolate, candied orange peel, and pistachios.

1. Place the mold in the freezer before starting.

2. Place ricotta and rum in a food processor fitted with the metal blade and process until smooth, about 30 seconds. Scrape into a mixing bowl.

3. Whip the cream until it holds a soft peak and refrigerate.

4. Combine egg whites and sugar in the bowl of an electric mixer and place over a pan of simmering water. Whisk constantly until egg whites are hot and sugar is dissolved, about 4 minutes. Remove bowl from water. Use an electric mixer fitted with a whip to beat until cooled and risen in volume, about 5 minutes.

5. Remove bowl of meringue from mixer and fold in ricotta mixture and chocolate pieces, candied peel, and pistachios. Remove whipped cream from refrigerator and rewhip if necessary. Fold into ricotta mixture.

6. Pour into the prepared mold and cover tightly with plastic wrap. Freeze overnight.

7. To unmold the cassata, have a chilled platter ready. Dip the pan in a bowl of warm water and remove the plastic wrap covering it. Cover the mold with chilled platter, invert, and lift off the mold. You may have to pull on the plastic wrap between the mousse and the mold to do this. The mold will come away as soon as the butter keeping the plastic wrap in place has softened or melted. If you are not going to serve the cassata right away, leave it covered loosely with plastic wrap and return to the freezer.

SERVING: Serve the cassata in ¾-inch slices with Chocolate Sauce, page 371.

STORAGE: Wrap and freeze any leftovers. To prepare the cassata in advance, double-wrap the mold in plastic wrap after it has frozen—you may keep it in the freezer for up to a month before serving.

SEMIFREDDO ALLA GIANDUJA

■ ■ ■

Makes about 1½ quarts frozen dessert,
8 to 10 servings

1 cup heavy whipping cream

1 cup hazelnuts, toasted, skinned,
and kept warm

2 tablespoons (¼ stick) unsalted
butter

8 ounces semisweet eating or
couverture chocolate, melted and
slightly cooled

4 large egg whites (½ cup)

¾ cup sugar

One 6-cup loaf pan, buttered and
lined with plastic wrap

Gianduja is a heavenly mixture of chocolate and hazelnuts. Here the two combine to flavor a smooth, velvety, and delicate-tasting frozen dessert.

1. Whip the cream until it holds soft peaks and set aside in the refrigerator.

2. Combine the warm hazelnuts (reheat them in the oven at 325 degrees for 5 minutes, if necessary) and butter in the bowl of a food processor. Pulse to grind, then run continuously about 2 to 3 minutes to make a paste. Scrape the hazelnut mixture into the chocolate, but do not mix them or the chocolate may begin to harden. Set aside.

3. Combine the egg whites and sugar in the bowl of an electric mixer and place over a pan of simmering water. Whisk constantly until egg whites are hot and sugar is dissolved, about 3 minutes. Use electric mixer to whip until cooled.

4. When the meringue is cool, fold the chocolate and hazelnut mixture into it, then fold that back into the whipped cream. Quickly scrape the mixture into the prepared pan and smooth the top. Cover with plastic wrap pressed directly against the surface. Freeze for at least 8 hours or overnight.

5. To unmold, have a chilled platter ready. Dip the pan in a bowl of warm water and remove the plastic wrap covering the semifreddo. Cover the mold with the chilled platter, invert, and lift off. You may need to pull on the plastic wrap between the dessert and the mold to free the mold. It will come away as soon as the butter keeping the plastic wrap in place has softened or melted. If you are not going to serve the dessert right away, cover loosely with the plastic wrap and return to the freezer.

SERVING: Serve the semifreddo in ¾-inch slices with some Chocolate Sauce, page 371.

STORAGE: Wrap and freeze any leftover semifreddo. If you want to prepare the dessert in advance, double-wrap the mold in plastic wrap after it has frozen—you may keep it in the freezer for up to a month.

FROZEN CHOCOLATE BOURBON SOUFFLÉ

∎ ∎ ∎

Makes one 1½-quart soufflé dish,
about 10 servings

2 cups heavy whipping cream,
   divided

¼ cup best bourbon, such as
   Jack Daniel's

12 ounces finest-quality bittersweet
   chocolate, melted

2 large eggs

4 large egg yolks

⅓ cup sugar

Cocoa powder for finishing

One 6-cup soufflé dish

This light mousselike mixture makes a wonderful frozen soufflé. If you don't feel like doing up a mold with a collar to present this as a frozen soufflé, freeze the mixture in a bowl or plastic container and serve it in scoops as you would ice cream—though it is both richer and lighter.

1. Cut a piece of aluminum foil long enough to go around the dish with a little overlap. Fold the foil in half the long way and wrap it around the dish to form a collar that extends about 4 inches above the rim. Tie or tape foil in place.

2. Set the prepared mold in the freezer while preparing the dessert. Whip 1½ cups of the cream until it holds a soft peak and refrigerate.

3. Bring the remaining ½ cup of cream to a simmer in a small saucepan over low heat. Whisk the cream, then the bourbon, into the chocolate. Set aside to cool.

4. Whisk the eggs, egg yolks, and sugar together in a heatproof bowl or the bowl of an electric mixer. Place over a small pan of simmering water and whisk constantly until the eggs are hot, increased in volume, and thickened. Use an electric mixer to whip until cooled to room temperature.

5. Fold the chocolate mixture into the egg mixture, then fold in the whipped cream.

6. Pour into the prepared dish and place in freezer. Cover with plastic wrap after the outside has frozen, about 2 hours after it is placed in freezer. Freeze overnight or for up to several weeks.

7. To serve, unwrap the dessert and remove the collar. Wipe the outside of the dish clean with a damp cloth if necessary and use a metal spatula to straighten the sides and top of the dessert. Return to freezer until serving time. Immediately before serving, dust top lightly with cocoa powder.

SERVING: Use two spoons to serve pieces of the frozen soufflé—don't try to cut it into wedges.

VARIATIONS

FROZEN CHOCOLATE CHIP SOUFFLÉ Use a small paring knife to cut 4 ounces of best-quality semisweet or bittersweet eating chocolate into ⅛-inch chunks. Or break the chocolate into 1-inch pieces and pulse it briefly in the food processor to chop. Fold the chocolate into the soufflé mixture along with the whipped cream.

FROZEN CHOCOLATE RUM SOUFFLÉ Substitute dark rum for the bourbon. Cognac or any other strong, nonsweetened spirits may also be substituted.

WHITE CHOCOLATE AND LIME FROZEN SOUFFLÉ Substitute white chocolate for the dark chocolate and white rum for the bourbon in the basic recipe. Reduce sugar to ¼ cup. Add 2 tablespoons lime juice to the egg mixture before heating it.

DOUGHS FOR PIES, TARTS, AND PASTRIES

• • •

Cocoa Cookie Dough for Tartlets
and Small Pastries

Vanilla Cookie Dough

Dark Sweet Chocolate Dough

Plain Sweet Dough

Flaky Chocolate Dough

Quickest Chocolate Puff Pastry

ROLLING DOUGHS AND FORMING PIE AND TART CRUSTS

• • •

BAKING AN EMPTY PIE OR TART CRUST

• • •

FORMING TARTLET CRUSTS

• • •

Chocolate Pecan Pie

Chocolate Custard Pie

Chocolate Banana Custard Pie

Old-fashioned Chocolate Cream Pie
(*Chocolate Meringue Pie*)

White Chocolate Coconut Cream Pie
with Chocolate Cookie Crust

Black Bottom Pie

Chocolate Ricotta Tart

Chocolate Banana Cream Tart

White Chocolate Strawberry Tart

Spicy Chocolate Tart

Chocolate Brownie Tart

Chocolate Apricot Tart

Chocolate Coconut Tart

Chocolate Velvet Tart

Chocolate Orange Cheese Tart

Chocolate Almond Tartlets

Tarteletas de Dulce
de Leche y Chocolate
(*Tartlets with Caramelized Milk
and Chocolate Filling*)

Chocolate Banana Tartlets

Chocolate Raspberry Tartlets

Pear and Chocolate Tartlets

Chocolate Cheese Tartlets

Chocolate Caramel Pecan Tartlets

Chocolate Palmiers

Chocolate Pistachio Mille Feuilles

Chocolate Pecan Straws

Cream Puff Truffles

*Profiteroles with Ice Cream
and Chocolate Sauce*

Chocolate Éclairs

Pâte à Choux
(*Cream Puff Pastry*)

Chocolate Paris-Brest

All the recipes in this chapter use pastry doughs. Don't let that stop you from trying them. Although preparing and using pastry doughs requires a certain degree of care—butter must be kept cold, mixing must be quick and deft—most of the doughs here can be prepared in the food processor.

Pies are desserts with a pastry crust baked in and served from sloping-sided pans. My preference for pie-baking is a 9-inch diameter Pyrex pie pan—they are available everywhere and give excellent results. Best of all, you can always tell when the bottom crust of your pie is baked.

Tarts are straight-sided desserts with a pastry crust usually baked in fluted metal molds with removable bottoms. All the recipes in this chapter may be baked in either a 9- or 10-inch diameter tart pan.

Tartlets are small versions of tarts. All the ones in this chapter use 2-inch diameter pans, which are relatively easy to find in kitchenware stores. I like to use rich fillings in tiny tartlets—fillings that might be too rich in a larger pie or tart but are sumptuous in only a bite or two.

Puff pastry, which is used in some of these recipes, is a multilayered dough. The puff pastry recipe here is for a chocolate version of the dough.

It is not to be confused with cream puff pastry (pâte à choux) also discussed in this chapter. The pastries made with this piped rather than rolled dough are delicate, versatile, and above all, easy to prepare.

DOUGHS FOR PIES, TARTS, AND PASTRIES

. . .

The emphasis in many of the recipes that follow is mainly on rich, smooth chocolaty fillings, but the doughs that form shells for these fillings are certainly important. The doughs considered here are standard recipes, except for the fact that they are—unusually—all chocolate. These recipes include a tender cookie dough, a dark chocolate sweet dough, a flaky chocolate dough, and one of my current favorites, a very quick chocolate puff pastry.

COCOA COOKIE DOUGH
FOR TARTLETS
AND SMALL PASTRIES

. . .

Makes enough to line about
24 small tartlet shells

12 tablespoons (1½ sticks) unsalted
   butter, softened

¾ cup confectioners' sugar

¼ teaspoon salt

2 large egg yolks

1½ cups all-purpose flour

⅓ cup alkalized (Dutch process)
   cocoa powder, sifted after
   measuring

1. Use an electric mixer to beat the butter, confectioners' sugar, and salt until mixed and somewhat lightened, about 2 minutes. Beat in yolks, one at a time, beating smooth after each addition.

2. Remove bowl from mixer and add flour and cocoa. Use a rubber spatula to stir the dry ingredients into the butter mixture. This will form a very soft dough.

3. Scrape the dough from the bowl and spread it in a rough rectangle on a piece of plastic wrap. Wrap and chill the dough until it is firm or for up to several days before using.

NOTE: If the butter is very soft, it is also possible to mix the dough by hand, beating it in with a rubber spatula in a mixing bowl.

VARIATION

VANILLA COOKIE DOUGH Substitute ½ cup extra flour for the cocoa powder. Add ½ teaspoon vanilla extract to the dough along with the egg yolks.

DARK SWEET
CHOCOLATE DOUGH
■ ■ ■

This recipe makes the right amount
of dough for any one-crust 9-inch pie
or tart in this chapter

1 cup all-purpose flour

3 tablespoons sugar

3 tablespoons alkalized (Dutch
   process) cocoa powder, sifted
   after measuring

⅛ teaspoon salt

¼ teaspoon baking powder

5 tablespoons cold unsalted butter,
   cut into 10 pieces

1 large egg

1. To mix the dough in the food processor, combine
the flour, sugar, cocoa, salt, and baking powder in
work bowl and pulse several times to mix.

2. Add butter to work bowl. Pulse to mix butter in
completely. When the butter is incorporated correctly
there should be no visible chunks of butter, but the
mixture should remain cool and powdery.

3. Beat egg with a fork and add to work bowl. Pulse
until dough forms a ball. If the dough does not easily
form a ball, add ½ teaspoon water, repeating if necessary, until it does.

4. Remove dough from processor, press into a disk,
and wrap in plastic. Chill dough until firm or for up
to several days before using.

5. To mix dough by hand, combine dry ingredients
in a mixing bowl and stir several times to mix. Rub
butter in, mixing it gently with fingertips, until it becomes a fine crumble. No
visible pieces of butter should remain, but mixture should stay cool and
powdery. Beat egg with a fork and stir into dough mixture. Continue stirring
until dough holds together in a mass. Wrap and chill as above.

6. To mix dough in a heavy-duty mixer, combine dry ingredients in mixer
bowl with paddle attachment. Beat on lowest speed until combined. Add
butter. Beat on low speed until butter is absorbed but mixture is still powdery,
about 1 minute. Beat egg in a small bowl and add to mixer bowl. Beat on low
speed until dough masses around paddle, about 30 seconds. Wrap and chill as
above.

VARIATION

PLAIN SWEET DOUGH   Substitute 1¼ cups flour for the flour and cocoa.
Proceed with recipe in the same manner.

FLAKY CHOCOLATE DOUGH

. . .

Makes a little less than 2 pounds dough

3 cups all-purpose flour

⅓ cup sugar

½ cup alkalized (Dutch process) cocoa powder, sifted after measuring

½ teaspoon salt

½ teaspoon baking powder

1½ cups (3 sticks) cold unsalted butter

6 tablespoons cold water

This is baked mostly as a thin sheet—see the recipes that use it on page 296. It is too fragile to form into a pie or tart shell.

1. To mix the dough in the food processor, combine the flour, sugar, cocoa, salt, and baking powder in work bowl and pulse several times to mix.

2. Divide each stick of butter into 5 pieces and add to work bowl. Pulse to mix butter in coarsely—in this dough there should be visible chunks of butter up to ¼ inch across throughout.

3. Add water to work bowl. Pulse until dough forms a ball.

4. Remove dough from processor, press into a disk, and wrap in plastic. Chill dough until firm or for up to several days before using.

5. To mix dough by hand, combine dry ingredients in a mixing bowl and stir several times to mix. Cut butter into 10 pieces and rub butter in, mixing it in gently with fingertips until it resembles a coarse meal. There should be visible chunks of butter up to ¼ inch across throughout. Stir in water with a fork and continue stirring until dough holds together. Wrap and chill as above.

6. To mix dough in a heavy-duty mixer, combine dry ingredients in the bowl of a mixer with paddle attachment. Mix on lowest speed until combined. Cut butter into pieces and add to mixer. Mix on low speed to mix butter in until it resembles a coarse meal. There should be visible chunks of butter up to ¼ inch across throughout. Add water to mixer bowl. Mix on low speed until dough masses around paddle, about 30 seconds. Wrap and chill as above.

QUICKEST CHOCOLATE
PUFF PASTRY

. . .

Makes about 24 ounces dough,
enough for the recipes on pages 295
and 298, which use this dough

1¾ cups all-purpose flour

3 ounces bittersweet chocolate, cut
  into ¼-inch pieces

2 tablespoons alkalized (Dutch
  process) cocoa powder, sifted
  after measuring

1 teaspoon salt

16 tablespoons (2 sticks) cold
  unsalted butter

½ cup cold water

This is a chocolate version of the quickest puff pastry that appears in my last book, *How to Bake*. To prepare this dough successfully you must use a food processor.

1. Combine flour, chocolate, cocoa, and salt in food processor and pulse repeatedly until mixture is reduced to a fine powder.

2. Cut butter into small cubes (cut each stick in half along the length, then across into cubes) and add to processor. Pulse twice.

3. Add water all at once and continue to pulse until dough forms a rough ball.

4. Scrape dough from work bowl onto a floured surface and pat into a rectangle, then roll the dough into a 10 × 15-inch rectangle.

5. Brush excess flour off dough. Fold the top third of the dough down over the center third and the bottom third up over them as you would a business letter. Starting from one of the short sides, roll the dough up into a fat cylinder. Press the top of the dough to flatten it into a square. Wrap well in plastic and refrigerate several hours before using.

PIES

ROLLING DOUGHS AND FORMING PIE AND TART CRUSTS
• • •

Place the dough on a floured surface and flour the dough. Press the dough with a rolling pin to soften it and make it thinner. Roll the dough, being careful not to roll over the ends in the same direction you are rolling (this makes the edges of the dough thinner and likely to stick). While you are rolling, move the dough frequently and add pinches of flour under and on the dough to prevent the bottom of the dough from sticking to the work surface and to prevent the rolling pin from sticking to the dough. When the dough is large enough (place the pie or tart pan on it to compare the size—the dough should be a few inches larger in diameter), fold it in half and transfer it to the pan, lining up the fold with the diameter of the pan.

For a pie crust, place the dough in a 9-inch Pyrex pie pan and unfold the dough to fill the pan. Press the dough well into the bottom and sides of the pan and trim away all but ½ inch of the excess dough at the edge of the pan. Fold the excess dough under, making the edge even with the rim of the pan. Flute the edge of the pie by pinching the dough from the outside with the thumb and index finger of the left hand and pushing the dough into the pinch from the inside with the index finger of the right hand. Chill the crust until you are ready to use it.

For a tart crust, place the dough in a 9- or 10-inch tart pan with fluted sides and removable bottom. Unfold the dough into the pan and press and fit the dough well into the bottom and sides of the pan. Let the excess dough hang over the top edge of the pan and roll over the pan with the rolling pin to sever the excess dough. Using the thumb and index finger of your right hand, press down with your index finger and in with your thumb at the top edge of the crust to make the edge straight and even. Chill the crust until you are ready to use it.

BAKING AN EMPTY PIE OR TART CRUST

. . .

To bake the crust before using it for a pie or tart, cut a disk of parchment or wax paper large enough to line bottom and side of the crust. Fill the crust with dried beans and bake the pie or tart crust on the middle rack of a preheated 350 degree oven for about 20 minutes, or until the dough is set and dull-looking. Remove paper and beans and return crust to oven if necessary to finish baking, up to about 10 or 15 minutes longer or until it is firm. Cool the baked crust in its pan on a rack before filling it.

FORMING TARTLET CRUSTS

. . .

Divide the dough into several small pieces and roll one at a time, keeping the remaining dough refrigerated. Use a plain or fluted cutter a little larger than the diameter of the tartlet pans to cut the dough, placing the disks of dough into the buttered tart pans as they are cut. Failing tiny tart pans, you may use mini-muffin pans to form tartlet shells. Press the dough firmly into the bottom and side of each little pan and arrange the lined pans on a jelly-roll pan. Chill until ready to use.

To bake the tartlet crusts in advance, fill them with dried beans and bake them on the middle rack of a preheated 350 degree oven for about 12 to 15 minutes. Cool the crusts for a few minutes, then invert the pans, beans, crust, and all. Later, after the crusts have cooled, you'll find that most of the beans have already fallen out and it is easy to remove the remaining beans. Line the baked, cooled crusts up on a jelly-roll pan and cover them loosely until time to fill them.

CHOCOLATE PECAN PIE

■ ■ ■

FILLING

1 cup dark corn syrup

⅓ cup sugar

4 ounces bittersweet chocolate, cut into ¼-inch pieces

4 tablespoons (½ stick) unsalted butter

3 large eggs

Pinch salt

2 tablespoons dark rum, optional

2½ cups pecan pieces, coarsely chopped

One 9-inch pie crust made from Dark Sweet Chocolate Dough, page 266, or Plain Sweet Dough, page 267, unbaked

The only thing better than pecan pie is chocolate pecan pie. This recipe works equally well with walnuts—but be sure to add the rum if you use them instead.

1. When ready to bake the pie, set a rack in the lower third of the oven and preheat to 350 degrees.

2. Combine corn syrup and sugar in a saucepan. Stir to mix. Bring to a boil over medium heat and remove. Stir in chocolate and butter and allow to melt. Whisk smooth. Whisk eggs with salt and rum, if desired, in a large bowl. Beat in chocolate/corn syrup mixture. Stir in pecans.

3. Pour filling into pastry-lined pan. Bake pie about 45 minutes, until set and somewhat puffed. Cool on a rack and serve at room temperature.

SERVING: Serve the pie with whipped cream or ice cream.

STORAGE: Keep loosely covered at room temperature up to several days.

CHOCOLATE
CUSTARD PIE

. . .

Makes one 9-inch pie, about 8 servings

CHOCOLATE CUSTARD

2½ cups half and half (or 1¼ cups
   each milk and cream)

⅓ cup sugar

5 ounces bittersweet chocolate, cut
   into ¼-inch pieces

4 large eggs

1 tablespoon dark rum

¼ teaspoon ground cinnamon

⅛ teaspoon ground cloves

One 9-inch pie crust made from
   Plain Sweet Dough, page 267,
   unbaked

This is an old-fashioned custard pie: a pie shell filled with a rich, creamy, just-set custard. I like this best with a plain crust because to my taste it frames the chocolate filling better than a chocolate one.

1. When ready to bake the pie, set a rack in the lower third of the oven and preheat to 350 degrees.

2. To make the filling, combine the half and half and the sugar in a saucepan. Whisk once or twice to mix and bring to a boil over medium heat. Remove from heat and whisk chocolate in smoothly. Continue to whisk until chocolate is melted.

3. In a large mixing bowl, whisk the eggs with the rum and spices. Whisk in the chocolate mixture. Whisk only until mixed. You want to avoid making a lot of foam on the custard.

4. Strain the custard into another bowl and skim any remaining foam off the surface. Pour the custard into the pie shell and bake the pie for about 45 minutes, or until all but the very center of the filling is set. Cool the pie on a rack.

SERVING: Serve with whipped cream or plain.

STORAGE: Keep the pie at a cool room temperature until it is served, then cover and refrigerate leftovers.

VARIATION

CHOCOLATE BANANA CUSTARD PIE Make sure your bananas are ripe and dotted with brown sugar spots. Reduce cream to 2 cups. Slice 2 or 3 large bananas into the pie shell before pouring in the custard cream. After baking, cool and chill pie and top with sweetened whipped cream and chocolate shavings.

OLD-FASHIONED CHOCOLATE CREAM PIE

Chocolate Meringue Pie

■ ■ ■

Makes one 9-inch pie, about 8 servings

CHOCOLATE FILLING

⅓ cup sugar

3 tablespoons cornstarch

2 cups milk

3 large eggs

6 ounces bittersweet chocolate, cut into ¼-inch pieces

2 teaspoons vanilla extract

One 9-inch pie crust made from Dark Sweet Chocolate Dough, page 266, baked

MERINGUE

4 large egg whites

⅔ cup sugar

Pinch salt

This is a classic, though no one seems to agree whether it should be covered with whipped cream or meringue. I like the idea of the meringue for this rich pie, but there are instructions for using whipped cream following the recipe if you prefer that topping.

1. To make the filling, mix the sugar and cornstarch in a heavy, nonreactive saucepan. Mix in the milk and place over low heat, stirring constantly with a wooden spoon until the custard thickens and comes to a boil. Remove pan from heat.

2. Whisk the eggs together in a small bowl, then whisk in about a third of the hot custard mixture. Whisk the egg mixture back into the hot custard mixture and return to a boil, stirring constantly. Remove from heat again, stir in the chocolate and vanilla until chocolate is melted and mixture is smooth. Scrape the cream into a bowl, press plastic wrap against the surface, and chill until it is cold or you are ready to assemble the pie.

3. When ready to assemble the pie, set a rack at the middle level of the oven and preheat to 400 degrees. Spread the cooled filling in the cooled pie shell.

4. To make the meringue, bring a small pan of water to a boil. Lower heat so the water simmers. Combine egg whites, sugar, and salt in a heatproof bowl. Place bowl over pan of simmering water and whisk gently for about 2 minutes, until egg whites are hot (about 140 degrees) and sugar has dissolved. Remove bowl from pan.

5. Whip meringue on medium speed until it has cooled and is able to hold a shape. But it should not be dry. Distribute spoonfuls of the meringue all over the top of the pie, then use the back of a spoon or a small offset metal spatula to spread the meringue evenly. It should cover the top of the pie and touch the edges of the crust all around. Here and there, bring up the surface of the meringue so that it has swirled peaks. Place the pie on a cookie sheet and bake for about 5 to 10 minutes, until the meringue is colored evenly. Cool on a rack.

SERVING: Serve in wedges; it needs no accompaniment.

STORAGE: Keep the pie at a cool room temperature until serving time—it tastes best if it is served after it has cooled on the day it is baked. Cover and refrigerate leftovers.

VARIATION

To top the pie with whipped cream instead of meringue, omit meringue. The pie won't need the second baking. Either top with sweetened whipped cream, page 56, or serve it alongside the pie. Sprinkle the whipped cream with chocolate shavings, page 392.

WHITE CHOCOLATE COCONUT CREAM PIE WITH CHOCOLATE COOKIE CRUST

■ ■ ■

Makes one 9-inch pie, about 8 servings

CHOCOLATE COOKIE CRUST

1 cup chocolate wafer crumbs, commercial or homemade

¼ cup sugar

½ cup finely ground almonds or pecans

8 tablespoons (1 stick) unsalted butter, melted

WHITE CHOCOLATE COCONUT FILLING

¼ cup sugar

¼ cup cornstarch

2 cups milk

3 large eggs

8 ounces white chocolate

1 teaspoon vanilla extract

2 cups heavy whipping cream

2 cups (about one 7-ounce bag) lightly toasted sweetened coconut, divided

One 9-inch Pyrex pie plate

CHOCOLATE

The best cookies for this crust are the Crisp Chocolate Wafers on page 177. To use them, just break up 12 to 16 cookies and pulse them in the food processor to make about 1 cup crumbs.

I. For the crust, set a rack at the middle level of the oven and preheat to 350 degrees.

2. In a mixing bowl, combine the cookie crumbs, sugar, and ground nuts. Mix well with a fork. Pour the melted butter evenly over the crumb mixture, then toss and stir with the fork. Scrape the crust mixture into the pie pan.

3. Use your fingertips to evenly distribute the crumb mixture all over the pie pan. Try to avoid thick or thin areas. Use the back of a spoon to smooth the surface if it is uneven. Scatter a few of the crumbs on the rim of the pan, but don't bother to try to make an even rim—it will only break apart when you are cutting the pie.

4. Bake the pie shell about 20 minutes, until it appears to be dry and not shiny. Cool on a rack.

5. To make the filling, mix the sugar and cornstarch in a heavy, nonreactive saucepan. Mix in the milk and place over low heat, stirring constantly with a wooden spoon until the mixture thickens and comes to a boil. Remove from heat. Whisk the eggs together in a small bowl, then whisk in about a third of the hot custard mixture. Whisk the egg mixture back into the hot custard mixture and return to a boil, stirring constantly. Off heat, stir in the white chocolate and vanilla and continue stirring until chocolate is melted. Scrape the custard into a bowl, press plastic wrap against the surface, and chill until it is cold or you are ready to assemble the pie.

6. To assemble the pie, whip the cream until it holds a firm peak. Remove the white chocolate filling from the refrigerator and fold in half the whipped cream and half the coconut. Scrape the filling into the cooled pie crust and smooth the top.

7. To finish the pie, spread the remaining whipped cream over the filling and sprinkle with the remaining coconut.

SERVING: Serve in wedges; it needs no accompaniment.

STORAGE: Keep the pie refrigerated until serving time—it tastes best if it is served on the day it is baked. Cover and refrigerate leftovers.

VARIATIONS

Substitute semisweet or milk chocolate for the white chocolate.

BLACK BOTTOM PIE

• • •

Makes one 9-inch pie, about 8 servings

CHOCOLATE AND VANILLA FILLINGS

½ cup sugar

⅓ cup cornstarch

3 cups milk

3 large eggs

6 ounces bittersweet chocolate, cut
    into ¼-inch pieces

2 teaspoons vanilla extract

One 9-inch pie crust made from
    Dark Sweet Chocolate Dough,
    page 266, baked

1 tablespoon dark rum, optional

¾ cup heavy whipping cream

FINISHING

Chocolate shavings, page 392

This is a combination of recipes given to me by several friends, among them Miriam Brickman and Allen Smith. The whole point of the pie, as far as I can determine, is to contrast chocolate and vanilla in one shell. I have substituted a chocolate pastry dough shell for the typical one made from chocolate cookie crumbs.

I. To make the fillings, mix the sugar and cornstarch in a heavy, nonreactive saucepan. Add the milk and place over low heat, stirring constantly with a wooden spoon until the mixture thickens and comes to a boil. Remove from heat. Whisk the eggs together in a small bowl, then whisk in about a third of the hot custard mixture. Whisk the egg mixture back into the hot custard mixture and return to a boil, stirring constantly.

2. Divide the cream evenly between two bowls. Stir the chocolate into one of the bowls and keep stirring until it melts. Stir the vanilla into the other bowl. Press plastic wrap against the surface of both creams and refrigerate them until they are cold or you are ready to assemble the pie.

3. When ready to assemble the pie, spread the cooled chocolate filling in the cooled pie shell.

4. Whip the cream and fold it along with the optional rum into the vanilla cream. Spread it over the chocolate filling in the pie shell and top with the chocolate shavings.

SERVING: Serve in wedges; it needs no accompaniment.

STORAGE: Keep the pie refrigerated until serving time—it tastes best if it is served on the day it is baked. Cover and refrigerate leftovers.

CHOCOLATE RICOTTA TART

■ ■ ■

Makes 10 to 12 servings

RICOTTA FILLING

32 ounces ricotta cheese

⅔ cup sugar

½ cup alkalized (Dutch process) cocoa powder

6 eggs

2 teaspoons vanilla extract

½ teaspoon ground cinnamon

1 cup (6 ounces) finely chopped milk chocolate or milk chocolate chips

2 batches Plain Sweet Dough, page 267

EGG WASH

1 egg, well beaten with a pinch of salt

One 9- or 10-inch-diameter layer cake pan, 2 inches deep, buttered

This typical Italian dessert is often served as an Easter specialty in southern Italy though it is excellent at any time of the year. The flavorings vary slightly according to the region, and toasted slivered almonds and grated lemon and orange zest are sometimes included. The dough here is a plain one, which accents the chocolate filling better.

1. Set a rack in the lower third of the oven and preheat to 350 degrees.

2. To make the filling, beat ricotta by hand until smooth. Stir in sugar, sift in the cocoa, then stir in the eggs, one at a time. Stir in remaining ingredients, being careful not to overmix.

3. To assemble, cut off and reserve one third of the dough. Roll the remaining two thirds into a 14-inch disk and line the prepared pan with it. Allow the dough to hang over the edge of the pan.

4. Pour in the ricotta filling and smooth it.

5. Roll the remaining dough into a 10 × 14-inch rectangle, then cut it into ten strips, 1 inch wide and 14 inches long. Paint the strips with the beaten egg. Paint the rim of the dough on the pan lightly with the beaten egg and, using the egg as glue, stick five strips of dough diagonally across the top of the pie. Stick the other five diagonally across the first to form a lattice. Trim away any overhanging dough and push the dough on the top rim back into the pan so there is no raised rim of dough.

6. Bake for about 45 minutes, or until puffed and slightly firm in the center. Cool in the pan on a rack before unmolding. To unmold, cover the pan with a flat plate or cutting board and invert. Remove the pan. Replace the pan with a platter and invert again. Remove top platter or board.

STORAGE: Keep loosely covered at room temperature on the day it is prepared. Wrap and refrigerate leftovers.

CHOCOLATE BANANA CREAM TART

■ ■ ■

Makes about 8 servings

CHOCOLATE FILLING

1 cup milk

¼ cup sugar

2 tablespoons cornstarch

3 egg yolks

4 ounces semisweet chocolate, cut into ¼-inch pieces

¾ cup heavy whipping cream

3 large bananas

1 batch Dark Sweet Chocolate Dough, page 266, lining a 9- or 10-inch tart pan, baked and cooled

FINISHING

1 cup heavy whipping cream

2 tablespoons sugar

1 teaspoon vanilla extract

Chocolate shavings, page 392

This melting dessert combines a lightened chocolate pastry cream with bananas and whipped cream.

1. To make the filling, bring the milk and sugar to a boil in a saucepan. Dissolve the cornstarch in a little water and beat in the yolks. Beat the boiling milk into the yolk mixture. Add yolks to the pan and whisk over low heat until boiling and thickened. Remove from heat and stir in chocolate to melt it. Scrape into a bowl. Press plastic wrap against the surface and chill to set.

2. To finish the filling, whip the ¾ cup cream and fold into the cooled chocolate mixture. Slice the bananas and fold them into the chocolate filling, then spread evenly in the cooled tart shell.

3. Whip the 1 cup heavy whipping cream with the 2 tablespoons sugar and the vanilla and spread over the surface of the filling. Cover with the chocolate shavings.

SERVING: Keep the tart refrigerated until time to serve it. Cut small wedges—this is a rich dessert.

STORAGE: Cover and refrigerate leftovers.

WHITE CHOCOLATE STRAWBERRY TART

• • •

Makes about 8 servings

WHITE CHOCOLATE FILLING

8 ounces white chocolate, cut into ¼-inch pieces

4 tablespoons (½ stick) unsalted butter

½ cup heavy whipping cream

2 large egg whites

¼ cup sugar

1 tablespoon kirsch

1 batch Dark Sweet Chocolate Dough, page 266, lining a 9- or 10-inch tart pan, baked

FINISHING

12 ounces white chocolate, melted and cooled

2 pints strawberries

White chocolate shavings, page 392

The whole berries garnishing this tart lend it an elegant and dramatic air.

1. To make the white chocolate filling, combine the white chocolate pieces with the butter in a heatproof bowl. Place over a pan of hot, but not simmering, water and stir to melt. Remove from the hot water and stir in the cream a little at a time. Keep stirring until the mixture is very smooth. Press plastic wrap against the surface and chill to set the filling.

2. To finish the filling, combine the egg whites and sugar in a heatproof bowl and place over a pan of simmering water. Whisk gently until the egg whites are hot and the sugar is dissolved. Remove the egg whites from the simmering water and use an electric mixer on medium speed to beat until whites are cool and have increased in volume. Meanwhile, beat filling to lighten it and beat in the kirsch. Fold the meringue into the filling and spread in the cooled tart shell.

3. Dip the berries in the prepared white chocolate. Place the coated berries on a paper-lined pan. Refrigerate to set white chocolate. Arrange the dipped berries on the filling. Sprinkle a few white chocolate shavings in the center.

SERVING: Cut the tart into wedges for serving.

STORAGE: Cover and refrigerate leftovers; return to room temperature for an hour before serving.

SPICY CHOCOLATE TART

. . .

Makes 8 servings

CHOCOLATE FILLING

⅔ cup milk

¼ cup sugar

6 tablespoons (¾ stick) unsalted
butter

6 ounces semisweet chocolate, cut
into ¼-inch pieces

3 large eggs

1 teaspoon ground cinnamon

½ teaspoon ground cloves

1 batch Dark Sweet Chocolate
Dough, page 266, lining a 9- or
10-inch tart pan, unbaked

This is a great dessert at any time of the year, but it is always most welcome in summer when we need the lift of a bit of spice.

1. Set a rack in the lower third of the oven and preheat to 350 degrees.

2. To make the filling, bring milk and sugar to a boil in a saucepan over medium heat. Add butter and continue beating until butter is melted. Off heat, whisk in chocolate. Whisk eggs with spices, then whisk in chocolate mixture. Pour into tart shell.

3. Bake for about 30 minutes, until well risen and firm. Cool on a rack.

SERVING: Unmold tart and serve with sweetened whipped cream.

STORAGE: Cover and refrigerate leftovers.

CHOCOLATE BROWNIE TART

▪ ▪ ▪

Makes one 9- to 10-inch tart,
about 8 servings

BROWNIE FILLING

2 ounces semisweet chocolate, cut
   into ¼-inch pieces

2 ounces unsweetened chocolate,
   cut into ¼-inch pieces

8 tablespoons (1 stick) unsalted
   butter

2 large eggs

Pinch salt

1 cup firmly packed dark brown
   sugar

½ cup all-purpose flour

1 cup pecan or walnut pieces,
   coarsely chopped

1 batch Dark Sweet Chocolate
   Dough, page 266, lining a 9- or
   10-inch tart pan, unbaked

Like a rich brownie baked inside a chocolate crust, this tart proves you can't be too thin, too rich, or have too much chocolate in one dessert.

1. Set a rack in the lower third of the oven and preheat to 350 degrees.

2. Bring a pan of water to a boil and remove from heat. Combine chocolates and butter in a heatproof bowl and place on the pan of water. Stir occasionally until melted. Remove bowl from pan of water.

3. In a large mixing bowl, whisk eggs with salt and sugar. Whisk in chocolate and butter, then with a rubber spatula, fold in flour and nuts. Scrape the filling into the prepared crust.

4. Bake for about 30 minutes, until well risen and firm. Cool on a rack.

SERVING: Unmold tart and serve sweetened whipped cream on the side.

STORAGE: Keep covered at room temperature.

CHOCOLATE APRICOT TART

■ ■ ■

Makes one 9- or 10-inch tart,
about 8 servings

COCOA ALMOND FILLING

¼ pound almond paste

¼ cup sugar

1 egg yolk

4 tablespoons (½ stick) unsalted
butter, softened

1 egg

1 tablespoon dark rum

3 tablespoons alkalized (Dutch
process) cocoa powder, sifted
after measuring

2 tablespoons flour

1 batch Dark Sweet Chocolate
Dough, page 266, lining a 9- or
10-inch tart pan, unbaked

12 ripe, fragrant apricots, about 2
pounds

¼ cup sliced almonds, about 1
ounce

GLAZE

½ cup apricot preserves

2 tablespoons dark rum

Try this with prune plums or raspberries when
they are in season.

1. Set a rack in the lower third of the oven and
preheat to 350 degrees.

2. To make the filling, use an electric mixer to beat
together almond paste, sugar, and yolk until smooth.
Beat in butter, scrape bowl and beater(s), then beat in
egg and rum. Continue beating until light. Stir in
cocoa and flour.

3. Spread filling evenly over dough. Rinse, halve, and
pit apricots. Slash each one three or four times
through the blossom end and arrange on filling, cut
side up in concentric circles. Place a piece of sliced
almond on each apricot half.

4. Bake the tart for about 40 minutes, until crust
and filling are baked through and apricots color at
the tips. Cool on a rack.

5. To make the glaze, combine preserves and rum in
a small pan and bring to a boil stirring over low heat.
Strain into another pan and simmer a few minutes to
thicken slightly. Brush hot glaze over the top of the
cooled tart.

SERVING: Serve in wedges with whipped cream or
Crème Anglaise, page 372, on the side.

STORAGE: Cover and keep leftovers at room temperature.

CHOCOLATE COCONUT TART

. . .

Makes one 9- to 10-inch tart,
about 8 servings

CHOCOLATE COCONUT FILLING

1 cup dark corn syrup

¼ cup sugar

4 ounces bittersweet chocolate, cut
into ¼-inch pieces

4 tablespoons (½ stick) unsalted
butter

3 eggs

Pinch salt

2 tablespoons white rum

One 7-ounce bag sweetened
shredded coconut

1 batch Dark Sweet Chocolate
Dough, page 266, lining a
buttered 9- or 10-inch tart pan,
unbaked

This rich, sticky tart is like a chocolate coconut
version of a pecan pie.

1. Set a rack in the lower third of the oven and
preheat to 350 degrees.

2. Combine corn syrup and sugar in a saucepan and
stir well to mix. Place over medium heat and bring to
a boil. Off heat, stir in chocolate and butter until
melted.

3. In a mixing bowl, whisk together eggs, salt, and
rum. Whisk in chocolate mixture until smooth. Stir in
coconut.

4. Scrape the filling into the prepared crust and
smooth the top. Bake for about 40 to 45 minutes,
until well risen and firm. Cool on a rack.

SERVING: Unmold tart and serve with sweetened
whipped cream on the side.

STORAGE: Keep leftovers covered at room temperature.

CHOCOLATE VELVET TART

. . .

Makes one 9- or 10-inch tart,
about 8 servings

CHOCOLATE VELVET FILLING

2 egg yolks

1 tablespoon instant espresso coffee

2 tablespoons kirsch

2 tablespoons dark rum

2 tablespoons crème de cacao

¼ cup praline paste, see Sources,
page 442

3 tablespoons melted butter

2 cups heavy whipping cream,
whipped

2 large egg whites

Pinch salt

2 tablespoons confectioners' sugar

¾ pound (12 ounces) semisweet
chocolate, melted

1 batch Dark Sweet Chocolate
Dough, page 266, lining a
buttered 9- or 10-inch tart pan,
baked and cooled

FINISHING

Chocolate shavings, page 392

The filling for this luscious tart is loosely based on the famous Chocolate Velvet dessert of the legendary Four Seasons Restaurant in New York. To prepare it you will need some praline paste. Since this is directly based on the recipe of my teacher, Albert Kumin, the opening pastry chef at the Four Seasons, it uses raw eggs, which I tend to avoid.

1. Set a rack in the middle level of the oven and preheat to 350 degrees.

2. For the filling, whisk the egg yolks, coffee, and liquors in a mixing bowl. Whisk in the praline paste and the butter. Remove whipped cream from refrigerator and rewhip if necessary.

3. Place egg whites and salt in bowl of electric mixer and whip on medium speed until white and opaque and able to hold a very soft peak. Increase speed to high and whip in confectioners' sugar in a slow stream. Whip the egg whites until they hold a soft peak.

4. Beat chocolate into egg yolk mixture, then quickly fold in egg whites followed immediately by whipped cream.

5. Scrape the filling into the tart shell and smooth the top, doming it up from the sides.

6. Sprinkle the top with chocolate shavings and refrigerate the tart until the filling is set. For advance preparation, cover tart with plastic wrap after filling is set. It can remain refrigerated for at least a day before it is served. Bring to room temperature before serving.

SERVING: This rich tart needs no accompaniment.

STORAGE: Keep in refrigerator, but bring to room temperature before serving. Wrap and refrigerate leftovers.

CHOCOLATE ORANGE CHEESE TART

• • •

Makes one 10-inch tart, about 8 servings

CHOCOLATE ORANGE CHEESE FILLING

16 ounces cream cheese, at room temperature

½ cup sugar

2 large eggs

3 ounces unsweetened chocolate, melted

1 teaspoon finely grated orange zest

3 tablespoons orange liqueur

1 batch Dark Sweet Chocolate Dough, page 266, lining a buttered 10-inch tart pan, unbaked

This tart, which is like a rich chocolate orange cheesecake, never fails to please.

1. Set a rack in the lower third of the oven and preheat to 350 degrees.

2. Use an electric mixer on lowest speed to beat cream cheese and sugar smooth. Add eggs, one at a time, scraping bowl and beater(s) well after each addition.

3. Combine chocolate, orange zest, and orange liqueur and stir well to mix. Scrape chocolate mixture into cheese mixture and beat only enough to combine evenly. Scrape the filling into the prepared crust and smooth the top.

4. Bake for about 35 to 40 minutes, until slightly puffed and firm everywhere but in the very center. Cool on a rack.

SERVING: Unmold tart and serve in wedges.

STORAGE: Wrap and refrigerate leftovers.

CHOCOLATE ALMOND TARTLETS

▪ ▪ ▪

Makes twenty-four 2-inch tartlets

CHOCOLATE ALMOND FILLING

    4 ounces almond paste

    ¼ cup sugar

    1 egg yolk

    4 tablespoons (½ stick) unsalted butter, softened

    1 egg

    2 tablespoons flour

    2 tablespoons alkalized (Dutch process) cocoa powder

    1 batch Cocoa Cookie Dough, page 266, lining twenty-four 2-inch tartlet pans, unbaked

CHOCOLATE CREAM

    ½ cup heavy whipping cream

    8 ounces semisweet chocolate, cut into ¼-inch pieces

MARZIPAN

    4 ounces almond paste

    1 cup confectioners' sugar

    2 tablespoons light corn syrup

    Red or pink food color

A simpler topping than the suggested marzipan hearts for these chocolate tartlets could be fresh raspberries and a sprinkling of confectioners' sugar.

1. Set a rack at the middle level of the oven and preheat to 350 degrees.

2. To make the chocolate almond filling, use an electric mixer to beat together the almond paste, sugar, and yolk until smooth. Beat in butter, scrape bowl and beater(s), and beat in egg. Continue beating until light. Sift and stir in flour and cocoa.

3. Fill a pastry bag fitted with a ½-inch plain tube (Ateco #6 or #806) with the chocolate almond filling and pipe into lined pans to about three-fourths full.

4. Bake the tartlets 20 to 25 minutes, until dough is baked through and filling is set. Cool in pans and unmold.

5. While the tartlets are baking, prepare the chocolate cream. Bring cream to a boil, remove from heat, and add chocolate pieces. Allow to stand several minutes, then beat smooth. Leave at room temperature to set. When cream is set, put it into a pastry bag with a medium star tube and pipe a large rosette onto each cooled tartlet.

6. To make the marzipan, combine almond paste, sugar, and corn syrup in food processor and pulse to mix. Knead smooth by hand. As you knead, add a small amount of the coloring. Roll marzipan out to a layer ¼ inch thick and cut heart shapes out of it. Top each rosette with a marzipan heart.

SERVING: These are great on a platter for a buffet with a few other desserts, or as the only dessert after a fancy meal. They need no accompaniment.

STORAGE: Cover and refrigerate leftovers.

TARTELETAS DE DULCE DE LECHE Y CHOCOLATE

Tartlets with Caramelized Milk and Chocolate Filling

■ ■ ■

Makes twenty-four 2-inch tartlets

DULCE DE LECHE

1 can evaporated milk, 12 ounces

1 can sweetened condensed milk, 14 ounces

4 ounces bittersweet chocolate, cut into ¼-inch pieces

1 tablespoon white rum

1 batch Cocoa Cookie Dough, page 266, lining twenty-four 2-inch tartlet pans, baked and cooled

FINISHING

Ground cinnamon or chocolate shavings, page 392

Though there are many different interpretations of dulce de leche (milk sweet or confection)—some dangerously rich and sweet—this one is simple and palatable. Using it as a filling for a tiny tartlet makes it seem lighter.

1. To prepare the dulce de leche, set a rack at the middle level of the oven and preheat to 350 degrees.

2. Combine the milks in a saucepan and bring to a boil, stirring occasionally so the milk does not scorch. Pour into a large, nonreactive baking pan, at least 3 inches deep, and bake for 30 minutes, scraping the side of the pan and whisking often. Remove from oven, whisk in chocolate and rum, then press mixture through a fine strainer into a bowl. Press plastic wrap against the surface and refrigerate until cold.

3. Line up the baked shells on a clean paper-lined pan. Fill each tartlet to the top with the dulce de leche. Sprinkle with cinnamon or shaved chocolate.

SERVING: Serve the tartlets as dessert or after dinner with coffee.

STORAGE: Keep the finished tartlets at a cool room temperature on the day they are served. Cover and refrigerate leftovers. For advance preparation, freeze the baked pastry shells between sheets of wax paper in a tin or other container with a tight-fitting cover.

CHOCOLATE BANANA TARTLETS

■ ■ ■

FILLING

1 cup heavy whipping cream

6 ounces bittersweet chocolate, cut into ¼-inch pieces

4 ounces milk chocolate, cut into ¼-inch pieces

2 large ripe bananas

2 teaspoons dark rum, optional

1 batch Cocoa Cookie Dough, page 266, lining twenty-four 2-inch tartlet pans, baked and cooled

FINISHING

24 large chocolate shavings, page 392

Confectioners' sugar

Though chocolate and banana are a wonderful flavor combination, bananas tend to darken and ruin their presentation. These tartlets solve that problem by placing the bananas under the chocolate filling.

1. To prepare the chocolate filling, bring cream to a boil, remove from heat, and add chocolates. Allow to stand several minutes until melted, then beat smooth. Leave at room temperature to set.

2. To assemble, slice the bananas ⅓ inch thick and place in a bowl. Toss quickly with the rum, if desired, and place a banana slice in each tartlet shell. Use an electric mixer to whip the cooled chocolate filling until it lightens. Put it into a pastry bag fitted with a ⅜-inch star tube (Ateco #4) and pipe a large rosette of filling into each tartlet, covering the banana. Top each tart with a large chocolate shaving and sprinkle very lightly with confectioners' sugar.

SERVING: Serve the tartlets as a dessert or after dinner with coffee.

STORAGE: Keep the finished tartlets at a cool room temperature on the day they are served. Cover and refrigerate leftovers. For advance preparation, freeze the baked pastry shells between sheets of wax paper in a tin or other container with a tight-fitting cover.

CHOCOLATE
RASPBERRY TARTLETS
■ ■ ■

Makes twenty-four 2-inch tartlets

FILLING

½ cup heavy whipping cream

1 tablespoon unsalted butter

1 tablespoon light corn syrup

6 ounces bittersweet chocolate, cut
   into ¼-inch pieces

1 tablespoon raspberry liqueur or
   eau de vie

1 batch Cocoa Cookie Dough, page
   266, lining twenty-four 2-inch
   tartlet pans, baked and cooled

1 half-pint basket fresh raspberries

FINISHING

Confectioners' sugar

Dark chocolate and raspberry are a classic combination, and just as good with the milk or white chocolate variations that follow the recipe.

1. To prepare the chocolate filling, bring cream, butter, and corn syrup to a boil, remove from heat, and add chocolate. Allow to stand several minutes to melt, then beat smooth, beating in raspberry liqueur. Leave at room temperature to set.

2. To assemble, spoon or pipe chocolate filling into tartlet shells to fill them. Arrange 3 or 4 raspberries on each tartlet. Dust with confectioners' sugar right before serving.

SERVING: Serve the tartlets as dessert or after dinner with coffee.

STORAGE: Keep the finished tartlets at a cool room temperature on the day they are served. Cover and refrigerate the leftovers. For advance preparation, freeze the baked pastry shells between sheets of wax paper in a tin or other container with a tight-fitting cover.

VARIATIONS

Substitute milk or white chocolate for the bittersweet chocolate in the filling and omit the corn syrup.

PEAR AND CHOCOLATE TARTLETS Use poached pears, page 240, well drained and cut into ½-inch dice, instead of raspberries, to cover the chocolate filling. Omit the raspberry liqueur and use a pear liqueur instead.

CHOCOLATE CHEESE TARTLETS

■ ■ ■

Makes twenty-four 2-inch tartlets

CHEESECAKE FILLING

12 ounces cream cheese, softened

⅓ cup sugar

2 large eggs

1 teaspoon vanilla extract

1 ounce unsweetened chocolate, melted

1 batch Cocoa Cookie Dough, page 266, lining twenty-four 2-inch tartlet pans, unbaked

These fun tartlets were inspired by Maida Heatter's bull's eye cheesecake, with alternating rings of plain and chocolate cheesecake batter. Here the tartlet shells are filled with plain batter, then a chocolate batter is piped into the center, so there are two different cheesecake flavors in the same little tart.

I. Set a rack at the middle level of the oven and preheat to 350 degrees.

2. To make the filling, use an electric mixer to beat together the cream cheese and sugar on low speed until smooth. Beat in the eggs, one at a time, mixing just until smooth. Scrape down bowl and beater(s) often to avoid lumps. Beat in the vanilla.

3. Remove ½ cup of the batter to a small bowl and stir in the melted chocolate.

4. Pipe or spoon plain cheesecake batter into each pastry-lined pan, filling it about half full. Put the chocolate batter into a pastry bag fitted with a small plain tube (Ateco #2 or #3). Insert the tube about ¼ inch down into the center of the plain batter in each filled tartlet. Pipe out a dab of the chocolate batter and withdraw the tube, leaving a chocolate circle in the center of the plain batter.

5. Bake the tartlets at 325 degrees for about 25 minutes, until dough is baked through and filling is set. Cool in pans and unmold.

SERVING: Serve tartlets as dessert or after dinner with coffee.

STORAGE: Keep the finished tartlets at a cool room temperature on the day they are served. Cover and refrigerate leftovers. For advance preparation, freeze the baked pastry shells between sheets of wax paper in a tin or other container with a tight-fitting cover.

VARIATIONS

Leave all the batter plain, or make all the batter chocolate by adding 2½ ounces more unsweetened chocolate.

Use the cheesecake filling as a base for fruit tarts, finishing the baked tarts with raspberries, strawberries, or other soft fruit.

CHOCOLATE CARAMEL PECAN TARTLETS

• • •

Makes twenty-four 2-inch tartlets

FILLING

⅓ cup sugar

1 teaspoon water

½ cup heavy whipping cream

1 tablespoon unsalted butter

6 ounces bittersweet chocolate, cut into ¼-inch pieces

2 teaspoons dark rum, optional

¾ cup toasted pecan pieces, coarsely chopped, about 3 ounces

1 batch Cocoa Cookie Dough, page 266, lining twenty-four 2-inch tartlet pans, baked and cooled

FINISHING

Toasted pecan halves

This caramel ganache filling is enriched—as if it needed it—with chopped toasted pecans.

1. To prepare the chocolate filling, combine the sugar and water in a saucepan and stir well to mix. Place over medium heat and, stirring occasionally, allow the sugar to color to a deep amber. Be careful not to let the sugar get too dark and bitter. To test, drop a little of the caramel onto a piece of white paper—it should just be a dark amber color. Off heat, add cream a little at a time—be careful, the sugar may splatter. Return pan to heat, add butter, and return to a boil. Remove from heat and add chocolate. Allow to stand several minutes, then beat smooth. Whisk in rum, if desired. Allow to set at room temperature. After the filling is cooled, fold in the chopped pecans.

2. To assemble, spoon or pipe in chocolate filling to fill shells. Arrange a pecan half on each.

SERVING: Serve the tartlets as dessert or after dinner with coffee.

STORAGE: Keep the finished tartlets at a cool room temperature on the day they are served. Cover and refrigerate leftovers. For advance preparation, freeze the baked pastry shells between sheets of wax paper in a tin or other container with a tight-fitting cover.

VARIATION

Substitute milk or white chocolate for the bittersweet chocolate in the filling.

CHOCOLATE PALMIERS

. . .

Makes about thirty 3-inch pastries

1 cup sugar

½ batch Quickest Chocolate Puff
Pastry, page 269

2 jelly-roll pans lined with
parchment or foil

This chocolate version of the beloved pastry uses Quickest Chocolate Puff Pastry. The flavor of the caramelized butter and sugar merges with the flavor of the delicate chocolate dough perfectly. These are even better when dipped in or streaked with tempered chocolate.

1. Scatter ½ cup of the sugar over the work surface and place dough on it. Scatter another ½ cup sugar over the dough. Use a rolling pin to press the sugar into the dough gently, about every ½ inch.

2. Roll the dough out into a 10-inch square. Turn the dough over often and make sure most of the sugar sticks to it.

3. Fold the top and bottom edges of the dough about a third of the way in toward the middle, then fold each edge over again toward the middle. Finally, fold over at the center to make a long, narrow package of dough.

4. Set a rack at the middle level of the oven and preheat to 350 degrees.

5. Slice the folded dough every ⅓ inch and dip the cut sides into any remaining sugar before placing the pastry, cut side down, on the pan. Leave at least 2 inches of space all around each palmier because they spread.

6. Bake about 20 minutes, until they are well caramelized. If the heat of the oven is uneven, it may be necessary to remove some of the pastries from the pan and return the others to the oven to finish baking. Let the color of the caramelized sugar be your guide; it should be a deep golden amber, not brown.

7. Cool the pastries in the pan on a rack and serve them while they are still warm for best flavor.

SERVING: Serve the palmiers as a cookie—with a fruit or custard dessert or with coffee.

STORAGE: Keep the palmiers in an airtight tin or plastic container with a tight-fitting cover.

CHOCOLATE PISTACHIO MILLE FEUILLES

. . .

Makes about thirty-five 2½-inch squares

1 batch Flaky Chocolate Dough,
   page 268

PISTACHIO CAKE LAYER

1 cup blanched pistachios

¾ cup all-purpose flour

4 large eggs, separated

¾ cup sugar, divided

½ teaspoon almond extract

Pinch salt

KIRSCH SYRUP

⅓ cup water

⅓ cup sugar

2 tablespoons kirsch

CHOCOLATE FILLING

1½ cups heavy whipping cream

⅓ cup light corn syrup

24 ounces semisweet chocolate, cut
   into ¼-inch pieces

2 tablespoons kirsch

FINISHING

Confectioners' sugar

Five 10 × 15-inch jelly-roll pans, 2
   lined with parchment or wax
   paper and 1 buttered and lined

Serve this rich dessert in small portions.

1. Divide the chilled chocolate dough in half and roll each to fit a paper-lined 10 × 15-inch pan. Prick dough all over with a fork, then cover each piece of dough with another piece of paper and another pan to weigh it down. Bake at 325 degrees until dry and crisp, about 30 minutes. Cool sheets of dough between pans to prevent warping.

2. To make the cake layer, grind pistachios in a food processor and add to sifted cake flour. Use an electric mixer to beat yolks with half the sugar and the almond extract. With clean beaters whip whites with salt until opaque, then whip in remaining sugar in a stream. Fold yolks into whites, then fold in pistachio and cake flour mixture. Spread batter in the buttered and paper-lined pan and bake at 350 degrees about 20 minutes. Cool on a rack.

3. To make the syrup, bring water and sugar to a boil in a small saucepan. Cool and stir in kirsch.

4. For filling, bring cream and corn syrup to a boil; remove from heat and add chocolate pieces. Allow to stand 5 minutes, then whisk in kirsch until mixture is smooth. At room temperature or in the refrigerator, cool until thickened and spreadable.

5. To assemble, turn one of the chocolate pastry layers out onto a board or the back of a pan, being careful to work gently because the baked pastry layer is fragile. Remove paper and spread with half of the filling. Paint top of pistachio cake layer with half the syrup and turn over onto filling. Pull away paper and moisten top of cake with remaining syrup. Spread with remaining filling. Top with remaining chocolate pastry layer and press layers so they stick together. Chill to set filling.

6. Trim sides even and cut into 2-inch strips. Cut each strip into 2-inch diamonds. Dust mille feuilles with confectioners' sugar.

SERVING: This rich dessert needs no accompaniment.

STORAGE: Keep the mille feuilles at a cool room temperature on the day they are served. Wrap and refrigerate leftovers.

CHOCOLATE PECAN STRAWS

· · ·

Makes about twenty-four
8- to 10-inch pastries

½ batch Quickest Chocolate Puff
Pastry, page 269

EGG WASH

1 egg, well beaten with a pinch
of salt

FILLING

⅓ cup sugar

½ teaspoon ground cinnamon

½ cup pecan pieces, finely chopped,
but not ground, about 2 ounces

One 10 × 15-inch jelly-roll pan
lined with parchment or foil

Another simple puff pastry is made richer and fancier by encrusting the dough with nuts and cinnamon sugar. Though you may use any nut, I find the sweetness of pecans works perfectly here.

1. Place dough on a floured surface, flour dough, and roll it out into a 12-inch square. Paint the surface of dough with egg wash.

2. Combine sugar, cinnamon, and pecans and spread them evenly over one half of the dough in a 6 × 12-inch rectangle. Fold the other half of the dough over the filling to cover it. Slide onto a pan and refrigerate until firm, about 15 minutes.

3. Set a rack at the middle level of the oven and preheat to 350 degrees.

4. Remove dough from refrigerator and roll out again into a 12-inch square. Use a cutting wheel to cut the dough into twenty-four ½-inch-wide strips. Twist the top of each strip one way and the bottom the other so they make a corkscrew shape. Place across the width (10-inch side) of the prepared pan and press the ends of each twist against the top edges of the pan so they stick. This keeps the straw from unraveling while they are baking.

5. Bake the twists about 20 minutes, until well puffed and well caramelized. Remove the pan from the oven and place on a rack to cool for 5 minutes. While the twists are still flexible and before they cool completely, trim off the ends with a sharp knife. If you wish, cut the twists in half to make two five-inch cookies from each.

SERVING: Serve the straws with a creamy dessert or as a tea pastry.

STORAGE: Keep the straws between sheets of wax paper in a tin or other container with a tight-fitting cover.

CREAM PUFF TRUFFLES

. . .

Makes about 24 small pastries

1 batch Pâte à Choux, page 303

CHOCOLATE FILLING

1 cup heavy whipping cream

12 ounces semisweet or bittersweet chocolate, cut into ¼-inch pieces

COATING

8 ounces semisweet or bittersweet chocolate, melted

FINISHING

8 ounces milk chocolate, finely grated

Confectioners' sugar

3 cookie sheets or jelly-roll pans lined with parchment or foil plus a 9 × 13-inch pan for the grated chocolate

This is a great way to dress up the humble cream puff. The little puffs are filled with a dark chocolate ganache similar to the center of a truffle. Then they are coated in melted chocolate and rolled in chocolate shavings—hardly humble anymore.

1. Set a rack at the middle level of the oven and preheat to 400 degrees.

2. Use a pastry bag fitted with a ½-inch plain tube (Ateco #6) to pipe twenty-four 1-inch-diameter puffs of the pâte à choux onto a prepared pan. Bake the puffs for about 15 minutes, then lower temperature to 350 degrees and continue baking 10 to 15 minutes longer, until puffs are firm, well colored, and crisp. Cool the puffs on a rack.

3. While the puffs are baking, prepare the filling. Bring cream to a boil in a medium saucepan over low heat. Remove from heat, add the chocolate, and allow to stand 3 minutes; then whisk smooth. Pour the cream into a heatproof glass or stainless steel bowl or pan. Press plastic wrap directly against the surface of the cream. Refrigerate about 1 hour, or until thickened but not hard. If filling becomes too firm, bring to room temperature, stirring and mashing occasionally with a rubber spatula, until of spreading consistency. Or stir over a pan of barely warm water to soften it.

4. To fill the pastries, use a chopstick or the sharp point of a vegetable peeler to make a small hole in the bottom (flat side) of each. Spoon the filling into a pastry bag fitted with a ¼-inch plain tube (Ateco #4). Pipe filling into the pastries and as each is filled place it, flat side up, on a clean pan.

5. To coat the pastries, place the pan with the filled choux on the left side of your work surface. (This is for right-handed people. If you're a southpaw, start on the right and spread your materials out to the left.) Immediately to its right place the bowl of melted chocolate. To the right of the chocolate, place the 9 × 13-inch pan of the grated chocolate arranged with a short side at the edge of the work surface. Finally, to the right of the shavings, place a clean jelly-roll pan lined with parchment, wax paper, or foil.

6. Dip your right hand into the bowl of melted chocolate and let it cover your palm. Pick up a chou in your left hand and drop it into the coated palm of your right hand. Roll it around until the pastry is covered with the chocolate. Drop the chou onto the grated chocolate pan, at the end closest to the edge of the work surface. Use a clean fork (held in your left hand) to roll the chou away from you to the other end of the pan. This will coat the pastry with the grated chocolate. As the choux accumulate in the shavings, use your left hand to lift them and set them, right side up so they are sitting on their flat bases, on the last empty pan. After all the choux are coated, refrigerate them to make sure the chocolate sets.

VARIATIONS

PROFITEROLES WITH ICE CREAM AND CHOCOLATE SAUCE This is a perfect dinner-party dessert. If you use the technique below and make the balls of ice cream in advance, the dessert is easy and quick to serve.

Makes 8 servings of 3 choux each

The baked unfilled choux, above
1 pint premium vanilla ice cream
1 batch Chocolate Sauce, page 371

1. Keep the baked choux at room temperature after they are made.

2. Using a small scoop, a melon baller, or a spoon, form 24 balls of ice cream. Place them, as they are made, in the freezer on a jelly-roll pan covered with plastic wrap. After all the ice cream has been scooped, cover with more plastic wrap and keep in freezer until serving time.

3. To serve the dessert, reheat the chocolate sauce over hot water.

4. Split the choux in half horizontally with a sharp knife. Place a scoop of ice cream on each bottom and cover with a top.

5. Arrange 3 on each plate and cover with the warm chocolate sauce; serve immediately.

CHOCOLATE ÉCLAIRS

• • •

Makes about 12 medium éclairs

1 batch Pâte à Choux, page 303

LIGHTENED VANILLA PASTRY CREAM

2 cups milk

⅔ cup sugar, divided

6 large egg yolks

Pinch salt

⅓ cup all-purpose flour

2 teaspoons vanilla extract

½ cup heavy whipping cream

GLAZE

1 batch Chocolate Glaze, page 44

1 cookie sheet or jelly-roll pan covered with parchment or foil plus 2 pans lined with parchment or wax paper

Just about everyone likes a chocolate éclair, whether it is filled with whipped-cream-lightened pastry cream, as this one is, or with simple sweetened whipped cream.

1. Set a rack at the middle level of the oven and preheat to 400 degrees.

2. Use a pastry bag fitted with a ½-inch plain tube (Ateco #6) to pipe twelve 4-inch finger-shaped éclairs onto the prepared pan. Bake the eclairs for about 20 minutes, then lower temperature to 350 degrees and continue baking another 10 to 15 minutes, until éclairs are firm, well colored, and crisp. Cool on a rack.

3. While the éclairs are baking, prepare the filling. In a medium, nonreactive saucepan bring the milk and half the sugar to a boil. Meanwhile, in a mixing bowl, whisk the yolks with the salt, then whisk in the remaining sugar. Sift over and whisk in the flour.

4. When the milk comes to a boil, whisk about a third of it into the yolk mixture. Return the remaining milk to a boil and whisk the yolk mixture back into it. Continue to whisk until the cream is thickened and returns to a boil. Continue cooking, whisking constantly, for about 30 seconds. Off heat, whisk in the vanilla. Scrape the pastry cream into a clean bowl and press plastic wrap against the surface. Chill until cold.

5. To finish, whip the cream until it holds a soft peak and carefully fold it into the chilled pastry cream.

6. To fill the éclairs, use a chopstick or vegetable peeler to pierce two small holes in the bottom (flat side) of each éclair, one at each end.

7. Spoon the lightened pastry cream into a pastry bag fitted with a ¼-inch plain tube (Ateco #4). Insert the tube into one of the holes in the bottom of an éclair and squeeze gently until the filling appears in the second hole. Place the éclairs, flat side up, on a clean pan covered with parchment or wax paper. Have ready a second pan.

8. To glaze the éclairs, allow the prepared icing to cool and thicken. Dunk the unpierced (top) side of the éclair ½ inch deep in the icing. Hold the éclair, icing

side down, over the pan of icing for 10 to 15 seconds to allow excess to drip off. Place éclair icing side up on empty prepared pan. Repeat with remaining éclairs. Reheat icing gently if it thickens too much.

9. Arrange the éclairs on a platter to serve.

SERVING: Éclairs are good not only as a dessert but also as a teatime pastry.

STORAGE: You can keep the baked pastry loosely covered at room temperature the entire day they are baked. They will have the best flavor and texture if they are served on the day they are made. For longer storage, wrap tightly and freeze; reheat at 350 degrees for about 5 minutes and cool before filling.

The filling may be made up to several days in advance and stored in the refrigerator. Fill the pastries no more than half an hour to an hour before you serve.

VARIATION

Fill the éclairs with sweetened whipped cream instead of the pastry cream.

PÂTE À CHOUX

Cream Puff Pastry

∎ ∎ ∎

Makes about 3 cups dough,
enough for about 12 to 18 small pastries

1 cup water

6 tablespoons (¾ stick) unsalted
   butter

¼ teaspoon salt

1 cup all-purpose flour

4 large eggs

This dough, used in many sweet desserts, is also often used for savory dishes.

1. Combine water, butter, and salt in a saucepan over medium heat and bring to a boil, stirring occasionally. As soon as it comes to the boil, remove from heat and sift in the flour and stir with a wooden spoon to combine smoothly.

2. Return to heat and cook, stirring constantly, until the paste dries slightly and leaves the sides of the pan.

3. Transfer the paste to a bowl and stir with a wooden spoon 1 minute to cool slightly.

4. Add eggs, one at a time, beating until each is absorbed before adding the next. Use pastry immediately.

STORAGE: The pâte à choux will puff better in the oven if it is freshly made. If you must keep the paste before baking it, press plastic wrap against its surface to prevent a skin from forming and store at room temperature for no more than 2 hours.

CHOCOLATE PARIS-BREST

■ ■ ■

Makes one 10-inch round pastry,
about 12 servings

1 batch Pâte à Choux, page 303

CHOCOLATE HAZELNUT FILLING

1½ cups heavy whipping cream

8 ounces semisweet chocolate, cut
 into ¼-inch pieces

8 ounces milk chocolate, cut into
 ¼-inch pieces

2 tablespoons dark rum

¾ cup hazelnuts, toasted, skinned,
 and coarsely chopped

FINISHING

Confectioners' sugar

1 cookie sheet or jelly-roll pan lined
 with parchment or foil, a 10-inch
 circle traced on the paper or foil,
 the paper then inverted

A Paris-Brest is a dessert named to commemorate a famous bicycle race. It consists of a ring of pâte à choux split, then sandwiched with a creamy filling. I use a crunchy chocolate hazelnut cream.

1. Set a rack at the middle level of the oven and preheat to 400 degrees.

2. Fill a pastry bag fitted with a ½-inch plain tube (Ateco #6) with the pâte à choux. Hold the bag perpendicular to the pan and about an inch above it and allow the pâte à choux to emerge from the tube in a stream the size of the opening in the tube. Pipe a ring of pâte à choux just inside, but touching, the traced line on the paper in the prepared pan. Pipe another ring inside the first one, then a third on top of and in between the first two.

3. Bake the Paris-Brest about 15 minutes, until well risen, then lower the oven temperature to 350 degrees and continue baking 20 to 30 minutes longer until well colored and risen. Slide the Paris-Brest onto a rack to cool.

4. To make the filling, bring the cream to a boil in a heavy, nonreactive pan. Remove from heat and add the chocolates. Allow to stand 3 minutes, then whisk smooth. Pour ganache into a bowl and allow to stand until cooled and thickened.

5. To fill the Paris-Brest, split it horizontally and place the bottom ring on a platter. Cut top ring into twelve to sixteen equal pieces. These will be replaced on the ring after the bottom is filled, but precutting avoids a crushing squish later when you are dividing the dessert into portions.

6. Use an electric mixer to whip filling until lightened. Whip in the rum and the hazelnuts. Use a pastry bag without a tube to pipe in a series of blobs of filling onto the bottom ring. Replace the pieces of the top and dust lightly with confectioners' sugar before serving.

SERVING: Serve small wedges of this rich dessert.

STORAGE: Keep leftovers covered at a cool room temperature.

GENERAL TECHNIQUES FOR TRUFFLES AND DIPPED AND MOLDED CHOCOLATES

• • •

Almond Clusters
Coconut Clusters
Walnut-Raisin Clusters
Hazelnut Clusters
Pecan Clusters
Pistachio Clusters
Macadamia Clusters
Caramelized Almond or Hazelnut Clusters

Almond Bark
Coconut Bark
Walnut-Raisin Bark
Hazelnut Bark
Pecan Bark
Pistachio Bark
Macadamia Bark

Chocolate-Covered Almonds
Chocolate-Covered Hazelnuts

Chocolate Tuiles

TRUFFLES

• • •

All-Purpose Truffles

Black and White Truffles

Truffes Champagne
(*Champagne Truffles*)

Truffes Ivoires
(*Ivory Truffles*)
White Raspberry Truffles
White Chartreuse Truffles
White Nougatine Truffles
Black Forest Truffles
Milk Chocolate Truffles

Truffes à l'Armagnac
(*Armagnac Truffles*)
Grappa Truffles
Bourbon Truffles

Pecan Bourbon Truffles
Hazelnut Rum Truffles
Walnut Nougatine Truffles

Espresso Truffles

Milk Chocolate Caramel Truffles
Milk Chocolate Date Truffles
Caramel Cream Truffles

Raspberry Chocolate Truffles
Cassis Truffles

Pistachio Marzipan Truffles

Nutmegs
Cinnamon Sticks
Earl Grey Truffles
Lemon Truffles

DIPPED CHOCOLATES

• • •

Carrés Pralinés
(*Praline Squares*)

Dark and Light Rum Fantasies

Palets d'Or
Nougatine Diamonds
Espresso Diamonds

Raspberry Tricolors

Carrés Framboise
(*Raspberry Squares*)
Carrés Cassis (Black Currant Squares)
Carrés Passion (Passion Fruit Squares)

Citronettes
Chocolate Orange Squares

Caramelines
(*Bonbons with Chocolate Caramel Centers*)

MOLDED CHOCOLATES
...

Praline Jewels
(*Molded Chocolates
with Praline Paste Filling*)

Chocolate Hazelnut Jewels
(*Bijoux Pralinés*)

Cherry Cordials

Pineapple Rum Fondants

Apricot Pistachio Fondants

Strawberry Fondants

Raspberry Fondants

Liqueur Fondant Molded Chocolates

Chocolate Mint Leaves

Petite Friture
(*"Small Fry"*)

White Chocolate Easter Eggs

Amandines
(*Almond and Kirsch–Filled
Molded Chocolates*)

Pistachio-Filled Molded Chocolates

Walnut- or Pecan-Filled Molded Chocolates

Milk Chocolate Rosettes

Marzipan Cups

SUGAR-BASED CONFECTIONS
...

Chocolate Caramels

Bittersweet Chocolate Caramels

Fondant

Chocolate Pecan Caramel Clusters

Cream Caramels

Nougatine

Hazelnut Nougatine

Walnut Nougatine

Almond and Hazelnut Nougatine

Hazelnut Feuilletés

Old-fashioned Butter Crunch

Recently European-style chocolate confections have become increasingly popular in the United States. American chocolate confections used to be mostly dipped chocolates with different flavors of fondant and butter cream inside, but now the public has been turned on to truffles and dipped chocolates with centers of different flavored chocolates, made of ganache, a mixture of chocolate and cream. The following is a list of the most popular chocolate confections and a brief description of the procedure for preparing them:

Dipped Chocolates: Sometimes referred to as bonbons, these are confections that begin with ganache poured into a frame or plastic-wrap-lined pan and allowed to set. After the ganache is set, a thin layer of chocolate is spread over it to make it easier to handle, then it is cut into uniform shapes. These shapes are dipped into tempered chocolate to give them a uniform coating and appearance.

Truffles: The first truffles were made from the scraps left over from cutting dipped chocolates into uniform shapes. At the end of the day, all the scraps would be combined, placed in a mixer, and beaten. The result was piped out into small irregular balls, chilled, roughly coated with tempered chocolate, and rolled in cocoa, so they looked like Périgord truffles covered with earth. Nowadays, ganache is prepared specially to make truffles. It is allowed to set, then whipped so it lightens. After that, the procedure is the same. The truffle centers are piped out and chilled, then coated with tempered chocolate and cocoa, confectioners' sugar, ground nuts, or pralin powder. Good truffles are always small and delicate and never the size of eggs or golf balls.

Solid Molded Chocolates: These are made by spreading tempered chocolate on a plaque indented with decoratively shaped cavities. After the chocolate sets, the plaque is turned over and the individual chocolates shaped by the cavities pop out.

Filled Molded Chocolates: These use the same sorts of plaques, but the cavities are filled with tempered chocolate and then turned over, so that most of the chocolate runs out and only a shell remains coating each. After the shells set, they are filled with a center mixture, which may be ganache, nut paste, or flavored fondant. Then another layer of tempered chocolate is added over the filling to cover and enclose it completely. The best molded chocolates have thin shells and delicate fillings.

Besides truffles, dipped, and molded chocolates the following confections appear in this chapter:

Molded Chocolate Cups: Empty shells made in molds. Cups are filled with a piped-in filling, which is not covered with chocolate.

Clusters: Simple chocolates made of nuts, dried fruits, or a combination mixed into tempered chocolate and formed into small clusters by being dropped onto pans with a spoon. Clusters may also be deposited into pleated paper cups.

Bark: Similar to clusters, but with fewer solid pieces. Bark is spread out flat and broken into irregular pieces after it has set.

Sugar-Based Confections: These involve cooking sugar (their main ingredient) beyond the boiling point. Some, such as fudge and chocolate caramels, contain chocolate. Others, liqueur bonbons and butter crunch, for example, are dipped in or coated with chocolate.

GENERAL TECHNIQUES FOR TRUFFLES AND DIPPED AND MOLDED CHOCOLATES

• • •

TRUFFLE TECHNIQUES

Forming Truffles: Whipped truffle ganache should be firm enough so that it holds its shape easily. If the ganache is too loose, the truffles will flatten when they are piped out. If this happens, stir the ganache over cool, not iced, water and rewhip briefly. Repeat if necessary. Pipe truffles onto a parchment-lined pan using a ½-inch plain tube (Ateco #6 or #806). In warm weather, chill the pan before you start piping. To pipe, hold the bag so that the tube is about ½ inch above the pan, and perpendicular to it. Squeeze once, gently, so that as the ganache emerges onto the pan it forms a ball with a slightly flattened bottom. Release pressure and twist a little to detach flow. Pipe the next center about ¾ inch away from the previous one. Chill centers thoroughly before you attempt to enrobe them.

Enrobing Truffle Centers: If the center is to be enrobed but not later encrusted, have a bowl of tempered chocolate ready (see pages 20–23). Place truffle center, right side up, on the surface of the tempered chocolate. Use a dipping fork to press the top of the center gently to submerge it in the chocolate. Slide fork under the flat side of truffle in the chocolate. Gently lift upward until the fork and bottom of truffle come to the top surface of the chocolate. Shake fork gently up and down to shake excess chocolate off truffle's surface. Keep the fork in contact with the surface of the chocolate. This helps to pull excess chocolate off truffle's surface. Lift fork off surface of chocolate and tilt it slightly, so that truffle hangs slightly off the edge of the fork. Scrape fork bottom against the rim of the bowl as you lift the truffle out of the bowl and deposit it on a paper-lined pan. To make a spiked surface, allow chocolate to set slightly, then roll truffle across a rack using a fork. Move the fork in a series of loops to make the truffle move across the rack and pull points in the chocolate covering.

Enrobing and Encrusting Truffle Centers: When truffle centers are to be enrobed and rolled in cocoa, confectioners' sugar, or ground nuts, follow this two-person procedure. Set up work surface with the pan of centers on far left, then the bowl of tempered chocolate to its right, and a pan of sifted cocoa or sugar to its right,

arranged so one of the short sides is against the edge of the work surface. To its right arrange a clean paper-lined pan for finished truffles. (This is if dipper is right-handed. If you are left-handed, start the series at the right and move left.) The first person picks up a center in his left hand; lays his right hand flat against the surface of the tempered chocolate to coat his palm; puts center in his right hand and closes his hand to coat the center with chocolate, then deposits it into a pan of cocoa at end of the pan closest to edge of work surface. The second person uses a fork to roll the truffle in the cocoa, pushing it to the far end of the pan, where the truffles are left until the coating sets. After a quantity have been coated, the second person lifts truffles with a fork to a paper-lined pan. After all the truffles are coated, they should be placed in a strainer, a few at a time, and shaken over the pan of cocoa to remove excess. They are then lifted from the strainer and placed in a storage pan. This step is only necessary when encrusting with cocoa or confectioners' sugar, not if ground nuts are used.

TECHNIQUES FOR MAKING DIPPED CHOCOLATES

Forming the Sheet of Center Mixture

1. Whip ganache until cooled, but still pourable and beginning to hold its shape. Line the bottom of a jelly-roll pan with a flat sheet of plastic wrap or parchment; chill pan.
2. Pour ganache onto the pan to a depth of ⅜ to ½ inch. With a small offset spatula, shape the edges of the sheet as straight as possible, so that the ganache is a neat 10-inch square. Chill to set.
3. Remove sheet from refrigerator and spread a *very thin* coat of tempered chocolate over the ganache, using a small offset spatula. This coating and the one on the other side makes the center mixture easy to cut and dip at room temperature. Return to refrigerator to set.

4. Invert the pan so the chocolate-coated side of the sheet is down on a clean, chilled, paper-lined pan and spread a thin layer of chocolate on the side now up. Chill until needed.

Cutting Centers from the Sheet

1. Slide sheet of center mixture to a chilled cookie sheet or the back of a chilled jelly-roll pan. Position the pan near the stove; heat a sharp knife briefly in a flame or over a heating element, then, using a ruler to keep width uniform, cut the sheet into ¾- to 1-inch strips. Wipe the blade clean after each cut and reheat the blade before each cut.

2. When all the strips have been cut, cut across them at ¾- to 1-inch intervals to make squares, rectangles, diamonds, or triangles. Keep centers at a cool room temperature before dipping. You could also use a heated 1-inch cutter with a simple shape, such as a circle, to cut centers. Heat cutter in a flame or over a heating element before each cut and wipe after every cut.

Dipping Cut Centers

1. To make plain dipped centers, set up work surface with the pan of centers on the far left, then the bowl of tempered chocolate and a clean, chilled, paper-lined pan at right. Again, reverse if you are left-handed.

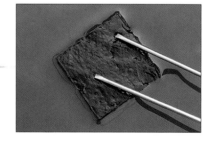

2. With left hand, place a center on surface of the chocolate in the bowl. With the fork held in the right hand, press the center into the chocolate so that the top of the center is at the top surface of the chocolate and is not completely submerged. Slide the fork into the chocolate and under the center and turn the center over so the coated side is now uppermost.

3. Withdraw the fork from under the center and with the side of the fork, sweep the excess chocolate from the top of the center in one movement, slide the fork back under the center, then shake the fork gently up and down to shake the excess chocolate off the dipped center. Keep the fork in contact with the surface of the chocolate, which helps to pull excess chocolate off.

4. Lift the fork off the surface of the chocolate, and tilt it slightly, so the dipped center hangs slightly off the edge of the fork. Scrape the fork bottom against the rim of the bowl as you lift it out and deposit the dipped chocolate on the paper-lined pan.

5. Use the side of the fork to score a decorative line on the surface of the chocolate and/or place a shred of a nutmeat or crystallized flower on it. Or, streak the surface of the dipped chocolates with a contrasting chocolate piped through a very fine opening in a paper cone.

TECHNIQUES FOR MAKING SOLID MOLDED CHOCOLATES

Preparing Molds: Buff cavities in molds with cotton or a very soft, clean cloth. Leave molds at room temperature before filling.

Filling Molds

1. Fill the cavities with tempered chocolate either using a large paper cone or by spreading chocolate onto the surface of plaque with an offset spatula, then sweeping excess into the bowl of chocolate.

2. Once the cavities have been filled, tap the bottom of the plaque against the work surface or tap the sides of the plaque with a rolling pin or the handle of a large wooden spoon to settle the chocolate into the cavities and eliminate air bubbles.

3. Scrape plaque surface clean with an offset spatula, sweeping excess into the bowl of chocolate. Set plaques aside until contents set.

Unmolding: After chocolate has set, turn the plaque over onto a clean, paper-covered pan and the chocolates will fall out easily.

Cleaning Molds: Run through dishwasher cycle. Drain well. Store upside down.

TECHNIQUES FOR MAKING FILLED MOLDED CHOCOLATES

Preparing Molds: Buff the cavities in the molds with cotton or a very soft, clean cloth. Leave molds at room temperature before filling.

Forming Shells

1. Fill the cavities with tempered chocolate either using a large paper cone, or by spreading chocolate on the surface of the plaque with an offset spatula, then sweeping away the excess into the bowl of chocolate. Tap the bottom of the plaque against the work surface or tap the sides of the plaque with a rolling pin or the handle of a large wooden spoon to settle the chocolate in the cavities and eliminate air bubbles.

2. Turn the plaque over the bowl of chocolate and tap gently on the bottom and sides of the plaque so that the excess chocolate drains into the bowl. Turn right side up, and scrape the surface clean with an offset spatula, sweeping the excess into the bowl of chocolate. Put the plaques aside to set the shells.

Filling

1. Use a paper cone or pastry bag fitted with a ¼-inch plain tube to fill shells. Be sure the filling in the cavities has a flat top surface and does not come to a point or rise higher than the shell. The easiest way to do this is to make sure the point of the cone or tube is inserted only about ⅛ inch into the shell and held steady while the cone or bag is squeezed.

2. When filling is at the proper level, release pressure on the bag and pull the tip away with a sideways motion to avoid leaving a point.

Sealing in Filling

1. With an offset spatula, spread a layer of tempered chocolate over the plaque, so the chocolate covers the areas over the filling.

2. Scrape the surface clean with an offset spatula, sweeping the excess into the bowl of chocolate. Set plaques aside to set the bottoms.

Unmolding: After the chocolate has set, turn the plaque over onto a clean, paper-covered pan and the chocolates will fall out.

ALMOND CLUSTERS

■ ■ ■

Makes about 30 candies

8 ounces tempered dark, milk, or white chocolate, pages 20–23

8 ounces (about 2 cups) lightly toasted slivered almonds, cooled

2 cookie sheets or jelly-roll pans lined with parchment or foil

These simple confections are a good way of using up the last bit of tempered chocolate left over after dipping or coating other centers.

1. In a bowl, combine chocolate and almonds. Stir thoroughly with a rubber spatula to coat almonds completely.

2. With a teaspoon, quickly drop 1½-inch mounds on the prepared pans and leave to set. For a different look, drop the clusters directly into pleated paper cups. If it is warm in the room, refrigerate the clusters briefly.

STORAGE: Place clusters in a tin or plastic container with a tight-fitting cover and keep at a cool room temperature for up to a month.

VARIATIONS

COCONUT CLUSTERS Substitute lightly toasted sweetened shredded coconut for the almonds. Make free-standing clusters or drop them into paper cups, as above.

WALNUT-RAISIN CLUSTERS Substitute equal parts of lightly toasted walnut pieces and dark raisins for the slivered almonds.

HAZELNUT CLUSTERS Substitute blanched, toasted, crushed hazelnuts for the slivered almonds.

PECAN CLUSTERS Substitute lightly toasted pecan pieces for the slivered almonds.

PISTACHIO CLUSTERS Substitute whole, blanched, lightly toasted pistachios for the slivered almonds.

MACADAMIA CLUSTERS Substitute unsalted, lightly toasted, crushed macadamias for the slivered almonds.

CARAMELIZED ALMOND OR HAZELNUT CLUSTERS: Coat the nuts with caramel as in Chocolate-Covered Almonds recipe on page 319, before continuing with the recipe.

ALMOND BARK

. . .

*Makes one 10 × 15-inch slab of candy
to be broken into irregular pieces*

8 ounces (about 2 cups) whole
blanched almonds, lightly
toasted and cooled

8 ounces tempered chocolate, pages
20–23, dark, milk, or white
chocolate

One 10 × 15-inch jelly-roll pan
covered with foil

Though this confection may be made with any type of nut, almonds are always popular and delicious.

1. Cut each almond into three or four pieces. In a bowl, combine chocolate and almonds, stirring thoroughly with a rubber spatula to coat almonds completely.

2. Scrape the mixture onto the prepared pan and spread it even with a metal spatula to a 10- to 12-inch square. Make sure the almonds are evenly distributed throughout the candy. Leave the bark to set. If it is warm in the room, refrigerate the bark briefly.

3. To serve the bark, break it into irregular pieces.

STORAGE: Place pieces of bark in a tin or plastic container with a tight-fitting cover and keep at a cool room temperature for up to a month.

VARIATIONS

In the following variations, it is necessary to cut up or crush only the hazelnuts and macadamias—all the other nuts are already small enough.

COCONUT BARK Substitute lightly toasted sweetened shredded coconut for the almonds.

WALNUT-RAISIN BARK Substitute a cup each of lightly toasted walnut pieces and dark raisins for the whole almonds.

HAZELNUT BARK Substitute whole, blanched, toasted hazelnuts for the whole almonds.

PECAN BARK Substitute lightly toasted pecan pieces for the whole almonds.

PISTACHIO BARK Substitute whole, blanched, lightly toasted pistachios for the whole almonds.

MACADAMIA BARK Substitute whole, unsalted, lightly toasted macadamias for the whole almonds.

CHOCOLATE-COVERED ALMONDS

• • •

Makes about 24 ounces candies

8 ounces (2 cups) whole blanched almonds

1 cup sugar

½ teaspoon lemon juice

8 ounces tempered bittersweet or semisweet chocolate, pages 20–23

2 cups alkalized (Dutch process) cocoa powder, sifted

1 roasting pan for the almonds, 1 oiled jelly-roll pan for caramelizing the almonds, and 1 large roasting pan for coating the almonds with cocoa

For a very special treat, try these mixed into French Vanilla Ice Cream, page 248.

1. Set a rack at the middle level of the oven and preheat to 325 degrees. Place the almonds in a roasting pan and bake until light golden, 15 to 20 minutes.

2. Remove the almonds from the oven and cover the pan with aluminum foil or a cookie sheet to keep the almonds warm.

3. To make the caramel, combine the sugar and lemon juice in a saucepan and stir to mix—it should look like wet sand.

4. Place over medium heat and stir occasionally until the sugar melts and begins to caramelize. When the sugar is evenly melted but is still light in color, move it off the heat and let it continue to color for a minute or two longer, or until it becomes a deep amber.

5. Stir the almonds into the caramel with a metal spoon or spatula. Stir well to make sure all the almonds are evenly coated. Pour the mixture into the oiled pan and, using two forks, separate each almond. If the caramel should harden before all the almonds are separated, place pan in oven set at 300 degrees. Watch closely, and when the caramel softens again you can separate the remaining almonds. Cool the almonds.

6. To coat the almonds with chocolate, have ready a roasting pan containing the cocoa. Stir the cooled almonds into the chocolate, then quickly pour the almonds into the cocoa powder. Again separate the almonds before the chocolate sets.

7. Place the almonds in a strainer and shake off excess cocoa.

STORAGE: Keep the coated almonds in a tin or plastic container with a tight-fitting cover in a cool place.

VARIATION

CHOCOLATE-COVERED HAZELNUTS Substitute blanched hazelnuts for the almonds. Because the hazelnuts are already toasted as they are being blanched, reheat them only before coating them with caramel.

CHOCOLATE TUILES

. . .

Makes about twenty 2½-inch tuiles

6 ounces (about 1½ cups) sliced almonds, lightly toasted and cooled

8 ounces tempered bittersweet, semisweet, or milk chocolate, pages 20–23

1 jelly-roll pan with several rolling pins resting across it for curving the tuiles

These are the shape of the curved cookies on page 150, except they are made of nothing but chocolate and almonds. First you spread rounds of the mixture on strips of paper, then you place the paper over a rolling pin or other curved surface, such as a bottle, to set. They will set curved. I suggest making some curved and some flat unless you have a large supply of rolling pins. Or save the cardboard tubes from the insides of rolls of paper towels and use them to shape the tuiles.

1. Prepare 6 strips of parchment or wax paper, each about 12 inches long and 4 inches wide, for shaping the tuiles.

2. Crush the sliced almonds with a rolling pin or chop them finely with a sharp knife.

3. Stir the almonds into the tempered chocolate. Quickly spread the mixture in 2½-inch rounds on one of the strips of paper, about four per strip, then immediately drape the paper over a rolling pin to curve the tuiles. Allow them to remain on the rolling pins until set. If the room is warm, place tuiles in refrigerator to set. Repeat with remaining mixture and papers.

4. When the tuiles are set, carefully peel the paper away.

STORAGE: Keep the tuiles in a cool place in a tin or plastic container with a tight-fitting cover.

VARIATION

Use any other type of chopped nuts for the tuiles.

TRUFFLES

. . .

Probably invented by Swiss confectioners during the last half of the nineteenth century, chocolate truffles have become a well-known and popular confection during the last quarter of the twentieth century. Cocoa-dusted truffles are supposed to imitate the aromatic fungus that grows under the ground in Périgord and Piedmont, but many truffles are also finished in other ways. Truffles may be encrusted with toasted nuts, grated chocolate, or confectioners' sugar, or they may even be left plain to show off their shiny chocolate coating. I usually recommend coating truffles with something—it can help hide the fact that the chocolate used for coating them is not in perfect temper.

Truffles are a practical chocolate confection to prepare if you don't feel like expending a lot of effort. The process of making the center mixture is easy and foolproof and forming the centers requires only a little care. Coating the truffles, especially if you use the quick tempering method (see "When you realy need to temper," page 22) is a breeze. You'll enjoy preparing these as much as you will eating them.

ALL-PURPOSE TRUFFLES

. . .

Makes about 35 to 50 truffles,
depending on size

CENTER MIXTURE

½ cup heavy whipping cream

2 tablespoons unsalted butter

1 tablespoon light corn syrup

8 ounces semisweet, bittersweet, or
milk chocolate, melted

COATING

12 ounces semisweet or bittersweet
chocolate

2 cups alkalized (Dutch process)
cocoa powder

2 cookie sheets or jelly-roll pans
lined with parchment or foil
plus a small roasting pan for
the cocoa

Use this recipe to make plain truffles from any type of chocolate. Fruit, liquor, liqueur, and other varieties follow.

1. To make centers, combine cream, butter, and corn syrup in a nonreactive pan and bring to a simmer over low heat. Remove from heat and allow to cool 5 minutes.

2. Add cream mixture to chocolate and whisk smooth.

3. Cool center mixture about 2 to 3 hours at room temperature, until it reaches about 80 degrees.

4. Whip the mixture using an electric mixer on medium speed, for about a minute, until it lightens in color. Spoon mixture into a pastry bag fitted with a ½-inch plain tube (Ateco #6 or #806). Pipe ¾-inch balls onto prepared pan. Chill the centers for at least an hour.

5. To coat the truffles, melt the chocolate, temper it according to the instructions on pages 20–23, or allow it to cool to about 90 degrees. Coat truffles, using your hand to cover truffles with chocolate (see page 312), depositing them into a pan of sifted cocoa.

6. Roll finished truffles in a strainer over wax paper to remove excess cocoa. Lift truffles from strainer and leave excess cocoa behind. (Sift cocoa through a fine strainer to remove any bits of chocolate and it may be reused.)

STORAGE: Place truffles in a tin or plastic container with a tight-fitting cover and keep at a cool room temperature for up to a week.

BLACK AND WHITE TRUFFLES

. . .

Makes about 35 to 50 truffles,
depending on size

CENTER MIXTURES

1 cup heavy whipping cream,
divided

8 ounces semisweet or bittersweet
chocolate, melted

2 tablespoons (¼ stick) butter,
divided

2 tablespoons light corn syrup,
divided

8 ounces white chocolate, melted

COATING

16 ounces semisweet or bittersweet
chocolate

3 cups alkalized (Dutch process)
cocoa powder

2 cookie sheets or jelly-roll pans
lined with parchment or foil
plus a small roasting pan for
the cocoa

These two-tone confections provide a bite of dark and white ganache in each truffle.

1. To make centers, bring ½ cup cream to a boil. Remove from heat and add dark chocolate, half the butter, and half the corn syrup; whisk smooth. Repeat with remaining cream, the white chocolate, remaining butter, and remaining corn syrup.

2. Scrape each ganache into a separate bowl, cover with plastic wrap, and cool several hours at room temperature, until set and firm, about 80 degrees.

3. Use an electric mixer on medium speed to whip the white mixture for about a minute, until it lightens in color. Spoon it into a pastry bag fitted with a ½-inch plain tube (Ateco #6 or #806). Pipe ½-inch balls onto the prepared pan. Repeat with dark ganache. Chill the centers for at least an hour.

4. After truffles have set, press one dark and one white together, base to base, to make a rough sphere.

5. To coat the truffles, melt the chocolate, temper it according to the instructions on pages 20–23, or allow it to cool to about 90 degrees. Coat truffles, according to directions on page 312, rolling them in cocoa.

6. Roll finished truffles in a strainer over a piece of wax paper to remove excess cocoa. Lift truffles from strainer and leave excess cocoa behind. (Sift cocoa through a fine strainer to remove any bits of chocolate and it may be reused.)

STORAGE: Place truffles in a tin or plastic container with a tight-fitting cover and keep at a cool room temperature for up to a week.

TRUFFES CHAMPAGNE

Champagne Truffles

■ ■ ■

CENTER MIXTURE

½ cup heavy whipping cream

2 tablespoons (¼ stick) unsalted
butter

1 tablespoon light corn syrup

9 ounces semisweet, bittersweet, or
milk chocolate, melted

1 tablespoon cognac or other fine
brandy

1 tablespoon dark rum

COATING

12 ounces semisweet or bittersweet
chocolate

2 cups alkalized (Dutch process)
cocoa powder

2 cookie sheets or jelly-roll pans
lined with parchment or foil
plus a small roasting pan for
the cocoa

The Champagne in this truffle refers to Fine
Champagne, a grade of cognac.

1. Combine cream, butter, and corn syrup in a nonreactive pan and bring to a simmer over low heat.
Remove from heat and allow to cool 5 minutes.

2. Add cream mixture to chocolate and whisk
smooth. Whisk in cognac and rum.

3. Cool center mixture 2 to 3 hours at room temperature, until it reaches about 80 degrees.

4. Use an electric mixer on medium speed to whip the
mixture for about a minute, until it lightens in color.
Spoon it into a pastry bag fitted with a ½-inch plain
tube (Ateco #6 or #806). Pipe ¾-inch balls onto the
prepared pan. Chill the centers for at least an hour.

5. To coat the truffles, melt the chocolate, temper it
according to the instructions on pages 20–23, or
allow it to cool to about 90 degrees. Coat truffles,
according to directions on page 312, rolling in cocoa.

6. Roll finished truffles in a strainer over a piece of
wax paper to remove excess cocoa. Lift truffles from
strainer so excess cocoa remains behind. (Sift cocoa
through a fine strainer to remove any bits of chocolate and it may be reused.)

STORAGE: Place truffles in a tin or plastic container with a tight-fitting cover
and keep at a cool room temperature for up to a week.

TRUFFES IVOIRES

Ivory Truffles

∎ ∎ ∎

Makes about 35 to 50 truffles,
depending on size

CENTER MIXTURE

12 ounces white chocolate, cut into
¼-inch pieces

4 tablespoons (½ stick) unsalted
butter

6 tablespoons heavy whipping
cream, cold

2 tablespoons orange liqueur

COATING

16 ounces bittersweet chocolate

3 cups confectioners' sugar

2 cookie sheets or jelly-roll pans
lined with parchment or foil
plus a small roasting pan for
the confectioners' sugar

These "ivory" or white truffles have an exquis-itely smooth center. Orange liqueur and rasp-berry eau de vie are my favorite flavorings for the centers.

1. Combine the white chocolate and butter in a heat-proof mixing bowl. Place over a pan of hot, but not simmering, water to melt, stirring constantly. Remove bowl from pan of hot water.

2. Use a whisk to stir in the cold cream, a little at a time, until smooth. Pour into a nonaluminum pan and press plastic wrap against the surface. Refrigerate until ganache is about 80 degrees and set.

3. Use an electric mixer on medium speed to whip the mixture about a minute, until it lightens in color. Spoon into a pastry bag fitted with a ½-inch plain tube (Ateco #6 or #806). Pipe ¾-inch balls onto the prepared pan. Chill the centers for at least an hour.

4. To coat the truffles, melt the chocolate, temper it according to the instructions on pages 20–23, or allow it to cool to about 90 degrees. Coat truffles, according to directions on page 312, rolling them in confectioners' sugar.

5. Roll finished truffles in a strainer over a piece of wax paper to remove excess sugar. Lift truffles from strainer so that excess sugar remains behind. (Sift confectioners' sugar through a fine strainer to remove any bits of choco-late and it may be reused.)

STORAGE: Place truffles in a tin or plastic container with a tight-fitting cover and keep at a cool room temperature for up to a week.

VARIATIONS

WHITE RASPBERRY TRUFFLES Replace the orange liqueur with framboise, raspberry eau de vie.

WHITE CHARTREUSE TRUFFLES Replace the orange liqueur with Chartreuse liqueur, whether clear, yellow, or green, or use another herb liqueur such as Benedictine, Galliano, or Strega.

WHITE NOUGATINE TRUFFLES Replace the orange liqueur with dark rum. Beat ½ cup ground or chopped almond nougatine, page 363, into the center mixture when aerating it. Enrobe the truffles in dark chocolate and roll them in finely chopped toasted almonds.

BLACK FOREST TRUFFLES Replace the orange liqueur with kirsch; fold 2 tablespoons chopped red candied cherries into the center mixture after it has been whipped. After dipping the truffles, coat them in cocoa powder.

MILK CHOCOLATE TRUFFLES Replace the white chocolate with milk chocolate in the master recipe or any variations that follow.

TRUFFES À L'ARMAGNAC

Armagnac Truffles

. . .

Makes about 35 to 50 truffles,
depending on size

CENTER MIXTURE

⅓ cup sweetened condensed milk

¼ cup Armagnac or other wine-
based brandy

2 tablespoons light corn syrup

12 ounces milk chocolate, melted

COATING

16 ounces bittersweet chocolate

3 cups confectioners' sugar

2 cookie sheets or jelly-roll pans
lined with parchment or foil
plus a small roasting pan for
the confectioners' sugar

The strength of the alcohol in these truffles is tempered by the sweetness of the milk chocolate. The use of sweetened condensed milk instead of cream makes them keep well.

1. In the bowl of an electric mixer, stir the sweetened condensed milk, Armagnac, and corn syrup into the melted chocolate. Use mixer with whip attachment to whip until completely cooled, about 5 minutes.

2. Cover bowl and refrigerate center mixture 10 minutes, until the temperature is about 80 degrees and the mixture is firm enough to pipe.

3. Spoon into a pastry bag fitted with a ½-inch plain tube (Ateco #6 or #806) and pipe olive shapes onto the prepared pan. Chill to set the centers.

4. To coat the truffles, melt the chocolate, temper it according to the instructions on pages 20–23, or allow it to cool to about 90 degrees. Coat truffles according to directions on page 312, rolling them in confectioners' sugar.

5. Roll finished truffles in a strainer to remove excess sugar. Lift truffles from strainer so that excess sugar remains behind. (Sift confectioners' sugar through a fine strainer to remove any bits of chocolate and it may be reused.)

STORAGE: Place truffles in a tin or plastic container with a tight-fitting cover and keep at a cool room temperature for up to a week.

VARIATIONS

GRAPPA TRUFFLES Replace the Armagnac with grappa, the clear Italian liquor made from the seeds, skins, and stems of grapes left over after wine making.

BOURBON TRUFFLES Replace the Armagnac with bourbon.

PECAN BOURBON TRUFFLES

• • •

Makes about 35 to 50 truffles,
depending on size

CENTER MIXTURE

½ cup heavy whipping cream

9 ounces semisweet chocolate,
melted

2 tablespoons (¼ stick) butter

1 tablespoon dark corn syrup

2 tablespoons bourbon

½ cup chopped lightly toasted
pecans, about 2 ounces

COATING

16 ounces semisweet chocolate

8 ounces chopped toasted pecans

2 cookie sheets or jelly-roll pans
lined with parchment or foil
plus a small roasting pan for
the pecans

The sweetness of the bourbon and the pecans is a perfect counterpoint for the bittersweet chocolate, and the contrast makes for an enticing truffle.

1. To make the center mixture, bring the cream to a boil and pour over the chocolate; whisk smooth. Whisk in the butter, corn syrup, and bourbon.

2. Cool the mixture to 80 degrees or until thickened.

3. Use an electric mixer on medium speed to whip the mixture about a minute, until it lightens in color. Then whip in the ½ cup chopped pecans. Spoon into a pastry bag fitted with a ½-inch plain tube (Ateco #6 or #806). Pipe ¾-inch balls onto the prepared pan. Chill the centers for at least an hour.

4. To coat the truffles, melt the chocolate, temper it according to the instructions on pages 20–23, or allow it to cool to about 90 degrees. Coat truffles, following directions on page 312, rolling them in the chopped pecans.

STORAGE: Place truffles in a tin or plastic container with a tight-fitting cover and keep at a cool room temperature for up to a week.

CONFECTIONS

VARIATIONS

HAZELNUT RUM TRUFFLES Replace the pecans in recipe with hazelnuts that have been toasted, blanched (see page 13), and chopped. Replace the bourbon with dark rum.

WALNUT NOUGATINE TRUFFLES Replace the chopped pecans in the center mixture with ½ cup finely chopped Walnut Nougatine, page 363. Replace the chopped pecans on the outside of the truffles with chopped, toasted walnut pieces.

ESPRESSO TRUFFLES

■ ■ ■

Makes 35 to 50 truffles,
depending on size

CENTER MIXTURE

½ cup heavy whipping cream

2 tablespoons (¼ stick) unsalted
butter

1 tablespoon light corn syrup

8 ounces semisweet or bittersweet
chocolate, melted

2 tablespoons instant espresso
coffee

½ teaspoon ground cinnamon

1 tablespoon dark rum

COATING

12 ounces semisweet or bittersweet
chocolate

2 cups confectioners' sugar

2 cookie sheets or jelly-roll pans
lined with parchment or foil
plus a small roasting pan for
the confectioners' sugar

These delicate truffles combine the rich flavors of coffee and chocolate, accented with a bit of cinnamon.

1. Combine cream, butter, and corn syrup in a nonreactive pan and bring to a simmer over low heat. Remove from heat and allow to cool 5 minutes.

2. Add cream mixture to chocolate and whisk smooth. Mix together espresso with cinnamon and rum and whisk in.

3. Cool center mixture 2 to 3 hours at room temperature, until it reaches about 80 degrees.

4. Use an electric mixer on medium speed to whip the mixture about a minute, until it lightens in color. Spoon into pastry bag fitted with a ½-inch plain tube (Ateco #6 or #806). Pipe ¾-inch balls onto a pan covered with parchment or wax paper. Chill the centers for at least an hour.

5. To coat the truffles, melt the chocolate, temper it according to the instructions on pages 20–23, or allow it to cool to about 90 degrees. Coat truffles according to directions on page 312, rolling them in confectioners' sugar.

6. Roll finished truffles in a strainer over a piece of wax paper to remove excess sugar. Lift truffles from strainer so that excess sugar remains behind. (Sift sugar through a fine strainer to remove any bits of chocolate and it may be reused.)

STORAGE: Place truffles in a tin or plastic container with a tight-fitting cover and keep at a cool room temperature for up to a week.

MILK CHOCOLATE CARAMEL TRUFFLES

· · ·

Makes about 35 to 50 truffles,
depending on size

CENTER MIXTURE

⅓ cup heavy whipping cream

⅓ cup sugar

1 tablespoon light corn syrup

2 tablespoons (¼ stick) butter

12 ounces milk chocolate, melted

COATING

12 ounces semisweet or bittersweet
chocolate

1 cup alkalized (Dutch process)
cocoa powder

2 cookie sheets or jelly-roll pans
lined with parchment or foil
plus a small roasting pan for
the cocoa

The caramel flavor blends well with the milk chocolate and contrasts with the dark chocolate and cocoa on the outside of the truffles.

1. Bring the cream to a boil and set aside, covered, to keep warm.

2. Combine the sugar and corn syrup in a 2-quart saucepan and stir well to mix. Place over low heat and allow to caramelize. Stir occasionally until a deep amber color, about 3 minutes longer. Carefully add the hot cream in several additions. (This is to keep the caramel from overflowing.) Be careful, caramel may splatter. Return to a boil, remove from heat, and stir in butter. Pour the hot mixture over the chocolate and whisk smooth.

3. Cool center mixture 2 to 3 hours at room temperature, until it reaches about 80 degrees.

4. Use an electric mixer on medium speed to whip the mixture about a minute, until it lightens in color. Spoon into a pastry bag fitted with a ½-inch plain tube (Ateco #6 or #806). Pipe ¾-inch balls onto a pan covered with parchment or wax paper. Chill the centers for at least an hour.

5. To coat the truffles, melt the chocolate, temper it according to the instructions on pages 20–23, or allow it to cool to about 90 degrees. Coat truffles, according to directions on page 312, rolling them in the cocoa.

6. Roll finished truffles in a strainer over a piece of wax paper to remove excess cocoa. Lift truffles from strainer so that excess cocoa remains behind. (Sift cocoa through a fine strainer to remove any bits of chocolate and it may be reused.)

STORAGE: Place truffles in a tin or plastic container with a tight-fitting cover and keep at a cool room temperature for up to a week.

VARIATIONS

MILK CHOCOLATE DATE TRUFFLES Add ⅓ cup finely chopped pitted dates to the center mixture, folding it in after the mixture has been whipped.

CARAMEL CREAM TRUFFLES Replace the milk chocolate with white chocolate.

RASPBERRY CHOCOLATE TRUFFLES

. . .

Makes about 70 truffles, depending on size

RASPBERRY PUREE

One 10-ounce package frozen raspberries

½ cup sugar

CENTER MIXTURE

¾ cup heavy whipping cream

16 ounces semisweet chocolate, melted

1 tablespoon butter

⅓ cup raspberry puree, see Step 1

1 tablespoon light corn syrup

1 tablespoon framboise (raspberry eau de vie)

FINISHING

8 ounces milk chocolate

8 ounces dark chocolate

2 cookie sheets or jelly-roll pans lined with parchment or foil plus a small roasting pan for the grated chocolate

These truffles have an exquisite raspberry scent. The raspberry puree here makes more than you need for the recipe, but the remainder may be used for flavoring butter cream or as a dessert sauce.

1. To make the raspberry puree, combine berries and sugar in a saucepan and bring to a simmer over medium heat. Allow to simmer about 15 minutes, until thickened. Puree in blender, then strain to remove seeds. Let cool.

2. To make the center mixture, bring the cream to a boil in a saucepan and remove from heat. Add all at once to chocolate and whisk smooth. Whisk in remaining ingredients in order, then cool to 80 degrees.

3. To form the truffles, use an electric mixer on medium speed to beat about a minute, until it lightens in color. Spoon into a pastry bag fitted with a ½-inch plain tube (Ateco #6 or #806) and pipe ¾-inch balls onto a parchment or foil-lined pan. Chill the centers.

4. To finish the truffles, grate milk chocolate in a food processor fitted with the grating blade. Place grated chocolate in the roasting pan. Melt the dark chocolate, temper it according to the instructions on pages 20–23, or allow it to cool to about 90 degrees, and coat the centers. With a fork, roll them through the grated milk chocolate, according to directions on page 313.

VARIATION

CASSIS TRUFFLES Replace the frozen raspberries with 1 cup frozen or bottled cassis puree (see Sources, page 442) and cook it with the sugar until thickened as with the raspberry puree. Use ⅓ cup of the resulting puree in the truffle center. Replace the raspberry eau de vie with crème de cassis. Enrobe the truffles in white chocolate and roll them in grated white chocolate.

PISTACHIO MARZIPAN TRUFFLES

• • •

Makes about 60 truffles

CENTER MIXTURE

½ cup heavy whipping cream

8 ounces bittersweet chocolate, melted

1 teaspoon almond extract

1 tablespoon butter

1 tablespoon light corn syrup

PISTACHIO MARZIPAN

8 ounces (about 2 cups) warm blanched pistachios, see page 13

4 ounces almond paste

1 cup confectioners' sugar

2 to 3 tablespoons light corn syrup

COATING

16 ounces semisweet or milk chocolate

16 ounces blanched pistachios, chopped

2 cookie sheets or jelly-roll pans lined with parchment or foil, plus a small roasting pan for the pistachios

This is a pared-down version of a rich Viennese confection called a Mozartkugel. Try to find the greenest pistachios possible so both the inside and the outside of the truffles will be brightly colored.

1. To make the centers, bring the cream to a boil and remove from heat. Whisk cream into chocolate. Whisk smooth, then whisk in extract, butter, and corn syrup. Cool the mixture to 80 degrees or until thickened.

2. To make the pistachio marzipan, place the blanched pistachios, still warm, in the bowl of a food processor. Process for a long time, scraping down frequently, until they form a paste. Pulse in the almond paste, then the confectioners' sugar. Add corn syrup as necessary, keeping the marzipan fairly soft. Remove from processor and knead smooth. Divide the marzipan into three pieces and roll each into a cylinder 12 inches long. Flatten ropes and roll them 2 inches wide.

3. Beat center mixture on medium speed about a minute to lighten and then spoon into a pastry bag fitted with a ½-inch plain tube (Ateco #6 or #806). Pipe down the center of each strip of marzipan. Bring the long sides of each piece of marzipan up around the ganache and press marzipan together along the center top of the ganache, enclosing it. Don't worry if the marzipan doesn't cover perfectly or completely. Cut each roll into ¾-inch lengths. Chill if necessary, then roll pieces into balls between the palms of your hands.

4. To coat the truffles, melt the chocolate, temper it according to the instructions on pages 20–23, or allow it to cool to about 90 degrees. Coat truffles, according to directions on page 312, rolling them in a pan of the chopped pistachios. Remove to a paper-lined pan and chill to set coating.

STORAGE: Place truffles in a tin or plastic container with a tight-fitting cover and keep at cool room temperature for up to a week.

NUTMEGS

. . .

Makes about 40 truffles

CENTER MIXTURE

½ cup heavy whipping cream

2 tablespoons (¼ stick) unsalted butter

1 tablespoon light corn syrup

1 teaspoon freshly grated nutmeg

8 ounces semisweet chocolate, melted

COATING

12 ounces semisweet or bittersweet chocolate

1 cup alkalized (Dutch process) cocoa powder

1 cup confectioners' sugar

2 teaspoons freshly grated nutmeg

2 cookie sheets or jelly-roll pans lined with parchment or foil plus a small roasting pan for the cocoa mixture

These spice-scented truffles are the creation of Hans Tschirren, proprietor of the beautiful Confiserie Tschirren in Berne, Switzerland. During my recent visit, he kindly gave me this recipe and the cinnamon variation that follows.

1. Combine cream, butter, corn syrup, and nutmeg in a nonreactive pan and bring to a simmer over low heat. Remove from heat and allow to cool 5 minutes.

2. Strain cream mixture into chocolate (to remove pieces of nutmeg) and whisk smooth.

3. Cool center mixture 2 to 3 hours at room temperature, until it reaches about 80 degrees.

4. Use an electric mixer on medium speed to whip the mixture. Spoon into a pastry bag fitted with a ½-inch plain tube (Ateco #6 or #806). Pipe ¾-inch olive shapes, to resemble whole nutmegs, onto the prepared pan, holding the bag at a 45-degree angle to the pan with the tube touching the paper. Squeeze and pull the tube toward you about an inch, then release pressure and pull away. Chill the centers for at least an hour.

5. To coat the truffles, melt the chocolate, temper it according to the instructions on pages 20–23, or allow it to cool to about 90 degrees. Sift the cocoa and confectioners' sugar into a roasting pan and stir in the nutmeg. Continue to stir the mixture together until it is evenly mixed. Coat truffles according to directions on page 312.

6. Roll finished truffles in a strainer over a piece of wax paper to remove excess cocoa mixture. Lift truffles from strainer so that excess cocoa and sugar remains behind.

STORAGE: Place truffles in a tin or plastic container with a tight-fitting cover and keep at a cool room temperature for up to a week.

FROM LEFT TO RIGHT: *Cinnamon Sticks, Pistachio Marzipan Truffles (page 333), Nutmegs*

CINNAMON STICKS Replace the ground nutmeg in both the center mixture and the coating with the same amounts of ground cinnamon. Pipe the whipped center mixture into long cylinders, as wide as the opening in the tube you are using to pipe, down the length of the prepared pan. Chill and cut the centers into 1½-inch lengths. Coat with chocolate and cinnamon-scented cocoa and confectioners' sugar.

EARL GREY TRUFFLES Replace the nutmeg in the center mixture with 2 teaspoons best quality Earl Grey tea leaves. Pipe the truffles into ¾- to 1-inch balls. Omit the nutmeg in the coating and just use cocoa and confectioners' sugar.

LEMON TRUFFLES Replace the nutmeg in the center mixture with the grated zest of 2 large lemons. Pipe the truffles into ¾- to 1-inch balls. Coat the truffles with milk chocolate and plain confectioners' sugar.

DIPPED CHOCOLATES

. . .

Unless you have had long experience tempering and dipping, these are some of the most difficult chocolate candies to make. But they are also among the best. Unlike truffles, which are almost always rolled in cocoa or some other powdery or crunchy substance, dipped chocolates are deliberately left bare to show off the beauty of the perfect, shiny, tempered chocolate coating. A dipped chocolate may have a tiny decoration, but it should serve only to accentuate the perfection of the surface further.

Here are a few suggestions to help you achieve success with this finicky chocolate.

- Divide up the work—make the centers one day and dip them the next.

- Make sure to use a real couverture chocolate (see page 10) for the coating—another type of chocolate could be too thick, which would make it almost impossible to dip the centers successfully.

- Make sure the room where you are dipping is cool, or the centers will become too soft to dip easily.

- Make sure centers are no cooler than 75 degrees or they may make their chocolate coat go out of temper and whiten.

- Above all, make sure you aren't distracted while you are trying to dip—it is a job that requires concentration.

- Review the directions on pages 314–15 before attempting to dip the centers you have prepared.

CARRÉS PRALINÉS

Praline Squares

■ ■ ■

Makes about thirty-six 1-inch squares

CENTER MIXTURE

10 ounces praline paste, see
Sources, page 442

16 ounces bittersweet chocolate,
melted

ENROBING

16 ounces bittersweet chocolate for
dipping, tempered, pages 20–23

Toasted, skinned, and chopped
hazelnuts for finishing

2 cookie sheets or jelly-roll pans
covered with plastic wrap

These are the least finicky of the dipped centers
and the easiest to prepare.

1. Place the praline paste in a bowl and stir it smooth
with a rubber spatula. Stir in the chocolate and turn
out onto a plastic-wrap-covered pan. Spread into a
square about 9 to 10 inches on a side. Refrigerate an
hour to set.

2. Remove the slab of center from the refrigerator
and, using a small offset metal icing spatula, spread a
thin layer of tempered chocolate, about 2 tablespoons, over the top. Quickly turn over onto another
plastic-wrap-covered pan and peel away the wrap the
slab was on. Quickly spread the top side with a thin
layer of chocolate as on the other side.

3. Cut the slab into ¾- to 1-inch squares, using a
sharp knife warmed in hot water and wiped before
each cut.

4. Dip the centers in the remaining tempered chocolate as in the instructions
on pages 314–15. Mark the top with your dipping fork or decorate the top of
each carré with a pinch of chopped hazelnuts.

5. Let the covering set.

STORAGE: Place bonbons in a tin or plastic container with a tight-fitting cover
and keep at a cool room temperature for up to a week.

VARIATIONS

Use milk chocolate or white chocolate for the coating.

Add ½ cup chopped hazelnuts to the filling along with the chocolate.

DARK AND LIGHT RUM FANTASIES

. . .

Makes about 60 candies

DARK CHOCOLATE CENTER

⅔ cup heavy whipping cream

11 ounces bittersweet chocolate, cut into ¼-inch pieces

2 tablespoons (¼ stick) unsalted butter, softened

2 tablespoons dark rum

WHITE CHOCOLATE CENTER

12 ounces white chocolate, cut into ¼-inch pieces

4 tablespoons (½ stick) unsalted butter

⅓ cup heavy whipping cream

2 tablespoons white rum

ENROBING

32 ounces bittersweet chocolate

Alkalized (Dutch process) cocoa powder

2 cookie sheets or jelly-roll pans lined with wax or parchment paper plus a pan for the cocoa

This confection combines dark chocolate and white chocolate with dark and white rum for a subtle effect.

1. To make the dark chocolate centers, bring the cream to a boil and remove from heat. Add cut chocolate, allow to stand 1 to 2 minutes, then stir until smooth. Beat in the softened butter and rum; cool to set.

2. Combine white chocolate with butter. Place over a pan of hot water and stir to melt. Remove from heat and beat in cream in several additions, until smooth. Beat in rum. Allow to set.

3. Use an electric mixer on medium speed to beat the dark center mixture. Spoon into a pastry bag fitted with a ½-inch plain tube (Ateco #6 or #806) and pipe the dark center mixture out in long cylinders the length of the paper-lined pans. Beat the white chocolate mixture and pipe the same way. Pipe in pairs so that each white chocolate cylinder touches a dark chocolate one. Chill to set the centers.

4. Use a small heated knife (see page 314) to cut the centers into 1-inch lengths.

5. To enrobe, melt and temper the chocolate (see pages 20–23) and dip the centers. Deposit them in a pan of cocoa and turn over to coat. Allow coating to set and shake off excess cocoa in a strainer.

STORAGE: Place bonbons in a tin or plastic container with a tight-fitting cover and keep at a cool room temperature for up to a week.

PALETS D'OR

. . .

Makes about 40 candies

CENTER MIXTURE

1 cup heavy whipping cream

2 tablespoons (¼ stick) unsalted butter

2 tablespoons corn syrup

16 ounces bittersweet chocolate, melted

ENROBING

16 ounces bittersweet chocolate, tempered, pages 20–23

FINISHING

Gold leaf

2 cookie sheets or jelly-roll pans lined with plastic wrap plus 1 cookie sheet covered with heavy acetate or polished aluminum foil

These chocolates are named for the shred of gold leaf that decorates them. To get the shiniest result from the covering chocolate, palets d'or are often placed on a sheet of stiff, shiny acetate to cool. After they are set, they are turned over so that the shiny side that dried against the acetate is on top. You can achieve the same results by drying them on a cookie sheet covered with a piece of aluminum foil, laid shiny side up and rubbed with a clean cloth to smooth out any wrinkles.

1. Bring cream, butter, and corn syrup to a simmer. Remove from heat and allow to stand 5 minutes. Whisk cream mixture into chocolate, then scrape center mixture into bowl of electric mixer.

2. Use whisk attachment to whip center mixture on slow speed until cooled and shiny. When it is, that means it is also well emulsified.

3. Spread the center mixture on a jelly-roll pan lined with plastic in a rectangle about 8 × 10 inches. Refrigerate an hour to set.

4. Remove slab of center from the refrigerator and use a small offset metal icing spatula to spread a thin layer of tempered chocolate, about 2 tablespoons, over the top. Quickly turn over onto the other pan covered with plastic wrap and peel away the wrap the slab was on. Quickly spread the top side with a thin layer of chocolate as you did the side now on the bottom.

5. Use a sharp knife, warmed in hot water and wiped before each cut, to cut the slab into ¾- to 1-inch squares. Or use a small round cutter to make rounds. Warm the cutter in a bowl of warm water and dry it before each cut.

6. After all the centers are cut, dip the centers in the remaining tempered chocolate as in the instructions on pages 314–15, depositing them on the cookie sheet covered with acetate or polished aluminum foil.

7. After the covering chocolate has set, turn each palet over so the shiny side is up and decorate it with a shred of gold leaf applied with the tip of a small knife.

STORAGE: Place bonbons in a tin or plastic container with a tight-fitting cover and keep at a cool room temperature for up to a week.

VARIATIONS

NOUGATINE DIAMONDS Add ½ cup chopped nougatine, page 363, to center mixture. Cut into diamond shapes. Dip as above and top with a pinch of chopped nougatine.

ESPRESSO DIAMONDS Add 3 tablespoons instant espresso coffee powder to the cream before heating it. Cut into diamond shapes.

RASPBERRY TRICOLORS

. . .

Makes about 50 candies

DARK CHOCOLATE CENTER

⅓ cup heavy whipping cream

6 ounces bittersweet chocolate, cut into ¼-inch pieces

1 tablespoon unsalted butter, softened

1 tablespoon framboise (raspberry eau de vie)

WHITE CHOCOLATE CENTER

8 ounces white chocolate, cut into ¼-inch pieces

2 tablespoons (¼ stick) unsalted butter

3 tablespoons heavy whipping cream

1 tablespoon framboise (raspberry eau de vie)

PINK CHOCOLATE CENTER

8 ounces white chocolate

2 tablespoons (¼ stick) unsalted butter

3 tablespoons heavy whipping cream

3 tablespoons thick unsweetened raspberry puree, see Note

ENROBING

32 ounces bittersweet chocolate

Alkalized (Dutch process) cocoa powder

1 cookie sheet or jelly-roll pan lined with parchment or foil plus a pan for the cocoa

Sometimes these are finished by brushing with tempered chocolate, then cutting with a hot knife to reveal the three colors of the center, instead of being cut and dipped individually.

1. To make the dark chocolate centers, bring the cream to a boil, remove from heat and add cut chocolate. Allow to stand 1 to 2 minutes and stir smooth. Beat in the softened butter and framboise; cool 2 to 3 hours at room temperature until set.

2. To make the white chocolate centers, combine white chocolate with butter in a heatproof bowl. Place bowl over a pan of hot water and stir to melt. Remove bowl from hot water and beat in cream in several additions, until smooth. Beat in framboise and cool at room temperature for 2 to 3 hours.

3. For the pink centers, proceed as for the white centers and beat in the puree instead of framboise.

4. To form, use an electric mixer on medium speed to beat white center mixture to aerate. Spoon into a pastry bag fitted with a ½-inch plain tube (Ateco #6 or #806). Pipe out in long cylinders, the length of the prepared pan. Repeat with dark center mixture, piping it next to and touching the white cylinders. Finally, beat pink mixture and pipe it on top of and in between the other two. Chill to set.

5. Cut the centers into 1-inch lengths with a small heated knife (see page 313).

6. To enrobe, melt and temper the chocolate (follow directions on pages 20–23) and dip the centers according to the instructions on pages 314–15. Deposit them in a pan of cocoa and turn over to coat. Allow coating to set and shake off excess cocoa in a strainer.

NOTE: Cook a 10-ounce package of frozen raspberries until thickened, then puree and strain to remove seeds.

CARRÉS FRAMBOISE

Raspberry Squares

• • •

Makes about 90 to 100 candies

RASPBERRY PUREE

One 10-ounce package frozen
   raspberries

½ cup sugar

CENTER MIXTURE

1 cup heavy whipping cream

2 tablespoons (¼ stick) unsalted
   butter

1 tablespoon light corn syrup

20 ounces bittersweet chocolate,
   melted

⅓ cup raspberry puree, see Step 1

2 tablespoons framboise (raspberry
   eau de vie)

ENROBING

16 ounces bittersweet chocolate,
   tempered, pages 20–23

2 cookie sheets or jelly-roll pans
   covered with plastic wrap
   plus 1 cookie sheet or jelly-roll
   pan lined with polished foil
   or acetate

Another cut ganache like the Palets d'Or, these
have a surprisingly strong raspberry flavor.

1. To make the puree, combine the raspberries and
sugar, bring to a boil, and reduce until very thick.
Puree and strain to remove seeds.

2. Bring cream, butter, and corn syrup to a simmer.
Remove from heat and allow to stand 5 minutes.
Whisk cream mixture into chocolate, then whisk in
raspberry puree. Scrape center mixture into bowl of
electric mixer.

3. Use whisk attachment to whip center mixture on
slow speed until cooled and shiny, which means it is
also well emulsified.

4. Spread the center mixture in a 10-inch square on
one of the jelly-roll pans lined with plastic.
Refrigerate an hour to set.

5. Remove slab of center from refrigerator and use a
small offset metal icing spatula to spread a thin layer
of tempered chocolate, about 2 tablespoons, over the
top. Quickly turn slab over onto the other pan
covered with plastic and peel away the wrap the slab
was on. Spread the top side of slab with a thin layer
of chocolate. Work quickly.

6. Use a sharp knife, warmed in hot water and wiped
before each cut, to cut the slab into ¾- to 1-inch
squares.

7. After all the centers are cut, dip the centers in the remaining tempered
chocolate as in the instructions on pages 314–15, placing them to dry on the
final prepared pan. Use the dipping fork to incise a line on the top of each
bonbon.

8. Let the covering of chocolate set.

STORAGE: Place bonbons in a tin or plastic container with a tight-fitting cover
and keep at a cool room temperature for up to a week.

CARRÉS CASSIS (BLACK CURRANT SQUARES) Substitute ¾ cup cassis puree, frozen or bottled (see Sources, page 442), for the raspberries. Cook with sugar until thick and use ⅓ cup for the center mixture.

CARRÉS PASSION (PASSION FRUIT SQUARES) Substitute passion fruit puree (see Sources, page 442) for the cassis puree, above.

CITRONETTES

▪ ▪ ▪

Makes about 90 to 100 candies

CENTER MIXTURE

> ¾ cup heavy whipping cream
>
> 2 tablespoons (¼ stick) unsalted butter
>
> 1 tablespoon light corn syrup
>
> Finely grated zest of 2 lemons
>
> 16 ounces bittersweet chocolate, melted
>
> 2 tablespoons (1 ounce) white rum

ENROBING

> 20 ounces milk chocolate, tempered, pages 20–23

FINISHING

> Thin ½-inch strips of candied lemon peel
>
> 2 cookie sheets or jelly-roll pans lined with plastic wrap plus 1 cookie sheet or jelly-roll pan lined with parchment or foil

The idea of combining the flavors of lemon and chocolate might seem bizarre at first, but one taste will convince that it can be a magnificent combination.

1. Bring cream, butter, corn syrup, and lemon zest to a simmer. Remove from heat and allow to stand 5 minutes. Strain cream mixture into chocolate, whisk smooth, whisk in rum, then scrape center mixture into bowl of electric mixer.

2. Use whisk attachment to whip center mixture on slow speed until cooled and shiny. When it is, that means it is also well emulsified.

3. Spread the center mixture in a 10-inch square onto one of the cookie sheets covered with plastic. Refrigerate an hour to set.

4. Remove slab from refrigerator and use a small offset metal icing spatula to spread a thin layer of tempered chocolate, about 2 tablespoons, over the top. Quickly turn slab over onto the other plastic-wrap-covered pan and peel away the wrap the slab was on. Spread the top side of the slab with a thin layer of chocolate. Work quickly.

5. Use a sharp knife, warmed in hot water and wiped before each cut, to cut the slab into ¾- to 1-inch squares. Or use a small round cutter to make rounds. Warm the cutter in a bowl of warm water and dry it before each cut.

6. After all the centers are cut, dip the centers in the remaining tempered chocolate as in the instructions on pages 314–15, and place them on the pan covered with parchment or foil. As each bonbon is dipped, place a piece of candied lemon peel on top.

7. Let the covering of chocolate set.

STORAGE: Place bonbons in a tin or plastic container with a tight-fitting cover and keep at a cool room temperature for up to a week.

VARIATION

CHOCOLATE ORANGE SQUARES Substitute the grated zest of 2 oranges for the lemon zest. Omit rum and add 2 tablespoons orange liqueur to the ganache before whipping it. Decorate the tops of the bonbons with candied orange peel.

CARAMELINES

Bonbons with Chocolate Caramel Centers

■　■　■

Makes about 90 to 100 candies

CENTER MIXTURE

 ¾ cup sugar

 ¼ cup water

 1 cup heavy whipping cream

 2 tablespoons (¼ stick) unsalted butter

 18 ounces bittersweet chocolate, melted

ENROBING

 16 ounces white chocolate, tempered, pages 20–23

FINISHING

Gold leaf

2 cookie sheets or jelly-roll pans covered with plastic-wrap plus 1 cookie sheet covered with heavy acetate or polished aluminum foil (see page 340)

These delicate centers, with just a hint of caramel, are the perfect discovery when you bite into their white chocolate coating.

1. To make the caramel, combine the sugar and water in a saucepan. Place over medium heat, stirring occasionally, until the sugar dissolves and the syrup boils. At the boil, cease stirring and cook until syrup is a deep amber.

2. While the sugar is cooking, bring the cream to a boil. When the caramel has achieved the right color, pour in the boiling cream. Allow to boil and blend. Remove from heat, add butter, and cool 10 minutes.

3. Whisk the caramel into the chocolate, then scrape center mixture into bowl of electric mixer.

4. Place whisk attachment on mixer and whip center mixture on slow speed until cooled and shiny. When it is, it also means it is well emulsified.

5. Spread the center mixture in a 10-inch square on one of the plastic-wrap-covered pans. Refrigerate an hour to set.

6. Remove slab from refrigerator and, using a small offset metal icing spatula, spread a thin layer of tempered chocolate, about 2 tablespoons, over the top. Quickly turn slab over onto the other plastic-wrap-covered pan and peel away the wrap the slab was on. Spread the top side of slab with a thin layer of chocolate. Work quickly.

7. Use a sharp knife, warmed in hot water and wiped before each cut, to cut the slab into ¾- to 1-inch squares. Or use a small round cutter to make rounds. Warm the cutter in a bowl of warm water and dry it before each cut.

8. After all the centers are cut, dip the centers in the remaining tempered chocolate as in the instructions on pages 314–15, and place them on the pan prepared with acetate or polished aluminum foil.

9. After the covering chocolate has set, turn each bonbon over and decorate it with a shred of gold leaf applied with the tip of a small knife.

STORAGE: Place bonbons in a tin or plastic container with a tight-fitting cover and keep at a cool room temperature for up to a week.

MOLDED CHOCOLATES

. . .

These are some of the most interesting chocolates to prepare at home. One caution: You must temper the chocolate completely—a quick tempering as for truffles won't work here. The resulting chocolates are always slick and spectacular-looking.

Finding molds is fairly easy—there are several companies that sell them listed in Sources, page 442. And it isn't necessary to have many different molds to have a great assortment of chocolates—the same molds may be used over and over with different chocolates and different fillings.

PRALINE JEWELS

*Molded Chocolates
with Praline Paste Filling*

• • •

Makes 25 to 50 molded chocolates,
depending on size of molds used

PRALINE PASTE FILLING

1 cup praline paste, about 10
ounces, see Sources, page 442

1 ounce milk chocolate, melted

2 tablespoons (¼ stick) unsalted
butter

MOLDING

16 ounces bittersweet or milk
chocolate, tempered, pages
20–23

2 plaques with deep round cavity
molds

These are the ultimate in rich molded chocolate. The smooth, rich filling perfectly complements a bittersweet chocolate shell—though it is also wonderful with milk chocolate. If you can't find praline paste easily in a retail store, see Sources, page 442.

1. To make the filling, heat the praline paste in a bowl over simmering water. Stir in the melted chocolate and the butter. Cool to room temperature, stirring occasionally.

2. Spread tempered chocolate in molds and shake to settle it, as in the directions on page 316. Turn molds over and allow excess chocolate to drain out. Scrape surfaces of plaques clean with spatula. Refrigerate to set, about 20 minutes.

3. Use a pastry bag fitted with a ¼-inch plain tube (Ateco #4 or #804) to pipe cooled filling into molds. Fill about seven-eighths full. Spread more tempered chocolate over filling and scrape away excess from surface of plaques with spatula. Chill again to set covering.

4. To unmold the chocolates turn the mold over—they should fall out easily. If they do not, gently tap the mold with the back of a long knife or a rolling pin to release them.

STORAGE: Place chocolates in a tin or plastic container with a tight-fitting cover and keep at a cool room temperature for up to a week.

VARIATIONS

Use the center mixture from any of the truffle recipes on pages 322–35 as a filling for a filled molded chocolate. You may use the filling immediately after it has cooled or aerate it by whipping, as in the truffles, before filling the chocolate-lined cavities.

CHOCOLATE HAZELNUT JEWELS

Bijoux Pralinés

. . .

Makes about 25 to 50 chocolates, depending on size of molds used

CENTER MIXTURE

½ cup heavy whipping cream

2 tablespoons (¼ stick) unsalted butter

6 ounces semisweet or bittersweet chocolate, melted

2 tablespoons dark rum

⅓ cup praline paste, about 3½ ounces, see Sources, page 442

MOLDING

16 ounces semisweet or milk chocolate, tempered, pages 20–23

2 plaques with deep round cavity molds

The center of these molded chocolates is made from a rum-spiked ganache flavored with praline paste.

1. To make center mixture, bring cream and butter to a boil. Remove from heat and cool 5 minutes. Whisk cream mixture into chocolate. Whisk in rum and praline paste. Cool to room temperature.

2. Spread tempered chocolate in molds and shake to settle as in the directions on page 316. Turn plaques over and allow excess chocolate to drain back into pan. Scrape tops of plaques clean with icing spatula. Refrigerate to set, about 20 minutes.

3. Spoon cooled filling into a pastry bag fitted with a ¼-inch plain tube (Ateco #4 or #804). Pipe into chocolate shells in molds. Fill each about seven-eighths full. Spread more tempered chocolate over filling to enclose it and scrape away excess with spatula. Chill again to set chocolate covering.

4. Turn the mold over to unmold the chocolates—they should fall out easily. If they don't, gently tap the bottom (now on top) of the plaque with the back of a long knife or a rolling pin.

STORAGE: Store chocolates in a tin or plastic container with a tight-fitting cover and keep at a cool room temperature for up to a week.

CHERRY CORDIALS

. . .

Makes about 25 to 45 chocolates,
depending on size of molds used

CENTER MIXTURE

½ cup Fondant, page 360

1 tablespoon light corn syrup

1 tablespoon kirsch

MOLDING

16 ounces semisweet or milk
chocolate, tempered, pages
20–23

Candied cherries—the same
number as cavities in the molds

2 plaques with deep round
cavity molds

This old-fashioned American chocolate has remained popular through many changes in chocolate fashion. For the filling I like to combine a good-quality candied cherry with fondant and kirsch.

1. To make center mixture, put the fondant in a heat-proof bowl and warm it, stirring constantly, over a pan of hot—not simmering—water, until it is softened and is about 100 to 105 degrees. Stir in the corn syrup and the kirsch, then remove the bowl from heat and cool the fondant to room temperature.

2. Spread tempered chocolate in molds and shake to settle, as in the directions on page 316. Turn plaques over and allow excess chocolate to drain back into pan. Scrape plaques clean with icing spatula. Refrigerate to set.

3. Spoon cooled fondant into a pastry bag fitted with a ¼-inch plain tube (Ateco #4 or #804) and pipe it into chocolate-lined molds, filling each about one-third full. Press a cherry into the fondant, then pipe on more fondant to fill the cavities to about seven-eighths full. Spread more tempered chocolate over filling to seal it in and, with the icing spatula, scrape away excess from surface of plaque. Chill again to set covering.

4. To unmold the chocolates turn the mold over—they should fall out easily. If they do not, gently tap the bottom of the mold (now on top) with the back of a long knife or a rolling pin.

STORAGE: Store chocolates in a tin or plastic container with a tight-fitting cover and keep at a cool room temperature for up to a week.

VARIATIONS

PINEAPPLE RUM FONDANTS Substitute cubes of candied pineapple for the cherries. Substitute white rum for the kirsch.

APRICOT PISTACHIO FONDANTS Substitute pieces of dried apricot for the cherries. Add half a pistachio to each cavity before filling with the fondant. Substitute dark rum for the kirsch.

STRAWBERRY FONDANTS Substitute pieces of fresh strawberries for the cherries. Serve these chocolates on the day they are prepared or the strawberries might ferment in the fondant.

RASPBERRY FONDANTS Substitute fresh raspberries for the cherries and framboise, raspberry eau de vie, for the kirsch. Serve these chocolates on the day they are prepared or the raspberries might ferment in the fondant.

LIQUEUR FONDANT MOLDED CHOCOLATES

■ ■ ■

Makes about 25 to 50 chocolates, depending on size

LIQUEUR FONDANT FILLING

½ cup Fondant, page 360

1 tablespoon light corn syrup

1 tablespoon liqueur, such as orange, raspberry, or one of the herb-flavored ones, such as Chartreuse, Strega, or Galliano

MOLDING

16 ounces bittersweet, semisweet, or milk chocolate, tempered, pages 20–23

2 plaques with deep round cavity molds

This is the easiest way to make candies with creamy liqueur centers.

1. To make center mixture, place the fondant in a heatproof bowl and warm it, stirring constantly, over a pan of hot, not simmering, water, until it is softened and is about 100 to 105 degrees. Stir in the corn syrup and the liqueur, then remove the bowl from the heat and cool the fondant to room temperature.

2. Spread tempered chocolate in molds and shake to settle, as in the directions on page 316. Turn plaques over and allow excess chocolate to drain back into pan. Scrape surfaces of plaques clean with icing spatula. Refrigerate to set, about 20 minutes.

3. Spoon cooled fondant into a pastry bag fitted with a ¼-inch plain tube (Ateco #4 or #804) and pipe into chocolate-lined molds. Fill each about seven-eighths full. Spread more tempered chocolate over filling to seal it in and scrape excess off plaques with spatula. Chill again to set chocolate.

4. To unmold chocolates turn the mold over—they should fall out easily. If they do not, gently tap the bottom of the mold (now on top) with the back of a long knife or a rolling pin to release the chocolates.

STORAGE: Store chocolates in a tin or plastic container with a tight-fitting cover and keep at a cool room temperature for up to a week.

VARIATIONS

Use a liquor such as rum or cognac or a fruit eau de vie such as kirsch or framboise as a substitute for the liqueur.

CHOCOLATE MINT LEAVES

■ ■ ■

Makes about 25 to 50 chocolates, depending on size of molds used

CENTER MIXTURE

½ cup heavy whipping cream

1 small bunch fresh mint, rinsed and coarsely chopped, about 1 cup

8 ounces semisweet or bittersweet chocolate, melted

4 tablespoons (½ stick) unsalted butter, softened

1 tablespoon crème de menthe

MOLDING

16 ounces semisweet or milk chocolate, tempered, pages 20–23

2 plaques with leaf-shaped molds

These molded chocolates have mint-flavored ganache centers.

1. To make center mixture, bring cream to a boil. Remove from heat and add mint. Allow to steep 5 minutes, then strain out mint. Whisk strained cream into chocolate and whisk in soft butter and crème de menthe. Cool to room temperature.

2. Spread tempered chocolate in molds and shake to settle as in directions on page 316. Turn plaques over and allow excess chocolate to drain back into pan. Scrape tops of plaques clean with icing spatula. Refrigerate to set, about 20 minutes.

3. Spoon cooled filling into a pastry bag fitted with a ¼-inch plain tube (Ateco #4 or #804). Pipe into chocolate-lined molds, filling each seven-eighths full. Spread more tempered chocolate over filling to seal it in and scrape away excess on surface of plaque with spatula. Chill again to set covering.

4. To unmold chocolates turn the molds over—the candies should fall out easily. If they do not, gently tap the bottom of the mold (now on top) with the back of a long knife or a rolling pin to release.

STORAGE: Place leaves in a tin or plastic container with a tight-fitting cover and keep at a cool room temperature for up to a week.

PETITE FRITURE

"Small Fry"

▪ ▪ ▪

Makes several dozen chocolates,
depending on size

½ ounce cocoa butter, cut into
¼-inch pieces, see Sources,
page 442

½ ounce chocolate liquor or
unsweetened chocolate, cut
into ¼-inch pieces, see Sources,
page 442

MOLDING

16 ounces white chocolate,
tempered, pages 20–23

2 plaques with assorted fish- and
shellfish-shaped molds, see
Sources, page 442

The name comes from the fish- and shellfish-shaped molds these are made in. Painting the molds with a dark transparent coating gives the chocolates molded in them a shiny, "antiqued" look because they are streaked with the darker color.

1. Combine cocoa butter and chocolate liquor in a small heatproof bowl. Place over a pan of hot, not simmering, water and stir occasionally until cocoa butter and chocolate liquor have melted. Remove bowl from heat and cool to 90 degrees.

2. Use a small, soft brush to coat the molds with a thin layer of the cooled mixture.

3. Fill the molds with the white chocolate, according to the instructions on page 316. Chill briefly to set the chocolate.

4. To unmold the chocolates turn the mold over—they should fall out easily. If they do not, gently tap the bottom of the mold (now the top) with the back of a long knife or a rolling pin.

STORAGE: Store chocolates in a tin or plastic container with a tight-fitting cover and keep at a cool room temperature—they will keep indefinitely.

VARIATIONS

Any chocolate can be used to mold novelty shapes such as these, but the dark cocoa butter and chocolate liquor coating really show up only when the cavities are filled with white chocolate.

WHITE CHOCOLATE EASTER EGGS Substitute a mold with small half-egg-shaped cavities for the molds above. If you wish, gently heat the flat sides of the unmolded eggs on a warm pan, two at a time, and stick them together.

AMANDINES

*Almond and Kirsch–Filled
Molded Chocolates*

■ ■ ■

Makes about 50 chocolates,
depending on size

ALMOND FILLING

½ pound (one 8-ounce can)
almond paste

4 tablespoons kirsch

4 tablespoons (½ stick) unsalted
butter, softened

MOLDING

16 ounces bittersweet chocolate,
tempered, pages 20–23

FINISHING

Slivered almonds, toasted

2 plaques with deep round
cavity molds

The filling in these delicate molded chocolates is simple but excellent. For a change of color and flavor try adding 1½ tablespoons cocoa powder to the filling.

1. To make the filling, use an electric mixer to beat the almond paste until it softens. Beat in the kirsch, then the butter. Continue beating to aerate, about 5 minutes. Reserve the center mixture at room temperature until needed.

2. Spread tempered chocolate in molds and shake to settle, as in the directions on page 316. Turn plaques over and allow excess chocolate to drain back into pan. Scrape tops of plaques clean with icing spatula. Refrigerate to set, about 20 minutes.

3. Spoon filling into a pastry bag fitted with a ¼-inch plain tube (Ateco #4 or #804), then pipe into shells filling each seven-eighths full. Spread more tempered chocolate over filling to seal it in and scrape away excess chocolate on surface of plaque with spatula. Chill again to set covering.

4. To unmold the chocolates, turn the mold over—they should fall out easily. If they do not, gently tap the bottom of the mold (now on top) with the back of a long knife or a rolling pin.

5. To decorate, dip the bottoms of almond slivers into melted and cooled chocolate and stick a few to the top of each unmolded chocolate.

STORAGE: Store chocolates in a tin or plastic container with a tight-fitting cover and keep at a cool room temperature for up to a week.

VARIATIONS

PISTACHIO-FILLED MOLDED CHOCOLATES Reduce almond paste to 4 ounces. Add 1 cup finely ground blanched pistachios (see page 13). Decorate each top with a pistachio half.

WALNUT- OR PECAN-FILLED MOLDED CHOCOLATES Reduce almond paste to 4 ounces. Add 1 cup finely ground pecans or walnuts. Substitute dark rum for the kirsch. Decorate each top with a shred of walnut or pecan.

MILK CHOCOLATE
ROSETTES
■ ■ ■

Makes about 24 chocolates,
depending on size

MILK CHOCOLATE FILLING

⅓ cup heavy whipping cream

2 tablespoons (¼ stick) butter

8 ounces milk chocolate, melted

MOLDING

12 ounces semisweet or bittersweet
chocolate, tempered, pages 20–23

FINISHING

Milk chocolate or white chocolate
shavings, page 392

2 plaques with cup-shaped molds
1 jelly-roll pan

This is a master recipe for making filled, molded chocolate cups. If you have no cup-shaped molds, then try using small pleated paper cups made for chocolates.

1. To make the filling, combine cream and butter in a saucepan and bring to a simmer. Remove from heat and cool 5 minutes. Whisk cream mixture into melted milk chocolate. Cool to room temperature, about 80 degrees.

2. Spread tempered chocolate in cup-shaped molds and shake to settle, as in the directions on page 316. Turn plaques over and allow excess chocolate to drain back into pan. Scrape surfaces of plaques clean with icing spatula. Refrigerate to set.

3. When the cups have set, unmold them by turning the plaques over—they should fall out easily. If they do not, gently tap the mold with the back of a long knife or a rolling pin to release them. Arrange cups on a clean jelly-roll pan.

4. If you don't have cup-shaped molds, use a small brush to paint a thin layer of tempered chocolate on the inside of pleated paper cups. Place coated papers on a jelly-roll pan and chill to set chocolate. When chocolate is set, peel away paper or leave it.

5. Use an electric mixer on medium speed to beat the filling. Spoon aerated filling into a pastry bag fitted with a medium star tube (Ateco #4 or #804). Pipe the filling into each cup to form a large rosette that rises above the top of the cup. Decorate the top of each rosette with a tiny chocolate shaving.

STORAGE: Store chocolates in a tin or plastic container with a tight-fitting cover and keep at a cool room temperature for up to a week.

NOTE: You may also use any of the truffle ganaches as fillings for these—just pipe them with a star tube as in the master recipe.

VARIATION

MARZIPAN CUPS Fill the chocolate cups with the almond filling as for Amandines, page 356. Dust the almond filling very lightly with cocoa powder and decorate with a shred of toasted slivered almond.

SUGAR-BASED CONFECTIONS

• • •

This section includes some of the most popular candies of all—fudge, caramels, butter crunch, and marzipan. Most of these recipes require cooking sugar to a temperature above the boiling point. Although cooking sugar can be complicated, if you follow these rules you shouldn't have any problems.

- Have a good, accurate candy thermometer. Use the type that looks like a ruler, at right, not the type with a stem and a round dial at the top. A ruler-type candy thermometer can touch the bottom of the pan and still give an accurate reading.

- Choose a dry day to cook sugar. Sugar absorbs moisture from the air very easily and many a batch of fondant has been ruined by excess humidity. If you must cook sugar in a humid climate, use only half the amount of cream of tartar or corn syrup called for in the recipe.

- Stir to help dissolve sugar up to boiling point, then cease stirring to avoid unwanted crystallization that agitation may cause.

- Use a metal spoon, not a wooden one that may contain odors or flavors of other foods it was used for.

- Be sure the sugar is dissolved before the mixture reaches the boiling point—this makes all the difference, for example, between smooth or grainy fondant.

- Use low heat to bring sugar to the boiling point, then raise heat to cook the syrup to the desired temperature.

- Always have a bowl of ice water handy to verify the consistency of the sugar syrup, to help ease burns, and to dip the bottom of the pan in to stop further cooking.

- Use a stainless-lined pan that has a copper or aluminum base. Do *not* use an all-stainless or tin-lined copper pan. The stainless pan conducts heat unevenly and the tin lining of the copper pan melts at high temperatures.

CHOCOLATE CARAMELS

• • •

Makes about one hundred
³/₄ × 1¹/₂-inch caramels

2 cups heavy whipping cream

1 cup light corn syrup

2 cups sugar

Pinch salt

16 tablespoons (2 sticks) unsalted
butter

8 ounces bittersweet or semisweet
chocolate, cut into ¼-inch pieces

Tempered chocolate for dipping,
pages 20–23, or cellophane for
wrapping

One 9 × 13 × 2-inch pan, buttered
and lined with buttered foil

These delicate, chewy treats are a little tricky to prepare—you need an accurate candy thermometer. I think they are best when dipped in chocolate, although they may also be wrapped, as is, in cellophane.

1. Combine cream, corn syrup, sugar, and salt in a saucepan. Bring to a boil. While mixture is coming to a boil occasionally wash sugar down sides of pan with a clean brush dipped in hot water to prevent sugar crystals from accumulating there and causing the batch to crystallize. Stir often.

2. When it comes to the boil, stop stirring and insert candy thermometer. Cook to 220 degrees.

3. Remove from heat and add butter and chocolate, allow to stand 2 minutes to melt, then stir to combine and replace on heat. Cook to the soft ball stage—until a teaspoonful of the mixture dropped into a cup of ice water forms a soft ball—240 degrees.

4. Pour mixture into prepared pan and allow to stand at room temperature until completely cool.

5. Unmold onto a cutting board and use a sharp knife to cut into ¾ × 1½-inch pieces. Dip or wrap.

STORAGE: Store dipped or wrapped caramels in a tin or plastic container with a tight-fitting cover and keep at a cool room temperature for up to a week.

VARIATION

BITTERSWEET CHOCOLATE CARAMELS Use 4 ounces unsweetened chocolate and 4 ounces bittersweet chocolate in the caramels.

FONDANT

. . .

Makes about 2 pounds fondant,
about 3½ cups

4 cups sugar

1⅓ cups water

¼ teaspoon cream of tartar or 1
tablespoon light corn syrup

½ teaspoon confectioners' sugar

One 12 × 18-inch marble slab or a
large stainless steel or enamel
roasting pan

The name means "melting" in French and this is the key to understanding this confection. Well-cooked fondant must have a soft, semisolid texture or it will be difficult to work with. Follow the instructions in the recipe carefully and you will get wonderful fondant to use for any of the fondant-based candies in this chapter.

1. Combine all the ingredients except the confectioners' sugar in a 3-quart saucepan.

2. Place the pan over low heat and stir the syrup with a clean metal spoon to dissolve the sugar crystals. As the syrup approaches boiling, wipe down the inside of the pan with a clean brush dipped in cold water to remove any sugar crystals. When the syrup reaches the boiling point, it may foam up in the pan because of the slight impurities in the sugar. Use a spoon to skim any gray foam from the surface.

3. Cover the pan and allow the syrup to boil for 2 minutes. Uncover the pan. Insert a candy thermometer and cook the syrup to 238 degrees. Remove from the heat and dip the bottom of the pan in ice water to stop the cooking. Immediately pour the syrup onto a marble slab or into a stainless steel or enamel roasting pan.

4. Cool the syrup, undisturbed, to approximately 110 degrees. At this point, the syrup will be warm to the touch. If you begin to work the syrup before it has cooled to this temperature it will form coarse crystals, which will make the finished fondant dull and grainy.

5. Using a stainless steel bench scraper or spatula, scrape the fondant up from the surface—of the marble or pan—and work it with a back-and-forth motion with the scraper. Occasionally, scrape all of the fondant together into a mass to make sure no part is being neglected. While the fondant is being worked it begins to whiten. Add the confectioners' sugar, which will speed up the whitening (or crystallization) of the fondant.

6. As the fondant continues to whiten, it will ultimately set into a very firm mass, and no longer be flexible enough to be worked with a spatula. Break small pieces the size of a golf ball off the hardened fondant and press and knead them with the heel of your hand, until they become smooth and semisolid.

7. Place the pieces of kneaded fondant in a dry bowl and sprinkle drops of water, *no more than* ½ teaspoon in all, over the surface. Put plastic wrap over the bowl and press it directly against the fondant. Then soak a paper towel in cold water, wring it out, and place that over the plastic wrap. Finally, cover the top of the bowl with plastic wrap. Allow the fondant to ripen about 24 hours at a cool room temperature or in the refrigerator.

STORAGE: After ripening, refrigerate the fondant until used. It keeps well indefinitely.

CHOCOLATE PECAN CARAMEL CLUSTERS
· · ·
Makes about 24 candies

CARAMEL

2 cups sugar

1 cup light corn syrup

¼ cup water

4 tablespoons (½ stick) butter

2 cups heavy whipping cream, scalded

½ teaspoon salt

2 teaspoons vanilla extract

FINISHING

16 ounces bittersweet or semisweet chocolate, tempered, pages 20–23

About 100 pecan halves

One 9 × 13 × 2-inch pan, buttered and lined with buttered foil plus 1 jelly-roll pan or cookie sheet covered with parchment or foil

These confections are worth their trouble.

1. Combine the sugar, corn syrup, and water in a large saucepan and place over medium heat. While mixture is coming to a boil, occasionally wash sugar down sides of pan with a clean brush dipped in hot water and stir often. Insert candy thermometer and cook to 305 degrees. Remove pan from heat and swirl in butter (be careful, the sugar will boil up in the pan), then add hot cream, a little at a time. Add salt and vanilla and return pan to heat. Insert thermometer and cook to 248 degrees. Remove from heat and allow to stop bubbling. Pour caramel into the prepared 9 × 13 pan and cool to room temperature. Wrap in plastic and continue cooling overnight.

2. To form the candies, drop half tablespoons of tempered chocolate onto the parchment-lined pan to form puddles about 3 inches apart. As soon as each chocolate is poured onto the paper arrange 4 pecan halves on each puddle.

3. Turn caramel pan over onto a cutting surface, remove foil and cut candy into twenty-four 2-inch squares. Roll each square into a ball then center it over a chocolate puddle and flatten it on top of the pecans. Drizzle remaining tempered chocolate over caramel on each candy.

STORAGE: Store candies in a tin or plastic container with a tight-fitting cover and keep at a cool room temperature for up to a week.

CREAM CARAMELS

. . .

Makes about one hundred
¾ × 1½-inch caramels

⅓ cup water

4 cups sugar

2 cups light corn syrup

4 ounces (1 stick) unsalted butter

4 cups heavy whipping cream,
scalded

½ teaspoon salt

1 tablespoon vanilla extract

Cellophane for wrapping or
tempered chocolate for dipping,
pages 20–23

One 9 × 13 × 2-inch pan, buttered
and lined with buttered foil

CHOCOLATE

These rich caramels are good as is, dipped in chocolate, or in chocolate pecan caramel clusters.

1. Combine the water, sugar, and corn syrup in a large saucepan over medium heat. While mixture is coming to a boil, occasionally wash sugar down sides of pan with a clean brush dipped in hot water and stir often. Insert candy thermometer and cook to 305 degrees.

2. Remove pan from heat and swirl in butter (be careful, the sugar will boil up in the pan), then add hot cream, a little at a time. Add salt and vanilla and return pan to heat. Insert thermometer and cook to 248 degrees. Remove from heat and allow to stop bubbling.

3. Pour caramel into prepared pan and allow to cool to room temperature. Wrap in plastic and continue cooling overnight.

4. Cut the caramel into ¾ × 1½-inch rectangles and wrap in cellophane or dip in tempered chocolate.

STORAGE: Store caramels in a tin or plastic container with a tight-fitting cover and keep at a cool room temperature for up to a week.

NOUGATINE

• • •

Makes about 60 pieces

2 cups sugar

½ teaspoon lemon juice

2½ cups sliced almonds,
 lightly toasted

16 ounces bittersweet, semisweet,
 or milk chocolate, tempered,
 pages 20–23, for dipping

Buttered 12 × 18 marble slab, or
 1 heavy jelly-roll pan, buttered

A popular confection in France and Italy, nougatine, crisp and fragile in texture, is a simple mixture of caramel and nuts. It is good on its own, or enrobed in chocolate.

1. Combine sugar and lemon juice in a saucepan and stir off heat with a clean wooden spoon until mixed—the sugar should look like wet sand.

2. Place the pan over medium heat and allow the sugar to begin to melt. Stir the sugar occasionally after it starts to melt. When the sugar is a uniform light amber color, remove it from the heat and stir in the almonds.

3. Immediately pour the nougatine onto a slab of buttered marble or a buttered jelly-roll pan and, using a buttered spatula or metal scraper, fold it back onto itself several times. Press it flat with a spatula, then use a buttered rolling pin to roll out into a thin sheet.

4. With a large, buttered knife cut the nougatine into 1-inch strips, then cut across each strip to make diamonds, squares, or rectangles. Allow to cool and harden.

5. If the nougatine hardens before all of it is cut, slide it onto a jelly-roll pan covered with parchment or foil and reheat until soft—just a few minutes—in a 300-degree oven, then finish cutting.

6. Dip the nougatine according to the directions on pages 314–15.

STORAGE: Store candies in a tin or plastic container with a tight-fitting cover and keep at a cool room temperature for up to a week.

VARIATIONS

HAZELNUT NOUGATINE Substitute toasted, skinned, and chopped hazelnuts for the almonds. After chopping the hazelnuts, shake them in a strainer to eliminate the dusty particles.

WALNUT NOUGATINE Substitute toasted and chopped walnut pieces for the almonds. After chopping the walnuts, shake them in a strainer to eliminate the dusty particles.

ALMOND AND HAZELNUT NOUGATINE Substitute 1¼ cups toasted, skinned, and chopped hazelnuts for half the almonds.

HAZELNUT FEUILLETÉS

• • •

Makes about one hundred and forty
1-inch squares

FEUILLETÉ

1 cup praline paste, about 10
    ounces, see Sources, page 442

3 cups sugar

2 teaspoons lemon juice

6 tablespoons (¾ stick) unsalted
    butter

Tempered semisweet chocolate,
    pages 20–23, for dipping,
    optional

One 6- or 7-quart stainless steel
    bowl, buttered, plus buttered
    12 × 18 marble slab or 1 heavy
    10 × 15-inch jelly-roll pan lined
    with buttered foil

These unusual confections have a flaky, fragile texture like puff pastry—hence the name. Feuilletés used to be prepared by rolling and folding the caramel and praline paste repeatedly as though it were a dough—a lengthy process that frequently resulted in burns to the cook and a mess to clean up. This simpler method, which folds the two mixtures together, is easier and produces excellent results.

1. Place the praline paste in a bowl over a pan of hot, not simmering, water to warm.

2. To make the caramel, combine the sugar and lemon juice in a 2-quart saucepan. Place over medium heat and allow to begin to melt. At the first sign of smoke, stir the caramel and continue stirring occasionally until the caramel is a golden amber. Off heat, stir in the butter and pour the caramel into a large buttered stainless steel bowl. Quickly add in the praline paste and fold the two mixtures together with a wooden spatula. Don't combine completely—they should remain streaky.

3. Pour the mixture out onto buttered marble and shape into a 10 × 15-inch rectangle. Cool slightly. Alternately, pour the feuilleté onto a 10 × 15-inch jelly-roll pan lined with buttered foil. Use a buttered rolling pin to roll the feuilleté out to a ¼-inch thickness and cut into 1-inch squares or diamonds. Cool the feuilletés.

4. Serve the feuilletés plain or dip them fully or half in tempered chocolate.

STORAGE: Store feuilletés in a tin or plastic container with a tight-fitting cover and keep at a cool room temperature for up to a week.

OLD-FASHIONED BUTTER CRUNCH

. . .

Makes about 3 pounds candy

BUTTER CRUNCH MIXTURE

16 tablespoons (2 sticks) unsalted butter

1½ cups sugar

3 tablespoons light corn syrup

3 tablespoons water

1 cup toasted almonds, chopped, about 4 ounces

TOPPING

12 ounces semisweet chocolate, tempered, pages 20–23

1 cup toasted almonds, chopped, about 4 ounces

One 12 × 18-inch pan, buttered and lined with buttered foil, plus 2 large cutting boards, jelly-roll pans, or cardboard pieces, covered with parchment

---

Always a popular confection, butter crunch successfully and enticingly combines chocolate, nuts, and sugar.

1. To make the butter crunch mixture, melt the butter in a saucepan. Remove from heat and stir in sugar, corn syrup, and water. Cook, stirring occasionally, until the mixture reaches 300 degrees on a candy thermometer. Remove from heat, stir in almonds, and pour out into prepared pan, spreading the mixture with the back of a spoon to fill the pan.

2. Before the butter crunch hardens, but when it is firm enough to handle, turn it out onto a large parchment-covered cutting board and peel away the foil. Allow the butter crunch to cool completely.

3. To finish the butter crunch, wipe the top surface of the candy with a damp paper towel to remove excess butter and allow to dry a few minutes. Have another cutting board or the back of a jelly-roll pan ready to turn the candy over onto.

4. Use a small offset metal icing spatula to spread half the tempered chocolate quickly over the butter crunch. Scatter half the chopped almonds over the chocolate. Cover this finished surface with a piece of parchment paper or foil and place another cutting board or the back of a large jelly-roll pan on the paper. Turn the candy over onto the second board or pan. Remove top board and paper and quickly spread with remaining tempered chocolate and scatter on remaining almonds (it isn't necessary to wipe the second side because it wasn't against a buttered surface). Refrigerate for 20 minutes to set chocolate.

5. Break the butter crunch into 2-inch pieces.

STORAGE: Store candy in a tin or plastic container with a tight-fitting cover and keep at a cool room temperature for up to a week.

SAUCES
...

Hot Fudge Sauce

Lean, Mean Hot Fudge Sauce

Chocolate Sauce

Chocolate Orange Sauce

Chocolate Syrup

Chocolate Fountain Syrup

Crème Anglaise

Lemon

Orange

Cinnamon

Coffee

Vanilla Bean

Chocolate

Liqueur

BEVERAGES
...

Sandra Church's Adult Hot Cocoa

French-Style Hot Chocolate

Bittersweet Hot Chocolate

Iced Mocha

Chocolate Caliente
(*Mexican Hot Chocolate*)

Chocolate Egg Cream

Chocolate Ice Cream Soda

SAUCES

. . .

These luscious liquids are among chocolate's crowning glories. Rich, gleaming sauces are treats to be savored in conjunction with plain desserts or to put rich ones over the top.

HOT FUDGE SAUCE

. . .

Makes about 2 cups

¼ cup water

1 cup light corn syrup

1⅓ cups sugar

¼ teaspoon salt

4 ounces unsweetened chocolate, coarsely chopped

½ cup alkalized (Dutch process) cocoa powder

4 tablespoons (½ stick) unsalted butter

¼ cup heavy whipping cream

1 tablespoon vanilla extract

This is one of those really rich hot fudge sauces that hardens as it hits ice cream. It's great to use as the sauce for a brownie sundae!

1. Combine water, corn syrup, and sugar in a nonreactive pan and bring to a boil, stirring often, until all the sugar crystals have melted. Boil 1 minute without stirring.

2. Remove from heat and add the salt and the chocolate. Allow to stand 2 minutes until chocolate has melted, then whisk smooth.

3. Sift the cocoa into a mixing bowl and stir in enough of the liquid mixture to make a paste, then stir the cocoa paste smoothly back into the syrup.

4. Whisk in the remaining ingredients.

5. Store the sauce in a tightly covered jar in the refrigerator. Reheat opened jar over simmering water before serving.

LEAN, MEAN
HOT FUDGE SAUCE

. . .

Makes about 2 cups

½ cup water

1 cup light corn syrup

1½ cups sugar

¼ teaspoon salt

1 cup alkalized (Dutch process)
   cocoa powder

1 tablespoon unsalted butter

1 tablespoon vanilla extract

Creating a hot fudge sauce with less fat and just as much taste was a challenge but I believe this is it. This is a great sauce to serve with rich ice creams and frozen desserts because it has so much flavor but adds only a few extra calories and grams of fat.

1. Combine water, corn syrup, and sugar in a nonreactive pan and bring to a boil, stirring often, until all the sugar crystals have melted.

2. Remove from heat and add the salt. Sift the cocoa into the hot syrup and whisk it in. There may be a few lumps—disregard them.

3. Replace the pan on low heat and whisk gently until smooth. Off heat, strain the sauce into a bowl and whisk in the butter and vanilla.

4. Store the sauce in a tightly covered jar in the refrigerator. Reheat opened jar over simmering water before serving.

CHOCOLATE SAUCE

■ ■ ■

Makes about 2 cups

1 cup heavy whipping cream

⅓ cup sugar

⅓ cup light corn syrup

12 ounces bittersweet chocolate, cut into ¼-inch pieces

Pinch salt

2 teaspoons vanilla extract or strong liquor, such as rum or brandy

This is an easy and delicious sauce to serve whenever a chocolate sauce is needed. It goes perfectly with ices and frozen desserts as well as with soufflés or any warm desserts.

1. Combine the cream, sugar, and corn syrup in a saucepan and place on low heat. Bring to a boil, stirring often.

2. Off heat, add chocolate and shake pan to submerge chocolate in hot liquid. Let stand 3 minutes until chocolate has melted, then whisk smooth.

3. Whisk in salt and vanilla.

4. Store the sauce in a tightly covered jar in the refrigerator. Reheat over simmering water before serving.

CHOCOLATE ORANGE SAUCE

■ ■ ■

Makes about 2 cups

1 cup heavy whipping cream

⅓ cup sugar

⅓ cup light corn syrup

12 ounces bittersweet chocolate, cut into ¼-inch pieces

Pinch salt

⅓ cup orange liqueur

This orange version of chocolate sauce takes on a new character when you use other liquors or liqueurs.

1. Combine the cream, sugar, and corn syrup in a saucepan and place on low heat. Bring to a boil, stirring often.

2. Off heat, add chocolate and shake pan to submerge chocolate in hot liquid. Let stand 3 minutes until chocolate has melted, then whisk smooth.

3. Whisk in salt and liqueur.

4. Store the sauce in a tightly covered jar in the refrigerator. Reheat over simmering water before serving.

CHOCOLATE SYRUP

. . .

Makes about 1½ cups

½ cup water

¼ cup sugar

⅓ cup light corn syrup

10 ounces bittersweet chocolate,
   cut into ¼-inch pieces

Pinch salt

2 teaspoons vanilla extract

This is a great, easy chocolate syrup, perfect for drizzling on ice cream or to use for making a quick chocolate drink.

1. Combine the water, sugar, and corn syrup in a saucepan and place on low heat. Bring to a boil, stirring often.

2. Off heat, add chocolate and shake pan to submerge chocolate in hot liquid. Let stand 3 minutes until chocolate has melted, then whisk smooth.

3. Whisk in salt and vanilla.

4. Store the sauce in a tightly covered jar in the refrigerator. Use the syrup as it is or reheat over hot water before serving.

VARIATION

CHOCOLATE FOUNTAIN SYRUP Use this to make a chocolate egg cream or ice cream soda, page 379.

Decrease amount of chocolate to 8 ounces and increase sugar to ½ cup for a slightly thinner and sweeter syrup.

CRÈME ANGLAISE

. . .

Makes about 3 cups

2 cups half and half or 1 cup milk
   and 1 cup heavy whipping cream

½ cup sugar

6 large egg yolks

2 teaspoons vanilla extract

This is a foolproof method for making this tricky sauce. The key to preparing a successful crème anglaise is organization. Have all utensils and ingredients ready before you start.

1. Before you start the crème anglaise, embed a heatproof bowl securely in another, larger bowl filled with ice. Place a fine wire-mesh strainer in the top bowl (if you have a conical French wire-mesh chinois, use it. If not, any fine strainer will do).

2. Combine the half and half and sugar in a nonreactive pan. Whisk once or twice, then place over low heat and bring to a boil. In the meantime, whisk the egg yolks in a bowl, just enough to make them liquid.

3. When the liquid boils, whisk about one third of it into the yolks. Return the remaining liquid to low heat and when it is about to boil again, whisk in the yolk mixture. Begin whisking before you pour in the yolk mixture or you'll scramble the yolks. Continue whisking for about 10 seconds—there will be a great burst of steam. It will not look very thick, but it will be visibly thickened, and you will feel a greater resistance on the whisk as the cream thickens.

4. Immediately remove the pan from the heat, still whisking constantly, and strain the sauce into the chilled bowl. Whisk for a minute or so after it has been strained.

5. Leave the sauce over the ice bath until it cools to room temperature, then whisk in the vanilla. Pour the sauce into a bowl, cover tightly with plastic wrap, and refrigerate immediately. Use the sauce within 24 hours.

HOW TO FLAVOR CRÈME ANGLAISE

Use the following flavors in addition to the vanilla extract.

LEMON: Add the grated zest of 2 lemons to the pan before bringing the liquid to a boil.

ORANGE: Add the grated zest of 2 oranges to the pan before bringing liquid to a boil; add 1 tablespoon orange liqueur with the vanilla.

CINNAMON: Add 2 crushed cinnamon sticks to the pan before bringing the liquid to a boil. At the boil, remove from heat and allow to stand 15 minutes. Bring back to a boil and continue with recipe—the cinnamon will be strained out after the sauce is cooked.

COFFEE: Replace ½ cup of the half and half with ½ cup very strong prepared coffee.

VANILLA BEAN: Omit the vanilla extract. Add a vanilla bean, split lengthwise, to the pan before bringing the liquid to a boil. (After the bean is strained out, rinse it and let it air-dry for a few hours. Wrap in plastic and store in the freezer—you may use it again.)

CHOCOLATE: Bring ½ cup milk to a boil and remove from heat. Add 6 ounces bittersweet chocolate cut into ¼-inch pieces to the hot liquid. Let stand a few minutes and whisk smooth. Whisk into cooled crème anglaise before refrigerating.

LIQUEUR: Whisk 2 tablespoons liquor or sweet liqueur into the crème anglaise before refrigerating it.

BEVERAGES

. . .

What could be better on a cold night than a cup of hot chocolate or cocoa? I like to distinguish between the two because hot chocolate should be made with solid chocolate, whereas hot cocoa is made with cocoa powder—an easier and less rich drink than hot chocolate.

With the advent of the espresso craze in the past few years, cold chocolate drinks have also come into their own. There are recipes for cold chocolate drinks as well as old-fashioned soda fountain specialties in this chapter.

SANDRA CHURCH'S ADULT HOT COCOA

. . .

Makes 3 or 4 demitasse servings

3 tablespoons sugar

3 tablespoons deluxe cocoa powder, such as Pernigotti or Valrhona

1 tablespoon instant espresso coffee powder

⅓ cup heavy whipping cream

1 cup boiling water

2 tablespoons cognac or brandy

My friend Sandra Church, who created the role of the young Gypsy Rose Lee in *Gypsy* during its first Broadway run, jokes that enough of this hot cocoa will make anyone want to strip!

1. Combine the sugar, cocoa, and coffee in a nonreactive pan and whisk in the cream until the mixture is smooth.

2. Whisk in the water, a little at a time, whisking smooth after each addition.

3. Place over low heat and cook, whisking often, until mixture is foamy and almost boiling (it will release large amounts of steam).

4. Remove from heat, whisk in cognac, and pour into warmed demitasse cups. Serve immediately.

FRENCH-STYLE HOT CHOCOLATE

. . .

Makes about 1 quart hot chocolate or
enough for 5 or 6 mugs

1 cup water

3 ounces French bittersweet
chocolate, cut into ¼-inch pieces

3 ounces French milk chocolate, cut
into ¼-inch pieces

¼ cup unsweetened alkalized
(Dutch process) cocoa powder

3 cups milk

1½ teaspoons vanilla extract

This is my approximation of the lusciously rich hot chocolate served at such famous Parisian establishments as La Maison du Chocolat and Angelina's.

1. Bring the water to a simmer in a small pan. Remove from heat and add the chocolates. Shake the pan to make sure all the chocolate is covered with hot water and set it aside for 5 minutes to melt the chocolate.

2. Sift the cocoa powder into another, larger saucepan, preferably an enamel-lined one. Add a few tablespoons of milk and stir to make a paste. This will keep the cocoa from lumping. Gradually whisk in the rest of the milk. Place the pan on lowest heat and bring the liquid to a simmer, whisking often.

3. Whisk the chocolates and water to a smooth paste and whisk into the cocoa and milk mixture. Continue to heat until very hot, but do not bring to a full boil. Keep whisking to make the chocolate frothy. Off heat, whisk in the vanilla and serve immediately.

BITTERSWEET HOT CHOCOLATE

• • •

Makes about 3 cups, or about 4 portions,
depending on the size of the cups

½ cup water

4 ounces bittersweet chocolate,
cut into ¼-inch pieces

2 cups milk

1 teaspoon vanilla extract, optional

This is a perfect chocolate drink for those who
don't like their hot chocolate too sweet.

1. Bring the water to a boil in a small saucepan and
remove from heat. Add chocolate and shake the pan
to make sure all the chocolate is covered and then set
it aside for 5 minutes to melt the chocolate.

2. In another, larger saucepan, preferably an enamel-
lined one, bring the milk to a simmer. Whisk the
chocolate and water mixture smooth and whisk it
into the milk. Continue to heat until very hot, but do
not bring to a full boil, whisking to make the chocolate frothy. Off heat, whisk
in the optional vanilla and serve immediately.

ICED MOCHA

• • •

Makes about 3 cups, or about 4 portions,
depending on the size of the glasses

½ cup heavy whipping cream or
milk

4 ounces semisweet chocolate, cut
into ¼-inch pieces

1½ cups strong brewed coffee,
cooled

8 ounces ice cream, chocolate,
vanilla, or coffee

Cocoa powder in a shaker for
finishing

This is a great summer chocolate drink—
especially for coffee lovers. Chill the glasses
before starting preparation.

1. In a small saucepan, bring the cream or milk to a
simmer, then remove from heat. Add the chocolate
and allow to stand a minute or two until the chocolate melts. Whisk smooth and whisk in half the
coffee.

2. Pour the chocolate and coffee mixture and the
remaining coffee into the container of a blender.
Cover and blend to mix. Add the ice cream and blend
smooth.

3. Immediately pour into chilled glasses and dust
lightly with cocoa.

CHOCOLATE CALIENTE

Mexican Hot Chocolate

• • •

Makes about 1½ quarts,
about 6 large portions

2 cups milk

3 cups water

8 ounces Mexican chocolate,
finely chopped

When the Conquistadores first arrived in Mexico during the sixteenth century, chocolate was served exclusively as a beverage. The beans were roasted and ground, then combined with honey, almonds, and spices and served hot. The type of chocolate used for this beverage survives today in the round tablets of flavored Mexican chocolate usually available in the Hispanic foods section of most markets.

To make an authentic pot of Mexican hot chocolate, you will need a *molinillo*, a carved wooden whip with rings around the handle that is rolled between the palms of the hands to aerate the mixture while it is heating. An ordinary wire whisk is, however, a good substitute. Heat cups before beginning preparation.

1. Combine milk and water in a nonreactive saucepan and bring to a simmer.

2. Remove from heat and add chocolate. Allow to stand several minutes to melt chocolate, then whisk smooth.

3. Return pan to low heat and whisk constantly until hot chocolate is near a boil and very foamy. Pour into heated cups and serve immediately.

CHOCOLATE EGG CREAM

▪ ▪ ▪

Makes 1 large drink

¼ cup Chocolate Fountain Syrup, page 372

⅓ cup milk

Cold seltzer (not club soda)

1 tall 12-ounce glass, ideally an old-fashioned soda fountain glass

A New York soda-fountain institution, the egg cream is famous for containing neither eggs nor cream. The foamy mixture of chocolate syrup, milk, and seltzer makes a refreshing and satisfying drink. The proportions here are only a guide—feel free to increase or decrease them to taste.

1. Combine the chocolate fountain syrup and the milk in the glass. Stir well to mix.

2. Pour in the seltzer slowly and carefully so the drink doesn't overflow. Stir once or twice with a long spoon and drink through a straw.

VARIATION

CHOCOLATE ICE CREAM SODA Before adding seltzer, add 2 scoops of chocolate ice cream. Add seltzer and stir once or twice. Serve with a straw and a long spoon. If you use vanilla ice cream (or a scoop each of vanilla and chocolate ice cream), you will make a black and white soda.

DECORATING
WITH CHOCOLATE

. . .

Chocolate Plastic

Dark, White, or Milk Chocolate Plastic

WORKING WITH
CHOCOLATE PLASTIC

. . .

Making Chocolate Ribbons, Ruffles, and Cigarettes

Making Leaves and Flowers

Glazing with Ganache and Chocolate

Tempered Chocolate Glaze

Multicolored Chocolate Glaze

Chocolate Cutouts for Decorating Cakes, Desserts, and Showpieces

Chocolate Sheet

Chocolate Shavings

Marbled Chocolate Bark

Chocolate Honeycomb

Chocolate Lace

Chocolate Filigree Decorations

Piping and Writing with Chocolate

Chocolate Enameling

Chocolate Curls and Large Shavings

Chocolate Curls Made from Melted Chocolate

DECORATING WITH CHOCOLATE

. . .

Chocolate is a wonderful medium for creating beautiful and, for the most part, easily made decorations. A professional could establish his reputation with the precision of the perfectly formed chocolate cylinders on his cakes. But there are many easier-to-achieve decorations that give as striking an effect.

Here are a few general suggestions for preparing and using chocolate decorations:

Plan Ahead: Many of the designs calling for tempered chocolate use only a small amount. Prepare them when you have tempered chocolate for something else. Then, with only a little extra effort, you will be able to make and store the decorations—they keep indefinitely in a cool, dry place.

Neatness Counts: Uniformity and neatness can be as important as artistic flair, especially if the decorative motifs or designs are repeated. Use cutters or patterns whenever possible.

Match the Decoration to the Dessert: Make sure the decoration you choose is appropriate for the dessert or cake on which it is used. Chocolate-dipped almonds or nougatine diamonds would be a handsome addition on an almond cake or mousse containing ground nougatine, but would be peculiar on a cake without either of those elements. Use plain chocolate decorations for simpler desserts that need dressing up.

Keep the Decoration Subordinate to the Dessert: Don't overwhelm the cake or dessert with decoration. Make the decoration smaller than the dessert so that it adds to, rather than detracts from, the beauty and symmetry of the dessert.

Above All, Have Fun with Chocolate Decorations: Minimize distractions so you can give your full attention to preparing the decorations and enjoying the process.

CHOCOLATE PLASTIC

∎ ∎ ∎

Makes about 1¼ pounds or enough
to decorate 2 or 3 desserts,
depending on their size

⅔ cup light corn syrup

16 ounces semisweet chocolate,
melted

1 cookie sheet or jelly-roll pan
covered with plastic wrap

This decorating paste—similar in some of the ways it is used to marzipan—makes lovely, dramatic cake decorations. Use it as you would marzipan to wrap an entire layer or roll cake, or to fashion ruffles and ribbons for delicate decorations.

1. Use a rubber spatula to stir the corn syrup thoroughly into the chocolate. Be sure to scrape the sides of the bowl to incorporate any unmixed chocolate clinging there.

2. Scrape the chocolate plastic out onto the prepared pan and spread it so that nowhere is it more than ⅓ inch thick. Draw the plastic wrap up around the chocolate to cover it completely.

3. Allow the chocolate plastic to set at a cool room temperature or in the refrigerator. In any case, wait several hours before using it.

VARIATIONS

Substitute white chocolate or milk chocolate for the semisweet chocolate. Reduce the corn syrup to ½ cup.

WORKING WITH CHOCOLATE PLASTIC

• • •

MAKING CHOCOLATE RIBBONS, RUFFLES, AND CIGARETTES

Follow these general instructions for rolling out ribbons from chocolate plastic.

1. Lightly dust the work surface and chocolate plastic with sifted cocoa powder.

2. Divide the batch into four pieces and pound each piece of the chocolate plastic with a rolling pin to soften it and make it pliable.

3. Shape each piece into a cylinder about 4 inches long, then flatten with the rolling pin or heel of your hand into approximately a 4-inch square. Lightly dust again with the sifted cocoa powder and roll each into a thin ribbon.

4. Or use a pasta machine to roll into thin ribbons. Pass each of the four pieces through every other setting, from the widest down to the next to last. (If it is extremely cool in the room, you might be able to pass the ribbons through the last setting. The result is a wonderfully thin, almost transparent ribbon.)

5. Use the ribbons to encircle a cake. Pleat some of the ribbons into ruffles for a beautiful effect (*right*), and cover the entire top of a cake with concentric circles of them.

6. Or mass the entire batch of chocolate plastic together, roll it out thinly, and use it to cover a cake or roll. Then dust it lightly with sifted cocoa powder.

7. To make cigarettes to decorate cakes or desserts, take a 3 × 5-inch piece of ribbon and roll it up tightly from one of the long ends (*right*).

1. To make leaves from the chocolate plastic, roll it out with the rolling pin or pasta machine, and cut into 1¼-inch-wide ribbons (*right*). Cut ribbons across to make diamonds, then press side angles in so sides curve into leaf shapes (*far right*).

2. To make carnations, roll out the chocolate plastic with a rolling pin or pasta machine, then cut it into ribbons 1 inch wide and 12 inches long. With the point of a paring knife, make cuts ¼ inch apart and ½ inch deep down one of the long

sides of the ribbon, so the ribbon looks like a fringe (*above left*). Begin from one of the short ends and roll up the uncut edge. When the whole fringe has been rolled up, hold the carnation between thumbs and forefingers of both hands and press in right under where the slashes end, to make the carnation open (*above right*). Pinch or cut away the excess chocolate plastic under the flower. Carnations are very effective when made in a variety of chocolate colors and massed together.

3. To make roses, proceed as above, rolling 12-inch-long ribbons. Then use a round cutter about 2 to 2½ inches in diameter to cut out petals (*top left*). Make conical rose bases by pressing the scraps together (*top right*), then wrap the petals around the base, as in the illustrations (*bottom left and right*). As in nature, make a closed bud first, then assemble several open petals around it.

4. To make bell-shaped flowers such as morning glories or petunias, shape about a ½-tablespoon piece of chocolate plastic into a sphere. Point one end, to make a cone with a curved end opposite the pointed one. Use a pencil or an awl to make a hole in the center of the shape from the rounded end. Revolve the awl around in the rounded end to enlarge the opening. Then withdraw it and use your fingertips to pinch the edges thinner. Pinch the pointed end to make it thinner. For a morning glory, open up the open end of the flower so that it is almost perpendicular to the pointed stem and pinch the thin edge in four places equidistant around the flower. For petunias, make a similar shape but more closed and pinch and frill the edge of the petals with your fingertips.

5. To make 4- and 5-petaled flowers, divide a tablespoon-size piece of chocolate plastic into four or five pieces. Form each into a sphere, then point one end of the sphere to make a cone with a rounded end and a pointy one. Press between fingertips to flatten to a teardrop shape. Repeat with the other pieces to make other petals. Mass the petals together at the pointy bases and press the bases together to keep the flower intact. Make a small sphere and flatten it, placing it in the center of the petals. Open the petals out and curve them slightly to give the flower some expression.

GLAZING WITH GANACHE OR CHOCOLATE

. . .

Makes about 2 cups glaze, enough for covering one 10-inch cake or several smaller desserts

1 cup heavy whipping cream

8 ounces semisweet chocolate, cut into ¼-inch pieces

A rack set in a jelly-roll pan for glazing

CHOCOLATE

The process for covering the entire outside of a cake or dessert with the ganache glaze that follows or with tempered chocolate is the same—only the material is different. Whichever medium is used it is important to have more glaze or chocolate than is actually necessary for coating the dessert so that one pour will cover it completely. You can touch up the sides with a spatula, but for the smoothest blemish-free effect the top shouldn't be touched again.

To ensure the best and smoothest glaze, the outside of the cake or dessert being glazed must be covered with a smooth medium that becomes firm when cold—butter cream, whipped ganache, or even a thin coating of marzipan or chocolate plastic. Just be sure to chill the dessert well before attempting to glaze it. If a glaze is poured on the bare surface of a cake, the cake will absorb the glaze and the result will be a rough surface.

Make sure the cake or dessert is on a cardboard disk, a tart pan bottom, or a springform base that does not protrude at the bottom of the cake for ease in moving the cake on and off the rack.

1. Bring cream to a simmer in a 1½- to 2-quart nonreactive saucepan over medium heat.

2. Remove from heat and add chocolate all at once. Gently shake pan to make sure all the chocolate is covered in the hot cream. Leave for 5 minutes.

3. Whisk the glaze smooth and put it through a fine wire mesh strainer into another nonreactive saucepan (the glaze is easier to pour from a pan with a handle—also it is handy to have the glaze in a pan in case you want to reheat slightly).

4. Let the glaze cool to room temperature. Be ready to pour the glaze just when it has cooled to room temperature. It is more liquid then and easier to pour. If the glaze gets too cool, it may set on contact with the chilled dessert and not run to cover it completely.

5. Place the well-chilled dessert on the rack in the jelly-roll pan (to catch runoff of glaze). Hold the pan so that the side from which the glaze will emerge is close to the top of the dessert, and begin to pour at the center of the top. Pour the glaze in a clockwise spiral. Pour slowly so that you can be sure you will have enough glaze left to coat the sides of the dessert. When you get to the outer edge of the cake pour the rest of the glaze around the rim and let it drip down to coat the sides. Quickly take a metal cake icing spatula and, holding it at about a 45-degree angle to the top of the cake, sweep once across the top of the cake. Don't press down, just sweep. Quickly turn the jelly-roll pan to check the sides of the dessert. It is easy to pick up a little of the glaze that has dripped into the pan with the edge of the spatula and touch up the sides.

6. Leave the dessert on the rack for 20 minutes at a cool room temperature before attempting to move it, so that the glaze sets. When you do, use a wide spatula. Slide it under the cardboard or other base the dessert is on and lift it from the rack. Use the point of a small knife to scrape away any drips at the bottom edge before you place the cake on a platter.

VARIATIONS

TEMPERED CHOCOLATE GLAZE You can use exactly the same technique to glaze a dessert with a pound of tempered bittersweet, semisweet, or milk chocolate. Have the dessert, on a cardboard or other base, covered with butter cream or ganache, as above, but remove it from the refrigerator to a cool room temperature at least an hour before glazing. If the dessert is too cold, the tempered chocolate will set immediately and you won't be able to even off the top or touch up any blemishes on the sides.

MULTICOLORED CHOCOLATE GLAZE To streak, feather, or marble the glaze, you will need a small amount of a contrasting color glaze made with milk chocolate or white chocolate. Prepare the glaze as above, using ¼ cup heavy whipping cream and 3 ounces of milk chocolate or white chocolate (the higher proportion of chocolate to cream is necessary because milk chocolates and white chocolates are softer than dark chocolate). If the background glaze and the streaking one are the same temperature, the lighter glaze will be absorbed by the background rather than staying above it, so the top of the glaze will be flat and neat. Place the strained glaze in a paper cone, squeeze bottle, or a nonpleated plastic bag. As soon as you have covered the top of the cake with the dark glaze, snip the end of the paper cone or the corner of the plastic bag and apply the contrasting color glaze using one of the following methods:

STREAKING: Pass the cone, squeeze bottle, or plastic bag back and forth across the top of the dessert. End each streak off the surface of the cake (so there won't be loops on the sides of the dessert). Place each streak at least ¼ inch from the previous one, until the whole top of the dessert is covered. If you wish, make the streaks farther apart and when top is covered turn the pan the dessert is on 45 degrees and add another layer of streaks diagonally to the first ones.

 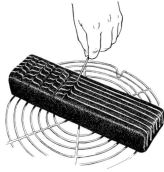

FEATHERING: Use the lighter glaze to make parallel lines ½ inch apart over the top. Use the point of a thin knife, a skewer, or a toothpick to pull from left to right across the lighter lines at 1-inch intervals. Working quickly, then pull the implement right to left between each of the left to right pulls, as in the illustration.

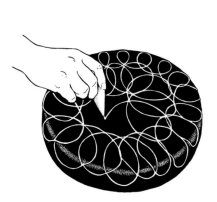 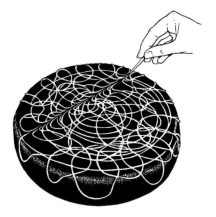

MARBLING: Use lighter glaze to streak the top of the dessert in a series of curves. With the point of a thin knife, skewer, or toothpick, draw a series of arcs across the lighter lines, as in the illustration.

CHOCOLATE CUTOUTS FOR DECORATING CAKES, DESSERTS, AND SHOWPIECES

. . .

Makes two 12-inch square sheets
to be cut into shapes

16 ounces bittersweet, semisweet, milk, or white chocolate, tempered, pages 20–23

2 cookie sheets or jelly-roll pans covered with parchment or heavy acetate

This is a simple way to achieve a beautiful three-dimensional effect on a cake or dessert. A series of cutout chocolate disks, half disks, or other shapes will give any dessert they are used on a tailored and neat decorated appearance. Mixing dark chocolate and white chocolate or milk chocolate decorations in the same dessert can also work well.

1. Spread tempered chocolate in a 12-inch square about 3/16 inch thick on back of the prepared pans. Streak surface with a decorating comb (a metal or plastic scraper with jagged teeth) if desired. Chill slightly, until chocolate begins to set. With a small paring knife, quickly cut the chocolate into 1-inch-wide strips, then cut the strips diagonally into diamonds. Allow chocolate to set completely before attempting to detach cutouts from paper. Use the same technique to cut squares, rectangles, triangles, or any plain, geometric shape.

2. You can also cut chocolate shapes with a cookie or other cutter. Dip the cutting edge into a bowl of warm water and dry it off before each cut. Be careful that the chocolate has not set completely or it will shatter when the cutter is pressed into it.

VARIATIONS

Use either the paring knife or the cutter technique, above, on Marbleized Chocolate Bark, page 394, or Chocolate Lace, page 395.

CHOCOLATE SHEET Leave the chocolate uncut. After it has set, break it into irregular pieces. These can be used to finish the top of a cake that has already been spread with butter cream or ganache, such as the Swiss Chocolate Hazelnut Cake, page 100.

CHOCOLATE SHAVINGS

• • •

4 ounces semisweet, milk, or white chocolate, preferably in a block cut from a large bar

Any of the following implements: box grater, food processor fitted with grating blade, old-fashioned vegetable peeler, melon-ball scoop, round cookie or biscuit cutter, or a miniature tart pan

1 jelly-roll pan lined with parchment or wax paper to catch the shavings

Many of the recipes in this book call for chocolate shavings. A single one is perfect to decorate the top of a small tart or the center of a whipped cream rosette; multiples can cover the top of a cake, pie, tart, or large cookie, or the sides or entire outside of a cake.

Place the chocolate on the prepared pan. Use a paper towel to hold the chocolate and grate it with the largest holes (not the slices) on the box grater. To use the food processor, fit the machine with the grating blade provided with the machine. Break the chocolate into ½-inch pieces and stuff into the feed tube. Turn on the processor and let the chocolate pass through the grating blade. Pour the shavings from the processor bowl into a lidded container for use or storage.

TO MAKE SHAVINGS WITH A VEGETABLE PEELER: Hold the chocolate with a paper towel and pass the vegetable peeler over the narrowest side of the chocolate. The chocolate will curl up like wood shavings.

TO USE A MELON BALL SCOOP, COOKIE OR BISCUIT CUTTER, OR MINIATURE TART PAN: Position the bar of chocolate on the paper-covered jelly-roll pan and hold it down with a paper towel. Scrape the melon-ball scoop or other instrument toward you, across the surface of the chocolate. You will get curved shavings. Continue until the chocolate breaks apart and the surface can no longer be shaved.

STORAGE: Keep the shavings in the lidded container in the refrigerator until needed. Leftover shavings keep in the refrigerator indefinitely.

NOTE: Any chocolate left over from making shavings may be used for another purpose. Wrap in foil and store with your other chocolate.

MARBLED CHOCOLATE BARK

• • •

Makes one 12-inch square, to be cut or broken into decorative shapes

6 ounces semisweet or bittersweet chocolate, tempered, pages 20–23

4 ounces milk chocolate or white chocolate, tempered, pages 20–23

1 cookie sheet or jelly-roll pan lined with parchment or heavy acetate

Please don't confuse this sheet of chocolate used for decorating desserts with the nut-chocolate candy on page 318. This bark may be made as simple or as elaborate as you feel up to attempting. Just remember that tempered chocolate sets fairly quickly, especially in a cool room, so you have a limited time to work with the chocolate.

1. Use an offset metal icing spatula to spread the dark chocolate in a 12-inch square on the paper or acetate.

2. Quickly streak the chocolate square with the lighter color chocolate. Apply it from the tip of a spoon, a paper cone, or a squeeze bottle in an irregular pattern.

3. Quickly and firmly tap the pan against the work surface to settle the layers of chocolate, then use a toothpick or skewer to pull a series of curved lines through the chocolates to marble them together, as in the illustration on page 390. Let chocolate set, then cut into shapes as for chocolate cutouts, page 391, or let set and break into irregular shapes to use for decorating cakes or desserts.

STORAGE: Keep the bark in a tin or plastic container with a tight-fitting cover between layers of wax paper. Store in a cool, dark place.

VARIATION

CHOCOLATE HONEYCOMB For a very impressive-looking one-color effect, spread tempered chocolate on the bubbly side of bubble wrap that has ½-inch bubbles or smaller. Press hard with an offset metal icing spatula and make sure chocolate falls between the bubbles, but does not cover them. Let set, then peel away the plastic and the chocolate will have a honeycomb pattern. Break into irregular pieces and use for decorating.

CHOCOLATE LACE

. . .

Makes one 10 × 15-inch rectangle of lace, to be cut or broken into smaller pieces

4 ounces semisweet, bittersweet, milk, or white chocolate, or a combination, kept separate, tempered, pages 20–23

One 10 × 15-inch jelly-roll pan lined with parchment or heavy acetate

Delicate lace patterns are easy to make with tempered chocolate—you pipe it from a paper cone, a squeeze bottle, or the snipped corner of a plastic bag.

1. Spoon the chocolate into a paper cone, nonpleated plastic bag, or a squeeze bottle with a small opening. If you are using the cone or plastic bag, snip the end with sharp scissors.

2. Hold the cone, bag, or squeeze bottle about 3 or 4 inches above the pan, and quickly pipe out the chocolate in a series of intersecting arcs, so that the paper is covered with thin curved lines of chocolate. Make sure not to cover the paper completely—what distinguishes the lace is its open quality.

3. Before the chocolate lace sets completely, use heated cutters or a small sharp knife to cut it into desired shapes. Or let the lace set completely and break it into irregular pieces.

STORAGE: Keep the lace in a tin or plastic container with a tight-fitting cover between layers of wax paper. Store in a cool, dark place.

CHOCOLATE FILIGREE DECORATIONS

• • •

Makes at least several dozen designs for decorating desserts

4 ounces semisweet or bittersweet chocolate, tempered, pages 20–23

1 cookie sheet or jelly-roll pan lined with parchment or heavy acetate

These are fun to make, but require a little practice. The best and easiest way to make filigree decorations is to draw the designs you want on a sheet of white paper using black ink or very dark pencil. Then place a sheet of acetate or thin parchment paper over the designs and pipe the chocolate onto that.

1. Draw the designs you wish to make on a sheet of white paper. See the illustration for ideas.

2. Slide the patterns under the acetate or parchment paper.

3. Use a paper cone, nonpleated plastic bag, or squeeze bottle to pipe the chocolate onto the paper, following the patterns. Hold the cone, bag, or bottle about 1 inch above the paper and straight up and down. Squeeze to let the stream of chocolate flow onto the designs. Stop squeezing to stop the flow and begin another pattern.

4. Let the chocolate set completely. Leave the decorations on the paper loosely covered with plastic wrap, until they are needed. Then peel the paper away from the decorations and use them. They are most effective when stuck into a small dessert or glass of mousse so the decoration stands straight up.

VARIATION

PIPING AND WRITING WITH CHOCOLATE Although chocolate doesn't need to be tempered to decorate a dessert or cake with chocolate piping or writing, the techniques are almost the same as making the filigree decorations above. I find it easiest to use chocolate diluted with some water—about 2 ounces of chocolate and 1 tablespoon water melted together works well. Practice by tracing the design over a written or drawn pattern as described above. Then, after you have practiced piping the design or message several times, you can execute it on the cake or dessert.

Templates are 50% actual size

CHOCOLATE ENAMELING

■ ■ ■

Makes several three-dimensional designs to use in decorating cakes or desserts

4 ounces dark chocolate, tempered, pages 20–23

6 ounces milk chocolate or white chocolate, tempered, pages 20–23

Several cookie sheets or jelly-roll pans lined with parchment or heavy acetate

A pretty variation on filigree piping, enameling means filling in piped chocolate outlines with solid areas of different colored chocolate. Outlines of dark chocolate look dramatic when filled in with white or milk chocolate. The outlines and filling don't necessarily have to be piped at the same time, so this is also a good use for those tail ends of tempered chocolate left after molding or dipping.

1. Draw the designs you wish to execute on white paper with black ink or dark pencil. Utilize most of the space on the pans. See the illustration for ideas.

2. Cover the designs with parchment paper or acetate and place in a pan.

3. First, use a paper cone, snipped nonpleated plastic bag, or squeeze bottle to pipe dark chocolate over the outlines of the designs.

4. Let the outlines set, then pipe in the lighter colored chocolate to fill them in. When the outlines are filled in, lift and tap the pan gently to make the flooded areas fill in and flatten.

5. Let the chocolate enameling designs set at a cool room temperature, then remove them from the papers. They look best when you place them with the bottom, or flat side, up.

Templates are 50% actual size

CHOCOLATE CURLS AND LARGE SHAVINGS

• • •

Makes at least 2 to 3 cups shavings,
even if you use the smallest bar

1 large bar or block of semisweet,
milk, or white chocolate

1 jelly-roll pan lined with
parchment or wax paper, plus a
cake cardboard or other piece of
corrugated cardboard, and a
large chef's knife

CHOCOLATE

To make these it is necessary to have a fairly large block or bar of chocolate, though it works well to use the Lindt 13.5-ounce bars and the Callebaut 18-ounce bars. If you can get a 2- or 3-pound piece cut from a 10- or 11-pound bar, or a whole 10- or 11-pound bar, even better.

These large shavings are easier to do than the ones that follow, for which you scrape away chocolate that has set against a marble or other nonporous surface. And they will be paper-thin and large or curled, depending on how you hold the knife.

Milk chocolate and white chocolate are naturally softer than dark chocolate and therefore easier to curl or shave.

1. Place the pan so that a short end is closest to the edge of the work surface nearest you, then put the narrowest end of the bar of chocolate at that same end of the pan. Stand close to the edge of the work surface and place the cardboard upright between you and the pan to protect you from the knife as you shave the chocolate.

2. To make shavings, hold the knife blade across the top of the chocolate, one hand holding the handle and the other the tip of the blade—hold this one with a folded kitchen towel. Scrape the blade toward you. This will make large flat flakes.

3. To make thin, rolled-up curls, change the position of the pan so that one of the long sides of the pan and the chocolate are now facing you. Hold the knife above as in Step 2, but lower it away from you, so that it is tilted at a 60-degree angle to the back of the chocolate bar. Scrape toward you, to make thin curls—the wider the bar of chocolate, the wider the curls.

4. As they are made, transfer the curls or shavings to a large container with a tight-fitting cover and refrigerate. If you intend to make a lot of either, layer them in the container between sheets of parchment or wax paper.

STORAGE: Keep the shavings in the refrigerator until you wish to use them.

CHOCOLATE CURLS MADE FROM MELTED CHOCOLATE

. . .

Makes about 18 or more curls,
depending on size

4 to 6 ounces dark chocolate,
melted

1 slab of marble at least 12 inches
square

These are the decoration sometimes called chocolate cigarettes. They aren't difficult to make, although it takes some practice to master the scraping movement required. Make sure the room where you are working is not too cold or the chocolate will set so quickly that it will not curl when you scrape it off the marble, but just shatter into pieces.

1. Cool the melted chocolate until it just feels slightly warm when you touch some of it to the bottom of your lower lip—it should be about 90 to 95 degrees.

2. Use a small offset metal icing spatula to spread half the chocolate in a strip the length of the slab, ⅛ inch thick and about 5 inches wide. Spread the chocolate as evenly as possible.

3. Let the chocolate stand for a minute or two, then press with a fingertip to determine if it has set all the way through—if it is not (you will see a crust on the outside and melted chocolate within), wait a minute longer and test again. The strip should be set but not completely hardened.

4. When the chocolate has set, turn the board so that one of the narrow sides of the strip is facing you. Position the knife or scraper about an inch away from the far end of the strip of chocolate and at a 45-degree angle away from you. Begin to scrape away from you over the strip of chocolate, scraping off a large curl that should roll up cylindrically as you scrape.

5. Quickly continue scraping curls off the strip of chocolate. Begin each curl an inch away from the end every time you scrape.

6. Quickly scrape off the board and spread the remaining chocolate into another strip; repeat above.

7. Carefully place the curls directly on the dessert they are to decorate, or place them in a container with a tight-fitting lid and refrigerate them.

DECORATING

U se these decorated masterpieces as special gifts or as the centerpiece of a special-occasion buffet. Each is complete in itself, though I think these all look best when they are the focal point of a selection of chocolate desserts or candies.

The photographs throughout this chapter show you most of the finished products of these next recipes. Don't be afraid to try these projects. Though they take time and effort to prepare, none of the following recipes is particularly difficult. Use the patterns provided with the recipes to produce neat, uniform results. And for the sake of practicality, don't try to complete the whole project at once. Leave yourself enough time to work on it at a leisurely pace over several days. This type of work can't be rushed.

MOLDING LARGE CHOCOLATE PIECES

• • •

Makes 1 or more large, hollow, molded chocolates, depending on size of molds

3 to 5 pounds dark or milk chocolate, tempered, pages 20–23

1 batch Chocolate Plastic, page 384

1 or more large molds

1 cookie sheet lined with parchment or foil, optional

Large molded chocolate items are more likely to be for display or decoration than to be eaten—although, of course, the chocolate they are made from is entirely edible. The large molds used for these creations are usually hinged, so that when they are closed the two halves automatically join together. I recommend clear plastic molds over any other type: They allow you to see when the chocolate is no longer stuck to the inside of the mold and has set completely—essential for neat unmolding.

Temper a large amount of chocolate—the leftover chocolate can always be reused. It will make the job easier if you don't have to skimp. It is also efficient, though not obligatory, to have several molds to coat. Remember that chocolate, after it has been molded, will keep well in a cool, dry place.

1. Buff the inside of the mold(s) with cotton or a soft cloth.

2. Use a brush or your fingertip to apply a thin coat of the chocolate to the inside of the mold, making sure that the chocolate covers any tiny, intricate parts of the mold's design. Quickly refrigerate the mold for a few seconds to set this initial coating.

3. When it is set, pour the tempered chocolate into each half of the mold. Tap the side of the mold with the back of a knife or spatula to make sure the chocolate settles into the mold and there are no air bubbles against the molded surface. Wait about 30 seconds, then pour the chocolate back into the bowl of tempered chocolate. With a knife or spatula scrape any chocolate off the mold where the two sides will join together and quickly close the mold. Secure it with its own clasp or with the large metal clamps used for paper.

4. Refrigerate the mold for 10 minutes. Preferably it should be standing so that the juncture, where the two sides come together, is vertical. If the mold has an open end, stand it in a pan covered with parchment or foil with the opening down.

5. When the chocolate has set, remove the mold from the refrigerator and stand it on a piece of parchment paper. Put on a pair of cotton or plastic gloves to avoid making fingerprints on the shiny chocolate surface. Release the clasp or clamps of the mold and open it—the chocolate will come away from the mold immediately. Remove the mold.

6. Always try to touch the surface of the chocolate as little as possible and only with gloved hands. With a small, sharp knife, trim the seam where the two sides of the mold come together so it is level with the molded surface.

7. Make a base for the molded chocolate using chocolate plastic. Roll it out about ¼ inch thick and cut it into a round or square, depending on the shape of the mold. Make the chocolate plastic about an inch larger all around than the base of the mold. A ¼-inch-thick round of chocolate molded in an engraved silver tray will also make a perfect base for a molded chocolate.

STORAGE: Keep the molded chocolate loosely covered in a cool, dark place until you intend to use it.

VARIATION

USING "FOUND" CHOCOLATE MOLDS Molded bowls or cups make great containers for chocolate truffles or other candies. They are also used as the container for the Bouquet of Chocolate Flowers on page 412.

Almost any metal, glass, or plastic vessel with a smooth, flat, shiny surface can make a good chocolate mold. Tempered chocolate will always shrink away from the surface of the mold as it cools—if the mold is nonporous and has a shiny surface the chocolate has nothing to stick to and will unmold beautifully. Initially, don't be too ambitious. Try something small—small stainless steel or glass bowls and small nonpatterned glasses are perfect. You can use an engraved silver tray to mold chocolate in and the patterned surface of the resulting chocolate tray will make a perfect base for a molded chocolate.

Mold as above, though the preliminary coating with fingertip or brush is only necessary in the case of an intricately engraved tray. When you refrigerate the chocolate to set it, stand the molds up as they will be used—don't stand a bowl or cup on its open side as with the large molds above. Mold a round of chocolate to serve as a base for your container, or make one from chocolate plastic, as in the instructions above.

FREE-FORM CHOCOLATE TULIP CUPS
. . .

Makes about 24 cups for mousse

24 ounces white chocolate,
  tempered, pages 20–23

4 ounces dark chocolate, tempered,
  pages 20–23

24 small thin round balloons

24 bulldog clasps, available in
  office supply stores

2 or 3 jelly-roll pans lined with
  parchment or wax paper

This technique for molding chocolate tulips on balloons was developed by my friend, Elaine Gonzalez, one of the foremost authorities on chocolate decorations and confections in the United States today. Her vast knowledge of chocolate is exceeded only by her kindness and generosity and I thank her for permission to share these instructions. For best results, be sure to use thin, shiny balloons, not the ones with a powdery coating.

1. Inflate the balloons about two-thirds full. Twist ends securely and fold over but don't knot. Secure end with bulldog clasp.

2. Pour ½ cup of white chocolate onto marble or countertop to make a small puddle. Dribble on three or four irregular streaks of dark chocolate from the end of a spoon. Position inflated balloon, rounded side down, at the edge of puddle. Roll the balloon five or six times in the puddle. Keep moving the balloon around until the rounded half is irregularly covered with chocolate. Place each balloon, chocolate side down, on paper-lined pan to set.

3. When the chocolate on the counter becomes muddy, scrape it away and replace with fresh white chocolate and more streaks. Continue with remaining balloons and chocolate.

4. To unmold tulips, release clips and deflate balloons gently; carefully remove deflated balloon. Store in a cool and dry place until they are filled.

SERVING: Fill the tulip cups with mousse, ice cream, or sherbet immediately before serving.

MOLDING CHOCOLATE SHAPES IN COCOA

• • •

This is a great way to make almost any smallish household item the positive for a chocolate mold. It's simple: You sift cocoa powder into a box or bowl to fill it, and level off the top. Then you press the model into the cocoa so it leaves its impression—anything without intricate detail works well. At a fancy chocolate store in Paris, I once saw a basket of chocolate wrenches, pliers, and other tools that had been molded this way. Another good positive for this type of molding can be a child's rubber bath toy.

Slowly fill the mold with tempered chocolate, piping it in from a paper cone or the snipped corner of a nonpleated plastic bag. Fill to the top and leave several hours to set. When it has, carefully, from underneath, lift the molded chocolate from the cocoa using your hands. Use a soft brush to clean away the excess cocoa, though some will remain stuck to the chocolate. The cocoa can be reused in any of the ways it might have been originally.

CHOCOLATE BASKET

. . .

Makes one 5- or 6-inch woven basket

2 batches Chocolate Plastic,
    page 384

Melted cocoa butter (see Sources,
    page 442) for finishing

A basket form or a 1-inch-thick
    square of Styrofoam, about 8
    inches square, and 15 new
    pencils, sharpened

2 cookie sheets or pans covered
    with parchment or foil

A platter or molded chocolate base,
    page 404

A pasta machine

This is fairly simple to do and makes a very pretty container for truffles, candies, or cookies. You will be weaving strips of chocolate, so you will need a basket form or *mandrin*—a wood or metal base with holes in it to hold vertical posts upright for weaving between. It is available from several equipment suppliers (see Sources). Or you can improvise a simple and economical solution with a piece of Styrofoam and some pencils.

1. If you are using a basket form, insert the vertical pieces into the holes in the base. If you are using the Styrofoam and pencils, draw a 5-inch circle or oval on the Styrofoam. If you want a straight-sided basket, stick a pencil, point down, into the Styrofoam about every inch around the circumference of the circle. Use all 15 pencils. If you want your basket to taper to the smaller base, insert the pencils at a slight angle, so they lean outward from the base.

2. Divide 1 batch of chocolate plastic into three parts. Place them on a work surface and pound them gently with a rolling pin to soften. Roll each into a 4-inch square. To make thin rectangles, pass the squares of chocolate plastic through the pasta machine, at the thickest setting. Continue passing the chocolate plastic through the pasta machine, decreasing the setting and making it thinner every time you pass it through. Continue until you have passed the chocolate plastic through the middle setting, halfway between the thickest and the thinnest.

3. If your pasta machine has a cutter, pass the sheets of chocolate plastic through the wide noodle cutter. If not, use a pastry cutting wheel or pizza cutter to cut the chocolate plastic into ⅜-inch-wide strips.

4. To weave the basket, starting at the inside of the form, pass a ribbon of chocolate in and out between the posts. When the ribbon ends, make sure it is inside the basket. Start the next ribbon from inside, attaching it to the end of the previous ribbon and continuing to weave in the same direction, as in the illustration. Continue weaving the ribbons onto the basket form until the basket is about 4 to 5 inches high.

5. Use a small brush to paint the inside of the basket with melted cocoa butter. Make sure to apply where the end of one ribbon meets the beginning of the next one. Let the cocoa butter dry for several hours.

6. To finish the basket, use about a third of the remaining batch of chocolate plastic to make the base for the basket: Pound the chocolate plastic with a rolling pin to soften it, then roll it about ⅜ inch thick. Cut the chocolate plastic into a round or oval a little larger than the bottom diameter of the basket.

7. Carefully pull up and remove the pencils or posts. Carefully pick the basket up and set it on the prepared pan. Place the prepared base inside the bottom of the basket. Press it flat against the pan and curve its edge up slightly around the inside bottom of the basket.

8. Roll more softened chocolate plastic into thin cylinders, a little smaller in diameter than the pencils or the basket form posts. Cut the cylinders so they are slightly longer than the height of the basket. Place the chocolate posts on a paper-covered pan and chill them for 15 minutes. Then insert the chocolate posts into the channels previously occupied by the posts or the pencils.

9. Use scissors to cut the posts even with the top of the basket. Melt the cocoa butter again and paint it over the places where the base and the bottom of the basket meet and onto the posts inside the basket. Leave for several hours to dry at a cool room temperature.

10. Use most of the remaining chocolate plastic to make two simple braids to finish the top and bottom edges of the basket. Roll a narrow cylinder ³⁄₁₆ inch in diameter and about twice as long as the circumference of the top of the basket. Double it back on itself and twist it so the two pieces curl around each other in a double corkscrew shape. Gently press the braid around the top edge of the basket, overlapping it slightly where it joins. Stand the basket on a platter or molded chocolate base. Make another braid to finish the bottom.

11. To make two ring-shaped handles: Form another twist as you did for the top of the basket and cut into two 5-inch lengths. Fashion into circles, overlapping the ends slightly. Use a piece of dried spaghetti to attach one ring to the basket under the top braid. Attach the other ring, opposite it, as in the illustration.

STORAGE: Keep the basket loosely covered with plastic wrap in a cool, dark place.

CHOCOLATE
MAGNOLIA SPRAY
▪ ▪ ▪

Makes 1 large flower

2 batches White Chocolate Plastic, page 384

1 batch Chocolate Plastic, page 384

1 cookie sheet lined with parchment or wax paper

This can be a spectacular decoration for a large cake or a platter of cookies, chocolates, or individual pastries. The flower this is meant to represent is the one on magnolia trees throughout the South and on the West Coast. In the Northeast and Midwest, a related species with less striking flowers, commonly called a tulip tree, is sometimes referred to as a magnolia but we're making the extravagant Southern bloom.

1. Use the drawings below to trace a pattern for the small and large petals and the leaves on cardboard or other stiff paper.

2. Divide 1 batch of the white chocolate plastic in half. Pound one of the halves gently with a rolling pin on a work surface. This will be used to make a base for the flower. Shape the white chocolate plastic into a ball, then form points at the top and bottom of the ball and press in on its equator to make an

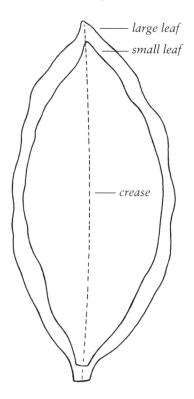

large leaf
small leaf

crease

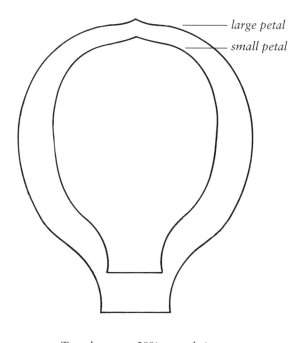

large petal
small petal

Templates are 50% actual size

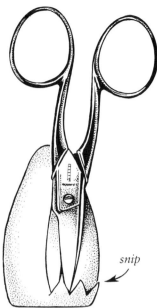

snip

elongated shape, pointed at top and bottom, about 3 inches high. Flatten the bottom point so that the base stands straight up in the prepared pan. Use a scissors, as in the illustration at left, to snip scales into the base. Then fashion tiny stamens of white chocolate plastic and use them to cover the top half of the base, as in the illustration below.

3. Roll the second half of that batch of white chocolate plastic into a rectangle about ⅛ inch thick and, from it, cut out 3 of the smaller petals. Set aside.

4. Divide the remaining batch of white chocolate plastic in half and roll out each half ⅛ inch thick. Cut 2 of the larger petals from each half. Then mass together all the scraps from cutting those petals as well as any left from the previous batch used for the smaller petals, and cut 2 more large petals.

5. To assemble the flower, shape the 3 smaller petals into cup shapes. Hold each petal between your thumb and first finger and with your thumbs inside the petal pull gently out from the center. Attach 1 of the petals close to and at the bottom of the cone-shaped base, almost perpendicular to the pan, by pressing with a fingertip to soften the white chocolate plastic and make it stick. Repeat with the other 2 petals, attaching them equidistantly from each other around the bottom of the base, so that the flower looks like the photograph on page 400.

6. Next curve out 3 of the large petals, as you did the smaller ones. Attach these three equidistantly around the bottom of the base, but so that they are lying on the pan, fully open below the small petals. Curve out the remaining 3 petals and arrange them between the 3 other large petals, but above them, between the smaller petals and the larger ones as in the photograph. Chill the flower while preparing the stem and leaves. If any of the groups of petals won't stay in place, fashion a ¾-inch band of white chocolate plastic and wrap the band around the base of the petals to keep them in place. Repeat with each row of petals, if necessary.

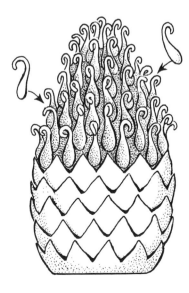

7. To form the stem, cut off a sixth of the batch of dark chocolate plastic and roll it into a thin "snake" about 8 inches long. Set aside.

8. Pound the rest of the dark chocolate plastic to soften it and roll it out into a large rectangle about ³⁄₁₆ inch thick. Cut four large and two smaller leaves from the chocolate. Immediately crease the leaves from point to point, folding them over gently and unfolding them.

9. Remove the flower from the refrigerator and place it on one end of the stem. Curve the stem around in an arc on the pan and attach the first 2 leaves opposite each other about an inch down the stem from the flower. Attach the next 2 leaves about 2 inches from the first ones in the same manner, then the last 2 leaves. Chill the flower, stem, and leaves to set them. After the chocolate plastic has dried for a few hours, it will be easy to lift the flower from the paper-lined pan.

USE: Use the magnolia spray on a cake or a platter to decorate it.

STORAGE: Keep loosely covered with plastic wrap in a cool dark place.

NOTE: If you can get some magnolia leaves, press the chocolate leaves against the tops of the magnolia leaves to vein them.

BOUQUET OF CHOCOLATE FLOWERS

• • •

Makes a 5- or 6-inch bowl of flowers

One 5- or 6-inch diameter
  chocolate bowl about 4 or 5
  inches deep, made from
  tempered chocolate according to
  the instructions on page 404

3 batches Chocolate Plastic,
  page 384, for flowers, leaves,
  and base

About 8 ounces chocolate,
  tempered, pages 20–23, for
  covering the stems

Thin bamboo skewers or florist
  wire trimmed to 5-, 6-, and
  7-inch lengths

1 cookie sheet covered with
  parchment

This particular piece can also be presented in a Chocolate Basket, page 407.

1. The chocolate bowl may be prepared weeks before you wish to assemble the decoration. Just keep the bowl loosely covered with plastic wrap in a cool, dark place. Use the rest of the tempered chocolate you used to make the bowl to cover the skewers or wire. Dip them into the chocolate, shake off the excess, and set the stems aside on the paper-covered pan.

2. Make the flowers: Use the instructions on pages 386–87 to make roses, carnations, and some simple, generic 4- and 5-petaled flowers. You'll need about 20 flowers in all. Also make about 40 to 50 leaves 1 to 1½ inches long.

3. Mass together any leftover chocolate plastic and roll it out to make a base for the bowl. Cut it about 2 inches larger around than the bottom of the bowl. Place the base on the prepared pan and press the bottom of the bowl against it. Use more leftover chocolate plastic to make a ball 3 to 4 inches in diameter. Press the ball into the bottom of the bowl. This will be used to anchor the flower stems.

4. One at a time, stick the tops of the stems into the flowers and the bottoms of the stems into the mound of chocolate plastic in the bottom of the bowl. Place the longer stems in the center of the arrangement and the shorter ones around them. After you press a stem in, attach 2 or 3 leaves to it under the flower. Put some of the leaves close to the flowers, others nearer the rim of the bowl.

USE: Use the bowl of flowers as the centerpiece, or on a tray of chocolates, cookies, or individual pastries.

STORAGE: Keep the bouquet of flowers loosely covered with plastic wrap in a cool dark place.

CHOCOLATE FLOWERS
WREATH CAKE
▪ ▪ ▪

One 10-inch cake, about 12 servings

2 batches Chocolate Plastic,
    page 384
1 batch Chocolate Walnut Crown,
    page 94, with the Chocolate
    Butter Cream Filling, but
    without the Walnut Praline
    Topping

This is an effective way of making a beautiful presentation of chocolate flowers without all the architectural stress of mounting them on stems in a bowl. You can make the flowers weeks ahead, and the cake and frosting the day before. Then all you have to do the day you intend to serve it is frost the cake and arrange the flowers on it.

I. Make the flowers: Use 1½ batches of chocolate plastic to make such flowers as roses, carnations, petunias, and some of the simple 4- and 5-petal flowers described on pages 386–87. Make about 30 flowers.

2. Use the remainder of the chocolate plastic to make 40 or 50 leaves in varying sizes ranging from 1 to 2 inches long, according to the instructions on page 385.

3. Prepare, fill, and frost the cake and place it on the platter from which it will be served.

4. Begin arranging the flowers. Place the first so they are standing straight up on the very top of the cake. Then arrange more flowers on the sides, facing outward. Space them well apart so there will be room for the leaves. After you have placed all the flowers, place the leaves between them at angles to the top and sides of the cake so they fill in all spaces and appear to be growing naturally.

5. Chill the cake to harden the chocolate plastic, then keep the cake in a cool, dark place until you are ready to serve it.

VARIATION

CHOCOLATE HOLLY LEAF CAKE This cake is a perfect centerpiece for a holiday buffet. Use a holly-leaf-shaped cutter to make about 100 holly leaves from dark or milk chocolate plastic, page 384, and make some holly berries at the same time. Or, stem, rinse, and carefully dry about 100 holly leaves. Paint tempered chocolate onto the shiny side of each leaf. Be sure not to get any chocolate onto the underside of the leaf. That makes it difficult to separate the finished leaves from the chocolate. Chill the leaves to set the chocolate, then carefully peel the leaves away from their chocolate imitations. This is fairly easy to do.

CHOCOLATE MARZIPAN WEDDING CAKE

• • •

Makes about 50 servings

12-INCH CAKE LAYER

16 tablespoons (2 sticks) unsalted butter, softened

1 cup sugar, divided

9 ounces semisweet chocolate, melted and cooled

12 large eggs, separated

2 cups ground almonds, about 8 ounces

1 cup dry bread crumbs

1 teaspoon ground cinnamon

Pinch salt

6-INCH CAKE LAYER

5 tablespoons unsalted butter, softened

⅔ cup sugar, divided

3 ounces semisweet chocolate, melted and cooled

4 large eggs, separated

⅔ cup ground almonds, about 3 ounces

⅓ cup dry bread crumbs

¼ teaspoon ground cinnamon

GANACHE FILLING AND FROSTING

24 ounces semisweet chocolate, cut into ¼-inch pieces

2 cups heavy whipping cream

¼ cup dark rum, optional

MARZIPAN

16 ounces (2 cans) almond paste

32 ounces confectioners' sugar, sifted

¾ cup light corn syrup

This is a perfect wedding cake for chocolate lovers. These instructions are for a two-day preparation, but the rich, moist layers may be made well in advance and kept frozen for up to a month. The recipe is based on one for a classic Viennese cake called Rehrucken (Saddle of Venison), so called because it is traditionally made in a ridged pan and the cake resembles a rolled and tied roast after it is unmolded.

The marzipan has a rich almond flavor and provides a neat, easy-to-prepare covering. The cake may be presented with a traditional ornament at the top, or decorated with chocolate, white, and variegated marzipan carnations and leaves.

MAKE THE CAKE LAYERS

I. Position a rack in the center of the oven and preheat to 350 degrees.

2. Use an electric mixer on medium speed to beat the butter until it is soft and light. Beat in half the sugar in a stream, and continue beating until the mixture whitens, about 3 to 4 minutes. Beat in the melted chocolate and scrape the bowl and beater(s).

3. Beat the egg yolks one at a time into the chocolate mixture. Continue beating on medium speed, scraping the bowl and beater(s) occasionally until the mixture is very light and looks like a chocolate butter cream.

4. Combine the ground nuts, bread crumbs, and cinnamon and stir them into the batter.

5. Pour the egg whites into a clean, dry stainless steel bowl. With a handheld electric mixer on medium speed and clean beaters beat the egg whites until they

⅓ cup alkalized (Dutch process) cocoa powder

One 12-inch round cake pan, 2 inches deep, buttered and bottom lined with parchment or wax paper

One 6-inch round cake pan, 2 inches deep, buttered and bottom lined with parchment or wax paper

Confectioners' sugar for dusting

are liquid, about 15 seconds. Add the salt and continue beating. Move the mixer all around in the bowl, and beat until the egg whites are very white and opaque and beginning to hold a very soft peak. Increase the speed to maximum and beat in the remaining sugar in a very slow stream. Beat the egg whites until they hold a firm peak.

6. With a rubber spatula stir one quarter of the beaten egg whites into the batter. Scrape the remaining egg whites over the batter and fold them in gently until no white streaks remain. Pour the batter into the prepared 12-inch pan and spread even with a spatula. Tap the pan a couple of times on a work surface to release any large air bubbles. Bake 40 to 45 minutes, until the cake feels firm when pressed gently with the palm of your hand and a cake tester or toothpick inserted into the cake about 2 inches from the center comes out clean. Cool the cake in the pan on a wire rack about 10 minutes. Run a knife around the edges of the cake layer to loosen it. Invert the cake onto a wire rack and leave the paper stuck to the cake. Invert again onto another rack, so that the cake is right side up. Cool completely. Wrap the cake layer in plastic and refrigerate overnight.

7. Combine the ingredients for the 6-inch cake layer, following the directions for the cake above. Bake this layer 30 to 35 minutes, until it tests done. Cool and wrap as for the 12-inch layer.

MAKE THE GANACHE

8. Place the cut chocolate in a mixing bowl. Bring the cream to a boil in a saucepan over medium heat. When the cream comes to a boil, pour it over the chocolate and allow to stand 3 to 4 minutes to melt the chocolate. Whisk the ganache smooth and stir in the rum if using. Press plastic wrap against the surface and refrigerate the ganache until needed.

MAKE THE MARZIPAN

9. Cut the almond paste into ½-inch pieces and place in food processor with the metal blade. Add half the sifted sugar and pulse until it forms fine crumbs. Add remaining sugar and pulse again until the mixture resembles cornmeal. Add half the corn syrup and pulse again. Test the consistency of the marzipan by removing a handful from the processor and kneading it. If the marzipan is smooth and supple, remove the rest from processor and knead it all until smooth. If the marzipan is too dry to knead, add half the remaining corn syrup and pulse and test again until the marzipan kneads smoothly. Do not over-process or the marzipan will be greasy and rough in appearance.

10. Cut off one quarter of the marzipan and knead the cocoa powder into it. If it becomes very dry, knead in a few drops of water. Form both the plain white and chocolate marzipan into cylinders, double-wrap in plastic, and keep in a cool place or in the refrigerator. This may be prepared up to 1 month in advance.

MAKE THE FLOWERS AND LEAVES

11. To make the leaves, roll one quarter of the chocolate marzipan into a rope. Divide the rope into four pieces, and roll each piece into a thin rope approximately 12 inches long. Cover the ropes with plastic wrap and a damp towel. One rope at a time, form the leaves. Flatten the rope against your work surface with the palm of your hand. Roll over it with a rolling pin to make a strip ¼ inch wide and about 16 inches long. Run a metal spatula or a knife under the strip to detach it from work surface. Cut the strip diagonally every 1 inch. Use the point of a knife to mark a central vein on each leaf. Shape the leaves by draping them against the inside rim of a jelly-roll pan, so they dry curved. Make more leaves with the remaining three ropes of marzipan. Allow the leaves to dry 24 hours, then store, placing the leaves between sheets of parchment or wax paper in a box with a tight-fitting cover. Once the marzipan has dried it will last several months in a cool, dry place. The leaves and flowers may be prepared months in advance.

12. To prepare to make the flowers, cut off one quarter of the white marzipan and rewrap the rest. Divide the piece of white marzipan in half. Wrap one of the pieces in plastic wrap; you will use it to make white flowers in Step 14.

13. Use the second small piece of white marzipan for variegated flowers as follows. Divide the remaining piece of chocolate marzipan into thirds. One piece will be used for variegated flowers with the second piece of white marzipan. To make variegated marzipan, roll each of the two colors into a long rope, then twist them together. With a rolling pin, roll the rope smooth. The chocolate will be unevenly distributed in the white marzipan for a variegated effect. Use the two remaining pieces of chocolate marzipan to make chocolate flowers.

14. To make the flowers themselves, roll half the chocolate marzipan into a rope about 12 inches long. Flatten the rope by pressing with the palm of your hand. Next use the bowl of a spoon to polish and flatten the rope into a ribbon about 16 inches long and 1 inch wide. Make the edge closest to you as thin as possible. Run a sharp knife or spatula under the ribbon to loosen it from the work surface. Make ½-inch slashes along the thin edge of the ribbon at ⅛-inch intervals. Divide the ribbon into two 8-inch pieces. Begin rolling up the ribbons, making sure that the slashed edge is straight and even. When the rolling is completed, with your fingertips, squeeze about ¼ inch under the slashes to open the flower. To dry the flower, stand it up in a tiny cup or an egg carton lined with aluminum foil. Make another chocolate flower with the other half of the same ribbon, then use the remaining chocolate rope to make another ribbon and 2 more chocolate flowers. Using the variegated marzipan, make 4 variegated flowers in the same way. Finally, make 3 white flowers with the reserved piece of white marzipan (it's smaller than the other pieces).

ASSEMBLE THE CAKE LAYERS

15. Cut out two cardboard disks, one 6 inches and the other 12 inches in diameter. These will form bases for each tier. Unwrap each layer and trim it so that the top is even. Turn the layers over and peel the paper from them. Slice each cake horizontally into two layers of equal thickness.

16. Remove the ganache from the refrigerator and heat the bottom of the bowl over hot water to loosen it. With a metal spatula, break the ganache into 1-inch pieces. Return the bowl to the hot water and allow one quarter of the ganache to melt. Remove from the water and beat the ganache smooth with a handheld electric mixer on medium speed. If the ganache is lumpy or grainy, reheat it briefly and beat.

17. Place one of the 12-inch layers on the 12-inch cardboard. Spread the top of the layer with about ¾ cup of the ganache. Place the other 12-inch layer over the first so that the smooth bottom of the layer is up. Set aside. Repeat with the 6-inch layers, using ⅓ cup of the ganache to fill them.

18. Use the remaining ganache to coat the outside of both tiers smoothly. Chill the tiers to set the ganache.

19. Cut a ¼-inch-thick dowel or chopsticks into three pieces, each equal to the height of the 12-inch tier. Trace a 4-inch circle on the center of the 12-inch layer. Embed the supports equally around the circumference of the 4-inch circle in the center of the 12-inch tier.

20. If the marzipan has been refrigerated, remove it from the refrigerator and allow it to come to room temperature for about 3 to 4 hours before rolling it. Keep the marzipan wrapped until just before you roll it.

21. For the 6-inch layer, cut off one third of the remaining white marzipan. Dust a work surface lightly with confectioners' sugar and knead the marzipan smooth. Form the marzipan into a round and dust it and the work surface very lightly with confectioners' sugar. Roll the marzipan out into an 11- to 12-inch round and center it on the tier. Let any excess marzipan drape down over the sides and carefully press against the sides of the tier to remove any pleats or creases. With a small sharp knife, trim away excess marzipan around the bottom. Reserve it to make a rope to finish the bottom of the tier. Reknead the remaining white marzipan and roll it out into a 16- to 18-inch round. Cover the 12-inch tier in the same manner as the 6-inch tier.

TIER THE CAKES

22. Choose a 14-inch plate or a cloth-covered plywood disk to hold the cake. Place the 12-inch tier on the plate, then center the 6-inch tier on the dowels.

DECORATE THE CAKE

23. Cut off one quarter of the reserved white marzipan scraps and roll into a thin rope about 16 inches long. Circle it around the base of the 6-inch tier. Trim the ends of the rope and press them together. With a pastry crimper or even a strawberry huller, crimp a series of diagonal lines in the rope, about ½ inch apart. Failing either of these, use the point of a knife, held at an angle, and press diagonal lines into the rope. Use the remaining scraps of white marzipan to make a 28-inch rope to finish the bottom of the 12-inch tier.

24. Place 6 of the flowers, with a leaf on either side, equidistantly around the top of the 12-inch tier and the sides of the 6-inch tier. Place 5 flowers interspersed with more leaves in a circle in the center of the 6-inch tier. Dip the bottoms of the flowers in heated corn syrup so they adhere firmly to the top tier.

CHOCOLATE RIBBON WEDDING OR ANNIVERSARY CAKE
▪ ▪ ▪

Makes 1 large two-tiered cake,
about 50 to 75 small portions

RUM SYRUP

1½ cups water

1 cup sugar

¾ cup dark rum

GANACHE

32 ounces heavy whipping cream

8 tablespoons (1 stick) unsalted
butter

½ cup light corn syrup

48 ounces bittersweet chocolate,
melted

3 batches Chocolate Genoise,
page 30, baked in three 12-inch
round layer pans, 2 inches deep

2 batches Chocolate Genoise,
page 30, baked in two 8-inch
round layer pans, 2 inches deep

4 cups white chocolate shavings,
page 392

2 batches Chocolate Plastic,
page 384

Confectioner's sugar for dusting

One 12-inch and one 8-inch round
cardboard for assembling the
cake

This two-tiered cake is perfect for a wedding or anniversary but may be served on any special occasion. The chocolate layers are moistened with a rum syrup and frosted with a delicate chocolate butter cream. Then the cake is completely masked in shaved white chocolate. After stacking the layers, the base of each is surrounded by a wide chocolate ribbon and the top of the cake is decorated with large chocolate ruffles.

1. To make the syrup, bring the water and sugar to a boil. Remove from heat and when it is cool, stir in the rum.

2. To make the ganache, bring the cream, butter, and corn syrup to a simmer. Remove from heat and cool 5 minutes. Whisk all the liquid at once into the melted chocolate. Refrigerate the ganache until it is of spreading consistency.

3. With a sharp serrated knife trim each layer so it is an inch high.

4. Place one 12-inch layer on the 12-inch cardboard. Use a brush to moisten with the syrup. With an offset metal icing spatula spread the layer with a thin coat of ganache. Top with another layer and repeat syrup and ganache. Top with last 12-inch layer, bottom side up. Moisten the top layer and cover the entire outside with the ganache. Press the white chocolate shavings against the sides of the cake with a flat spatula. Repeat with the 8-inch layers.

5. To stack the layers, embed four wooden skewers in a 4-inch square in the center of the 12-inch layer. Use sharp scissors to snip them so they are even with the top of the cake. Center the 8-inch cake on the supports.

6. Make ruffles of chocolate plastic (see instructions on page 385) and arrange them on the top of the 8-inch cake. Start at the outside rim and work toward the center so that the last ruffles added are perpendicular to the cake. Cover the area between the edge of the 8-inch cake and the rim of the 12-inch cake with more ruffles. Start at the outside edge of the 12-inch layer and finish against the bottom of the 8-inch cake.

7. Right before serving, dust a very small amount of confectioners' sugar over the ruffles.

COCOA DOUGH FOR DECORATING

. . .

Makes about 3 pounds dough

6 cups all-purpose flour
1 cup alkalized (Dutch process)
    cocoa powder
1 teaspoon salt
½ cup vegetable oil
1 cup dark corn syrup
4 egg whites
1 whole egg
Water

Use this dough for any of the recipes that follow.

1. In the bowl of an electric mixer fitted with the paddle attachment, blend the flour, cocoa, and salt on low speed. Pour in the oil and continue mixing on low speed until absorbed, about 4 to 5 minutes.

2. In a 2-cup measure, combine the remaining ingredients and add water to make 2 cups; whisk briefly to blend. Pour into the dry ingredients and mix on low speed until a moist, sticky dough is formed.

3. Turn dough onto countertop, scraping bowl to remove it all, and knead briefly, 15 to 20 seconds, until dough is smooth. Dough will be smooth, shiny, and very pliable. Form into a thick log, cut log in half, and wrap each half tightly in plastic. Let rest 15 minutes.

STORAGE: Keep the dough, double-wrapped in plastic, for 1 or 2 days in a cool place but not the refrigerator.

CHRISTMAS TREE CENTERPIECE

■ ■ ■

Makes I large decoration

3 batches Cocoa Dough for Decorating, page 423

Dark corn syrup for adhering

1 batch Chocolate Plastic, page 384

½ cup silver or gold dragees

Four 11 × 17-inch cookie sheets or jelly-roll pans

8 sheets parchment paper, cut to fit the cookie sheets or jelly-roll pans

Nontoxic wood glue

This spectacular tree is easy to make with the Cocoa Dough for Decorating. All the pieces may be baked in advance and assembled later. Because the baked dough is dry and hard, you can make the tree weeks in advance.

I. Photocopy the pattern on page 426 on a copy enlarger. The tree pattern should be 12½ to 13 inches high and the widest width approximately 11½ inches. Cut out the pattern. Trace the cutout onto stiffer paper, such as poster board or a thin cardboard; make three of these. Cut these with an Exacto knife or a single-edged razor. Cut out the center axis from each of the three patterns as in the guides on page 427. Enlarge and cut out the disk templates on page 427 and make a pattern of the star on the same page.

2. Make the cocoa dough. Preheat oven to 350 degrees. Dust a work surface with cocoa powder and after the resting time, unwrap one sixth of the dough and place on cocoa. Dust the top of the dough lightly with more cocoa powder, then press with a rolling pin to flatten. Press many times, working across the entire surface of the dough. Begin rolling the dough out, dusting with more cocoa powder if it sticks to the pin. Roll the dough into a rectangle ⅛ inch thick (or slightly more) and at least 14 inches long and 12 inches wide. Transfer the dough to one of the prepared pans. Dust lightly with cocoa powder and place the stiff tree pattern on the dough. Hold pattern in place, and cut around it with a sharp, thin knife tip (or Exacto knife). Follow the outside edges of the complete pattern. Use the pattern or a 1½-inch star cutter to cut stars from the excess dough. Cut more stars from the excess dough of the other trees for a total of about 20 stars. Slide the parchment paper with the dough onto another cookie sheet and place another sheet of parchment on top of the dough, then another cookie sheet. Bake for 12 minutes. Remove pans from oven and work swiftly; remove top pan and top parchment and slide the dough and bottom parchment onto a large cutting board and quickly cut a slot out of the center of the tree panel according to the illustrations and dimensions given. (When cutting hot dough, with one hand press down on a firm straight edge, such as a ruler, while cutting along its edge with the other.) Slide the parchment and dough back into one of the cookie sheets, replace top parchment and second

CHOCOLATE

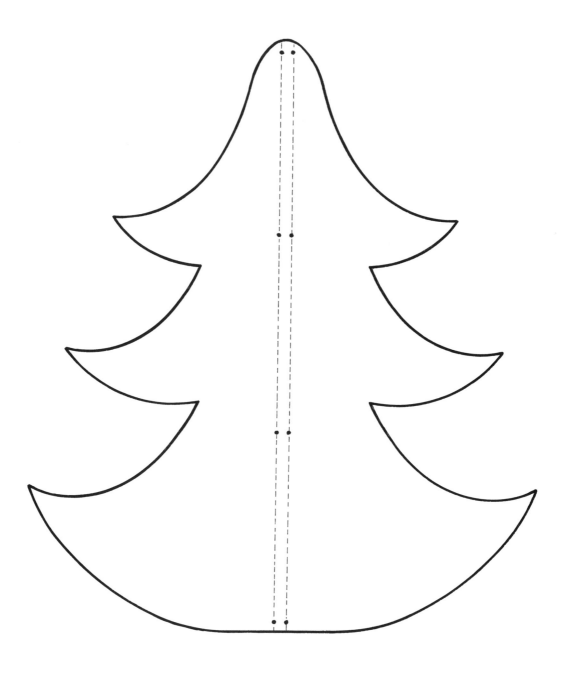

Template is 50% actual size

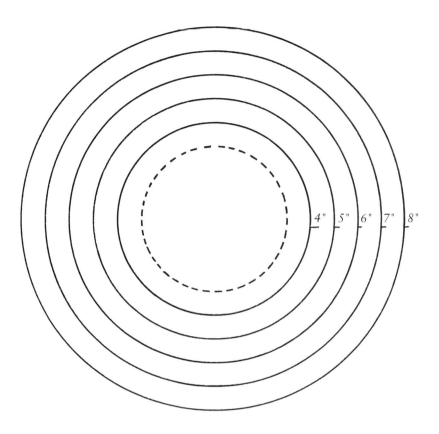

4" 5" 6" 7" 8"

Template is 50% actual size

Template is actual size

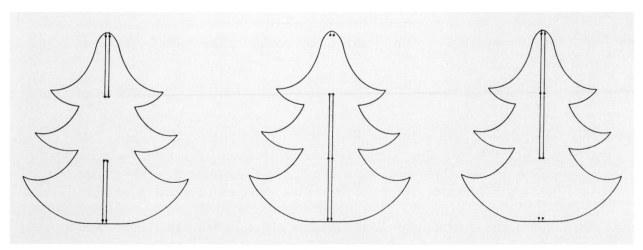

Guides for cutout patterns
(template on opposite page)

sheet, and return to oven for 12 to 15 minutes, or until dough is firm to the touch. Remove from oven and cool dough between pans on a wire rack.

3. Cut out and bake the other two tree panels. Use a fresh section of dough each time, cutting stars from the excess dough. The center slot is cut differently for each panel. Follow the illustrations. There will be three tree panels, one of each illustration.

4. Form another one sixth of the dough into a rectangle and roll out ¼ inch thick. Using the pattern or cake pans, trim two disks, one 8 inches in diameter, the other 4 inches in diameter. Bake as you did the panels, between two cookie sheets with parchment, for 40 minutes. Cool between pans on a wire rack. Roll the remaining two sixths to ¼-inch thickness and cut out rounds of 7 inches, 6 inches, and 5 inches. Place as many rounds on a cookie sheet as will fit without touching and bake as above.

5. Bake the stars as for the tree panels, about 20 minutes.

ASSEMBLE THE BASE

6. Spread some corn syrup onto the largest round, stopping 1 inch short of edges. Center the next largest round on top, and press down firmly. Spread with more corn syrup and repeat with increasingly smaller rounds, ending with the smallest on top. Set aside to dry.

7. Fill a paper cone or nonpleated plastic bag with nontoxic wood glue and snip the end. Place one tree panel flat on a work surface and apply a very small dot of icing to it. Press a silver dragee into the dot—use tweezers if necessary to handle the dragees. Repeat, avoiding about 1 inch down the center length of the panel, until the surface is covered with dragees, approximately ¾ inch apart. Repeat with the other two panels. Return to the first panel and very gently turn it over onto a dry dish towel. Apply dragees in the same manner to the other side. Repeat with the other two panels. Allow to dry before assembling.

ASSEMBLE THE TREE

8. Take about ½ cup of chocolate plastic and form into a round, 3 inches across and ½ inch thick. Spread a small amount of dark corn syrup on the bottom of the chocolate plastic disk and center it on top of the base and press firmly. Use the edge of a ruler to press a deep indentation straight across the center of the top of the chocolate. Make two more indentations, evenly spaced across the first, so that all three lines cross in the center. Brush a small amount of dark corn syrup into the indentations. Pick up the tree panel that has the single slot cut down from the top. Center the bottom of the panel over the first indentation and gently press it down into the corn syrup.

9. Next pick up the panel with the two slots, one from the top and one from the bottom. Center the bottom slot of the panel over the top slot of the first panel and turn it so that the two panels are at 90-degree angles to one another. Carefully slide the second panel over the first, turning it slightly so that the bottom can be pressed into one of the cross indentations. (Before pressing down on the bottom, align the points at the top of the two panels, and hold them together with one hand, while pressing the bottom with the indentation.)

10. Repeat with the third panel, the one with the slot from the bottom up. Angle the bottom so it is in line with the last cross indentation before sliding the last panel over the first two. Again, align the points at the top, then press down gently. Once all three panels are in place, gently press on the chocolate plastic between the bottom of the panels to tighten the support. Use the wood glue to apply more dragees along the top edges of each "branch."

11. Decorate the side of the base by rolling out long, thin ropes of chocolate plastic and wrapping them around each level. Use the back of a knife to indent the ropes as in the illustration. Attach with dark corn syrup. Dab the bottom two points of baked stars with corn syrup, then stand them around the outer rim of the largest base round. Decorate each star with a dragee in the center.

CHOCOLATE COBBLESTONE HOUSE

■ ■ ■

Makes one 9 × 6 inch house

3 batches Cocoa Dough for
　Decorating, page 423

Alkalized (Dutch process)
　cocoa powder

Egg wash: 2 eggs beaten with
　1 teaspoon water

½ batch Milk Chocolate Plastic,
　page 384

½ batch White Chocolate Plastic,
　page 384

Silver dragees

1 batch Royal Icing, page 179

Corn syrup for gluing decorations

Four 11 × 17-inch cookie sheets
　or jelly-roll pans

8 sheets parchment paper,
　cut to fit the cookie sheets

Large cutting board

Ruler

2 cardboard boxes, at least
　11 inches tall and 10 inches wide

Nontoxic wood glue

This chocolate house more closely resembles a typical gingerbread house and will make a great centerpiece for a holiday table.

1. Enlarge house patterns, pages 433–34, on a photocopier until the dimensions are: front and back— 9 inches tall and 6 inches wide; sides—6 inches tall and 9 inches long; roof—10 × 10½ inches (these will be cut in half to make two roof pieces, each 5 inches wide and 10½ inches long). Cut out all patterns, including the door and window openings. Trace the cutout patterns onto a stiffer paper, such as poster board or a thin cardboard.

2. Use an Exacto knife or a single-edged razor blade to cut out the patterns.

3. Make the cocoa dough and wrap each batch separately. Preheat oven to 350 degrees. After the resting time, unwrap one batch of the dough and divide into three equal pieces. Rewrap two of the pieces in the plastic. Dust a work surface with cocoa and place the unwrapped dough on the cocoa. Dust the top of the dough lightly with more cocoa, then press a rolling pin onto the top of the dough to flatten it. Press up and down the entire surface of the dough.

4. Place one sheet of parchment on the work surface and dust with cocoa, then transfer the dough to the center of the parchment. Roll the dough out to the size of the parchment. The dough will be very, very thin. Trim any excess and transfer the parchment and dough to a cookie sheet. Cover the surface of the dough with plastic wrap and set aside. Repeat with one other piece of dough.

5. Unwrap the remaining one-third batch of dough, pinch off small handfuls and roll with the palm of your hand into long ropes, the width of a pencil. Use a small knife or bench scraper to cut the ropes into small ⅜-inch "cobblestones." As you go, chop the pieces into a large (4-cup) measuring cup, measure, place in a bowl and cover with plastic. Repeat with some dough from the second batch until there are about 6 cups of cobblestones.

6. Uncover one of the thinly rolled sheets of dough and slide the parchment and dough onto a clean work surface. Brush the entire surface of the dough with the egg wash. Distribute half the cobblestone pieces to cover the dough in a single layer. Use the rolling pin to press and flatten the pieces slightly, then firmly roll over the surface a couple of times. Slide the parchment and dough back onto the cookie sheet. Bake, uncovered, 30 minutes.

7. Remove pan from oven and, working quickly, slide the parchment and dough onto a large cutting board. Place the front/back pattern onto the dough. Position it near one side as two pieces will be cut from this one sheet. Use a ruler or other straight edge to press down along one side of the pattern while you cut along that edge with the tip of a sharp knife. Cut two identical pieces from this pattern for the front and back of the house, then cut the window and door out of one of the pieces. This will be the front of the house. The back piece can have a window cut out, if you want. Remove all cut away dough and reserve.

8. Slide the parchment with the house pieces back onto the sheet and return to oven for 25 to 30 minutes, or until the dough is very firm. Remove from oven, cover with another sheet of parchment and another cookie sheet or pan. Place a slight weight (such as a large book) on the top pan. Let the pans cool on a wire rack.

9. Add the cobblestones to the second thinly rolled sheet of dough, bake, and then cut out the two sides of the house. Cool in the same manner.

10. Divide the third batch of dough in half and roll one half to the size of the cookie sheet. The dough will be thicker than previously. Slide the parchment and dough onto a pan, cover with another sheet of parchment, then another pan.

11. Bake for 15 minutes, remove from oven, and cut roof pieces. Return to the pan and bake for another 20 to 25 minutes. Remove from oven and let cool between pans on a wire rack.

12. The unbaked dough for the base should be trimmed prior to baking. Bake in the same manner as the roof pieces, but leave in the oven for 20 minutes after flipping the two pans over. Remove from oven and cool between the pans.

13. Assemble the cobblestone house in the same manner as the Chocolate Victorian Cottage Cookie Box, page 436. The only difference is that after the four house sides have been glued together and to the base and allowed to dry thoroughly, the roof pieces are glued onto the top of the house. Glue one side of the roof on with the wood glue, hold firmly in place for 2 to 3 minutes, then repeat with the other side of the roof and allow to dry thoroughly.

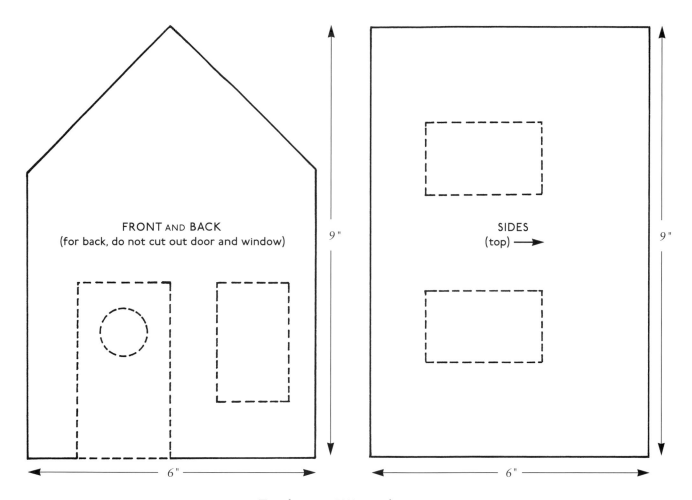

FRONT AND BACK
(for back, do not cut out door and window)

9"

6"

SIDES
(top) →

9"

6"

Templates are 50% actual size

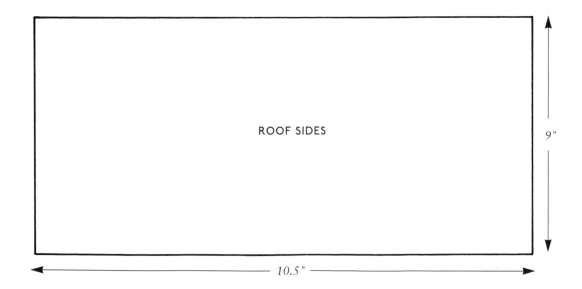

ROOF SIDES

9"

10.5"

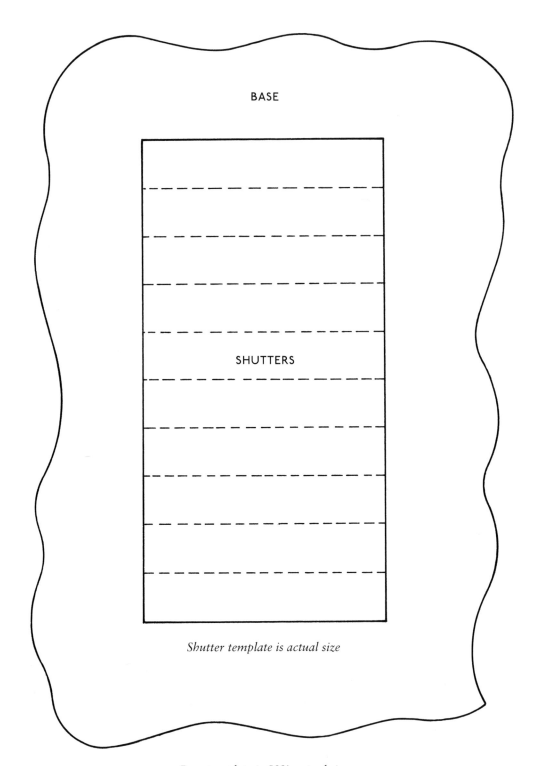

BASE

SHUTTERS

Shutter template is actual size

Base template is 50% actual size

DECORATE

14. For the door, take the piece of dough from the door cutout and turn it so that the smooth side is facing out. Run a line of wood glue down one long edge and both short edges of the door. Position door so that it stands open slightly.

15. Use the white chocolate plastic to make a wreath. This will go on the door or the peaked area at the front of the house. Snip with scissors for texture.

16. Make a wreath bow with the milk chocolate plastic and glue it on with corn syrup. Attach dragees, if desired. Glue the wreath to the door or house with corn syrup.

17. Use the milk chocolate plastic to make shutters and ledges for the windows. Roll out a rectangle of the chocolate plastic and cut it into 1×2-inch rectangles to finish off the top of the roof, as in the illustrations below. For snow, spoon the royal icing into a nonpleated plastic bag or paper cone. Snip end and apply "snow" to the rooftop and window ledges, if you want it.

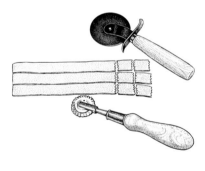

CHOCOLATE VICTORIAN COTTAGE COOKIE BOX

. . .

Makes one 9 × 9 × 10-inch cookie box

3 batches Cocoa Dough for
   Decorating, page 423

1 batch Milk Chocolate Plastic,
   page 384

1 batch White Chocolate Plastic,
   page 384

Dark corn syrup for gluing

Four 11 × 17-inch cookie sheets or
   jelly-roll pans

8 sheets parchment paper, cut to fit
   the cookie sheets

1 or 2 cardboard boxes, at least 10
   inches high and 10 inches wide

Nontoxic wood glue

Sheets of gelatin or cellophane

Confectioners' sugar

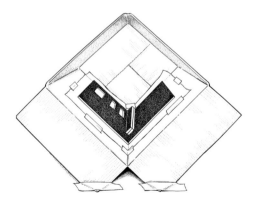

ASSEMBLE THE COTTAGE

This cottage is based on my friend Mary Risley's Pacific Heights Victorian cottage in San Francisco.

1. Photocopy cottage pattern, page 439, on a copy enlarger until it is a height of 10 inches and a width of 9 inches. Cut out the pattern, including the door and window openings. Trace the cutout pattern onto a stiffer paper, such as poster board or a thin cardboard. Using an Exacto knife or a single-edged razor blade, cut out the pattern, including the door and window openings. This one pattern will be used for all four sides of the cottage. The door and windows will be on the front wall only. The other three walls will be solid. Roll the dough and cut the base piece and the "lid," page 438, which will be 10 × 10 inches square, using a ruler.

2. Preheat oven to 350 degrees. Roll cocoa dough as in Step 2 of directions for Christmas Tree Centerpiece (see page 424). Transfer rolled-out but uncut dough to one of the prepared pans and top with paper and another pan. Bake about 20 minutes, cutting around pattern squares while dough is hot. There will be three solid 9 × 10-inch rectangles. Cut doors and windows out of fourth rectangle. Cut any remaining baked dough into eight 1-inch wide strips. Return dough to pan and replace top paper and pan. Bake for 30 minutes or until dough is firm. Cool between pans on a wire rack.

3. Roll out and bake the last two pieces of dough the same way, cutting the squares with a ruler, after baking, to measure 10 × 10 inches after baking. Cool in the same manner as the walls

4. If your cardboard boxes have lids, cut those off. Place the box on one side. Use books, tape, or towels to prop the box up so that it is resting on a corner (see illustration, above). Line the inside of that corner with wax paper and

place the front piece (with the door and windows), against one side, with one 10-inch edge resting in the wax-papered corner (see illustration, page 436). Place it so that the outside of the front is against the box, and the wax paper is under the dough. Squeeze a line of nontoxic wood glue along the inside of the 10-inch edge of the dough in the corner. Rest a second 10×9-inch square of dough against the adjoining wall of the box so that one 10-inch edge is pressing against the glued edge of the front piece. Hold firmly in place for 2 to 3 minutes.

5. If a second box is available, repeat with the other two 10×9-inch pieces. The corners may be reinforced with blocks of dough made from the 1-inch strips cut from the baked sheets. If the strips are longer than 8 to 9 inches,

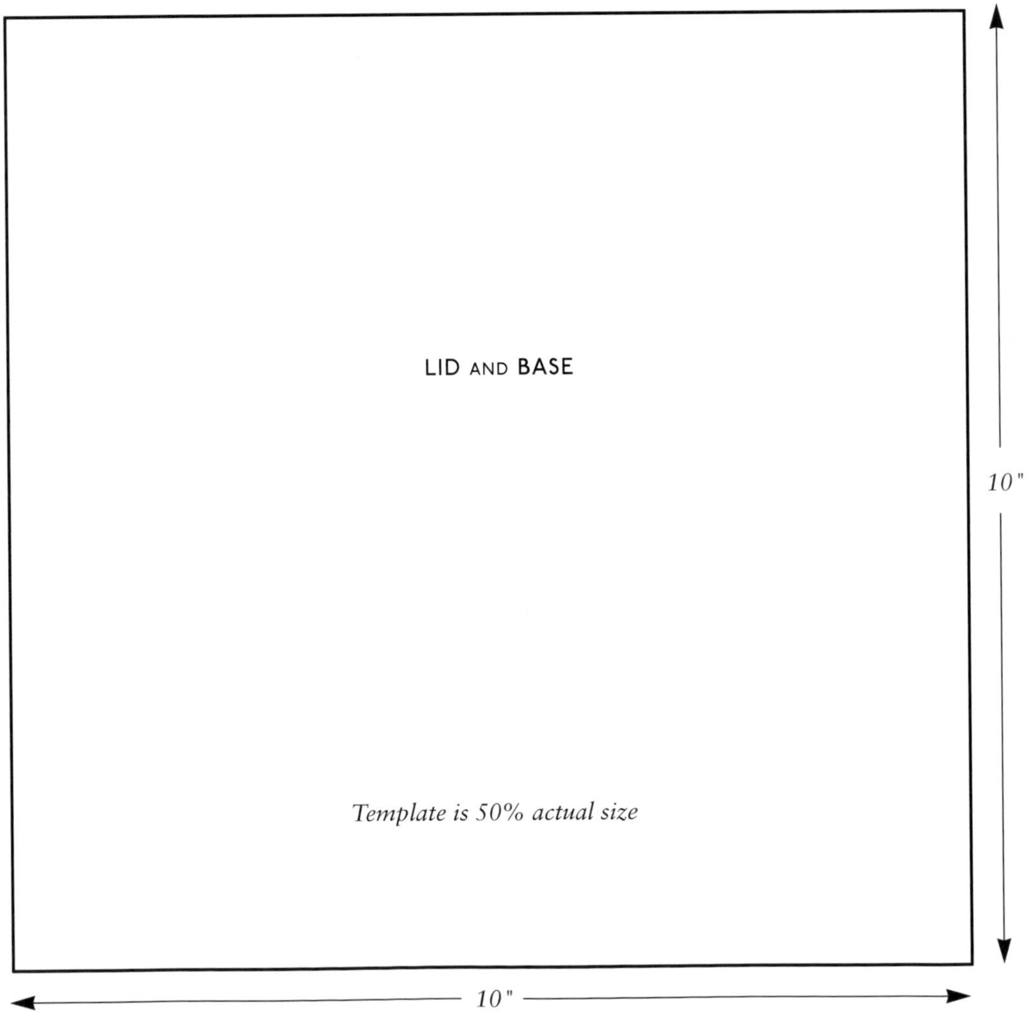

LID AND **BASE**

10 "

Template is 50% actual size

10 "

break them off to that length (shorter is okay). Glue two strips together to form a column. Apply more glue to the inside corner of the cottage pieces in the box and press the dough column into the corner. Hold firmly in place for 2 to 3 minutes. Allow the glue to dry thoroughly—overnight, if possible.

6. Place one 10 × 10-inch square of dough on the work surface. Carefully lift one of the corners from a box. Remove the wax paper if it has stuck. Place it on the inside of one corner of the square (see illustration, page 436). Don't glue yet. Repeat with the other corner piece, placing it on the square base opposite, so that a box is formed. Remove one corner piece and apply glue to the bottom edges. Replace the piece where it had been. Remove the other corner piece and apply glue to both the bottom edges *and* to the two side edges. Replace the

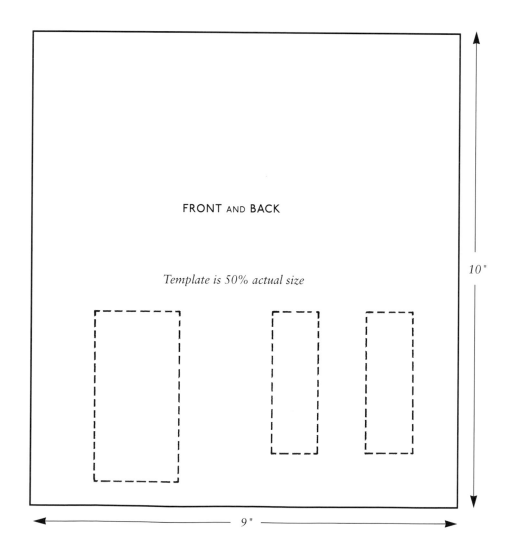

FRONT AND BACK

Template is 50% actual size

10"

9"

piece on the base square so that the two glued side edges are firmly against the side edges of the first corner piece, again forming a box. As you press the second piece against the base, also press the two glued pieces together firmly for 2 to 3 minutes. (If desired, these corners may also be reinforced with dough columns, as above.) Allow all pieces to dry thoroughly.

DECORATIONS

7. Glue sheets of gelatin or cellophane over the inside of the windows. Glue door cutout into doorway. Use the milk chocolate and white chocolate plastics to decorate the front of the cottage as illustrated, page 437.

TO MAKE THE WHITE PLASTIC DECORATIONS

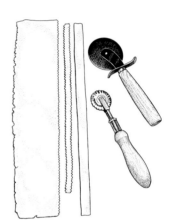

8. Dust the work surface with confectioners' sugar and roll the white chocolate plastic out to approximately 1/16 inch or thinner. Using a ruler's edge and a rolling cutter or the tip of a sharp knife, cut out the strips for between the windows, as in the illustration at right. Glue the decorations on with corn syrup. The wide cornice above the window and door decoration is made by placing a strip cut with a serated cutting wheel over a wider one cut with a straight wheel. The brackets are formed by hand; see the illustrations on facing page. Pinch off a small amount of white plastic and form it to the shape desired. The tip of a knife may be used to score further decoration into the brackets or window frames.

TO MAKE THE MILK CHOCOLATE DECORATIONS

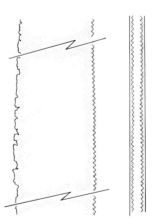

9. The window awnings are made by forming a small handful of the milk chocolate plastic into the desired shapes. Use a ruler to measure the width of the windows and door as this will determine the width of the awnings (see illustration on facing page). The impressions of "tiles" on the awnings are made by pressing with only half the round bottom edge of a metal piping tip. Let all the glue dry thoroughly, then fill with cookies, if desired, and place lid on top.

DOOR AWNING

Templates are actual size

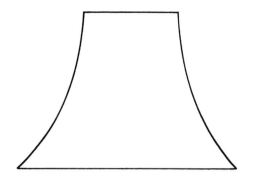

WINDOW AWNING

DOOR CROWN

DOOR AND WINDOW BRACKETS

SOURCES

American Chocolate Mould Co., Inc.

*3194 Lawson Boulevard
Oceanside, NY 11572
(516) 766-1414*

Catalog available; chocolate temperers and metal molds.

Balducci's

*424 Sixth Avenue
New York, NY 10011
(800) 572-7041; (212) 673-2600*

Catalog available ($3.00, refundable with first order); food products of all kinds.

Bazzini

*339 Greenwich Street
New York, NY
(212) 334-1280*

Nuts and nut products.

Bridge Kitchenware

*214 East 52nd Street
New York, NY 10022
(212) 688-4220*

Catalog available ($3.00, refundable with first order); tart pans, tartlet pans, basket forms, chocolate molds, and assorted pastry equipment and cookware.

Chandre Corporation

*14 Catherine Street
Poughkeepsie, NY 12601
(800) 324-6252*

Sinsation Chocolate Tempering Machine.

Concepts in Candy

*8832 Shirley Avenue, Unit 1
Northridge, CA 91324
(818) 609-1445; (818) 993-7920*

Retail catalog available; plastic candy molds.

Country Kitchen Sweetart

*3225 Wells Street
Fort Wayne, IN 46808
(800) 497-3927; (219) 482-4835*

Catalog available ($5.00, coupon for $6.00 off first purchase); variety of molds, equipment, chocolate, and assorted items necessary for candy making.

Dean and De Luca

*560 Broadway
New York, NY 10012
(212) 226-6800*

Will special-order passion fruit and cassis purees, also chestnut spread, and chestnuts in syrup, Mexican and other imported chocolates.

Hilliard Chocolate Systems

*275 East Center Street
West Bridgewater, MA 02379
(508) 587-3666*

Chocolate tempering machine.

Kitchen Glamor

*39049 Webb Court
Westland, MI 48302
(800) 641-1252*

Free catalog available; cookware, bakeware, chocolate.

New York Cake and Baking Distributors (formerly The Chocolate Gallery)

*56 West 22nd Street
New York, NY 10010
(212) 675-2253*

Catalog available ($3.00); eighty-page catalog offers chocolate, cocoa butter, chocolate liquor, praline paste, basket forms, cake cardboards, 4-ounce aluminum foil cups, chocolate molds, dipping forks, chocolate thermometers, and a full line of pans and decorating equipment.

Penzeys, Limited, Spices and Seasonings

*P.O. Box 933
Muskego, WI 53150
(414) 574-0277*

Free catalog of herbs, spices, and extracts.

Sepp Leaf

381 Park Avenue South,
Suite 1301
New York, NY 10016
(212) 683-2840

Gold leaf.

Sur la Table

Pike Place Farmers Market
84 Pine Street
Seattle, WA 98101
(800) 243-0852; (206) 448-
2244

Catalog available; tart pans, tartlet pans, and assorted pastry equipment and cookware.

Sweet Celebrations (formerly Maid of Scandinavia)

7009 Washington Avenue
South
Edina, MN 55439
(800) 328-6722

Catalog available; wide variety of decorating supplies, including chocolate and gelatin.

Tomric Plastics, Inc.

136 Broadway
Buffalo, NY 14203
(716) 854-6050

Catalog available; molds.

Williams-Sonoma

100 North Point Street
San Francisco, CA 94133
(800) 541-2233

Catalog available; tart pans, tartlet pans, assorted pastry equipment and cookware, and imported chocolates.

Wilton Industries, Inc.

2240 West 75th Street
Woodridge, IL 60517
(800) 323-1717; (708) 936-
7100

Catalog available; bakeware and baking and decorating products.

BIBLIOGRAPHY

Abrahamson, E. M., and A. W. Pezet. *Body, Mind and Sugar.* New York: Holt, Rinehart and Winston, 1951.

All About Home Baking. New York: General Foods Corporation, 1937.

Bachmann, Walter. *Swiss Bakery and Confectionery.* London: Maclaren & Sons Limited, 1949.

Baggett, Nancy. *The International Chocolate Cookbook.* New York: Stewart, Tabori & Chang, 1991.

Barnachon, Maurice, and Jean-Jacques Barnachon. *La Passion du Chocolat.* Paris: Flammarion, 1985.

Beard, James. *American Cookery.* New York: Little, Brown, 1972.

Book of American Baking. New York: American Trade Publishing Company, 1910.

The Book of Cookies: Recipes and Sales Ideas. Chicago: Baker's Helper Company, 1940.

Coady, Chantal. *Chocolate: The Food of the Gods.* San Francisco: Chronicle Books, 1993.

Coe, Sophie D., and Michael D. Coe. *The True History of Chocolate.* London: Thames and Hudson, 1996.

Constant, Christian. *Du Nectar à l'Ambroisie le Chocolat.* Paris: Nathan, 1988.

Consumer Guide, editors. *The Perfect Chocolate Dessert.* New York: Beekman House, 1981.

Cook, L. Russell. *Chocolate Production and Use.* New York: Magazines for Industry, 1963.

Culinary Art and Traditions of Switzerland. Vevey: Nestlé, 1992.

Dorchy, Henry. *Le Moule à Chocolat: Un Nouvel Objet de Collection.* Paris: Les Éditions de L'Amateur.

Edden, Gill. *Harrod's Book of Chocolates & Other Edible Gifts.* New York: Arbor House, 1986.

Escriba-Serra, Antonio. *Felices Pascuas.* Barcelona: Antonio Escriba-Serra, 1967.

Ghirardelli: Originial Chocolate Cookbook, Second Edition. San Leandro, Calif.: Ghirardelli Chocolate Company, 1983.

Gonzalez, Elaine. *Chocolate Artistry: Techniques for Molding, Decorating, and Designing with Chocolate.* Chicago: Contemporary Books, 1983.

Hadda, Ceri. *Coffeecakes.* New York: Simon & Schuster, 1992.

Hamelecourt, Juliette Elkon. *The Chocolate Cookbook.* New York: Macmillan, 1985.

Hepp, Antoine. *La Confiserie.* Colmar, France: Editions S.A.E.P.

Hershey's: Make It Chocolate! Hershey, Pa.: Hershey Foods Corporation, 1987.

Hirsch, Sylvia Balser, and Morton Gill Clark. *A Salute to Chocolate.* New York: Hawthorn Books, 1968.

Hoffman, Mable. *Chocolate Cookery.* New York: Dell Publishing Company, 1978.

Jordan, Stroud. *Confectionery Standards.* New York: Applied Sugar Laboratories, 1933.

Lambert, Robert. *Fantasy Chocolate Desserts.* San Francisco: Chronicle Books, 1988.

Leaver, Alec. *Making Chocolates.* New York: Weathervane Books, 1975.

Leighton, Alfred E. *A Text Book on Candy Making.* Oak Park, Ill.: Manufacturing Confectioner Publishing Company, 1952.

Linxe, Robert. *La Maison du Chocolat.* Paris: Robert Laffont, 1982.

McCully, Helen, and Eleanor Noderer. *Just Desserts.* Obelensky, 1957.

Marcus, Adrianne. *The Chocolate Bible.* New York: G. P. Putnam's Sons, 1979.

Mattle, Josef von. *Praline Passe-Partout.* Zürich: Schweizerischen Bäckerei und Konditorei-Personal-Verband, 1986.

Moreau, Charles. *Manuels-Roret: Nouveau Manuel Complet du Confiseur et Chocolatier.* Paris: Editions Baudouin.

Morton, Marcia, and Frederic Morton. *Chocolate: An Illustrated History.* New York: Crown Publishers, 1986.

144

Myers, Barbara. *Chocolate Chocolate Chocolate: The Ultimate Chocolate Dessert Cookbook*. New York: Penguin Books, 1983.

Neil, Marion H. *Candies and BonBons and How to Make Them*. Philadelphia: David McKay Publisher, 1913.

Orban, Olivier. *Le Guide des Croqueurs de Chocolat: Les 170 Meilleurs Chocolatiers de France*. Marie-Helene Orban, 1988.

Pasley, Virginia. *The Holiday Candy Book*. Boston: Little, Brown, 1952.

Pope, Antoinette, and François Pope. *Antoinette Pope School Cookbook*. New York: Macmillan, 1948.

———. *Antoinette Pope School: New Candy Cookbook*. New York: Macmillan, 1967.

Das Pralinen-Buch. Basel and Lorrach: Coba-Bucherei, 1933.

Richemont Pastry School. *A Guide to Perfect Bakery and Confectionery*. Lucerne: Bakery and Confectionery Craft School Richemont, 1989.

———. *Swiss Confectionery*. Lucerne: Bakery and Confectionery Craft School Richemont, 1985.

Rubinstein, Helge. *The Ultimate Chocolate Cake and 110 Other Chocolate Indulgences*. New York: Congdon & Weed, 1982.

Scarborough, N. F. *Sweet Manufacture: A Practical Handbook on the Manufacture of Sugar Confectionery*. London: Leonard Hill Limited, 1933.

Seranne, Ann. *Delectable Desserts*. Boston: Little, Brown, 1952.

Urquhart, D. H. *Tropical Agriculture Series: Cocoa*. London: Longmans, 1961.

Villiard, Paul. *The Practical Candymaking Cookbook*. New York: Abelard-Schuman, 1970.

SELECTED RECIPE INDEX

INDEX

INDEX

454

459

INDEX

461

462